OUTDOOR RECREATION IN AMERICA

Fourth Edition

Clayne R. Jensen

Brigham Young University
Provo, Utah

 Burgess Publishing Company
Minneapolis, Minnesota

Acquisitions editor: Wayne E. Schotanus
Assistant editor: Sharon B. Harrington
Development editor: Anne E. Heller
Copy editor: Greg Breining
Art coordinators: Melinda Radtke, Barbara Horwitz
Composition: Dacon Engineering
Cover photograph: Dennis Tasa
Cover design: Barbara Horwitz
Production: Pat Barnes, Morris Lundin, Judy Vicars

Library of Congress Cataloging in Publication Data

Jensen, Clayne R.
    Outdoor recreation in America.

    Includes bibliographies and index.
    1. Outdoor recreation–United States. 2. Outdoor
recreation–United States–Management. 3. Outdoor
recreation–Government policy–United States.
4. Natural resources–United States. I. Title.
GV191.4.J46   1984   790'.0973   84-7709
ISBN 0-8087-1082-6

Burgess Publishing Company
7108 Ohms Lane
Minneapolis, Minnesota 55435

J I H G F E D C B A

Contents

PART IV   MANAGEMENT PRACTICES AND CONSIDERATIONS

Preface

The forests, prairies, streams, lakes, skies, and shorelines were once abundant with pleasant scenery and wild game, fish, and fowl. The streams ran clear as they sought the rivers that funneled into the scenic Atlantic and Pacific. Nature's gifts to Americans were rich and abundant, perhaps unequaled anywhere. But owing to lack of appreciation, foresight, and planning, these gifts were abused, mismanaged, and lost–not to be restored, no longer living symbols of life in America.

One hopes that the chronicles of history will not include such a statement–that we will be wise enough to conserve, protect, and retain a fair share of nature's gifts, even though retaining them has become difficult and will be even more so in the future.

For many Americans, open space no longer lies in the backyard or around the corner of the next block. In fact, a great majority now live in urban and suburban environments, and more than half of our people live in large cities. Yet our thin coat of modern civilization has not squelched the basic desire for contact with nature and benefit from its renewing capacities. As a result, the demand for outdoor recreation has continued to increase. People from all walks of life travel long distances to enjoy a huge variety of activities in outdoor settings and to visit a multitude of scenic and interesting places that add meaning to life.

Because of the dramatic upsurge in outdoor recreation during recent years, many agencies and organizations have undertaken programs of preservation, conservation, education, and management to guarantee continued enjoyment derived from contact with nature–to ensure high-quality outdoor recreation. Numerous government agencies at federal, state, and local levels are involved with recreation as either a primary or a secondary function. In the private sector, many individuals and enterprises have become involved in a variety of ways. The total field of outdoor recreation is becoming ever more extensive and complex.

The first edition of *Outdoor Recreation in America*, published in 1970, came at the end of America's greatest decade of attention to the recreational use of outdoor resources. The content of the first edition was especially pertinent to the times and was well received. The second and third editions appeared in 1973 and 1977, and they were bolstered by new information about the developments of the 1970s, which formed the second great decade of national concern for the outdoor environment.

The content of the three previous editions, combined with further significant developments pertaining to outdoor recreation during the late 1970s and early 1980s, set the stage for an expanded fourth edition. Enough new information became available to justify the addition of five chapters on topics that were not included in the third edition. Further, some topics previously included were expanded to form separate chapters so that the new edition includes a total of seven new chapters and four new appendices. Among the new topics in this edition are: (1) the natural-resource base for outdoor recreation, (2) resources of critical concern, (3) planning procedures, (4) management policies, and (5) legal aspects. Topics that were expanded significantly include: (1) the involvement of federal agencies, (2) participation trends, (3) economic factors, and (4) educational programs. Further, all of the chapters have been updated to include the most current information. This fourth edition is clearly an improvement over the earlier editions, and it is believed to be the most complete and up-to-date text on this topic.

The content of this edition was especially selected for college students who are preparing for professional work in park and recreation management, or one of the several areas of natural-resource management. The focus of the book involves a balance between: (1) the outdoor-recreation interests of people, and (2) management of the resources that are used for recreational pursuits.

The chapters have been arranged into four groupings according to how they relate to each other, and to form a logical sequence. Part I includes information about the meaning, development, and significance of outdoor recreation. Part II deals with the various government agencies, resources, and programs. Part III covers the nongovernment facet of outdoor recreation—the private sector. Part IV includes policies, practices, and considerations pertaining to the management of resources, programs, and people.

The book should be especially useful to: (1) teachers and students in recreation, natural-resource management, and outdoor education, (2) employees of resource-management agencies, both government and private, (3) park and recreation administrators, and (4) laypeople concerned with the use of natural resources for the enjoyment of people.

I wish to express sincere appreciation to my colleagues who reviewed the manuscript for the fourth edition and helped to shape the content with their useful suggestions and comments. Also, appreciation is expressed to the past and present users of the text for finding ways to apply its content effectively in the teaching process, and especially those users who have provided constructive feedback to help design this improved edition. Further, I recognize the important contribution of those editorial and production staff members of Burgess Publishing Company who worked on the book, particularly Anne Heller, the Senior Development Editor.

Numerous photographs and charts have been acquired from several government agencies and from private individuals. Special appreciation is expressed for the use of these materials. Each photograph and chart is given a credit line where appropriate.

PART I

The Basis for Outdoor Recreation

CHAPTER 1

Important Meanings and Concepts

The Declaration of Independence proclaims that "the pursuit of happiness" is a basic human right. In addition to that important proclamation, many papers have been written and speeches given on what we should achieve for ourselves and help others to achieve. One obvious answer seems to be the achievement of satisfaction, enjoyment, and well-being, a condition known as happiness. The pursuit of true happiness is today, as it has always been, a principal concern of the human race.

This book is based on the thesis that wholesome recreation along with meaningful work contributes significantly to the lives of people. Furthermore, the book proposes that an intellectual treatment should be given to the study of recreation and the factors that influence it. Such an approach requires serious consideration of such topics as (1) our time and how we use it, (2) socioeconomic forces that influence work and leisure, (3) organizations and agencies involved with outdoor recreation, (4) supply of and demand for outdoor recreation resources, (5) impact on resources, (6) management policies and procedures, (7) economic factors related to recreation, and (8) our future expectations.

The focus of the book is on our recreational use of natural resources–land, foliage, water, wildlife, open space, and scenery–not only now but also in the future.

Before we can effectively discuss outdoor recreation, we must understand some basic meanings and concepts. For instance, what is leisure time? What determines whether an activity is recreational? What have past and present leaders said about the significance of leisure and recreation?

TIME AND LEISURE

Time can be divided logically into three classes: (1) time for existence–biological requirements such as sleeping, eating, and personal care, (2) time for subsistence–economic requirements such as working on one's job, and (3) free time–the time remaining. For the typical

American adult, this classification of time may be represented on a 24-hour scale, as shown below.

Existence	Subsistence	
Biological requirements	Work and travel	Free time
10 hours	9 hours	5 hours

Some writers view free time as different from leisure time, and some fine distinctions can be made. For the purposes of this book, however, *free time, leisure time,* and *choosing time* are terms that are used interchangeably.

IMPORTANCE OF LEISURE TIME

The amount of time we have and how we use it have great significance. The final test of a civilization has been said to be the ability to use time wisely. Further, how people choose to use time clearly influences the making and unmaking of individuals, communities, and nations, and helps to determine the final quality of life itself.

Bertrand Russell said, "To be able to fill leisure time intelligently is the last product of civilization." A century earlier, Benjamin Disraeli stated, "Increased means and increased leisure are the two civilizers of man." Long before that, Socrates said, "Leisure is the best of all possessions." Time to do as one pleases—to create, to play, to do things enriching and satisfying—has long been a dream of the common man. The dream to be freed from the heavy burden of his work has come at least partly true; and there is the promise of greater freedom yet. With freedom of time, however, must come understanding of its potential for good and for bad.

Arnold Toynbee, one of our most renowned historian-philosophers, stated that the three great dangers facing the contemporary American society are world warfare, overpopulation, and too much free time. David Sarnoff said that free time—not labor—will be a great problem in the years ahead.

For the first time in our history, free time has become a strong integrating force in the life of the average person. It has become a dominating factor in our life-styles and offers potential for personal development and self-realization that was heretofore unachieved. Leisure time has become abundant enough to require that both individuals and society take it seriously, much as we always have done with work, and use it to add perspective to life. Free time, according to Thomas Desmond, "can be a real friend if you know how to use it, or a formidable enemy if you abuse it."

LEISURE TIME VERSUS LEISURE

Some authors have viewed *leisure time* and *leisure* as different. They interpret leisure not as a block of time but as a state of being or a condition in which the person exists, and claim that certain people are ill-prepared to achieve leisure even when an abundance of time is available. In his discussion of leisure, Sebastian de Grazia reviews the serene concept of leisure that some ancient philosophers held. He does not equate leisure with unproductiveness. He claims that free time is thought of as the opposite of work and therefore is unproductive. He expresses that leisure and free time are entirely different, stating that "today's time is considered free when not at grips with work. Work is the antonym of free time. But not leisure. Leisure and free time live in two different worlds."[1]

Aristotle said leisure is "the first principle of all action" and that "leisure is better than work and is its end." Leisure has also been called the greater part of a free life and the nurse of civilization. Like virtue and unlike labor, leisure is its own reward. The quality of any society's leisure defines its version of the good life.

THE DANGER OF CHOICE

A basic problem associated with free time is that it is not inherently good or bad, but has tremendous potential for either. It is a key that unlocks a new door but brings no guarantee of reward or improvement. Leisure time requires the making of choices, and to ensure wise choices, people must be adequately prepared. For example, one must decide how much to eat and drink, whether to seek spiritual sustenance, how to maintain a sense of physical well-being, or what recreation to pursue.

One fallacy about leisure time is the idea that people have only two alternatives–a good choice and a bad choice. Usually a multitude of alternatives lie between the extremes. Further, different individuals have different ranges of choice, depending on their resources and abilities. Most individuals have a tremendous potential for creativity, but to realize it, one must accept challenge, seek new experiences, and strive for higher achievements.

MEANING OF RECREATION

Recreation is derived from the Latin word *recreare*, which means to create anew, to become refreshed and invigorated–the act of re-creating or rebirth. Some typical phrases used to explain recreation are these:

1. The pleasurable and constructive use of leisure time
2. Activity that rests one from work, often by providing a change or diversion
3. Activities in which we engage because of inner desire and not because of outer compulsion

Some common elements among the several definitions distinguish the term *recreation:* (1) voluntary participation, (2) leisure time, (3) enjoyment and satisfaction, and (4) positive results for the individual.

Recreation is not simply an activity. It is a personal response and a psychological reaction. Many so-called recreation pursuits are not recreation, but are only amusers, or time-wasters, which are detrimental rather than constructive and which "decreate" rather than re-create.

Recreation takes several forms, and it is so varied that any of a great number of activities may be recreational to someone at some time. Activities that are recreational to one person may not interest another. Furthermore, recreation that interests an individual at one time may

---

1. DeGrazia, Sebastian, *Of Time, Work, and Leisure,* Doubleday, Inc., Garden City, New Jersey, 1964, p. 233.

have a different effect at another time. For instance, a person who is physically fatigued has little need for vigorous recreation, and one who is mentally exhausted is not attracted to activities that require heavy concentration. Recreation at its best often takes the form of diversion and helps bring one's life into balance.

Because people have various interests they enjoy different pursuits, even in the same setting and with the same resources. For instance, some outdoor enthusiasts enjoy hunting and fishing, but others prefer to photograph and study wildlife. To some, a park is a place for games; to others, it is for quiet meditation or the enjoyment of beauty. Some want to preserve resources in their present state; others see little value unless the resources are used in some activity or to make products.

MISCONCEPTIONS ABOUT RECREATION

Several misconceptions about recreation are common. Let's discuss some of them.

Recreation is only the antithesis of work. It is true that for many people the hours of employment are repetitive, boring, and exhausting. Today relatively few people find recreation in their work, but there are some whose vocations are absorbing and satisfying. It is said that Thomas Edison gave himself so completely to creative work that he apparently felt little need for diversion. It is not uncommon to find scholars engaged in research or businesspeople involved in a new enterprise whose work yields the kind of excitement and satisfaction commonly associated with recreation. In general, however, recreation takes place during off-the-job hours, and it usually involves a form of diversion from work.

Leisure time and recreation are the same or inseparable. Recreation is generally a leisure time activity, but not all leisure time is spent on recreation. *Leisure time* does not necessarily imply either participation or outcome. Conversely, recreation depends on individual involvement and individual results–it is not a block of time.

Recreation must be earned through the work process. This belief implies that recreation is not valuable except as a recuperative interlude between periods of work. It echoes the work-play-work cycle and fails to recognize the significant nature and vital purpose of recreation itself–a desirable state of being whether in preparation for work or not.

Recreation is only a means of alleviating personal and community problems. True, recreation can be a means of achieving these and other useful individual and social objectives. However, these are not the primary reasons people enter recreational pursuits. Fortunately, the concept that recreation has value per se and the concept that it produces positive social results are by no means incompatible. In fact, a recreational experience is likely to bring greater satisfaction to an individual if it also contributes to the betterment of himself and his community.

Recreation can be accurately defined in terms of specific activities. Recreation involves a state of mind as well as a kind of activity. Even though certain activities frequently yield pleasure to many people, they are merely means of achieving recreation and are not recreation themselves. Recreation is a result, not an activity.

Recreation, unlike education, is essentially without purpose or discipline. This misunderstanding occurs because recreation is identified with relaxation or pleasurable involvement. In many forms of recreation there is a high degree of concentration, physical exertion, and mental application. Some forms are keenly challenging and press the participants almost to their limits. Such activities certainly result in individual development. Recreation is often a functioning laboratory for the practice and implementation of personal interests and useful skills. Many people who have routine jobs use recreation as a means of self-actualization.

It is desirable to divide the field of recreation into two distinct segments—parks and recreation. Certainly this has some logic, provided the dichotomy is not carried too far. Parks *are* for recreation of particular kinds, and recreation often occurs in parks. While it is logical to have specialists in *resource management* and *program administration*, these specialists need to understand their close relationships to each other and work closely together.

CLASSIFICATION OF RECREATIONAL PURSUITS

Because of the great variety of activities included under the term *recreation*, a classification plan can be meaningful. Recreation may be classified into two broad categories: (1) *resource oriented* and (2) *activity oriented*. Resource-oriented recreation includes those forms that depend largely on the use of natural resources and take place in natural settings, such as nature study, the enjoyment of natural scenery, camping, hiking, fishing, boating, and hunting. Activity-oriented recreation includes activities that are normally done in nonnatural or improved surroundings and that involve performance, or the witnessing of a performance, such as athletic sports and games, dramatics, music, art, crafts, and so on.

Some activities seem to fall in between the two extremes, and these in-between activities form the *intermediate* class. Examples are waterskiing, snow skiing, and sailing. These activities use natural resources and are done in basically natural settings, but they require skill in an activity, and one in particular requires the use of motorized equipment. Naturally, gray areas exist between the three categories, but such classification does help to comprehend the total field of recreation.

The U.S. Forest Service has used a classification that divides recreation participation into three categories. These categories cover only the kinds of recreation done in the national forests; therefore, all three categories align closely with *resource-oriented* recreation, and they range from primitive to modern recreational use of forests.

Primitive recreation involves (1) basic outdoor skills, (2) achievement of satisfying outdoor experiences without mechanized access by the user, (3) minimum controls and restrictions on the use of natural resources, and (4) a feeling of closeness to nature and isolation from civilization.

Intermediate recreational pursuits include: (1) outdoor skills at a moderate level, (2) enough controls and restrictions to provide a sense of attachment and security while the participant still has an adequate amount of freedom, (3) a balance between being close to nature and experiencing social interchange, and (4) opportunities to participate in small groups and use skills such as rock climbing, organized backpacking, cross-country skiing, and canoeing.

Modern recreational activities involve: (1) a feeling of being associated with nature but not close to it, (2) extensive opportunities to use outdoor skills in developed or supervised areas such as alpine skiing, picnicking, organized camping, and supervised waterfront activities, including waterskiing, boating, and swimming, (3) feelings of security arising from controls, supervision, and the presence of other people.

This absolute freedom gives every hour an intense lucidity. (National Park Service, U.S. Department of the Interior, photograph by Richard Frear)

Aldo Leopold[2] took a related approach, which differed from actual classification. He talked of five important components of outdoor experiences. More than one, and possibly even all of the components, can be present in a single experience.

The first of Leopold's components was a collection of physical objects. This can be thought of as a trophy-seeking experience, and the trophies might be unique or spectacular photographs, rare forms of rocks, sea shells, wood pieces, antlers, insects, fish, or game animals. Pursuing, obtaining, and displaying the collected items brings satisfaction to the recreationist. Some kinds of collection must be controlled if the resource is to survive.

2. Leopold, Aldo, *A Sand County Almanac,* Oxford University Press, New York, 1966, p. 213

Second, Leopold mentioned a feeling of isolation in nature. An occasional experience of isolation is an absolute necessity for some people and a valuable experience for almost everyone. However, a few feel no need for it and are even frightened by such an experience. A feeling of solitude in nature is a fragile condition that is easily destroyed with mass pursuit. Ironically, this kind of experience becomes increasingly important and at the same time less available as our country becomes more densely populated.

Third are fresh air and scenery. This component can withstand mass pursuit without much dilution. Those who travel along recreational corridors by either water or land can get an abundance of fresh air and scenery even when many others in the vicinity are seeking the same rewards.

Fourth is the perception of natural processes. It is more than simply observing or being entertained or amused by natural phenomenon. It is gaining a feeling for the rhythm and interdependence of nature, including the tremendous dependence of humanity itself on the natural world. Fortunately, this sort of study does not contribute to the destruction of the natural environment. In fact, the more people understand nature, the more likely that the environment will receive care and protection.

Leopold's final component is a sense of husbandry. This component is closely related to the preceding one, because a person is more likely to feel a sense of husbandry if he has a keen perception of natural processes. Leopold considers this component to be the most valuable and satisfying element of recreational experiences. It means that the recreationist feels a personal obligation toward the natural environment and for the maintenance and care of areas and facilities.

OBJECTIVES OF OUTDOOR RECREATION

Recreation leaders of the past have been charged with conducting pigmy programs amid giant opportunities. This criticism is still somewhat valid, though much progress has been made. Certainly a weakness of the recreation profession has been that its leaders have not agreed on well-defined goals for themselves. Professional objectives have not been clearly defined or well established.

I believe that the objectives of outdoor recreation should include at least the following and that these objectives should be adopted by the various agencies involved.

1. *Appreciation of nature.* Most people in our urban society have limited opportunities for contact with the great outdoors. Thus, people find it difficult to become interested in the conservation and preservation of natural resources. For increasing numbers of people, contact with the natural environment occurs only during an occasional trip to the country or a visit to a nearby scenic or historic area. In view of this, it is important that outdoor recreation be aimed toward increasing people's understanding of nature and their awareness of the importance of sound conservation and preservation practices.

2. *Personal satisfaction and enjoyment.* People participate in outdoor recreation for enjoyment and satisfaction. Outdoor recreation agencies should try to enhance these

opportunities. Each agency ought to be aggressive about developing resources that can induce a feeling of enjoyment and satisfaction in people. Among these are areas that are significant from the standpoint of aesthetics, history, geology, archeology, and biology (including wildlife). Also significant is simple "open space."

3. *Diversion and relaxation.* One reason people go to the outdoors is to divert themselves from their usual rapid pace, routine patterns, and the various restrictions under which they ordinarily live. Agencies should help them to achieve this much-sought-after diversion. The accomplishment of this will become more difficult as the number of users continues to increase. In the outdoors, people must find the opportunity to relax, to live at their own desired pace, to find time to understand their place in the scheme of things, and to renew themselves in preparation for their return to usual patterns of living.

4. *Physiological fitness.* The increasing lack of physiological fitness has been recognized as one of the crucial problems facing Americans, and much emphasis is being placed on improving this situation. Many forms of outdoor recreation are vigorous and tax participants far beyond their usual levels of performance. For instance, hiking, climbing, cycling, swimming, skiing, and canoeing provide unusual physical challenges. In many instances, participants in such activities precondition themselves to meet the occasion. Special attention should be given to promoting fitness through outdoor recreation. This can be accomplished by providing attractive opportunities and encouragement for people to do wholesome amounts of hiking, cycling, swimming, and other forms of vigorous outdoor activities.

5. *Positive behavioral patterns.* The fact that today's outdoor recreationist must share the resources with many other people requires the development of desirable patterns of outdoor conduct. There was a time when an individual going to the outdoors could be alone, but for the most part those days are gone. Today's typical outdoor participant finds many people wherever he or she goes—driving most of the way to the destination on a superhighway and passing thousands of cars in a day, fishing on a lake where boat traffic must be strictly controlled, hunting where more hunters than game animals are seen, and camping within a colony of other campers. Attitudes of courtesy, consideration, and sincere interest in each other should be fostered. Each recreationist needs to recognize that others have come for essentially the same reasons. Agencies involved in outdoor recreation can be helpful by encouraging desirable social patterns.

6. *Sense of stewardship.* Experiencing a sense of stewardship can be one of the most satisfying aspects of one's experiences with nature. This feeling of husbandry is a much-needed characteristic which will increase in importance with the continued growth of our nation. Its prerequisite is a keen perception of nature's processes, and its practice involves conservation and preservation. A sense of stewardship can vastly improve the rewards of one's association with the outdoors. The development and perpetuation of such a sense among the resource–users could be a boon to the protection and care of all aspects of the natural environment. Fostering a sense of stewardship should be important to all outdoor–recreation agencies, and it should be among the objectives of every professional in the field.

THE TOTAL RECREATION EXPERIENCE

At first thought a recreation experience appears to be confined to the block of time during which participation actually occurs. But with further analysis, it becomes apparent that the total experience extends far beyond the time of actual participation. The value and usefulness of the experience may be part of a person's life long before and remain long after the event itself. Thus, a recreation experience may be divided into four phases: anticipation, planning, participation, and recollection.

The *anticipation phase* is that time during which the person considers the activity, decides to go ahead with it, and eagerly awaits the day when the dream will become a reality. The person anticipates catching a big trout, climbing a high mountain, or bagging a deer. Some trips never progress beyond the anticipation. Even so, this phase makes some contribution to one's life, stimulating reading, study, and conversation.

The *planning phase* involves the actual preparation for the trip–gathering equipment and supplies, preparing food and clothes, and making travel arrangements. If done well, this can be an educational experience, and sometimes it is a social event.

The *participation phase* is the actual experience of fishing, hunting, canoeing, swimming, camping, boating, skiing, or hiking. It extends from the time of departure to the time of return and thus includes travel as well as the activity itself. Often this phase is relatively short compared to the other phases, and it may seem almost insignificant in terms of time. Yet it is the core around which the other three phases are built.

The *recollection phase* is the thinking, telling, and showing about the experience. It may take the form of expression in oral or written form, or displaying pictures, slides, or movies. Fortunately, there is no time limit on this phase.

Sometimes anticipation, planning, and recollection are more exciting than the participation itself, but it takes all four phases to make the recreational experience complete.

Discussion Questions

1. Leisure time is one of man's most cherished conditions, yet David Sarnoff has said that leisure time will be one of the great problems in the years ahead. Why could leisure time be a problem? What can be done to prevent that from happening?
2. It has been stated that increased leisure time presents an opportunity to succeed to greater heights or fail in the attempt. If the result is failure or partial failure, could we say it would have been better if the leisure time, and the challenge of using it appropriately, had never existed?
3. What elements distinguish recreation from other activities? Discuss their relative importance.
4. Aldo Leopold considers "a sense of husbandry" to be the most valuable component of outdoor recreation. Do you agree? Why or why not?
5. Is it possible for outdoor recreational resources to serve the interests of all people? If not, is it right that some people be deprived while others are not? Who should make the decisions about the development and use of these resources?
6. In the management of natural resources, what might be meant by managing for the greatest good for the greatest number of people? Is this a sound concept? Why or why not?
7. What are the different elements of a total recreation experience? What is their relative importance?

Recommended Readings

"Attitudes Toward Outdoor Recreation Development: An Application of Social Exchange Theory." *Leisure Sciences*, Vol. 3, No. 2, 1980, p. 169.

"Basic Dimensions of Leisure." *Journal of Leisure Research*, September 1979, Vol. 4, No. 4, p.15.

Chubb, Michael, and Holly R. Chubb. *One Third of Our Time.* New York: John Wiley & Sons, 1981. Chapters 1, 3, 8.

"The Four-Day Workweek: An Assessment of Its Effects on Leisure Participation." *Leisure Sciences*, 1 November 1979, p. 55.

Harper, William. "The Experience of Leisure." *Leisure Sciences*, Vol. 4, No. 2, 1981, p. 113.

Jensen, Clayne R. *Leisure and Recreation: Introduction and Overview.* Philadelphia: Lea & Febiger Publishing Co., 1977, Chapter 1.

Jensen, Clayne R., and Jay H. Naylor. *Opportunities in Recreation and Leisure,* 2nd ed. Skokie, Illinois: National Textbook Co., 1983.

"Job Burnout." *U.S. News and World Report,* 18 February 1980, p. 71.

Knudson, Douglas M. *Outdoor Recreation.* New York: Macmillan Publishing Co., 1984, Chapter 1.

"Leisure When No Recession Is in Sight." *U.S. News and World Report,* 15 January 1979, p. 41.

Murphy, James. "Leisure Concepts in a Changing Society." *Journal of Physical Education, Recreation and Dance,* October 1981, p. 40.

"Why the Four-Day Workweek Hasn't Caught On." *U.S. News and World Report,* 6 October 1980, p. 92.

CHAPTER 2

The Value of Outdoor Opportunities

It seems that people have always needed a sanctuary of unspoiled land—a place of solitude where they may turn their thoughts inward and wonder at the miracles of creation. That we live in a world that moves crisis by crisis does not make contact with nature any less important. In fact, these circumstances increase the significance of nature in our lives.

The outdoors is a great laboratory for learning, a museum for study, a playground for wholesome fun and enjoyment. It affords a special kind of fulfillment not available in other settings. It has meaning in the lives of individuals and importance in the welfare of our nation. The outdoors lies deep in the American tradition and is the basis of tales of discovery and hard-won settlement. When we look for the meaning of our past, we seek it not in ancient ruins but in mountains, forests, rivers, and seacoasts.

Throughout history people have treasured experiences in the outdoors, and in one way or another tracts of land and water have been reserved for their pleasure. For example, such areas were not uncommon in the great civilizations of Thebes, Greece, and Rome, and during the Renaissance a revival of interest in the beauties of nature was expressed largely in the development of formal gardens. In hunting and fishing is an extremely strong affinity between primitive and present concepts of outdoor recreation.

Modern recreation on wild lands in the United States has some similarity to medieval practices in Great Britain. In feudal England some forests were more important for game than for timber, and certain lands were reserved for the recreation of the nobility. Such recreational privileges of the ruling classes, greatly extended by William the Conqueror and other Norman kings, were not modified until after the adoption of the Magna Carta in 1215. Today the Forest of Dean, west of Gloucester, and New Forest, near Southhampton, are remnants of the Norman preserves.

The first great lovers of the outdoors in America were the Indians. The outdoors was their heritage in the truest sense, and nature was a part of every phase of their lives. They lived directly from the products of the land. Their diets were geared to the vegetation of their particular locale. Their clothing and utensils were made of the materials at hand. The land and its resources surely had special meaning to these people.

The great days of the American Indians are gone, and with them went an era of rugged outdoor living. Since then, we have moved through other eras. The conquering of the wilderness, the isolated farm or plantation, the self-contained country town, and detached neighborhoods are relics of the American past.

In its short history the United States changed from a rural nation to an urban one. At the same time, despite the advantages inherent in urban living, something apparently is lacking in city life—the fundamental values of nature, the concept of the wholeness of life, the satisfaction of seeing things born and nurtured, and the observation of nature's marvelous processes. Today these elements are not common in the lives of most Americans, and indeed, to many they are not even accessible.

Through all of this we have learned some important lessons. For example, in terms of human modification of natural areas, bigger is not always better, slower may be faster, and less may well mean more in the long run. We have learned that too many people in too little space always results in some form of poverty. This is true whether it is a city street, a playground, or an outdoor area. Further, we have found that the quality of the environment, like freedom and justice, must be protected and achieved anew by each generation.

A century ago John Muir made this meaningful observation: "Each year thousands of nerve-shaken, overcivilized people find that going to the mountains, forests, and deserts is sort of like going home. These areas are useful not only as fountains of timber and water but as fountains of life."

Former Secretary of the Interior Stewart Udall said, "Every generation of Americans has a rendezvous with the land." If our generation is to meet this rendezvous, we must show special respect for the fundamental values of nature and of natural beauty, and we must pay special attention to the way these relate to the good of people and society. We must remember that man cannot live by science and technology alone. The natural world is the human world. Having evolved in it for many centuries, we are not far removed by the flimsy barrier of civilization.

Work meets many of our psychological, social, spiritual, and material needs. We must also be re-created to maintain a healthy balance. Recreation and work together contribute to fullness. We will be more effective if we plan some time for contemplation and renewal.

CHALLENGE AND ADVENTURE

The need for challenge and adventure carries young and old to indoor contests and to athletic fields. These same drives take people to mountaintops, tropical forests, deserts, and the Arctic, as well as into the air and under the sea. People endure hardships during long travel and in lonely places devoid of modern comforts. They willingly encounter heat, cold, and insects to find outdoor adventure and challenge.

In earlier times these forms of adventure and challenge were built into everyday life. People had trees to fell, animals to tame, streams to ford, mountains to climb, wilderness to explore, and wildlife to pursue. Through everyday adventure they achieved some alliance and

Before 1945, only about 100 people had challenged the white water course of the Grand Canyon. Now this number exceeds 14,000 per year. (Photo by Douglas Nelson)

dependence. Today life is much different, but people still can find meaningful challenges through a multitude of outdoor activities. Let us teach people skiing, swimming, sailing, marksmanship, mountain climbing, outdoor living skills, and survival techniques.

Above the entrance of an old Greek palaestra was the phrase "strip or retire," which meant get into action or leave, enter the race or step aside. We should not be advocates of unnecessary or unreasonable danger, but we should recognize that absolute safety and security have never been man's greatest need. Adventure and challenge with a reasonable chance for success have always ranked ahead of these.

CULTURAL VALUES

Scenic parks and well-preserved natural areas do much to promote love of country. Imagine the listlessness that would prevail in a country of wholly functional plowed fields, grazed pastures, and colorless cities. A drab country produces drab people; a beautiful country helps to keep the human spirit high.

Throughout history people have gradually added beauty to utility. The first pots or vessels were made for utility alone; then a touch of decoration was added. As civilization advanced, pots became treasured more for beauty than utility. The same pattern has followed in architecture, design of cities, and many other things created, used, and treasured by people.

There was a time in history when our natural resources were valued almost exclusively for their utility, for the goods they provided. Little by little, priority of beauty over utility has occurred in the use of certain resources, as it has in other phases of life. The beauty in this case is described in our use of nature for enjoyment, the enrichment and fulfillment of life. Essentially, this is what outdoor recreation is all about—the use of the outdoors for fulfillment of life.

Some ultramodern individuals have lost their roots in the land and assume that they have discovered what is important—a gadget-ridden society pent up by economic enterprise. Others recognize that the natural world will always be important in giving definition and meaning to all aspects of human endeavor. Aldo Leopold added meaning to the cultural dimension of nature when he made a plea for the preservation of some tag ends of wilderness as museum pieces for the edification of those who may one day wish to see, feel, or study the origins of their cultural inheritance.

PSYCHOLOGICAL VALUES

Some of our wisest leaders have emphasized that the goals of life should be the full unfolding of a person's potentials; what matters is that a person is much, not that he or she has much.

Retaining a feeling of significance is becoming ever more difficult in our society of giant enterprises, in which the individual gradually becomes a smaller cog in a bigger machine. In many cases, people find themselves economic puppets who dance to the tune of automation and detached management. They become anxious, not only because their economic security depends directly on others but also because they fail to derive satisfaction from their everyday involvement. In too many cases people live and die without having experienced the fundamental realities that are vital in human existence.

Experiences with nature provide a partial solution to this dilemma. Not merely the scenery, the mountain breeze, or the open spaces are satisfying. The outdoors embodies history, primitive experiences, and elements capable of lifting the spirit. Intangible and imponderable qualities abound in nature. The outdoors has greatly influenced America's character, but the greatest impact is its contribution to the health and sanity of man. Said John Muir:[1] "Everybody needs beauty as well as bread, places to play in and pray in, where nature may heal and cheer and give strength to body and soul alike."

A great comforting influence comes from our being in contact with nature. We become aware of a presence beyond and around us which manifests itself in nature's process—the marvel of the smallest snowflake, the grandeur of the Milky Way. These are all evidence of the order and creation of which we are a part. In nature, these daily miracles are visible on every side, and they enhance a feeling of security and contentment. The awareness of interactions and relationships in the balance of nature is essential to all of us. Robert Frost said it well: "Here are your waters and your watering place. Drink and be whole again beyond confusion."

---

1. "Writings of John Muir," *Mountains of California* (Sierra ed.), Houghton Mifflin Company, Boston, 1916, p. 286.

"In a pleasant spring morning, all men's sins are forgiven. Such a day is a truce with vice."
–Henry David Thoreau (National Park Service)

SOCIOLOGICAL VALUES

In most people there exists an innate drive for adventure, excitement, and challenge. If this drive is not satisfied by high-quality activities, then it will be satisfied by less desirable ones. When a young boy was brought before a renowned judge on a charge of theft, the judge said, "This boy should have been stealing second base." He implied that the boy ought to be challenged through socially acceptable activities. The same statement could have been made about an adventure to the top of a mountain, the pursuit of a large fish, a vigorous hike through the woods, the study of nature, or one of many other wholesome outdoor experiences.

Another social aspect of outdoor activities is that people of like interests draw close together, causing them to develop friendships. Often, a person's circle of friends is developed around a special recreational interest.

Still another aspect is learning desirable behavior and conduct. Learning to keep camp and picnic areas clean, to avoid marring the landscape, and to be considerate of the rights of others are important social attributes, and they are rapidly becoming more important in outdoor recreation because of the tremendous increase in participants.

> Climb the mountains and get their good tidings. The winds will blow their freshness into you and the storms, their energy. Your cares and tensions will drop away like the leaves of autumn.
> —John Muir, *Our National Parks*,
> Houghton Mifflin Company, Boston, 1901, p.56.

PHYSIOLOGICAL VALUES

Heart disease in the United States is a national disaster. Every year about 1 million Americans die from cardiovascular disorders—a death rate higher than that of any other country. About 100,000 people die from coronary disease alone. Millions more are partially crippled by heart attacks. To make matters worse, the disease seems to be killing younger people. Men in their 40s and even in their 30s are dying at an alarming rate, and as in most everything else, women are catching up with men. Partly because of heart disease the longevity of American men is 17th and that of women is 20th among the major developed nations of the world.

To a large extent the health problem relates to lack of exercise. In homes and factories and even on farms, machines now supply the power for most of the work. Mechanized devices have virtually eliminated the necessity of extensive walking, running, lifting, or climbing. One modern machine—TV—holds Americans in captive idleness for an average of 22 hours a week. One of the best opportunities for dealing with this lack of exercise is through the active use of leisure time.

A nation is no stronger than its people, and physical vigor is as much a part of the nation's strength as a good education is. Outdoor recreation has a contribution to make in this regard. Hiking, mountain climbing, canoeing, bicycling, skiing, and swimming tax the body beyond its usual levels. If more of us were rugged outdoorsmen, the average fitness of Americans would certainly be improved.

Perhaps the best thing resource management agencies could do to improve physical fitness would be to encourage the simple pleasures of walking and cycling. In one sense it is a tribute to Americans that they engage in as much cycling and walking as they do, for little has been done to encourage these activities, and a good bit to discourage them.

> Walking, especially walking in scenic surroundings, can be one of the great activities in life—walk for fun, for adventure, for health, and for inspiration.

EDUCATIONAL VALUES

Outdoor recreation has educational values that are essential to the health of society. The outdoors provides a part of education that strengthens people's minds as well as their bodies, that broadens their understanding of the laws of nature, that sharpens their appreciation of its manifold beauties, that fortifies their most precious possession—the spirit that gives life its meaning.

"To those devoid of imagination, a blank place on the map is a useless waste; to others, the most valuable part."–Aldo Leopold, *A Sand County Almanac,* **Ballantine Books, New York, 1978, p. 294. (U.S. Fish and Wildlife Service, photo by Marvin Lee)**

The outdoors offers a laboratory in living where people can make discoveries that vest life with value. Discovering things for oneself is one of the most satisfying occupations. Each of us is on a separate voyage of exploration, and there is no limit to the exciting things we can find when we place ourselves in an environment where we can discover and observe first-hand the wonders of nature.

A few of the specific educational values that may be obtained through outdoor experience include an awareness of life's natural processes, geological formations of soil and rock, the practices of conservation and preservation, beautiful scenery and the joy of experiencing it, one's own self through being alone with nature, good outdoor manners, and the benefits of outdoor skills.

Aldo Leopold[2] put correct emphasis on education in the outdoors when he said, "Every woodland or forest in addition to yielding lumber, fuel, and posts, should provide those who frequent it with a liberal education about nature. This crop of wisdom never fails but unfortunately it is not always harvested." He went on to explain that man is only a cog in the ecological mechanism. If we work with the mechanism, we can both survive and flourish, but if we work against it, it will gradually grind us down. He stressed that recognizing nature as a community is a basic concept of ecology, but knowing that nature is to be loved and respected is an extension of ethics.

A further educational consideration is to recognize that some students who are bored in the classroom are provoked to learn through outdoor experiences. The observation of wildlife, for example, can instill a desire to learn more about biology and ecology.

SPIRITUAL VALUES

In outdoor experiences as in no other way, save a good home or a good church, spiritual values may be realized. Everybody needs beauty as well as bread, places where nature may heal and cheer and give strength to body and soul. Through outdoor recreation a person may feel freedom, serenity, humility, inner warmth, and a sense of security. Experiences in outdoor settings are renewing. To quote Ralph Waldo Emerson:

> Whoso walketh in solitude,
> and inhabiteth the wood,
> Choosing light, wave, rock, and bird,
> Before the money-loving herd,
> Into that forester shall pass,
> From these companions, power and grace.

Of the various outdoor settings that have special meaning, rivers are among the most unique. Rivers flow deep through our nation's heritage. They accommodated the native Americans for hundreds of years, and later they beckoned settlers to explore a new continent and build a nation. Now these same rivers are used in a multitude of other fashions, including enjoyment, renewal, and recreation. Following are some thoughts that help one to understand the variety and uniqueness of rivers.

2. Leopold, Aldo, *A Sand County Almanac*, Oxford University Press, New York, 1966, p. 213.

RIVERS

There is water to feed and cleanse, and water to quicken the earth. Water is in all shapes and sizes from babbling brooks to the great sea. But a river is the friendliest of the waters. It bears life and stimulates life, and protects life; it is a traveler and a joy to all who share its presence.

Long before a river acquires enough authority, it earns a name and a place on the map. Maybe it is a child of the Rocky Mountains, shimmering through green-sided valleys. It may be a daughter of the Cascades made of milk water, hurrying down the church aisle to marry the sea. Or it might be a sentry of the great plains, meandering slowly toward the ocean as it keeps its watch over all of life that depends upon it. It passes 50 towns or more and witnesses every kind of land and living thing. It seems to say, "Let all who will come seeking; no treasures shall be hidden."

Before a river settles in its summer bed, early spring campers come to its side to shed the bonds of winter. The fresh smell of snow-fed waters holds a promise for new beginnings. Man, child, and river reunite for another long season of sunlight and blooming.

Along a western river freshly watered horses carry adventurers alongside a swift stream as they weave their way upward to the high country, and they see the river gradually dwindle as it branches into tributaries that vanish under snowbanks near mountain peaks.

The trout angler seeks a river's loneliness and a touch-and-go acquaintance with a speckled life. He comes to claim the river, and in perfect privacy he stands in the current, hypnotized by the river's voice,

Every river is a world of its own, unique in pattern and personality. **(U.S. Forest Service, photo by Melvin H. Burke)**

"A river is more than an amenity–it is a treasure."–Oliver Wendell Holmes (U.S. Department of Agriculture, Soil Conservation Service, photo by R. B. Branstead)

listening to the monologue of his thoughts; and he calls this fishing. In the chilliness and mist of a mountain valley is another river, swift, deep, and cold, where strong salmon test an angler's tackle and skill. This river holds no easy prize.

Rushing down a deep gorge of the high country is a special kind of river that jumps, thrusts, strikes, and whirls. Its violence and speed cause men to want to conquer it. After the first river riders came down alive, one of them said, "It's ours now; we have mastered the river."

In a less violent setting, a lazy river, clear as window glass, meanders along the valley, showing off its sapphires and emeralds to the sky, sliding over limestone, stealing catnip in Missouri on its way to Arkansas. Slow travelers follow this river as they drift in their boats and explore and dream.

Look across the middle of the land and there are wild hills and prairies divided by another river. It is steady and dependable, and long ago it provided the buffalo with drink. After the buffalo, long-horned cattle grazed on the same banks, and now the longhorns are also gone. Beneath the hoof marks and deep in the hills, lie fossils of life long ago. Prehistoric mammals trace close to the surface. Scientists listen and learn what the earth has been preaching. The river is a museum guarding records of voyageurs who came with rifles and traps, and traders who came to sell pelts of mink and beaver.

Today another kind of voyageur comes by canoe to the same place, trading a few hours of youth for a reunion with the past. For this generation of traders, there is only a trace of the olden days on the river, but other things have changed only in small ways. This is a river, serenely independent and timeless. "Come back when you can," it says, "I'll be waiting."

"There is no music like a little river's . . . . It takes the mind out-of-doors . . . and . . . it quiets a man down like saying his prayers."
–Robert Louis Stevenson
(U.S. Forest Service, photo by Leland J. Prater)

One cannot say that aimless hours were wasted on the river. One can only make sure that the river is a fit companion. (U.S. Forest Service, photo by Paul T. Steucke)

In the East, a person in no hurry can take his stand in a johnboat and ease along the river straight into American history. The scene has changed some since the first person floated down. Fences along the river signify a quiet partnership of man and river. The twinkling surface sparkles in the sun like specks of gold in a prospector's pan. Here the dreamer could ask no more than time and the river's music.

Somewhere in late September a river comes to a lonely, quiet time. Summer slips away into the mist like the wake of a canoe on a foggy day. Schoolchildren return to their more practical errands, and the waterfowl rehearse their journey to the South. Now the late hikers discover the river's summer handiwork, the driftwood. This is the time when a river flows through the countryside, a thin thread of nature appealing for a thicker screen of trees and a wider apron of beauty to guard its privacy and enhance its charm.

The smartest of the curious are brought to the river to make one final probe of driftwood and pebble before the days turn dark too soon. Shopping for an autumn wardrobe, the river borrows colors and textures from the sky and shore, altering them with taste and wearing them with originality. It settles in the haze of Indian summer and paints its dream on liquid canvas. The anglers who never say die return in the golden flame of the autumn for one more cast—just one more.

Then the shortening days loosen the chilling air, preparing the river for a long season of meditation and mending, anticipating the first deep frost and perhaps an overcoat of snow. Now the river seems to slow in its tracks, as though looking backward to its birthplace and to friends across the years, pioneers in past centuries, vacationers last month. Then, seemingly aware of the dependence of all life upon its progress and purity, the river rolls on to its appointment with another springtime.

Discussion Questions

1. In what way is the outdoors an important part of the American tradition?
2. Former Secretary of the Interior Stewart Udall said, "Every generation has a rendezvous with the land." What does this mean, and why is it important to outdoor recreation?
3. "A nation is no stronger than its people." Do you agree? Why or why not? What contributions can outdoor recreation make in creating a nation of strong people?
4. The opportunity to elevate and renew the human spirit has been said to be essential in productive human growth. How can outdoor recreation experiences contribute to this need?

Recommended Readings

"America Shapes Up." *Time*, 2 November 1981, p. 94.

"Americans Get the Trail-Blazing Urge." *U.S. News and World Report*, 11 August 1980, p. 52.

Arnold, Nellie D. "Cultural Bridges." *Journal of Physical Education, Recreation and Dance*, October 1981, p. 51.

Ball, Edith L. "Dynamic Values." *Journal of Physical Education, Recreation and Dance*, October 1981, p. 35.

Barnett, L.A., and B. Storm. "Play, Pleasure and Pain: The Reduction of Anxiety Through Play." *Leisure Sciences*, Vol. 4, No. 2, p. 161.

Chubb, Michael, and Holly R. Chubb. "Changing Human Elements." *Journal of Physical Education, Recreation and Dance*, October 1981, p. 42.

"Factors Associated with Camping Satisfaction in Alberta Park Campgrounds." *Journal of Leisure Research*, Vol. 4, No. 4, p. 292.

"Job Burnout." *U.S. News and World Report*, 18 February 1980, p. 71.

Thoreau, Henry David. *Walden*. Columbus, Ohio: C.E. Merrill, 1969.

"Why More Vacationers Rough It." *U.S. News and World Report*, 21 July 1980, p. 71.

Wilderness Challenge. Washington, D.C.: National Geographic Society, 1980.

CHAPTER 3

Historical Development
of Outdoor Recreation

Recreation activities are as old as recorded history, and the idea of parks for people's enjoyment has been traced to the Sumerians. In *A History of Garden Art*, Marie Luise Gothein[1] refers to the cedar woods of Humbaba with their straight cared-for paths and their neatness as the starting point of art history. She traces the western Asiatic parks from the vineyards and fish ponds of the Sumerian King Gudea (about 2340 B.C.) to the hanging gardens of Babylonia (about 1000 B.C.) and the introduction of flowers in parks in the seventh century B.C.

Centuries after the Sumerians, Greek writers told of the parks and gardens of Persia. Says Gothein:

> The Persians were also familiar with the chase in open country. A grand hunting ground was given to the young Cyrus by his grandfather, in the hope that it would keep him at home, but he despised it, and, fired with longing, summoned his companions and went off, for in this park there were so many animals that he felt as though he was only shooting captive creatures.

In ancient India there were not only parks for the kings but great recreation and park areas for communities as well. In the 12th century B.C. a park in the city of Polonnaruwa in Ceylon included, according to Gothein,

> Spouts of water, conveyed thither in pipes and machines, made the place appear as though clouds were incessantly pouring down drops of rain. There was a great array of different baths that delighted masters and men. We hear also of other parks and other baths, and even of gardens that the rich made for the recreation of the poor.

---

1. Gothein, Marie Luise, *A History of Garden Art*, 2 vols., ed. Walter P. Wright, J. M. Dent & Sons, Ltd., London, 1913. Quoted in Charles B. Doell and Louis F. Twardzik, *Elements of Park and Recreation Administration*, 3rd ed., Burgess Publishing Co., Minneapolis, 1973.

The growth of the Greek games caused the need for outdoor gymnasiums. One form of the gymnasium became the academy, and the academy became the seat of learning, actually the home of Greek philosophers. Hippodromes, gymnasiums, and academies became portions of Greek parks.

Wealthy and influential Romans were noted for having large villas, and many of these had characteristics of parks with special emphasis on hunting. Gothein notes:

> Quintus Hortensius had already made a park of fifty yokes of land, and enclosed it with a wall, and on this estate he had set up on the higher ground a shooting-box where he entertained his friends in a peculiar way. He had a slave dressed like Orpheus who sang before them, and then sounded a horn, whereupon a whole crowd of stags and boars and other quadrupeds came up, so that to him who told the tale the spectacle seemed more delightful than the hunt itself.

Generally speaking, throughout the Roman Empire the villas were on the outskirts of the towns or in the country. In ancient Rome itself, however, the estates occupied the municipality so that the city was spotted with gardens. This was the first significant move to bring the country into the city. Also, the ingenious Romans invented the floral greenhouse, using mica for windowpanes. During the first century of the Christian era the Romans expanded their empire northward, and their great villas and hunting parks began to appear in what is now France and Germany—some of them even as far north as England.

During the early Christian era before the fall of Rome, little was new in the historical development of parks. The thousand years following the fall of Rome, commonly known as the Middle Ages and sometimes called the Dark Ages, were truly dark from the standpoint of park and recreation development. The idea of parks was barely kept alive—largely in the monasteries, which frequently were the former villas of the nobility and later possessed by the church.

The kings of England formerly had their forests "to hold the king's game" for sport or food . . . Why should not we . . . have ours or shall we, like villains, grub them [game] all up, poaching on our own national domain?

—Henry David Thoreau

Gradually some of the barons began to acquire sizable estates, and the art of gardening grew from the simple chore of raising fruit and plants to designing gardens of interest and beauty. By the 13th and 14th centuries there were many such villas, and a popular feature of most of the gardens was the maze, a network of hedges constructed as a puzzle.

By the end of the 13th century in Italy, public grounds were established for the pleasure of common people. These took the form of walks and public squares, frequently decorated with statues.

During the 1500s, in the early phase of the Renaissance, the private grounds and estates of many of the noble and wealthy developed in fabulous fashion. In the period between 1500 and 1700 the central European and Scandinavian countries, and even Russia to some extent, made great progress toward the development of parks and gardens. Among the popular facilities were private fishing and hunting reserves, summerhouses, grottos, and formal gardens. Water displays, including canals, ponds, and elaborate fountains (some with extravagant statues), all became part of the numerous parks and villas. Outdoor theaters, much like those of the early Greek and Roman eras, were reintroduced, as were facilities for certain games—tennis courts, archery ranges, race courses, and lawn-bowling greens. Music became part of the entertainment in many of the gardens. This was the period when several still-famous parks were established, such as the Tuileries and Luxembourg in Paris and the Parque de Madrid in Spain. This new movement, which had its origin in Italy and especially in Florence, crept northward into France and the Low Countries, then Germany, Scandinavia, and England.

By the latter part of the 18th century, England had developed a park and garden character of its own, which in turn influenced other countries of the continent. The English gardens assumed the appearance of informal walks and plantings. Rock walkways were developed and greens were provided for bowling. The bowling greens of England became the "boulingrins" of France. It was during the late part of this era that parks and gardens became more accessible to the commoners.

By the late 19th century, public grounds were established in Italy for the leisure of all people. Gothein writes:

> Not only for shooting but for other sport, places were provided, and especially for ball games which developed in the 15th century, chiefly in England; later they spread all over the continent in the form of football, croquet, and lawn tennis, and when people had more room these games were introduced in private gardens with properly laid out squares and courts.

The trend toward public parks inside communities spread to France and Germany, and then to other countries in both northern and southern Europe.

COLONIAL PERIOD AND AFTER

In the historical sense, municipal parks as we know them today appeared late in the development of community life in America. In the New England colonies the common public ground (or village green) that had become traditional in England appeared again under a new setting. The Boston Common was set aside near the middle of the town in 1634, and in 1640 the Boston city officials took action to protect it from future encroachment. Throughout Massachusetts, Connecticut, and New Hampshire numerous examples still exist of commons of various origins and in various states of preservation.

The commons in the early New England communities were not solely recreation areas. They were plots owned by the community and used for a variety of purposes, some of which were recreational. Other uses included selective harvesting of timber, the grazing of livestock, community work projects, and political, business, and social activities. Usually the community buildings were placed on the commons and often it was also the location of the community's church.

It is natural that England exerted the strongest influence on the early phases of the park and recreation movement in America. As our country developed, however, it established a character of its own. In some respects, the United States has now become the world leader in

An early hunting, fishing, and forest recreation scene. (Library of Congress, originally published by Currier and Ives)

the provision of park and recreation areas. This is especially true concerning recreation on wild lands.

Fortunately, our nation's early abundance of natural resources seemed to prompt the romantic efforts of poets, writers, artists, philosophers, and explorers. For example, the writings of George Catlin, William Cullen Bryant, James Fenimore Cooper, and John Muir certainly have contributed to the protection of pristine areas. Emerson, Thoreau, and Leopold, too, communicated a philosophy toward nature that has aided in saving aesthetic resources.

Organized conservation efforts started in the United States as early as 1626, when the colony of Plymouth passed an ordinance that prohibited the cutting of timber on colony land without official consent. In 1710 the town of Newington, New Hampshire, acquired a 110-acre (44-ha) community forest to be used by the townspeople for acquiring lumber for public buildings. In 1799, Congress appropriated $200,000 to purchase timber lands. These beginnings of forest management were based primarily on the need for ready access to lumber for ships and public buildings. These actions automatically set the stage for a large number of other acts of conservation and preservation that have had a tremendous effect on the availability and use of natural resources for recreational purposes.

By the time of the Revolutionary War, 12 of the 13 colonies had enacted closed seasons on certain game. In 1844 the first association for the protection of game was formed in New

York. In 1871 Congress passed a much-needed bill for the protection of bison. The next year a law was passed in New York naming a seven-member commission to study the advisability of reserving wild lands for watershed preservation. By 1873 New York had purchased 40,000 acres (16,000 ha) of forest land. This is accepted as the first substantial purchase of state forest reserves, which now total more than 2.5 million acres (1 million ha) in that state, mostly in the Adirondack and Catskill mountains.

These acts were among the first significant responses to the mounting evidence that natural things should not be taken for granted. It had become clear to the wise that with population growth and industrial expansion, nature easily could be tipped off balance and in certain aspects damaged beyond recovery.

On 10 April 1872 in Nebraska, Arbor Day was declared to create an awareness of the need for trees in metropolitan areas. In that same year Yellowstone National Park was reserved as a "pleasuring ground," and this marked the beginning of the national park system in the United States (and in the world). In 1874 Dr. Franklin D. Hough, at a meeting of the American Association for the Advancement of Science, presented a paper entitled "The Duty of Government in the Preservation of Parks."

The decade from 1875 to 1885 brought increased emphasis to conservation, which was highlighted by the writings and efforts of Theodore Roosevelt. Much of his conservation philosophy was expressed in his book *The Wilderness Hunter*, and he and his close associate Gifford Pinchot gave significant national leadership during the late 1800s.

During that same era citizens paid increased attention to wildlife management. California and New Hampshire established state game commissions in 1878, and in 1883 the American Ornithologists Union was organized.

President Benjamin Harrison created the first national forest reserve in 1891–the Yellowstone Timberland Reserve, now part of the Shoshone National Forest. Before his term expired he had set aside other forest reserves totaling 13 million acres (5.3 million ha).

On 31 March 1891, the Park Protection Act was passed to protect wildlife in the national parks. In 1898 Gifford Pinchot was named head of the Federal Government Forest Division, and the forest conservation movement began to expand greatly under his leadership. He brought the word "conservation" into popular usage in application to natural resources. In 1899 Congress allowed the recreational use of forest reserves. This was the first law to recognize officially the recreation value of forests.

The states began to take a more active role as Niagara Falls, New York, was set aside as a public reservation in 1885. In the same year Fort Mackinac was transferred from the federal government to the state of Michigan to mark the beginning of that state's system of recreation areas. In 1885 New York instituted the first comprehensive state forestry act in America, and that same year California, Colorado, and Ohio created state boards of forestry.

EARLY 1900s

The conservation movement progressed significantly in the first decade of the 20th century. The passage of the Reclamation Act in 1902 provided for government aid to help develop water resources. The first national wildlife refuge was established in 1902 on Pelican Island off the coast of Florida. In 1905 the Bureau of Biological Survey, the predecessor of the U.S. Fish and Wildlife Service, was established. The Division of Forestry in the Department of

A golf game during the sport's early beginning in the United States. (Library of Congress, printed by W.T. Sniedley)

Agriculture was changed to the U.S. Forest Service, and this new agency took over the forest reserves that had been administered by the General Land Office of the Department of the Interior.

The Antiquities Act of 1906 paved the way for setting aside national monuments by presidential proclamation. Also in 1906, President Theodore Roosevelt signed 33 proclamations that added more than 15.6 million acres (6.32 million ha) to the forest reserve. In 1908 Roosevelt appointed a national conservation commission, with Gifford Pinchot as chairman, to study ways to save the country's natural resources. In 1909 the commission published an inventory of natural resources in the United States.

By 1916 several national parks and monuments had been set aside under the preservation concept, and during that year the National Park Service was established to administer these areas. According to the document that established it, the purpose of the Park Service is to "promote and regulate the usual federal areas known as national parks, monuments, and reservations, to conserve the scenery and natural and historic objects and the wildlife, and to provide for the enjoyment of the same in such manner and by such means as will leave them unimpaired for their enjoyment for future generations."

Other noteworthy developments of the early 1900s were these: the passage by Congress of the Term-Lease Law of 1915, which authorized issuance of long-term permits for summer homes, lodges, and other structures needed for recreation and for public convenience on national forest lands; the establishment of the Rocky Mountain National Park in Colorado; and the establishment of the Gila Wilderness in New Mexico in 1924.

During the 1920s the U.S. Forest Service and the National Park Service gave increased emphasis to outdoor recreation. Stephen Mather, the first director of the Park Service, claimed that recreation was a primary function of the agency. Forester William Greeley wrote in *Outlook* in 1925 that "outdoor recreation ranks today as one of the major resources of the national forests."

The depression years of the 1930s were boom years for outdoor recreation. The emergency conservation work programs of the federal government, debatable though they were, fulfilled certain definite needs. They created a demand for trained personnel through the work projects of the Public Work Administration, Works Progress Administration, and the Civilian Conservation Corps. Needed outdoor recreation facilities were constructed, and federally funded positions for 26,500 recreation workers were made available.

Also in the 1930s, wildlife management began to gain recognition as a science. Aldo Leopold's book, *Game Management,* was published during that decade, and it continued for a long time to serve as an important guide to wildlife-management personnel.

The Migratory Bird Hunting Stamp Act of 1934 provided for acquiring lands for national wildlife refuges. Congress established an advisory board on national parks, historic sites, and monuments. The Soil Conservation Service was established during the early 1930s. The Forest Service continued to designate wilderness areas within the national forest reserve. The National Resources Committee was appointed by President Franklin D. Roosevelt in 1935 to investigate the country's natural resources and to plan for their development and use. Also in that year, Congress passed the Fullmer act, which established federal aid to the states to acquire state forest lands.

In 1940 the Bureau of Biological Survey and the Bureau of Fisheries merged and became the U.S. Fish and Wildlife Service, located within the Department of the Interior. In 1941 several states passed enabling legislation to enhance the establishment of state, city, town, and school forests. A few states already had state forests. In 1943 comprehensive interagency river-basin planning began with the organization of the Federal Interagency River Committee.

POSTWAR YEARS

After World War II, the growing public demand for resource-oriented recreation and sharpening competition for the various uses of natural resources became a matter of increasing national and international concern. The United Nations sponsored a conference on the conservation and use of natural resources in 1949. The Dingell-Johnson Act of 1950 provided federal aid to state fisheries, and the Watershed-Protection and Flood-Prevention Act of 1954 authorized the Department of Agriculture to cooperate with state and local agencies in planning and making improvements on small watersheds. The Recreation and Public Purposes Act of 1954 authorized state and local governments and nonprofit organizations to acquire certain federal lands for recreational use and for other public purposes. Congress amended the Coordination Act of 1958 to specify that wildlife and fishery conservation should receive equal consideration and should be coordinated with other features of water-resource development. Also of major significance was the initiation in 1956 of the ten-year Mission 66 facility-improvement program of the Park Service. In 1957 the U.S. Forest Service launched a five-year special improvement program called Operation Outdoors.

We are now living through the second great divide in human history, comparable in magnitude only with that first break in historic continuity—the shift from barbarism to civilization.
—Alvin Toffler, *Future Shock*, Bantam Books, New York, 1971.

Recognizing the need for a nationwide study of these programs, Congress established in 1958 the Outdoor Recreation Resources Review Commission to survey the outdoor recreation needs of the people for the next 40 years and to recommend actions to meet those needs. The report of the commission consisted of 27 informative volumes. Several significant legislative acts and nationwide programs have resulted from the commission's report.

The Multiple-Use Sustained-Yield Act of 1960 made outdoor recreation an official function of the National Forest Service on the same basis as the other four identified functions. This was really more a formality than a significant official action, because the national forests had been managed under the multiple-use concept for many years.

The establishment of the Bureau of Outdoor Recreation within the Department of the Interior in 1962 was a major development. In 1965 the Land and Water Conservation Fund Act was passed, with the provisions of the act to be administered by the Bureau of Outdoor Recreation. This act provides matching grant-in-aid funds to the states and their political subdivisions for planning, acquiring, and developing outdoor recreational areas.

Also in 1964 the Wilderness Act was passed, authorizing the creation of a national wilderness system that originally contained 9 million acres (3.6 million ha) of national forestland.

In 1965 the Highway Beautification Act went into effect, and it provided government grants for highway aesthetics and recreation development. The Wild and Scenic Rivers Act of 1968 authorized a program of protection of free-flowing rivers by placing them in the national system. During this same year, the National Trails System Act was approved; the Pacific Crest and the Appalachian trails were the two initial entries into the system.

The Land Law Review Commission released a report in 1970 recommending a larger recreational role for federal lands. That same year the administration rejected the first nationwide outdoor-recreation plan because of its high cost and urban emphasis. The following year the Legacy of Parks program was initiated to accelerate acquisition of additional national park lands.

In 1972 the Water Pollution Control Act decreed that all water must be safe for fishing and swimming by 1983. Also, the National Park Centennial Year was celebrated by adding 14 units to the national park system, including the Gateway National Recreation area close to San Francisco.

The second Nationwide Outdoor Recreation Plan, published in 1973, was entitled "A Legacy for America." In 1974, a landmark bond issue at the state level was passed in California, issuing $250 million of bonds for parks, recreation, and wildlife. In 1976 the Federal

Ice-skating in Central Park during the early 1800s. (Library of Congress, originally published by Currier & Ives)

Land Policy Management Act formalized the multiple-use management policy for the Bureau of Land Management.

The National Parks and Recreation Act of 1978 provided $1.2 billion for the improvement of urban and national parks. That same year the Alaska Lands Bill failed in Congress; so the president used his authority under the Antiquities Act to proclaim more than 50 million acres (20 million ha) for national monuments in Alaska. This was by far the largest single addition to the national park system. At the same time, the president added 40 million acres (16 million ha) in Alaska as national wildlife refuges.

In 1978 the Bureau of Outdoor Recreation was combined with other divisions of the Department of the Interior to form a new agency, the Heritage Conservation and Recreation Service. This agency lasted only three years; in 1981 it was dissolved and its responsibilities were absorbed by the National Park Service.

The era of the 1960s and 1970s was considered the most productive in resource conservation and outdoor recreation. A significant amount of major legislation was passed. Many important government programs were initiated, and more emphasis than ever before was placed on outdoor recreation by private enterprise and the public in general.

The opposite was true during the end of the 1970s and the early 1980s. These were years of constraint and caution. The recession, high unemployment, heavy pressure to cut back government spending, and continuation of the fuel shortage created a highly conservative atmosphere that resulted in little action and few new programs. In fact, some programs were eliminated and the funding was reduced for others at various levels of government. Moreover, because of financial constraints, free enterprise in the recreation industry found producing a profit and staying in business to be difficult. Leaders in the 1980s appear to be emphasizing caution and concern about waste and the abuse of resources.

RECREATION ORGANIZATIONS

The first association representing the natural resource interests of the nation was the American Forestry Association, organized in Chicago in 1875. This association has exerted a strong influence on forest management during the past century. A second influential group with strong interest in recreation is the Sierra Club, founded in 1892 by John Muir, its director for two decades. The club was most influential in having Yosemite established as a national park. The dedicated members of this group frequently join forces with other associations, magazines, and newspapers to further their cause. For example, Mount Rainier became a national park in 1899 through the combined efforts of the Sierra Club, the National Geographic Society, the American Association for the Advancement of Science, the Geographical Society of America, and the Appalachian Club. Other organizations that have provided significant support to the parks movement, especially national parks, are the American Museum of Natural History, established in New York in 1869; the National Audubon Society, started in 1905; and the Wilderness Society, organized in 1935.

The first professional organization for persons directly involved in the parks movement was formed by a group of municipal park superintendents in New England. The New England Association of Park Superintendents first convened in Boston in 1898. By 1904 this group had become a national association and changed its name to the American Association of Park Superintendents. In 1921 a broader constitution was adopted, recognizing that parks were not only places to be viewed but also places where people could participate in various recreational pursuits. The reorganization also included a change of title to the American Institute of Park Executives.

Other organizations that have left their mark on the outdoor-recreation movement are the Boy Scouts of America and the Camp Fire Girls, both organized in 1910; the Girl Scouts, 1911; the American Society of Landscape Architects, 1916; and the American Camping Association, 1924.

The National Parks Association was formed in 1919 to promote the system of federal parks. This association became the National Park and Conservation Association in 1968.

The Izaac Walton League was established in 1922 as a national conservation organization. The league has consistently spoken out for the recreational use of natural resources.

The National Conference on State Parks was formally organized in 1928, and it has served traditionally as the professional association for park and recreation professionals at all levels of government.

During the 1930s the American Wildlife Institute, the National Wildlife Federation, and the American Wildlife Society were founded. The first North American Wildlife Conference was held during that decade.

Other organizations that have spoken out for improved outdoor recreational opportunities are the Conservation Foundation, established in 1948, and Resources for the Future, organized in 1952.

The International Recreation Association was established in 1956 and changed its name to the World Leisure and Recreation Association in 1973. In 1958 the Association of Interpretive Naturalists was formed.

The National Recreation and Park Association was created in 1965 by the merger of six national organizations–the American Association of Zoological Parks and Aquariums, the American Institute of Park Executives, the American Recreation Society, the National Association of State Park Directors, the National Conference on State Parks, and the National recreation Association. This was a milestone in the history of the outdoor-recreation movement, and its significance is explained by Alfred B. LaGasse and Walter L. Cook.[2]

The broad park and recreation field has moved through three phases: (1) the stage of unity, when recreation was pursued on the estates of large landholders without thoughts of whether it dealt with parks, planning and design, recreation, forestry, wildlife, or related natural resources, (2) the stage of separation when those in organized recreation, parks, and forestry pursued their individual fields of endeavor with little thought for the others, and (3) the stage of moving the three streams of development toward unity.

Descriptions of the numerous organizations associated with outdoor recreation appear in Chapter 15.

LEADERSHIP PREPARATION

The increased emphasis on conservation and resource management gradually resulted in demands for more knowledgeable personnel. As a result, universities began to offer instruction in resource management. Eventually, colleges of forestry were established at Yale in 1873 and Cornell University in 1874. By 1910, 19 universities had schools of forestry, but none of them had curricula specifically in the field of outdoor recreation. People with experience in planning and design or horticulture filled most park superintendent positions. In 1911, however, the New York State College of Forestry at Syracuse University became the first to offer a program to prepare professionals in park administration and city forestry.

Beginning in 1915, several annual American game conferences were held under the auspices of the American Game Protection and Propagation Association. In 1919 the American School of Wildlife Protection was established in McGregor, Iowa. In 1924 the first national conference on outdoor recreation, held in Washington, D.C., was attended by 309 delegates representing 128 organizations.

During the 1930s several institutions began educating people in the management of natural resources for recreation use. The landscape architecture department of the University of Massachusetts played a leading role in this regard, and by the mid-1930s the forest management department of Utah State University offered three classes in recreation. A course in national park management was introduced in the College of Forestry at Colorado State Uni-

---

2. LaGasse, Alfred B., and Walter L. Cook, *History of Parks and Recreation*, Management Bulletin No. 56, National Recreation and Parks Association, 1965, p. 33.

versity. Also, courses having to do with wildlife management were added in colleges of forestry. In 1935 a recreation major was started in the Department of Forestry at Michigan State University, and in 1936 a four-year undergraduate curriculum in wildlife management was established at the University of Massachusetts.

Immediately after World War II a number of colleges and universities added recreation curricula. North Carolina State University established an option in park administration. Colorado State University organized a department of forest recreation and wildlife conservation, and the Great Lakes Park and Recreation Training Institute was established. In the early 1950s the Southeastern Park and Recreation Training Institute and the Southwest Park and Recreation Institute were added. Subsequently, numerous other such regional institutes have been established.

During the 1950s noticeable changes took place in the philosophy underlying recreation curricula. It became more apparent that those managing natural resources should be better informed about people's use of the resources, while those prepared in municipal recreation should be more knowledgeable about natural resources. As a result, the base of many of the curricula began to broaden.

In the mid-1950s a park management and municipal forestry curriculum was organized in the Department of Land and Water Conservation at Michigan State University, replacing a similar program established at that university in the Department of Forestry in 1935. A curriculum in park management was started in the Department of Horticulture and Park Management at Texas Tech University. Also, a park management curriculum was started at Sacramento State College in 1959.

In 1953 the American Association for Health, Physical Education, and Recreation started an Outdoor Education Project, and the association also sponsored national conferences on professional preparation in 1954, 1956, and 1958. The American Alliance for Health, Physical Education, Recreation, and Dance[3] also sponsored a national conference, Education for Leisure, in 1957 and another, Leadership for Leisure, in 1963.

In 1962 the National Recreation Association began the Recreation Management Institute at Indiana University, and in 1965 the Park Management School was started at Oglebay Park, West Virginia.

Also in 1965 the American Institute of Park Executives completed research indicating that at least 99 curricula in recreation or park administration existed. There were also 28 accredited and 18 nonaccredited schools of forestry, of which 8 reported curricula or options in forest recreation. There were 29 colleges with curricula in soil conservation, 33 with curricula in wildlife management, and several with curricula in other recreation-related fields.

When the National Recreation and Park Association was organized in 1965, the Society of Park and Recreation Educators became one of the divisions. This society provided the academic profession for the first time with a common platform. The most recent significant event in the educational chronology of parks and recreation was the beginning of *The Journal of Leisure Research*. After a timid start, it is now accepted as the most important leisure-oriented research journal.

3. This organization formerly was called the American Alliance for Health, Physical Education and Recreation. In 1980 its name was changed to reflect its growing involvement in dance. The abbreviation AAHPERD will be used for all references to the organization in this text, regardless of its actual name at the time.

In 1968, the American Alliance for Health, Physical Education, Recreation, and Dance and the National Recreation and Parks Association sponsored a national conference in Washington, D.C., entitled Outdoor Recreation in America. In 1973 the two organizations published a booklet listing more than 300 colleges and universities that offered curricula in the park and recreation field. Some of these schools offer specialties in outdoor recreation. In 1974 the Bureau of Outdoor Recreation sponsored a national conference on outdoor-recreation research.

Additional historical information appears in other chapters and in Appendix A.

Discussion Questions

1. Recreation participation is as old as recorded history. Have people's recreation objectives changed through time? What factors have possibly influenced change?
2. In the early history of leisure, certain forms of recreation seemed to be limited to the wealthy. Why? Is the same true today?
3. Who were some of the early American philosophers and writers who enhanced man's appreciation for the outdoors? Discuss the particular contributions of some of these leaders.
4. What were some of the early acts of conservation of natural resources in the United States, and what were the essential circumstances surrounding these acts?
5. Why were the depression years of the 1930s boom years for outdoor recreation in some aspects? Explain some of the positive results.
6. With increased emphasis on resource conservation and management, greater demands have arisen for more knowledgeable personnel. What organizations and institutions have sought to meet these demands, and how much success have they had?
7. The 1960s and 1970s formed an era of tremendous concern and action on behalf of outdoor recreation. Why was this so? What were some of the more important results?

Recommended Readings

Brockman, Frank, William R. Catton, Jr., and Barney Dowdle. *Recreation Use of Wildlands*, 3rd ed. New York: McGraw Hill, 1979. Chapters 3, 4, 5.

Chubb, Michael, and Holly R. Chubb. *One Third of Our Time*. New York: John Wiley & Sons, 1981. Chapter 2.

Dulles, Foster Rhea. *A History of Recreation: America Learns to Play*. New York: Appleton-Century-Crofts, 1965.

Jensen, Clayne R. *Recreation and Leisure Time Careers*. Skokie, Illinios: National Textbook Co., 1983.

Van Doren, Carlton, and Louis Hodges. *America's Park and Recreation Heritage–a Chronology*. U.S. Department of the Interior, 1981.

CHAPTER 4

Sociological Trends and Influences

Ours is a fast-moving technological society where the watchword is "change." Change follows change with bewildering rapidity, and this influences our lives in various respects, including our leisure and recreational patterns.

One thing that is new is the prevalence of newness, the scale and scope of change itself, so that the world alters as we walk in it, so that the years of a man's life measure not some small growth or rearrangement or moderation of what he learned in childhood, but a great upheaval.

–Robert Oppenheimer, *The Population Challenge*, U.S. Department of the Interior, Washington, D.C., 1967, p. 23.

In the past most people were able to go through life with a set of attitudes and beliefs appropriate to the age in which they were born. The rate of change in science, technology, education, and social values was slow enough that those disciplines changed little throughout one's lifetime. Even then each generation expressed its frustration with the common phrase, "What is the world coming to?" In our day and age there are many interesting questions about what the world is coming to in terms of population growth, urbanization trends, work and leisure time, mobility, technology, income, education, and changing philosophies.

POPULATION

Resource managers are very concerned about the demands being placed on our natural resources, and an increase in population implies still more use. Moreover, more people

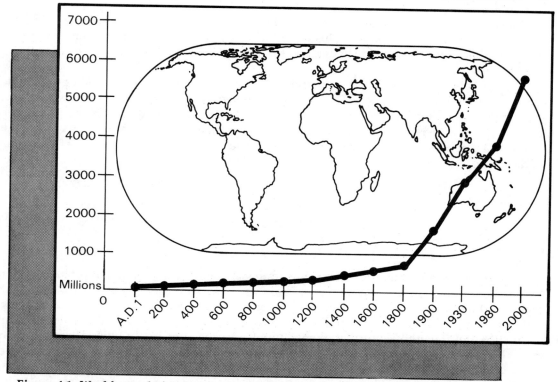

Figure 4.1. World population trends, A.D. **1–2000. (Source: Bureau of the Census,** *Population Projection Series II)*

require more residential, commercial, and industrial space, and this results in fewer natural areas. There is a point of population beyond which the resources cannot satisfy the demand for outdoor recreation, at least of the kind and quality to which we are accustomed.

It is estimated that from the year A.D. 1 until 1930 the world population doubled from 750 million to 1.5 billion. Then during the next 35 years (1930–1965) it redoubled, increasing to 3 billion. The U.S. Commission on Population has stated that it could almost redouble again by the year 2000, thus approaching 6 billion people (the 4 billion mark was reached in 1976).[1] It has been calculated that if the present rate of annual growth had existed since the beginning of the Christian era, we would now have an average of 1 square yard of earth for each person. That would be hardly enough for mountain climbing, skiing, and long golf drives (Figure 4.1).

Each minute 220 babies are born, while 140 people die. Each time your heart beats the world's population increases by one. Human multiplication is self-accelerating. Like compound interest, it spurts upward in geometrical progression.

---

1. Much of the information about early population trends was obtained from the U.S. Commission on Population, Washington, D.C. Current population figures and future estimates were obtained from the Bureau of the Census.

Most of the world's population is in underdeveloped countries or countries where the natural resources are badly depleted. This contributes to social unrest and political instability, and it smothers efforts to develop better lives for millions of people who are ill-fed, ill-clothed, and ill-housed.

Currently North America and Western Europe have about 17% of the world's population and 64% of the income, as measured in goods and services produced. Asia has 56% of the population and 14% of the income. Ironically, the deprived and underprivileged portion of the population is increasing faster than the affluent portion. The "hunger belt" of Africa and South Asia accounts for four of every five births, while this area produces only one fifth of the world's food.

We'll all be a doubling, doubling, doubling
We'll all be a doubling in 32 years.
    —Pete Seeger, "A Population Ballad."

It is especially important for Americans to recognize that the population problem is not confined to faraway places; our own predicted rate of increase is only slightly less than that of the world in total. In 1800 the U.S. population was less than 5 million. Fifty years later it had increased by five times, to 25 million. By 1900 the population reached 85 million, and in the first half of the 20th century, it almost doubled, surpassing 151 million. There are now more than 235 million people in the United States, and the population continues to grow at a rate of 2 million to 3 million annually.

Even though the percentage of increase is less than a decade ago, never before have our numbers risen so rapidly—not even during the peak of the immigration flood just before World War I, when a million immigrants were added to the population each year (Figure 4.2).

The population explosion is a matter of simple mathematics, and it is well illustrated by this true story.[2]

On the eve of his 95th birthday, John Eli Miller died in Middlefield, Ohio, leaving to mourn his passing a large number of living descendants. He was survived by 5 children, 61 grandchildren, 338 great-grandchildren, and 6 great-great-grandchildren—a total of 410 living descendants.

John Miller actually had seen with his own eyes a population explosion. His data were not statistics on a graph or chart, but the scores of children at every family gathering who ran up to kiss Grandpa, so many that it confused him. His confusion can be forgiven, for there were among them 15 John Millers, all named in his honor. What man could remember the names of 61 grandchildren and 338 great-grandchildren?

The remarkable thing about this large clan was that it started with a family of only seven children. John Miller's family was not unusually large. It is just that he lived long enough to find out what simple multiplication can do.

At the time of John Miller's death, 61 of his 63 grandchildren were still living. Of the 341 great-grandchildren, only 3 had died. All 6 of his great-great-grandchildren were born during

2. *Population Profile.* U.S. Government Printing Office, Washington, D.C., 1964.

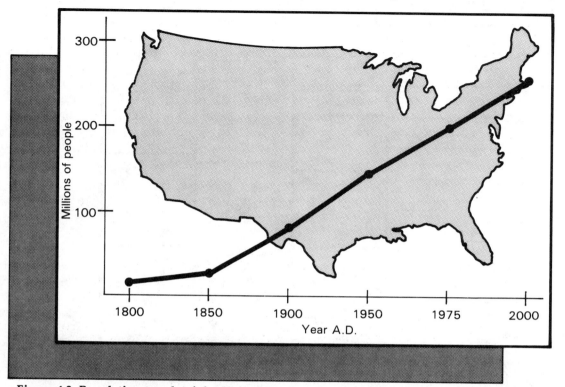

Figure 4.2. Population trends of the United States, 1800–2000. (Source: Bureau of the Census, *Population Projection Series II)*

the last year of his life and were healthy infants. Thus, a major factor in the worldwide population crisis was vividly evident in John Miller's family: A very high percentage of children born in the 20th century, who enjoy the benefits of modern medicine, are growing up to become adults and to have families of their own.

What did John Miller think about his family? Did it worry him to see it growing so large? Indeed it did. His concerns were the very ones that the demographers, economists, sociologists, and other serious students of the world population have been voicing. He was not an educated man, but John Miller summarized it in one simple question he constantly repeated, "Where will they all find good farms?"

The population increase (excluding immigration) is an expression of the ratio between births and deaths. In 1900 the annual death rate was 17.2 per 1000 Americans. Now it has been reduced to 9.1 per 1000. On the average a male child born in 1900 could expect to live 46 years, whereas now one's life expectancy is 72 years. For females the gain has been even greater, from 48 in 1900 to 78 years. What will life expectancy be in the year 2000 and beyond?

Furthermore, the age distribution of the U.S. population is changing. In 1940, 7% of the population was age 65 or more. Currently this figure is 12%. The proportion of older members

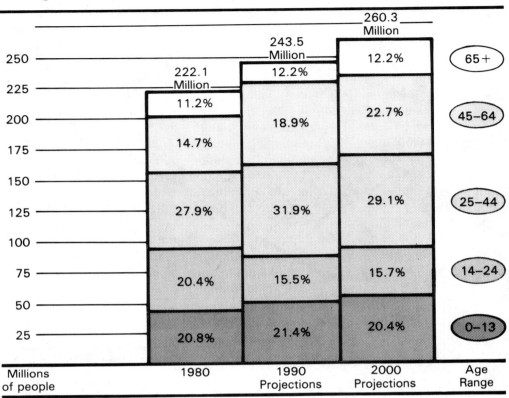

Figure 4.3. Population age structure of the United States. (Source: Bureau of the Census, *Population Projection Series II)*

of the population has increased, while the proportion of working age has decreased (Figure 4.3).

Still another interesting point is that the average household size is getting smaller. It is presently about 2.65 persons, as compared to 2.75 in 1980. This is a big drop from 3.14 persons per household in 1970. It is projected that by 1995 the average household size will be 2.39. One reason for the drop is the decline in birth rate. Other reasons are the higher divorce rate, and persons' waiting longer to get married.

In addition to total population and age distribution, the population density in particular geographic locations is an important consideration, which leads us to the topic of urbanization trends.

URBANIZATION

For most Americans the days are gone when inspiring natural beauty could be found at the end of the street or around the corner of the block. First came villages and towns, then cities, and sprawling metropolitan areas, and finally metropolitan areas joined together to form megalopolis regions. Like inflating balloons, the small communities founded a century or two ago have grown larger, and as they have grown, problems that the founding fathers never foresaw have been generated.

The American society was originally agrarian. In fact, some of our institutions are still geared to seasons and harvests. But because of startling advances in agriculture, the average farm worker today can produce enough food for 70 other persons. At the time of the Revolutionary War 92% of our population were farmers, while today this figure is about 3%, and some economic experts predict that by the year 2000 fewer than 2% of our population will be farmers and that they will produce a surplus of farm products. This means that each year more people leave the rural areas and go to cities to live and work.

At the time of the first U.S. census (1790) only 5% of the 4 million population lived in cities of 2500 or more, and these cities were small by today's standards. At the time of the Civil War we were 20% urban; by World War I we had become 45% urban; and in 1930, for the first time more than half of our population lived in cities or towns. In 1950 the census showed that 60% of the population was urban, by 1960 it was 68%, and now it exceeds 75%. Demographic experts predict that by the turn of the century, 80% of our population will live in urban and suburban areas (Figure 4.4).

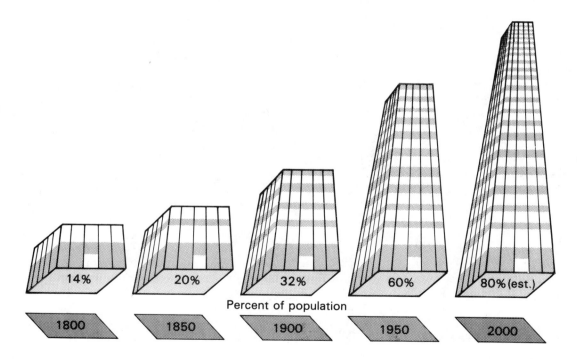

Figure 4.4. Trends toward urbanization of the U.S. population, 1800–2000. (Source: Bureau of the Census, *Population Projection Series II)*

While the steady movement of people to urban locations has been under way, there have also occurred some major changes within the urban complexes. The old districts and central portions of the cities have grown little in recent years and some have lost population. In contrast, the surrounding suburbs have expanded. As a result, almost everyone in the United States has firsthand experience with some area of land which was in a farm or a forest a decade ago and today it is covered with suburban housing, a shopping center, or an industrial complex.

A significant feature of the metropolitan pattern in the United States is its low density. This applies not only to residential areas but also to industries, business, and schools. We have emphasized rambling structures surrounded by large areas for parking. A century ago when a community increased by 1000 people it urbanized about 10 acres. Thirty years ago 30 acres were needed. Today in suburban areas over 100 acres are required to absorb 1000 additional population. It is not implied that this sprawling style of development is totally undesirable, but it does require a tremendous amount of land, and open land is becoming more precious every year.

Because of our sprawling suburbs some metropolitan areas are taking on dimensions of 100 square miles (260 km²)or more, thus forming megalopolis regions. In the future, the Atlantic Seaboard, the Great Lakes region, the Pacific Coast from San Francisco to San Diego, and the Florida peninsula will take on strong megalopolis characteristics (Table 4.1).

Gradually, the whole world is becoming urbanized. This Revolutionary War fort, Castle Clinton, provides welcome open space that thousands of visitors enjoy each year. (National Park Service, photo by Richard Frear)

**Table 4.1. Populations of Selected
Megalopolis Regions of the United States**

Area	Population
Boston-Lawrence-Lowell	3,710,000
Chicago	8,056,000
Cleveland-Akron-Lorain	3,180,000
Detroit-Ann Arbor	4,982,000
Houston-Galveston	2,322,000
Los Angeles-Long Beach-Anaheim	10,600,000
New York-Newark-Jersey City	18,020,000
Philadelphia-Wilmington-Trenton	5,936,000
San Francisco-Oakland-San Jose	4,770,000

Bureau of the Census, Population Profile 1982, p. 146.

Despite advantages enjoyed by urban dwellers, there is much criticism of large cities as places to live and work. They are often criticized for their congestion and poor sanitation and their lack of order and unity. The central core often suffers from blight and is a breeding place of disaffection and violence. Furthermore, movement into the cities for work and away from them for recreation and other qualities of life contributes to severe transportation and pollution problems.

The number of people living in urban areas is expected to double during the next 30 to 40 years. The open spaces currently surrounding the cities will turn into suburban developments, with emphasis on condominium and high-rise apartment complexes. Single-family units will become scarce and costly.

Nature and its inspiring effects will become even more remote from people's day-to-day lives. As this trend develops, the great migration to the country during weekends and vacation periods will continue to demonstrate our attraction to nature. Increasing numbers will own two homes—one in the city and one in the country. But, despite strong efforts to cling to our rural heritage, urban living will dominate the lives of a great majority, and urban values will prevail.

WORK AND LEISURE TIME

The line between leisure and labor has always been tenuous and shifting. Nevertheless, since early civilizations leisure time has been available to at least a portion of the people. Leisure and work are two sides of our shield. The one side, labor, enables us to live while the other side, leisure, makes living more meaningful. "We labor in order to have leisure," said Aristotle. Work can ennoble a person, but leisure provides an opportunity to develop perfection and enrichment of character.

In the well-established societies throughout history, such as ancient China, Egypt, India, Sumeria, Greece, and Rome, leisure and labor became well defined, and both had increasing importance. Labor produced material wealth, and the wealth was concentrated in the hands of a few. Leisure became the prize of the few who possessed wealth, while labor remained the lot of the great majority. Many of those who controlled the wealth put their leisure to use in a variety of sportive activities and in the pursuit of the aesthetic and the intellectual. As a result, cultural trends were established and civilizations advanced.

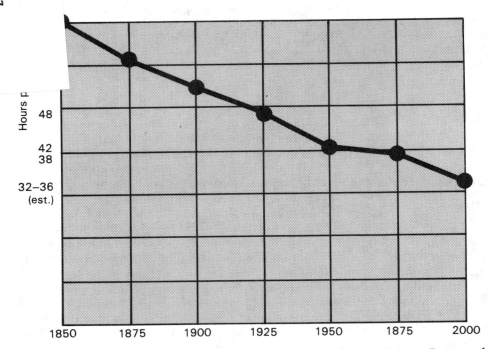

Figure 4.5. Changes in average work week for Americans, 1850–2000. (Source: Bureau of the Census, *Statistical Abstracts of the U.S.*, 103rd ed., p. 369)

During the past century, tremendous shifts have occurred in the work life of the typical American. The sunup–to–sundown working day that was standard in the early 1800s is now as rare as a horse-drawn buggy. This is true both in the United States and in other developed countries of the world. Most full-time employees in America now work about 40 hours a week, as compared to 60 hours a century ago (Figure 4.5).

The work week is still moving downward, although the rate of reduction is much slower now. In the future, many workers in organized labor will have work weeks of 36 hours and, later, 32 hours. Management and professional personnel will not experience such decreases until later, but even for these occupational groups, the work week will gradually get shorter.

There is presently some experimentation in certain occupational areas with a work week of four 10-hour days instead of five 8-hour days. Also, there is experimentation with four 9-hour days. A four-day work week would reduce the travel time and expense, and result in a three-day weekend. A reduction in travel would help with the problems of gasoline shortage, traffic congestion, and pollution from automobiles. Further, those who favor three-day weekends claim that (1) families would have more time together, (2) there would be opportunities for more significant leisure pursuits, and (3) there would be increased job efficiency and better morale. Whether any of these potential advantages would occur is unknown.

While the work week becomes shorter, vacation periods become longer. Two-week vacations were once a rare privilege, but now the trend is toward three or four weeks of vacation. At the same time, people are retiring earlier. When we add up the shorter work week, increased vacations, and earlier retirement, it is apparent that Americans today spend significantly less time on the job and more time at leisure than was the case 25, 50, or 100 years ago. Some leaders believe that our leisure has increased faster than our ability to use it properly.

The four kinds of leisure that are built around the work schedule include daily, weekly, annual, and retirement leisure. *Daily leisure* is represented by the amount of time left over each day after economic and biological requirements have been met. For the typical American, this amounts to a potential of about 5 hours. Eight hours of work and 11 hours for sleeping, eating, commuting to work, and other duties leave 5 hours of uncommitted time. This 5-hour period is choosing time–time when a person can participate in recreation of one kind or another, do service projects, or whatever else he chooses.

Weekly leisure usually occurs on weekends. Currently we think of this as two whole days, enough time to engage in significant projects or to take a short trip. However, weekend leisure is often interrupted by chores postponed during the week. Nevertheless weekends do permit many pursuits that are impossible during the week.

Vacation leisure has increased tremendously since the turn of the century. It is largely a product of the industrial revolution combined with improved work benefits in industry and business. It represents a block of time which workers often feel they have earned by a year of labor and which they have the right to apply in some unusual and often adventurous manner. To most working Americans the vacation period represents a segment of the year when time is not the greatest limitation. This period affords time to travel or to become involved in some extensive project.

The fourth kind of leisure is in the form of *retirement*. Most Americans now retire from their regular occupations at about age 65. However, many are retiring earlier and the trend toward younger retirement is continuing.

The average American now lives to about age 75, with women living an average of six years longer than men. Therefore, most people reaching retirement age will have substantial time on their hands, and some will have two or three decades.

The cumulative effect of the increases in the four forms of leisure has had a significant impact on the amount of choosing time that people have, and the impact will be even greater in the future. In turn, this will have a marked effect on the recreation opportunities that people need and want.

It should be clarified at this point that there are some trends which dilute the amount of apparent leisure. These include moonlighting, do-it-yourself projects, housework, and commuting time.

Too many people have never learned to use leisure time effectively, and therefore, it is largely a waste for them. For some it is even destructive. Conversely, other people try to engage in too much. A person may possibly buy more of everything but lack the time to do more. For example, to belong to a golf club, a sailing club, and a hunting club requires too much time to participate in each fully. Further, because of the cost of belonging to all of these, one may have to work more and have even less time to enjoy them. Emerson expressed this idea when he said, "If I keep a cow, the cow will milk me."

Many people become slaves of possessions instead of creative users of their time. Most of us know neighbors or friends whose material goods for leisure (boats, campers, snowmobiles, ski equipment, vacation homes) are so extensive that their lives are dominated by sustaining them. Apparently for some the pleasure is in possessing, and the joy of participation is not their main incentive.

Even with an abundance of leisure and with the promise of still more to come, all of us must remain highly selective about how we use the time for it to serve us well. Leisure can truly be a blessing, but unfortunately for some, it becomes a sort of curse because of boredom or overindulgence.

MOBILITY

The miraculous progress that has been made during the past century in travel represents one of the most dramatic changes in the history of man. Certainly one of the distinct features of life in America is our high rate of mobility. Whether we choose land, air, or sea, and whether we travel long or short distances, comfortable and rapid modes of transportation are available.

At the time of the Declaration of Independence horseback was the fastest method of travel for such great men as Washington and Jefferson. As recently as 100 years ago horseback and horse-drawn carriage were still the primary modes, aside from walking, although a few people of that era did ride on crudely built trains and steamboats. At that time it took nearly two weeks to travel to Yellowstone National Park from the nearest train station (Figure 4.6).

Recreation became a problem with a name in the days of President Theodore Roosevelt, when the railroads began to carry city-dwellers, en masse, to the countryside. It soon became apparent that the greater the exodus, the smaller the per capita ration of peace, solitude, wildlife, and scenery and the longer the migration to reach them.

The automobile has spread this once small problem to the outermost limits of good roads; it has made scarce in the hinderlands the solitude once abundant on the back forty.

It was not until the 1920s that the new look in travel began to take shape. Some people of that era owned automobiles, and even though there were no transcontinental highways, people were doing much of their travel by car. As the trend continued, tourist attractions began to spring up in all parts of the country, and there was more car travel being done for business. As a result extensive highway systems began to develop. The way became paved for the automobile to become the king of travel in America.

Today our most common carrier by far, as measured by passenger miles, is the automobile. This is followed respectively by air, train, and boat. Automobiles, like people, are appearing in great numbers. In America alone more than 9 million cars are produced each year, and the number of privately owned cars now exceeds 100 million. If all of the existing automobiles were placed end to end on all of the paved highways in the United States, there would be one car every 200 yards. The present population of the United States could be comfortably seated in these cars, and the average would be only 2.2 persons per car (Table 4.2). Four out of five American families now own cars, and in suburban and rural areas nine out of ten families own cars. Further, a high percentage of all families own two or more cars.

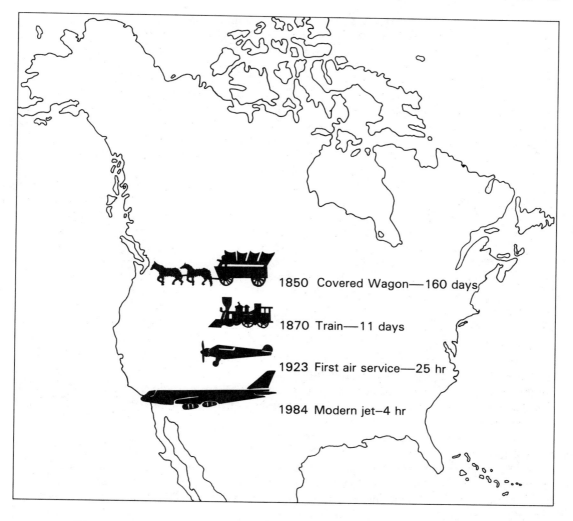

1850 Covered Wagon—160 days

1870 Train—11 days

1923 First air service—25 hr

1984 Modern jet—4 hr

Figure 4.6. Comparison of travel time across the United States, 1850–1984.

Within the United States there are more than 5 million miles (8 million km) of highways, roads, and streets. This system connects in many places to the highways of Canada and Mexico. But even with this extensive highway system, traffic is sometimes slowed to a snail's pace. To relieve travelers from passing through cities, the vast interstate system now provides over 45,000 miles (73,000 km) of freeways, and there are many local freeways in addition. Surely the pressures resulting from the increased use of automobiles will severely test the resourcefulness and skills of the nation's road builders, traffic specialists, automakers, and energy experts.

**Table 4.2. Number of Passenger Cars
and Average Population Per Car in Selected Countries**

Nation	Number of Cars in Use	Number of Persons Per Car
Industrialized		
United States	114,453,000	2.1
New Zealand	1,271,000	3.0
Canada	9,313,000	3.1
Australia	5,548,000	3.1
France	17,041,000	3.2
West Germany	20,139,000	3.2
United Kingdom	15,073,000	4.0
Japan	19,400,000	6.1
Developed		
South Africa	2,277,000	12.2
Brazil	6,666,000	18.4
Mexico	2,773,000	25.6
Soviet Union	5,943,000	46.3
Underdeveloped		
India	840,000	782
Bangladesh	21,000	4,028
China	52,000	17,328

Washington, D.C., Transportation Statistics—1982, p. 21.

Even though the automobile is the king of travel, other modes have become increasingly important. Airplane passengers in the United States increased from 2.5 million in 1940 to 91 million in 1984, and it is predicted that this number will soon exceed 100 million. The 600-mile-per-hour (1000-kph) jetliner has revolutionized air travel in all parts of the nation and the world. It has put major cities within a few hours of each other. There are more jetliners in the United States than all other countries combined, and we have nine of the world's ten busiest airports.

Already supersonic transports travel faster than the speed of sound, and some experts predict they will become popular. Short-route helicopter systems will be used more, especially in metropolitan areas, and rooftops will be used for landing pads. Also, there is a real possibility that individual flying devices will come into use in large numbers, thus permitting individuals to fly almost anywhere we now can drive or walk. It is speculated that the aircraft of the future will be fueled by liquid hydrogen or some other nonpetroleum product and the engines will be more efficient and produce less pollution and noise.

Even though some of these methods of travel are not imminent, information from transportation experts would indicate that many of us will live to see airliners cross the continent in 90 minutes, trains travel at 200 miles per hour (322 kph) over a cushion of air, and ships skim the water at 75 knots. In the future our great mobility will enable people in large numbers to test their skills and pursue their interests in exciting leisure activities in all parts of the world. They will be delivered to the doorsteps of outdoor recreation areas everywhere. Obviously, this will have an immense impact on our natural resources and our recreation patterns.

Even surfing has been influenced by technology. The sport has been revolutionized by the development of fiberglass. (National Park Service, photo by Richard Frear)

TECHNOLOGY

In the *Republic* Plato built his ideal society with thousands of slaves to perform the work so that a few at the peak of the social structure could develop their intellectual, physical, and spiritual qualities and thereby improve the society. It is estimated that at the peak of the Athenian culture there were 15 slaves for each citizen. Automation experts estimate that the average American has at his or her disposal, the equivalent of 500 human slaves. Our slaves have become available through technology, which is the development and use of mechanical devices and their energy sources. A great variety of mechanical instruments perform an increasing number of functions for us with unmatched precision and rapidity. Computers, engines, electrical appliances, and other implements perform a phenomenal amount of work that saves human time and energy.

Visualize, for example, the amount of slave energy that would be needed to propel an automobile at 60 miles per hour (100 kph) for just 1 mile. Most of us drive an automobile several miles each day and sometimes we drive several hundred miles. Further, visualize the human energy that would be required to generate and deliver the electricity used for running the several electrical appliances, lighting, heating (or air conditioning) in an average American home over a 24-hour period. Think of the thousands of hours that would be spent making calculations that can be accomplished on a computer in just 30 minutes. Even more impressive is the equivalent energy spent on a four-engine jetliner streaking through space at 600 miles per hour (1000 kph), or a 100-car freight train traveling at 50 miles per hour (80 kph).

Skydiving is an adventurous activity that relates directly to technological advances. (U.S. Army, photo by Joe M. Gonzales)

These kinds of automation are largely responsible for the increased leisure that is presently available. At the same time other technical devices influence how we use our leisure in recreational pursuits. For example, powerboating and waterskiing are relatively newfound pleasures that depend directly upon technology. The same is true of downhill skiing, motorized underwater exploration, driving for pleasure, the recreational use of various aircraft and off-road vehicles. Many other recreational pursuits are influenced less directly, but substantially, by the availability of electricity; better modes of travel, and better gear.

Technology experts predict that we shall make far more technological progress in the next 20 years than we have in any equivalent period in the past. A generation of expanded computer use is coming on fast and strong. The computers of the future will do a decade of work during a lunch hour, and their impact will be felt not only by blue-collar workers but by technicians and managers as well.

Further, American scientists are expressing optimism about electric automobiles powered by lithium batteries, nonpetroleum aircraft fuel, abundant solar energy units for heating buildings, computers that will be cheap enough to be in almost every office and many households (in addition to the midget computers that almost every individual can own). Also, significant strides will continue in the improvement of household appliances and tools, and this will make home management less time consuming and leave more free time for other activities. Further, there will be continuing improvements in almost all kinds of recreation gear. Technologists are truly significant contributors to our life-style—both on and off the job.

INCOME

There are few aspects of life in this country more impressive than the tremendous amount of goods and services produced. The total market value of these for a particular year is referred to as the gross national product (GNP). The GNP is generally accepted as an indication of the economic well-being of the nation.

In 1952 the GNP was estimated at a little over $329 billion. Thirty-two years later, in 1984, it had increased to about $1.2 trillion. Even when changes in population and the effects of inflation are considered, the actual purchasing power (money to buy goods and services) of Americans per capita has approximately doubled since 1952.

To relate the increased economy more closely to the individual American citizen, consider the increase in annual per capita income (Figure 4.7). In 1930 the average income per person was $1224. This has increased rather steadily until now the average is more than five times the 1930 amount in actual dollars.

Further, more than half the American families currently enjoy annual family incomes in excess of $15,000, and 25% of the families have incomes of $18,000 or more. However there are also those on the lower end of the income scale. In 1984 more than 12 million families received incomes of poverty level or less. These families represent about one fifth of the population.

Increased income per individual has resulted in greater expenditure in all phases of life. The greatest increase in spending, however, has not been on food, clothing, and shelter but on enrichment activities, including outdoor recreation.

It is logical to assume that in the future we will have even more purchasing power, and if this turns out to be true, it is safe to expect that we will spend more on hobbies, sports, adventure activities, and other recreation. Many of us will own two homes, of which one will be in a resort area. Many families will become three-car families, and the cars will be used more for pleasure than necessity. Boats, ski equipment, athletic gear, hunting and fishing supplies, and other recreational goods will appear in ever-increasing amounts. People will travel more miles and spend more time in recreation places using these luxury goods.

EDUCATION

In a general sense the purpose of education is to prepare individuals to live successfully in society and contribute toward its improvement. Thus, the content of education is influenced by local values and living patterns, and by the knowledge, skills, and attitudes that people need to earn a living and perpetuate traditions and cultural values.

Education is of two general kinds: preparation to *earn* a living and preparation *for* living. We can be reasonably sure that work in the future will be more specialized, more automated, and require more education. At the same time there will be a need for better social understanding, and the pressures of our fast-moving society will bring increased attention to the psychological aspects of learning and adjustment. All of this will contribute to the increased complexity of education and to the increased need for it.

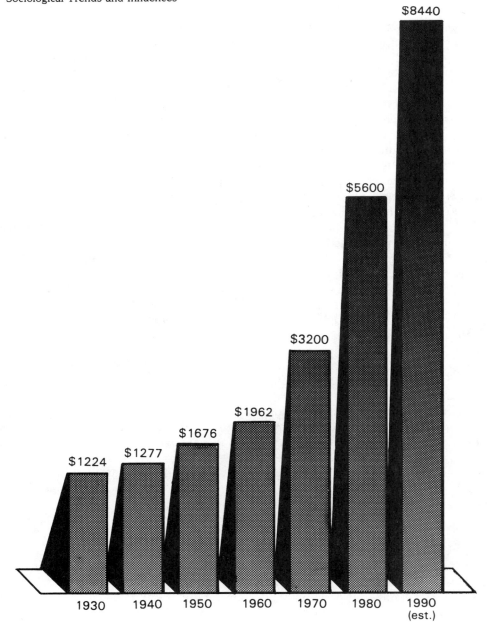

Figure 4.7. Changes in per capita income for Americans in actual dollars, not adjusted for inflation. (Source: Bureau of the Census, *Statistical Abstracts of the U.S.*, 103rd ed., p. 463)

    Citizens have realized that a high level of education is essential if they are to live effectively in our present-day society. As a result, not only has the number of students increased;

so has the average level of education. For example, in 1910 only 63% of school-age children (5 to 18 years) were enrolled in school. By 1952 it had risen to 78%; it now exceeds 88% (Table 4.3).

A greater number of students are going on to college. College enrollments increased from 2.5 million in 1950 to 3.2 million in 1960 to 6 million in 1970. College enrollment now exceeds 10 million students. In the early 1950s only 27% of college-age students were enrolled; this percentage is now about 45%. Additional education also has increased greatly among adults of all ages.

This increased attention to education has two startling effects on our planning for outdoor recreation. First, education is a key to higher personal income, and higher income influences what people do for recreation and where they go to do it. Second, additional education advances people's interests, appreciations, and skills in recreational pursuits. Therefore, educated people tend to have more interests, and also more means with which to pursue them.

CHANGING PHILOSOPHY

It has already been pointed out that Americans are experiencing rapid changes in life. This is particularly true in terms of basic values. These changes are being prompted by a unique mixture of scientific research, engineering skills, technological advancements, and mass production, which all contribute to automation. Despite many urgent problems, the changes have brought with them leisure time. We live in an era characterized by freely disposable time and materials. As we have become freed from labor, we have found ourselves with greater opportunity for personal enrichment and service. We have more time to think, feel, and exercise without being burdened by the necessities of survival.

Release from excessive work affords people the opportunity "to become," but only those who have enlarged their minds and tamed their hearts can profit significantly from material competence.

Further, sociologist Karl Mannheim raised doubt about the real value of increased leisure when he pointed out that comparative studies in the use of leisure show that a higher position, larger income, and increased security do not necessarily lead to cultural development. The average citizen, according to Mannheim, is unsuccessful in inventing new uses for his or her leisure.

This view strongly suggests that to use leisure time effectively, desirable philosophical concepts, appreciations, and skills must be taught. It emphasizes the need for education,

Table 4.3. Percentage of School-Age Youth Enrolled in Schools in the United States, 1952–1982

Year	Elementary and Secondary Schools (Ages 5–18)	Colleges and Universities (Ages 18–21)
1952	78	27
1962	84	35
1972	87	43
1982	89	45

Source: Unpublished data, National Education Association, Washington, D.C.

which will lead to the worthy use of leisure time, along with the development of a wholesome philosophy about leisure.

In our society work has traditionally been associated with more than material accomplishment or economics; it has been a source of social and moral recognition. Modern concepts do not and should not minimize the values of work, but they do indicate a greater appreciation for leisure and recreation. Generally people now realize that wholesome recreation may contribute to a well-rounded personality and add to life a spirit of adventure and enrichment. Even though individuals have traditionally made their marks on society through long hours of work, they have often done so with the hope that something better is to come. This "something better" resides in the idea that leisure time affords the opportunity to pursue interests and activities of one's own choosing, which will add enrichment and satisfaction.

For this really to happen there has to be adequate leadership, part of which must be in the form of connoisseurs, educators, and managers who have insight into "the good life," who know much about the needs of people, and who have the ability to help large numbers of people achieve the things that contribute to enrichment.

> The fact that we live in a world that moves crisis by crisis does not make a growing interest in outdoor activities frivolous, or ample provision for them unworthy of the nation's concern.
> –John F. Kennedy, *It's Your World–Grassroots Conservation Story*, U.S. Department of the Interior, Washington, D.C., 1969, p.88.

Discussion Questions

1. In your personal life, how have work and recreation contributed to your positive development? Be specific.
2. Some authors believe that our leisure has increased faster than our ability to use it properly. Do you agree? Why?
3. Many people have never learned to use leisure time effectively. What are some of the undesirable uses of leisure time, and what are the potential results?
4. With increased mobility, a larger number of people can achieve a greater variety of outdoor recreation experiences. This is generally viewed in a positive light. But what are some of the disadvantages of this fact?
5. What forms of outdoor recreation have been influenced significantly by recent technology? What seems to be the potential for further technological influence on recreation in the future?
6. Do you believe there is a population explosion crisis? What relationship exists between population and outdoor recreation? What is the possible future impact of this relationship?
7. Increased income affects the quantity, quality, and variety of one's recreation. Are all forms of outdoor recreation influenced by income? How prominent is income in determining one's outdoor recreation patterns?
8. What are the four categories of leisure time available during one's lifetime? Explain each kind and discuss the trends in each category.

Recommended Readings

Chubb, Michael, and Holly R. Chubb. *One Third of Our Time.* New York: John Wiley & Sons, 1981. Chapters 4, 5, 6, 7.

"Comeback for Cities–Woes for Suburbs." *U.S. News and World Report,* 24 March 1980, p. 53.

Fenstermacher, George C. "Elderly Sunbelt Migrants." *Journal of Physical Education, Recreation and Dance,* October 1981, p. 57.

"The Four-Day Workweek: An Assessment of Its Effects on Leisure Participation." *Leisure Sciences,* Vol. 2, No. 1, p. 55.

"The Growing Problem of World Population." *Technology Review,* November–December 1980, p. 80.

"How Cities Are Luring People Back." *U.S. News and World Report,* 24 March 1980, p. 64.

Howe, Christine Z. "From the Leisure Ethic to Reindustrialization." *Journal of Physical Education, Recreation and Dance,* October 1980, p. 38.

"How Long Will You Live?" *Time,* 2 November 1981, p. 37.

Kelly, John R. "Leisure and Family Change: 1960–1990." *Journal of Physical Education, Recreation and Dance,* October 1981, p. 47.

Knudson, Douglas M. *Outdoor Recreation.* New York: Macmillan Publishing Co., 1984. Chapter 5.

"Leisure: Where No Recession Is in Sight." *U.S. News and World Report,* 15 January 1979, p. 41.

Masnick, George, and Mary Jo Bane. *The Nation's Families: 1960–1990.* Cambridge, Massachusetts: Joint Center for Urban Studies of Massachusetts Institute of Technology and Harvard University, 1980.

Miller, Tyler. *Living in the Environment,* 2nd ed. Belmont, California: Wadsworth Publishing Co., 1979. Chapter 7.

Murphy, James F. "Leisure Concepts in a Changing Society." *Journal of Physical Education, Recreation and Dance,* October 1981, p. 40.

Toffler, Alvin. *The Third Wave.* New York: William Morrow and Co., Inc., 1980.

Underhill, A. H. "Population Dynamics and Demography." *Journal of Physical Education, Recreation and Dance,* October 1981, p. 33.

U.S. Department of Commerce. *Statistical Abstracts of the U.S.,* 103rd ed. Washington, D.C.: Bureau of the Census, 1982.

"U.S. Living Standards Still Tops." *U.S. News and World Report,* 17 March 1980, p. 41.

Van Doren, Carlton S., George B. Priddle, and John E. Lewis. *Land and Leisure: Concepts and Methods in Outdoor Recreation.* Chicago: Maaroofa Press, Inc., 1979. Chapters 3, 4.

Van der Tak, Jean, Carl Haub, and Murphy Evans. "A New Look at the Population Problem." *The Futurist,* April 1980, p. 39.

Vaske, Jerry J., and Maureen P. Donelly. "Workstyle Choices and Recreation Patterns." *Journal of Physical Education, Recreation and Dance,* October 1981, p. 44.

"Where Supercities Are Growing Fastest." *U.S. News and World Report,* 30 June 1980, p. 52.

CHAPTER 5

Economic Factors

Outdoor recreation is big business. Consider for example the impact of recreation on the sale of products by Wilson Sporting Goods Company, Mercury Marine Division of Brunswick Corporation, Head Division of AMF, Polaris Industries, Coleman Company, Eastman Kodak Company, Remington Arms Company, Kampgrounds of America, and a host of other large corporations and companies.

A recent article in *U.S. News and World Report*[1] stated that $1 of every $8 earned in this country goes for leisure activities–a larger share than for housing construction or national defense. This amount of spending is of crucial importance to the economy. Additionally, 1 of every 15 jobs in the United States is directly related to leisure pursuits.

Statistics from the U.S. Department of Commerce (Bureau of the Census) show that leisure expenditures have grown from $58 billion in 1965 to $292 billion in 1984. This is an increase (adjusted for inflation) of 48% in 19 years. With an expected average increase of $20 billion annually (8% annual increase), the rate of expenditure by 1990 will be well over $400 billion (Figure 5.1).

Data from the Department of Commerce indicate that the biggest participant activities are the following (listed in order of the greatest number of participants): swimming, bicycling, camping, fishing, boating, jogging, and tennis. The data also show that when the economy tightens people's patterns of expenditure change only slightly. They still go on about the same number of vacations but the trips are shorter, and they buy less of the expensive equipment such as boats and motor homes. It also was found that the high cost of gasoline has reduced the sales of motor homes, camp trailers, campers and large motorboats.

The purchase of recreation goods penetrates deep into the economic system, causing the total effect to be greater than the direct expenditure. For example, consider a recreationist who

1. "America Plays, Even With the Economy in a Spin," *U.S. News & World Report*, 8 September 1982, p. 76, Vol. 87.

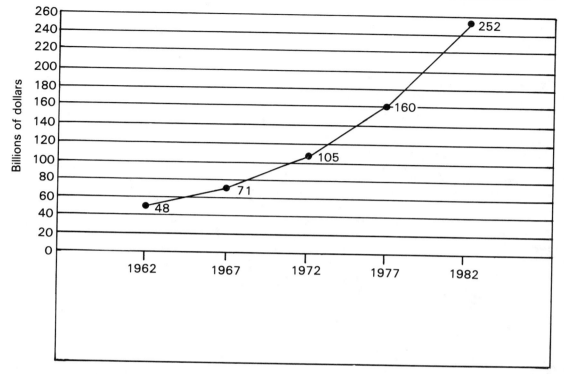

Figure 5.1. Spending trends for leisure in the United States, 1962–1982. (Source: Bureau of the Census, *Statistical Abstracts of the U.S.*, 103rd ed., p. 469)

buys a powerboat from a boat distributor for $10,000. The boat was made by a manufacturer who purchased parts from various suppliers. The parts were purchased from other suppliers who developed the products from raw materials.

What this adds up to in terms of economics is an astonishing picture of millions of Americans participating in outdoor recreation. Behind the scenes serving the ever-increasing number of participants are millions more Americans making their living from recreation.

ECONOMICS OF THE RECREATION EXPERIENCE

As explained in Chapter 1, the total outdoor recreation experience includes four phases: *anticipation, preparation, direct experience,* and *recollection.* Each of the phases has its own economic impact, although the impact is nowhere nearly equal for all phases. The second and third phases have the greatest economic significance.

During the anticipation phase a person may purchase printed information, but for the most part the anticipation phase involves little expenditure.

The preparation phase typically ranks second in economic impact. During this phase a person may make rather large expenditures for equipment and supplies.

Leisure time activities make possible one of the largest and fastest growing industries in America. (Bureau of Reclamation, photo by E. E. Hertzog)

The direct experience extends from the time one leaves home until he or she returns. Money is spent for travel, food, lodging, equipment, special services, and other things. This phase is typically the one involving the greatest expenditure.

The recollection phase is relatively insignificant in terms of economic impact, but it does have some relevance. Film may be processed and one might be prompted to purchase a projector for showing the film. Trophies taken in hunting and fishing are sometimes mounted, and various other expenses may be incurred in one's effort to keep alive the memories of the experience. Also, after the experience there are often expenditures for equipment repairs and maintenance and the replenishment of supplies.

ECONOMICS OF TOURISM

Tourism has a significant impact on the economy in general, and especially in certain states, such as California, Hawaii, Florida, and Colorado. In these and several other states the state tourist agency spends well over $1 million a year to attract tourist trade. Some states have been ambitious in developing state parks and other scenic attractions to stimulate tourism by state residents and out-of-state visitors. The advantages of this are clear. It causes the residents of the state to spend their money within the state's boundaries, and it brings in tourist dollars from outside the state, both of which increase the flow of money, stimulate the economy, and produce more tax revenue.

It is estimated by the tourist industry that an average tourist spends $40 per day, a figure that varies widely among individuals and also with location and kind of activity. Some forms of tourism are relatively inexpensive, but other forms are costly. Also, some localities are more expensive than others. People staying in hotels and eating in restaurants spend much more than backpackers do.

MULTIPLIER EFFECT

Once a tourist dollar is spent, it is redistributed almost immediately to others who provide goods and services secondhand. This has an accumulative influence on the initial expenditure and it is known among economists as the multiplier effect. The direct expenditures for such items as food, lodging, and gasoline have an initial economic benefit. Some of the dollars received are paid to others for supplies and services, while a certain amount of each dollar remains with the original merchant as net profit. Some of the money goes to suppliers or workers in the local area, and some will be transferred out of the region. Jack L. Knetsch[2] points out that if money is spent for lodging a greater portion stays in the local area than if the same amount is spent for gasoline. In the case of lodging, a large portion is passed on to local suppliers and workers, whereas with gasoline most of every dollar spent locally is used to import the gasoline from outside the region. The money that stays in the area further aids the local economy as it is spent and respent.

Each time the dollar turns over, it contributes toward continuation of the economic chain. The net effect is expressed as a multiplier of the original expenditure. Charles B. Garrison[3] found that in a small area $1 spent by a tourist may produce an economic effect of $1.53 in the region. William B. Byers[4] calculated that if the whole nation is considered instead of a local region, the multiplier effect of the tourist dollar is $3.02. His findings indicate that there is considerable leakage of the multiplier effect from the local area, but very little leakage from the national economy as a whole.

It was determined in a study of tourism at the Olympic National Park that visitors spent $21.8 million in 1981 in connection with their visits to the park. About $18.3 million of this was spent in Washington, but only $8 million was actually spent on the Olympic Peninsula.

When the multiplier effect was applied it was determined that the $21.8 million expenditure produced the effect of $66 million nationwide. The majority of this total effect stayed in

2. *Technical Report WO-2*, U.S. Forest Service, Washington, D.C., 1977, pp. 17–18.
3. Garrison, Charles B., "A Case Study of the Local Economic Impact of Reservoir Recreation," *Journal of Leisure Research*, Vol. 6, No. 1, pp. 7–19.
4. Byers, William B., *An Economic Impact Study of Mount Rainier and Olympic National Parks*, University of Washington, Seattle, 1970, p. 32.

Outdoor beauty is one of our most popular forms of tourist attractions. (National Park Service)

Washington, whereas slightly less than half of it remained in the area of the Olympic Peninsula.

A relatively high ratio of tourism expenditures is for services, and this contributes significantly to employment. It was calculated that the annual expenditure at Olympic National Park created 2800 jobs in Washington with a high percentage of these being on the peninsula or close to it. Moreover, the expenditure supported several hundred jobs outside of the state.[5]

One of the ways that Indian tribes have improved their economy is through the development of recreation attractions for tourists. For example, when the $110 million Kinua Dam and Reservoir was planned for western Pennsylvania, the Bureau of Indian Affairs assisted the Seneca tribe in developing a huge tourist program including shops, lodges, museums, an Indian village, a motel, a 100-boat marina and outdoor and indoor theaters for Indian ceremonial and folklore festivals. This new development has attracted several hundred thousand tourists each year.[6]

5. Unpublished data from the Public Affairs Office, National Park Service, Washington, D.C., 1983.
6. *Tourism Planning Bulletin*, Bureau of Indian Affairs, Department of the Interior, Washington, D.C., 1981, p. 18.

EFFECTS OF RECREATION PROJECTS

Money begets money. For example, the construction of a ski resort can increase the amount of money spent in the local area on ski-related items. Snow skiers in the United States, now an estimated 6 million in number, are increasing at a rate of 15% annually. Ranked as lavish spenders, they plunk down approximately $1.3 billion each season getting to the ski slopes and for equipment, lodging, lift passes, and entertainment. Thus, the development of a popular ski resort can cause a boom in the local economy. This kind of economic boom has recently occurred in the area of Park City, Utah, by the addition of Deer Valley, a major ski resort and a significant tourist attraction. Similar situations occur in various parts of the country every year.

The same effect can result from the construction of a major reservoir. Many such projects have been built by the Bureau of Reclamation and the Corps of Engineers. One example is a five-county area of Oklahoma where several artificial lakes have been constructed since 1950. These lakes attract thousands of campers, boaters, and fishers. The increase in sales-tax receipts for those counties during the five years following completion of the lakes was almost triple the increase for the rest of the state.[7]

When the Grand Teton National Park in Wyoming underwent its last major expansion, the total assessed valuation of property in Teton County approximately doubled in eight years. During the same period sales-tax receipts more than doubled, and bank deposits approximately doubled. Certainly not all of this could be attributed to the enlargement of the park, but the park was a major influence.

To get further insight into the nature of the economic impact of outdoor recreation, the whole topic can be divided into phases. Assume the development of a major recreational attraction, such as a large reservoir, a national recreation area, or a major ski resort. Consider the impact on the following factors.

Land Prices

If an area has recreation features that attract people, the land in that area becomes more in demand. Some people may want to build vacation homes near the recreation site. Others will want to build commercial establishments, and some may want to own land for speculative purposes. This means that the simple law of supply and demand will cause land prices to escalate. In some cases land near recreation developments skyrockets; in other cases the escalation is gradual. In any case, landowners stand to gain financially.

Construction Projects

People want vacation homes and recreation cabins near attractive sites, and this in turn increases the need for commercial establishments. Real-estate transactions increase. It also spurs local construction, creating a demand for construction materials and workers. These improvements cause property values to increase, and this enlarges the tax base in the local area.

---

7. Unpublished data from the Bureau of Reclamation, Department of the Interior, Washington, D.C.

Goods and Services

The influx of recreationists and workers increases the purchase of food and lodging, gasoline, clothing, recreation equipment, and a host of other goods. Such purchases can be a real boon to the business establishments near major recreation complexes.

With more people visiting the area, there is need for more employees to provide services. Also, additional jobs are created for real estate and construction. In many cases the recreation operation itself provides new opportunities for employment. At a national park, for example, a number of people are employed to manage and maintain the park. Often concessionaires are needed and guides and outfitters are in demand to provide tours and excursions.

Effects on Nearby Communities

While boat docks, motels, restaurants, campgrounds, picnic sites, access roads, and the like are being constructed in the recreation area, nearby towns undergo a shift in economics, and sometimes in social and political structure. Broadly speaking, the shift is away from an economy devoted to serving only local residents to one serving both residents and visitors. Many of the outsiders have an urban point of view and expect goods and services equal to urban standards. Because local citizens usually want to put their best foot forward, they become more conscious of unpaved streets, sidewalks in poor repair, limited stores, and the absence of good restaurants and motels. Often newcomers arrive and start new enterprises or improve old ones. If the long-time community leaders fail to heed the new demands for improvements, they may find their positions eroded. The extent to which all of this actually happens depends, first, on the nature and extent of the recreation development and, second, on the ability of the nearby communities to accommodate the needs of the visitors.

ECONOMIC IMPACT OF VACATION HOMES

Researchers from the Department of the Interior conducted a study to determine the extent to which occupants of vacation homes in northern New England (including Maine and parts of Vermont and New Hampshire) participate in outdoor recreation and the amounts they spend in connection with their vacation homes. The following are some pertinent facts resulting from the study:

1.   More than 50% of the vacation homes are located on less than 1 acre (0.4 ha) of land, but because some are on large estates, the average size is 16.4 acres (6.64 ha).
2.   The real value of the homes and the property on which they are located ranges from a few hundred dollars to well over $200,000.
3.   Only 37% of the homeowners reside in the northern New England states. The other 63% live in various regions of the eastern United States.

There were 28,140 vacation homes in the particular New England region included in the study. On the average each homeowner spent $2425 per year locally and $180 elsewhere within the region. Thus, approximately $73.3 million is spent each year in the region by the occupants of the vacation homes.

It has been estimated by economists that $1000 of direct expenditure by out-of-the-region vacation visitors adds 1.55 times that amount to the region's total economy. This would mean that the total economic impact of the vacation homes in the region is about $113.6 million annually (1.55 times $73.3 million of direct expenditures).

TEXOMA RESERVOIR PROJECT

Texoma Reservoir, a large artificial lake on the Texas-Oklahoma border, was developed in 1945 by the Corps of Engineers, primarily for flood control and power production. Almost immediately it became a major recreation attraction. Two years after its completion, 2 million people visited the lake. Five years later the annual visits were 4 million. By 1957 annual attendance had reached 8 million. Now between 12 million and 16 million recreationists visit the reservoir each year.

The counties surrounding the lake were historically capital poor. In such cases local leaders usually consider lack of capital to be a prime reason for their economic difficulties. But the underlying problem might also be seen as a lack of opportunity for capital to be profitably employed. It can be argued that if the right combination of natural resources and human talent had been present capital would have been forthcoming.[8]

The completion of the reservoir illustrates the point. It provides an opportunity for capital to be profitably used in developing recreation businesses and in associated investments.

The Texoma project attracts outside dollars to bolster the local economy in at least three ways: (1) it brings in visitors who spend large sums at lakeshore resorts and elsewhere in the area, (2) it induces private investors and government agencies to invest money in accommodations, and (3) it attracts newcomers who have homes and cabins constructed for their own use on or near the lakeshore.

In the five counties touching Texoma, direct expenditures by visitors now exceed $40 million annually. When the 1.55 multiplier explained in the previous case study is applied, the total expenditure impact equals $62 million per year.

PEARL RIVER PROJECT

One of the best case studies of rising land prices was provided in the U.S. government publication *Recreation Land Price Escalation*. It describes a well-documented situation in the Pearl River Reservoir near Jackson, Mississippi. A detailed analysis was made of 304 sales involving over 25,000 acres (10,121 ha) of land near the planned reservoir project. An analysis for the same period of 101 sales transactions covering more than 11,000 acres (4,453 ha) in a comparable area not influenced by the project served as a control for the study. The average price paid per acre of land adjacent to the project showed an average annual increase of slightly less than 9% before announcement of the project. After the project was announced, prices increased 165% the first year, 191% the second year, 216% the third year, 236% the fourth year, and 258% the fifth year. The price per acre of the control area for the same period of time continued to increase between 8 and 10% per year.

ECONOMIC VALUE OF A PARK

Placing values on parks in economic terms was for a long time purely an academic exercise. For the most part there has been no practical need for establishing a price because parks are not sold in the marketplace. Parks have traditionally been a class of public holdings that

8. Unpublished data from the Water Projects Division, Corps of Engineers, Washington, D.C., 1983.

symbolized the land's character and permitted breathing room within the city and outside cities and would last indefinitely.

Like practically all else in today's world, parks have lost their "eternal permanence" and there are attempts to evaluate them on the basis of economics. Therefore, it is of practical necessity to try to find some economic measures by which to justify the existence of at least some of the parks. This is true of state and federal parks as well as municipal parks.

It has been implied by economists that the immediate value of a park can be roughly measured by surveying the users of the park and finding out how much each one would be willing to pay per use. By determining the ratio of users that would pay each amount and by knowing the total number of users it can easily be calculated how much the users would be willing to pay if payment was necessary. In other words this tells how much revenue the park would produce if fees were charged. In one sense this could be interpreted as the immediate financial value of the park to the public. However, this procedure does not take into account related values such as the escalation of adjacent property values and the influence that the park has on land even farther away, say a half-mile or mile. Neither does it take into account the general positive feeling that parks cause members of a community to have, even those who never use the parks. The fact that the parks are available and part of the total community plan seems to be a source of social satisfaction. Also, it does not consider the importance of parks in terms of heritage.

Another approach that is sometimes used in the case of state parks or national parks is to calculate the approximate amount of money spent in and near the park by those who come to visit–in other words, the effect that the park has on the local commerce. This again deals with only one aspect of the value of the park, but it is important information.

Certain government agencies, including the Corps of Engineers and the Bureau of Reclamation have estimated the value of visits by fishers, boaters, and campers to calculate the economic impact of the recreational characteristics of a project. This procedure provides substantial economic information, but still does not include all the economic values that accrue from recreation.

In the final analysis it seems that the value of a park is what the managing agency and the public think it is, and is willing and able to pay for it. This is essentially the same as saying that a rare work of art is worth whatever a buyer is willing to pay. It is not a very precise method of pricing, but in most cases it is the most meaningful one and the one that prevails. However, it is true that some of the procedures of making economic estimates described here might influence the amount that the governing agency is willing to pay, and how persistent the agency might be toward acquiring or holding the park in the face of pressures to do otherwise.

THE ECONOMY OF MORE PARKS

There is almost always some resistance toward public park and recreation areas because public ownership takes the land off the tax rolls. But a contrasting idea was outlined in a series of articles in the *San Francisco Chronicle*. The articles called upon the Bay Area to save its open spaces, hillsides, and forests from the economic strangulation that is sure to come if they are covered with houses. The following is a summary of the articles.

The usual thought that property should not be taken off the rolls is valid only if the property returns more in taxes than it costs in services. Most subdivisions built today do not. The city comes out fairly well with the development of residential areas, the property taxes returning slightly more than the costs. But after the cost of schools and community services is considered, a house on a typical city lot comes nowhere near paying its way in property taxes. It is for this reason that some recreation planning experts say government saves money by building parks up to a certain level.

There are other major, but possibly less obvious, benefits from having extensive open space around cities. For example, property values are higher and the social environment is typically better in neighborhoods where parks and open spaces are abundant.

Certainly we must have homes, and the argument in favor of parks cannot be carried too far and still be valid. The important thing is to plan wisely and plan now, to set aside the parks where they should be before the land is swallowed up for subdivisions and other purposes.

COST-BENEFIT ANALYSIS

Sometimes a cost-benefit projection is used to determine whether a proposed project is justified. Often recreation is only one of the possible benefits included in such an analysis. Different approaches are used by different agencies of government and private consultants to try to arrive at a sound cost-benefit ratio. It would be normal practice, for example, for Congress to require a detailed cost-benefit analysis on a proposed Bureau of Reclamation project before allocating funds to support it. Such an analysis would usually involve identification of the various benefits and an estimation of their value.

After the total process was completed the benefits would be compared to the estimated cost, and the comparison would produce a ratio. If the ratio equaled 1 it would mean the project would produce a dollar's worth of benefit for every dollar of cost over the calculated life span of the project, taking into consideration the initial investment and a reasonable rate of interest. If the ratio were 0.8 it would mean the calculated benefits would be 80% as great as the cost, and the project probably would not be funded. If the ratio were 1.5 the calculated benefit would be 50% greater than the cost.

ADDITIONAL ECONOMIC FACTS

Following are some interesting findings that pertain to the economics of recreation:

1. The Internal Revenue Service reported that in 1982 more than 15,000 corporations were involved in amusement and recreation services, producing income taxes of about $200 million. In addition, there were over 250,000 nonincorporated firms involved with recreation services. Altogether, these industries generated more than $330 million in income taxes.
2. The U.S. Travel Data Center reports that outdoor recreation travel accounts for about 11% of total expenditures for trips greater than 200 miles (320 km) round trip, accounting for about $15 billion in travel costs.

Major ski areas are excellent examples of the economic effect of outdoor recreation. (Photo courtesy of Snowbird Ski Corporation, Alta, Utah)

3.   Recreation businesses have relatively minor impact on the environment; they do little to pollute air or water. Furthermore, the industry consumes relatively little in natural resources or fuel.

4.   The National Tourism Resources Review Commission reported that just 80 families visiting an area each day produce more than $5 million per year of direct revenue to a community through their expenditures for local goods and services.

5.   Vanderbilt University reported that for every 10 park jobs created by a Tennessee state park, between 1.6 and 3.3 additional jobs were created in nearby local economies–primarily through park visitors who purchase from local businesses.

6.   In Philadelphia every acre of a large urban park was found to generate $3400 in increased property values.

7.   The "leisure year" is 123 days long now, one third of the calendar year, with seven 3-day weekends and an average of 16 days vacation per worker. This represents more available time than ever before.

8.   Outdoor-recreation equipment rentals have a significant impact on the economy. Watercraft of various kinds and ski equipment are among the leaders in recreation rentals.

9.   A recent survey by the U.S. Fish and Wildlife Service showed that one out of every two adult Americans (nearly 100 million people) engaged in some form of outdoor

activity involving fish and wildlife. Through involvement in these activities, the participants spend over $40 billion annually, making fish and wildlife in America truly big business.

10. An analysis by the U.S. Department of Commerce of spending for recreation showed that households in the middle of the family life cycle spend more money than those on either extreme. Additionally, the education level is positively related to recreation spending. Urban households spend more than the rural ones, and those in the western region of the United States spend more than those in other regions. Also, the changing role of women has resulted in more leisure spending, and this relates closely to the rapid escalation of participation by women in outdoor activities.

SOME PRECAUTIONS

Outdoor recreation and tourism have been among the most rapidly expanding sectors of our national economy since the early 1960s. Nonetheless, a high percentage of small firms that have attempted to capitalize on this trend have been only moderately successful, according to information provided by the Small Business Administration of the Department of Commerce.

One reason for this lack of success is that many of the firms are seasonally oriented and therefore operate only a part of the year. Further, many of the small businesses in outdoor recreation and tourism are involved with retail trade and services to patrons. This is the phase of the industry that has had the most difficulty with business success.

Small firms in this field are faced with the same basic problems as small businesses in general: (1) a lack of capital, (2) a lack of long-term financing under reasonable terms, and (3) inadequate management.

Poor management has been a particular problem with outdoor recreation enterprises. One reason for poor management is that many of the owner-managers are more interested in a recreation experience than in making a profit. As a result, sound business practices are often neglected while the manager spends time enjoying the activities with which the business is concerned.

Other factors hindering the success of small recreation enterprises are: (1) a high rate of owner-managers who are first-time operators or retired persons, (2) a preoccupation with other enterprises, which limits their time in the recreation business, and (3) short operating seasons.

Financial data from the Small Business Administration show that the average net profit for small businesses in outdoor recreation during recent years was 5% of gross revenues, whereas an average net profit of 10% was achieved by the total sample included in the study. Again, the Small Business Administration attributed this poor showing of outdoor recreation to lack of efficient management and the seasonal nature of these businesses.

Among the recreation businesses surveyed, the Small Business Administration emphasized campgrounds and ski resorts (most ski resorts are not small businesses, but some are). Both of these kinds of enterprises are seasonal and both require fairly large investments, especially ski areas. The agency found that both campgrounds and ski areas produce relatively low profit ratios but have fairly good long-term potential if they are managed well.

This information points out that despite the marked increase in outdoor recreation and tourism, making a profit by providing services to patrons is not easy. It can be done only in situations where there is sufficient demand over an adequate portion of the year and where the enterprise is well managed. No one should have the impression that outdoor recreation provides a mecca for making a profit.

GOVERNMENT EXPENDITURES

It is difficult to determine and describe the economic impact of government expenditures in the field of recreation. Certainly, it would be erroneous to claim that such expenditures are economic gains, because it simply amounts to public spending of public money. However, it is a fact that government expenditures have direct economic benefits in the particular areas where the expenditures occur. So the particular placement of expenditures has potential benefit for that locality, with some effect outside the immediate area.

Federal Government Expenditures

Information from the Department of Commerce shows the magnitude of leisure time spending in the total economy to exceed $250 billion annually. This dwarfs the $5 billion spent on recreation each year by federal, state, and local governments. However, a substantial but undetermined portion of the total volume of spending could not occur in the absence of the publicly provided recreation lands, facilities, and programs.

Direct outlays by federal agencies for recreation and parks have tripled in the last 30 years from about $500 million to approximately $1.5 billion per year. The largest federal contributor to recreation spending is the Department of the Interior, which administers the Land and Water Conservation Fund and manages a large area of land. The Department of Agriculture is also much involved with recreation, primarily through the management of national forests. The Department of Labor, through its Comprehensive Employment and Training Act (CETA), also makes large expenditures in recreation. Figure 5.2 shows the percentages of federal recreation expenditures by function. Figure 5.3 shows the amount of expenditure at the different levels of government.

State Expenditures

Several states have special programs to help finance outdoor recreation. For example, the Massachusetts Self-Help Program provides reimbursement up to one half the cost for acquisition of land and the planning of outdoor facilities in an effort to help less affluent communities use Federal Land and Water Conservation Fund money. New Mexico provides supplementary funds with the federal conservation grants to help communities of less than 15,000. Connecticut has a similar program. There are many other states that provide money by some kind of matching formula in connection with Land and Water Conservation Fund grants.

Other states have used several different methods for raising funds. Montana assesses a tax on all coal mined in the state. A percentage of the tax is available to communities affected by coal mining for the acquisition and development of recreation sites. Also, part of the tax is provided for acquisition of land for state parks.

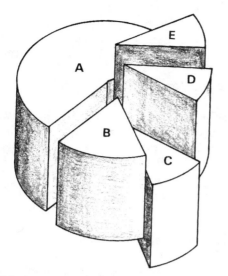

Function

A Grants–55%
B Operation, Mainte-
   nance, and Manage-
   ment–21%
C Development and
   Construction–11%
D Land Acquisition–7%
E Other–7%

Figure 5.2. Approximate federal outdoor-recreation expenditures by function.
Percentages vary slightly from year to year. (Source: U.S. Department of the Interior, *Third Nationwide Outdoor Recreation Plan,* revised 1983)

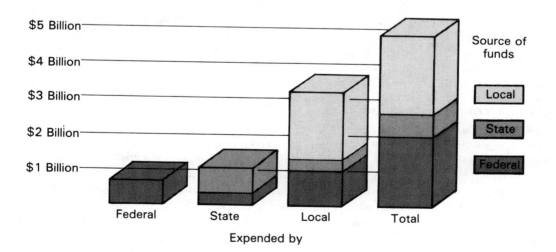

Figure 5.3. Approximate park and recreation expenditures at federal, state, and local levels in 1983. The level of the expenditures has remained fairly constant since the late 1970s. (Source: U.S. Department of the Interior, *Third Nationwide Outdoor Recreation Plan,* revised 1983)

Nebraska, Utah, Colorado, and several other states have instituted user fees for state parks, and the funds collected are invested in the expansion and development of state parks.

Texas recently approved a cigarette tax which yields over $20 million per year to help with the development of state and local parks.

Missouri has made a move that will add $25 million per year to expand fish, wildlife, and forestry programs through a small increase in the state sales tax.

In some cases states have earmarked special funding sources for particular kinds of recreation development. For example, several states use revenue generated from powerboat licensing, gasoline, taxes, and other income from water recreation. Most states collect a large amount of money annually from hunting and fishing licenses, and this goes back into the management of fish and wildlife.

Several of the northern states collect a substantial amount through snowmobile licensing, and in some cases this money is being used to develop snowmobile trails and for the enforcement of safety regulations.

State bond elections in support of both park expansion and wildlife development have been quite successful, and many states are in the process of upgrading these programs by use of funds from bond issues. Among the states that have recently approved bonding for recreation developments are Nevada, Minnesota, Montana, Missouri, Kansas, and Nebraska.

New Jersey is perhaps the best example of a state that emphasizes bonding for parks and recreation. It approved bond issues in 1961, 1971, 1974, and 1978. The 1974 bond issue included $100 million for recreation development and $100 million for acquisition in non-urban areas. The 1978 bond issue included $200 million for acquisition and development with the option of using some of the money in urban areas.

It is apparent that every state collects money through various fees, charges, special taxes, and bond issues to supplement appropriated funds to provide outdoor recreational opportunities. Even though all of this is public money, regardless of its source, and even though it is spent on projects to serve the public, it still must be viewed as an economic factor of considerable significance. How great the impact and exactly how it is applied varies considerably among the states.

Local Government Expenditures

According to the National Recreation and Park Association, about 2.3% of local government appropriations go into the recreation and park budgets. This percentage has remained relatively constant over the past 10 years, even though it has fallen off slightly since 1978. The annual per capita outlay for local recreation and park expenditures is now at about $22.

Information from the National Park Service shows that young dynamic cities spend a larger share of their recreation money on acquiring and developing new areas and facilities, whereas the large cities, which have long-established recreation systems, put more emphasis on operating and maintaining their existing facilities and programs.

Naturally there is a large variation in the total dollars spent for recreation by the different communities across the country. But, it is a fact that practically every community of much size has a recreation and park budget, and hundreds of millions of dollars are spent each year by these local agencies. This spending has a tremendous economic impact in the form of employment, purchases, and land acquisition.

Discussion Questions

1. Of the four major phases of a recreation experience described in Chapter 1, which phase has the greatest economic impact? Give examples of how each phase can affect the economy.
2. What is meant by the multiplier effect of tourism, and how does this affect the economy?
3. How and why does the development of a major recreation attraction affect surrounding land prices, local employment, and the sale of goods?
4. How and why does the tax base change in a local area because of the development of a recreation attraction?
5. What is meant by a cost-benefit analysis of a resource-improvement project? How is it calculated?
6. What are some of the factors that often hinder the success of small private recreation enterprises? How can these disadvantages be removed or reduced?
7. Because of the proven economic advantages of a major recreation development, can you identify reasons why a community should not welcome such a development? What conditions or controls are necessary for such a project to be highly beneficial?

Recommended Readings

Brockman, Frank, et al. *Recreation Use on Wildlands,* 3rd ed. New York: McGraw Hill, 1979. Chapter 13.

Business Research Division, Graduate School of Business. *The Cost of Recreation and Leisure Activities.* Boulder, Colorado: University of Colorado, 1980.

Dardis, Rachel, et al. "Cross-Section Studies of Recreation Expenditures in the United States." *Journal of Leisure Research,* Vol. 13, No. 3.

Epperson, Arlin F. *Private and Commercial Recreation.* New York: John Wiley & Sons, 1977.

Federal Outdoor Recreation Fee Program Report. Washington, D.C.: U.S. Department of the Interior, 1982.

Gunn, Clare A. *Tourism Planning.* New York: Crane Russak Publishers, 1979.

Hawkins, Donald, et al. *Tourism Marketing and Management Issues.* Washington, D.C.: George Washington University Press, 1980.

Hawkins, Donald, et al. *Tourism, Planning and Development Issues.* Washington, D.C.: George Washington University Press, 1980.

Kitchen, James W., James E. Miller, and James W. Graves. *Recreation Expenditures by U.S. Consumers, 1929–1979.* Lubbock, Texas: Texas Tech University, College of Agricultural Sciences, August 1982.

Knudson, Douglas M. *Outdoor Recreation.* New York: Macmillan Publishing Co., 1984, Chapter 6.

"Leisure: Where No Recession Is in Sight." *U.S. News and World Report,* 15 January 1979, p. 41.

Owen, Elizabeth. *The Growth of Leisure Markets and Its Impact on the U.S. Economy.* Washington, D.C.: U.S. Department of Commerce, Office of Consumer Goods and Services Industry, 1978.

Pennsylvania Department of Environmental Resources. *Overview of Economic Significance of Recreation in Pennsylvania.* Harrisburg: October 1982.

"Recreation Real Estate Market for Rural Property." *Journal of Leisure Research,* September 1979, p. 4.

U.S. Department of Agriculture. *Growth Potential of the Skier Market in the National Forests.* Forest Service Research Paper WO-36, U.S. Government Printing Office, 1980.

U.S. Department of Agriculture. *Outdoor Recreation: Advances in Application of Economics.* Forest Service, General Technical Report WO-2, 1977.

U.S. Department of Commerce. *Statistical Abstracts of the U.S.*, 103rd ed. Washington, D.C.: Bureau of the Census, 1982.

Van Doren, Carlton S., George B. Priddle, and John E. Lewis. *Land and Leisure: Concepts and Methods in Outdoor Recreation.* Chicago: Maaroofa Press, Inc., 1979. Chapters 9, 17, 18.

Wilder, Robert L. *Parks and Recreation: An Economic Justification.* National Recreation and Park Association, 1981.

CHAPTER 6

Natural Resource Base for Recreation

Because of the various trends explained in the previous chapters, and certain other factors as well, the demand for outdoor recreation has increased at an astonishing rate. Further, there are strong indications that the high rate of increase will continue. A crucial concern then is whether we have an adequate base of outdoor recreation resources, and how well it will last.

The area of the United States is 3.62 million square miles (9.38 million km²); 98% is land and 2% is inland water. Just what portion of this is suitable for outdoor recreation of one kind or another is difficult to determine. But, it is certain that a good amount of it has some recreation value in its present state and much of it could be improved to have additional value. Trees and grass can be grown, parks and golf courses can be laid out, and in certain localities lakes can be created on rather ordinary land. Such improvements add greatly to the recreation potential of a particular area. Also, within certain limitations, fish and game can be propagated, ski areas developed, and some forms of scenery improved. But, features like wilderness and natural streams cannot be manufactured with any amount of time and effort. Once these resources are gone they will never return.

Many people believe that the nation's resources are badly deteriorating as a result of continued urban growth, industrialization, and environmental abuse. This view is supported by the ongoing destruction of wildlife habitat, conversion of open space to domestic uses, impoundment of free-flowing streams, destruction of wetlands, discharges of toxic chemicals into waterways, and continuing reduction of the nation's forests. All of this supports the need for more restrictions on development and better efforts to protect the resource base.

Conversely, there are supporters for the view that the nation's resources are in a healthy state. Although traditional beliefs about endless abundance have been modified, there are still many who advocate that the undesirable trends pertaining to resource abuse are under control and some trends have been reversed.

Regardless of one's point of view about the patterns of resource use, it is a fact that our resource base has been altered drastically during the past several decades, and the alterations will continue. Further, these alterations have had and will have a combination of positive and negative effects.

It should not be assumed that all of the resources covered in this chapter are either suitable or available for recreation. Some resources already are used in a way to prohibit or restrict recreational use. One question that will deserve careful attention in the future is which resources really will be available in light of (1) the use priorities placed on the resources and (2) the barriers that restrict people's use. Fortunately, the potential use of the basic resources can be increased to some degree by changing the use priorities and by changing people's circumstances to reduce barriers to use.

Another factor of importance is the maldistribution of government-owned areas as compared to the population. Figure 6.1 illustrates that in a general sense most of the government's natural resources are in the West, while most of the people are in the East. This means that the mere existence of outdoor areas and their availability to the public are by no means synonymous. More is said about this in the last section of this chapter.

For the purpose of discussion outdoor resources are organized under three major categories: water resources, land resources, and living resources.

WATER RESOURCES

Water is the lifeblood of the biological community. Without an adequate supply of water all forms of life would become extinct. Because of this and other reasons as well, the protection and wise use of water are absolute necessities.

Water has three natural forms—liquid, solid, and vapor. Scientists believe that all of the earth's original water supply is still present—in the atmosphere, on the earth's surface, or beneath the surface. The earth's total water supply is estimated at 326 million cubic miles (1.37 billion km³). A small percentage of the total supply (less than 0.05%) is in motion at any one time in the hydrostatic cycle in the form of liquid or vapor. More than 97% of the total is held in the oceans, about 2.1% is frozen in glaciers and polar caps, and the remainder (less than 1%) forms the earth's lakes, rivers, streams, and underground reservoirs.[1]

The hydrostatic cycle takes the water from the earth's surface into the atmosphere and then redeposits it in the form of rain and snow. Most of it falls into the ocean, though a small portion falls on land and either soaks into the soil or follows the land's drainage system, which returns it to the ocean. During this process some water evaporates from lakes and streams. In various geographical areas, great differences occur in the rate of evaporation and precipitation because of climatic and topographic influences.

The vast majority of the total water supply is not usable by humans either because of its salty or polluted condition or its geographic inaccessibility. The supply that is available is held in delicate balance and is subject to drastic influences by humans who sometimes use it in manners incompatible with nature's processes. How we treat this precious resource will determine whether there will be sufficient usable water for future generations of humans, and for the other forms of life on earth.

1. U.S. Department of the Interior, *The River of Life*, Conservation Yearbook Series, Vol. 6, 1970, pp. 6–15.

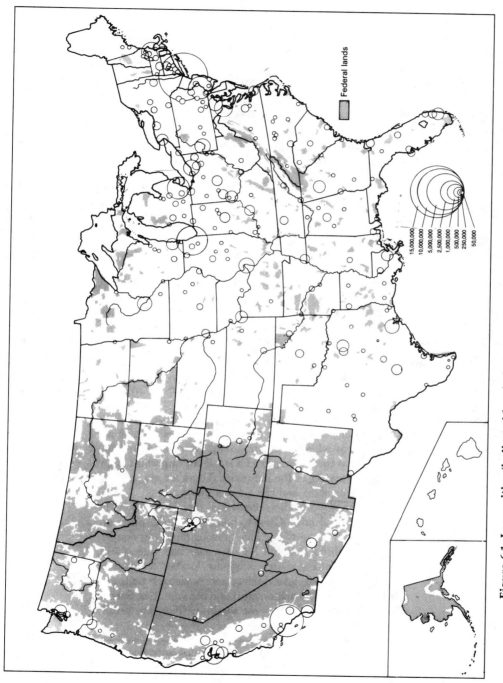

Figure 6.1. Large cities (indicated by circles) generally are far from federally owned lands.

River Corridors

Within the continental United States there are approximately 3.25 million miles (5.24 million km) of rivers and tributaries, ranging from free-flowing streams in wilderness terrain to greatly altered channels through urban areas. A recent inventory by the Department of the Interior indicates that most of our nation's rivers (about 90%) are found in short segments of less than 25 miles (40 km).[2]

The meeting place between land and water attracts and supports numerous biological species. Also, most river corridors provide a high concentration of scenic and geographic interests. Serving as trails and transportation routes, rivers have played an important role in the exploration and settlement of the nation. As a result the river corridors also contain many historic and cultural sites.

A wide range of water-based recreation can take place along rivers. Swimming, boating, and fishing are popular activities that have been encouraged by recent improvements in the water quality. Some streams provide unique opportunities for white-water rafting, kayaking, and canoeing. However, rivers have an even broader recreational appeal based on scenic qualities that provide a desirable setting for camping, hiking, picnicking, and other land-based activities.

Rivers serve many important functions in addition to their role as a recreation resource. They provide water for irrigation and hydroelectric power. Further they serve as thoroughfares for shipping raw materials and manufactured goods. About 25,000 miles (40,300 km) of the nation's rivers are considered commercially navigatable waterways.

Unfortunately, during the past rivers have provided a convenient place to dispose of the waste and pollutants generated by urban and commercial development. The Mississippi, Hudson, and Detroit rivers are prime examples of this. These major waterways have been polluted in almost every conceivable manner. Some pollutants can be assimilated by water without obvious impact on recreation use. But recreation values can be destroyed by overdoses of toxic chemicals, sewage, industrial discharges, and litter ranging from cans to abandoned automobiles. Several other competing uses also threaten the recreational use of rivers. Withdrawals of water for domestic, agricultural, and industrial supplies can reduce stream flow, change salinity, or substantially affect water temperature. Similarly, impoundments to generate power or control floods can interfere with natural processes and reduce downstream recreational opportunities. Threatening the scenic qualities of river corridors are many unsightly industrial areas and commercial enterprises, especially near cities.

The careless use that we have made of our streams has resulted in several legislative acts and other forms of government involvement in efforts to correct these abuses. Perhaps the two most significant actions in recent times revolve around the Clean Water Act and the Wild and Scenic Rivers Act, both passed in 1968. The importance of these and other legislative acts is discussed elsewhere in this book.

Although rivers are frequently thought of as narrow water-filled channels, there are two other elements of rivers to consider in terms of recreation potential. These elements add significantly to the overall importance of river corridors. They are (1) the *floodplain* along the

2. *The Third Nationwide Outdoor Recreation Plan: The Assessment,* 1979, p. 89.

River corridors provide a variety of recreation opportunities. They can accommodate many people without seeming crowded. (National Park Service, photo by Richard Frear)

> The real way to know a river is not to glance at it here or there in the
> course of a hasty journey, nor to become acquainted with it after it has
> been partly civilized and spoiled by too close contact with the works of
> man. You must go to its native haunts; you must see it in youth and
> freedom; you must accommodate yourself to its pace, and give yourself
> to its influence, and follow its meanderings withersoever they may lead
> you.
>
> –Henry Van Dyke

river, which is sometimes underwater, and (2) the larger *river basin* or drainage defined by topographic features that collect water that flows into the corridor.

Wetlands

The term *wetlands* is used to describe areas such as marshes, swamps, sloughs, bogs, wet meadows, and shallow ponds. Wetlands are transition zones between dry land and aquatic environments.

In some areas wetlands cover thousands of square miles and are the dominant characteristic of the landscape. Examples are the Everglades, Hackensack Meadowlands, the Great Dismal Swamp, and the Okefenokee area. However, wetlands are usually small parcels lying between open water and dry land. They often border estuaries, coastal areas, rivers, and lakes.

The most significant role of wetlands is their highly productive environment for fish and wildlife. Spawning grounds for many species of both ocean and freshwater fish are found in these areas. Wetlands also support both permanent and migratory waterfowl and numerous other animals that feed, nest, breed, and mature in wetlands. These populations are supported by the tremendous capacity of wetlands to produce basic plant materials and nutrients.

The wetland environment provides opportunity for a variety of recreation activities including nature study, fishing, hunting, trapping, bird watching, hiking, canoeing, and photography.

Numerous competing uses threaten wetlands. Often viewed in the past as wastelands, many wetlands have been drained and filled for agricultural, industrial, and residential development. Most of us can see examples of this in or near our own communities. Wetlands have provided cheap sites for dumps, sanitary landfills, power lines, airport runways, and industrial complexes. Intrusions by railways, discharges of toxic chemicals, and alterations of natural drainage patterns have destroyed the natural conditions of many wetlands.

The U.S. Fish and Wildlife Service has estimated that about 127 million acres (51.4 million ha) of wetlands existed at one time in the continental United States. The current estimate of area is about 75 million acres (30 million ha). The difference indicates a dramatic loss of valuable natural areas. It is claimed that during the past decade we have lost 300,000 wetland acres (121,000 ha) per year to the various forms of encroachment.

Shorelines and Islands

The Atlantic, Pacific, Gulf, and Alaskan coastlines of the United States total more than 88,000 miles (142,000 km). There are an additional 11,000 miles (17,700 km) of U.S. coastline bordering the Great Lakes. In addition there are several thousand miles of coastline surrounding the islands of Hawaii, the various territorial islands such as Guam, Samoa, and the Virgin Islands, and the dozens of small islands that lie along the coastal regions.

The federal government owns most of the coastline of Alaska. But aside from Alaska, about 70% of our shorelines are privately owned. State and local governments own 19%, and 11% are owned by federal agencies. Much of our coast is no longer in its wild state, but a large portion is still relatively undeveloped. Slightly less than 10% is available for public recreation.

The nation's coastlines are characterized by considerable diversity. Consider, for example, the rugged and rocky shores of New England and Alaska, the wide sandy beaches of the southern Atlantic states and southern California, the dunes and cliffs of the Great Lakes, the coral reefs of the Florida Keys and Virgin Islands, and the South Pacific beaches of Hawaii, Samoa, and Guam.

These diverse coastal zones provide a key link in the complex ecological web. Coastlines include beaches, dunes, marshes, tidal creeks, barrier islands, and inlets that serve as natural harbors. With all of these features, our shorelines provide popular settings for a great variety of recreational activities. Swimming, boating, fishing, surfing, and skin diving are a few of the water-based activities that occur there. Recreationists who picnic, hike, camp, study nature, and pursue other land-based activities are also attracted to the water's edge by the sense of openness, scenic beauty, and forms of wildlife.

Coastal shorelines with high public-recreation potential are often attractive for various competing economic uses. Hotels, resorts, condominiums, and town houses are popular along scenic coastlines. Also, numerous historic sites are located along the shores.

The coast is often a place of beauty and serenity, but it is also a site of struggle between the land and the water. Gradually shifting sands as well as devastating storms make some coastal areas impractical and even hazardous for permanent development. Human efforts to stabilize shorelines with dikes and walls have frequently been ineffective as well as expensive.

Ports and harbors are important uses of coastal lands. Increasing energy needs have imposed new demands on coastal areas for refineries, pipelines, terminals, and staging grounds to support exploration in the outer continental shelf. Pressures for development along the remaining virgin coastlines have increased rapidly, threatening to disrupt the coastal ecosystem and spoil much of the remaining natural beauty. The waters of the coastal zones that support the diverse ocean life are threatened by chemicals, oil slicks, and other pollutants.

Lakes and Reservoirs

In round figures there are 100,000 natural lakes in the United States ranging from prairie ponds to high mountain craters and from glacier reservoirs to the expansive Great Lakes system. These inland waters provide opportunities for many different recreation activities, such as swimming, boating, waterskiing, sailing, fishing, camping, hiking, picnicking, and sightseeing.

It is estimated, according to Department of the Interior statistics, that in the United States there are 22 million surface acres (8.8 million ha) of fresh water available for recreation. In the heavily populated areas the amount available is already insufficient, and the National Water Resources Council has calculated that nationwide the amount of surface area is less than optimal.

In addition to the 100,000 natural lakes, there are thousands of large and small reservoirs that have been constructed by government agencies and private individuals for flood control, irrigation, and electrical power. These are discussed in Chapter 9.

Natural lakes are called on to serve many functions other than recreation. Water to meet domestic and agricultural needs is often drawn from natural lakes as well as from reservoirs. Other competing demands come from industry and homes, both of which often use lakes as convenient dumping places for trash and pollutants.

Natural lakes have been especially subject to despoilment. Consequently, the federal Water Pollution Control Act of 1972 gives special attention to the quality of water in lakes as part of achieving the national clean-water goals. The act requires each state to:

1. identify and classify according to eutrophic conditions all publicly owned freshwater lakes within the state,
2. prepare procedures, processes, and methods including land-use requirements to control pollution of lakes, and
3. develop methods and procedures to restore the water quality of lakes.

Shorelines of the major reservoirs frequently are managed by a federal, state, or local agency. Within the limits of authorizing legislation, these agencies can restrict or encourage public access. Conversely, much of the land near natural lakes is privately owned and subject to various state or local regulatory programs which can help protect the natural and recreational values. As the nation continues to develop, the three most crucial issues in terms of recreation on inland waters are (1) the loss of resources as the demand for their use increases, (2) controlling pollution and the many ills that result from it, and (3) providing adequate public access to the various water areas.

LAND RESOURCES

The land area of the United States (excluding surface water) is 2.2 billion acres (.88 billion ha). Of this, 58% is in private hands, 34% is owned by the federal government, 6% is held by state and local governments, and 2% is allocated to Indian tribes (see Figure 6.2).

The uses of the land are far from static. For example, we continue to grow more crops on fewer acres each year. Between 1963 and 1983 cropland acreage fell 8%, but we increased the total production of food and fiber and the amount per acre. Forest acreage also decreased during that period. Pasture and rangeland increased, and much rural land was taken over for urban and suburban developments.

Rural land use shifts back and forth. During the past 20 years millions of acres went from crops to pasture and millions more from pasture to crops. Trees were cleared from 11 million acres (4.5 million ha) to make way for crops, while millions of cropland acres reverted to commercial forests (Table 6.1).

A large portion of the total land area has some recreation value, either direct or indirect. Private crop and pasture lands help support wildlife which fits into the outdoor recreation

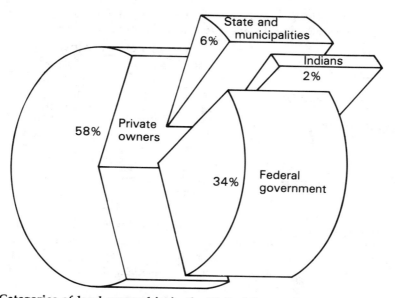

Figure 6.2. Categories of land ownership in the United States. (Source: Bureau of Land Management, *Public Land Statistics*, 1983)

scheme. Wetlands also support wildlife and, in some cases, have scenic value as well. Of course, there are multiple recreational uses of forests, alpine regions, deserts, and seashores.

There is much confusion between land and country. Land is the place where corn, gullies, and mortgages grow. Country is the personality of the land, the collective harmony of its soil, life, and weather. Country knows no mortgages, alphabetical agencies, no tobacco road; it is calmly aloof to these petty exigencies of its alleged owners.

—Aldo Leopold, *A Sand County Almanac*,
Ballantine Books, New York, 1978, p. 177.

Forests

The forests that once covered most of the North American continent have receded greatly in the face of consumptive use of an expanding population. Only about one third of our nation's land is still forested. These forests range from the towering redwoods of the Pacific coast to the dwarf pines of New Jersey.

Forest areas provide a wide range of recreation–hiking, horseback riding, alpine and cross-country skiing, snowmobiling, camping, hunting, fishing, nature study, and picnicking. Forests also provide habitat for wildlife and serve important ecological functions by protecting watersheds from erosion.

Table 6.1. Trends in Land Use in the United States
(Includes United States, Puerto Rico, and Virgin Islands; Excludes Alaska)

Land Use	Millions of Acres (ha) 1963	1983	% Change
Cropland	446 (180.49)	410 (165.92)	− 8
Pasture, native pasture, and range	492 (199.11)	549 (222.18)	+12
Forestland	440 (178.07)	360 (145.69)	−18
Urban land (over 10 acres)	59 (23.88)	99 (40.06)	+76
Small areas of open water	7 (2.83)	9 (3.64)	+29
Other	64 (25.90)	80 (32.38)	+27
Total	1,501 (607.45)	1,498 (606.23)	

Source: Unpublished data from the Land Statistics Office, Soil Conservation Service, 1983.

Forest resources are subject to considerable pressures for economic development. The same forests that provide natural beauty and a home for wildlife also supply lumber for houses, pulp for paper, and wood for alternate sources of energy. The demand for coal, oil, and other minerals beneath forested land continues to rise. Residential and agricultural developments also continue to encroach on our forests.

During the early development of our country, forests were seen as inexhaustible resources that frequently had to be cleared to make way for settlement. Gradually it has become apparent that the United States could soon suffer a shortage of good forests, and eventually the shortage could become critical, as it is already in many of the older nations of the world.

According to the U.S. Forest Service, there are about 748 million acres (303 million ha) of forestland in the United States. Surprisingly, most of the nation's forests–420 million acres (170 million ha)–are privately owned. However, much of the high-quality forestland is within national forests, which include 187 million acres (75.7 million ha). About 30 million additional acres (12 million ha) of forests are found within the national park areas, wildlife refuges, and other federal lands. State and local government agencies own about 38 million acres (15 million ha) of forestland.

Forests are vastly different in character in the several regions of the country. Hardwood forests are concentrated in the East, Southeast, and Midwest, while the more arid areas of the West produce largely softwoods–spruce, fir, and pine. Also, the terrain and the elevation vary considerably, with forests in the East being at relatively low elevations and on mild terrain as compared to the forests in the West. Almost all of these forests are high in recreation value. Considerably more is said about this topic in the section about the U.S. Forest Service in Chapter 8.

Grasslands

Tall-grass prairies once covered 400,000 square miles (1 million km²) of North America, according to the Bureau of Land Management. This vast area was dominated by bluestem and Indian grass which exceeded 6 feet (1.8 m) and supported millions of bison, antelope, and other grazing animals. Tall-grass areas extended from the Appalachian plateaus throughout an area known as the Central Lowlands, including parts of Ohio, Indiana, Illinois,

There must always be nature–desirable places to discover the wonders of nature and our dependence upon it. (National Park Service, photo by Richard Frear)

Iowa, Missouri, Oklahoma, Texas, and the Great Lakes states. The moist tall-grass prairies were fertile and provided ideal cropland. As a result, agricultural uses have taken over most of America's scenic grassland areas.

The western Great Plains were originally covered with varieties of short grasses that could thrive with average annual precipitation of 10 to 20 inches (25–50 cm). Mixed-grass prairies extended through the Great Plains region and the Rocky Mountain states. Grasslands also were found in the coastal plains of Louisiana, Texas, California, and in parts of the Northwest. Great expanses of these areas have been converted to agricultural production, made possible through reclamation projects. Most of the native grassland areas that are uncultivated have been altered by extensive livestock grazing.

Some grasslands have been protected in conjunction with other resources. Representative remnants of mixed-grass prairies are found in several national parks, and there are 3.8 million acres (1.5 million ha) of national grasslands that are managed by the U.S. Forest Service. Also, remnants of grasslands remain on Indian reservations, on Bureau of Land Management areas and in wildlife refuges. Further, some grassland plots are protected for research projects and by private conservation groups. A Great Plains Grasslands National Park has already been proposed, and there appears to be growing interest in preserving other sections of native grasslands for scenic, scientific, and educational uses.

Even though grasslands are limited in their recreational value, they do serve some purpose in this regard. Grasslands are vital to the preservation and propagation of certain wildlife, and some grasslands are quite scenic. Moreover, in grassland areas there are oases of heavy vegetation around water sources, and these areas often have high recreation potential.

Despite the significant reduction of our native grasslands, the trend is still toward converting this kind of resource into agricultural production wherever the economic conditions and the availability of water make it feasible.

Deserts

Lands receiving less than 10 inches (25 cm) of annual precipitation are generally classified as desert. Deserts of the United States range from high, dry mountains and plateaus to deep canyons, dry lake beds, and sand dunes. These areas were originally seen as inhospitable wastelands to be avoided or tolerated in the westward march of civilization. In recent years, however, the desert has become a significant attraction for recreation. Despite the scorching daytime heat and sometimes uncomfortably cool nights, people go to the deserts in large numbers to hike, camp, hunt, photograph, sightsee, picnic, ride horses, and drive off-road vehicles, such as dune buggies and motorcycles. In addition to these pursuits, the desert has become attractive for such dramatic recreational activities as parachuting, sand sailing, and hang gliding.

Numerous parks and monuments have been established to focus on the desert's scenery and to help preserve its natural state. Among these are sites in the West and Southwest such as Death Valley, White Sands, Saguaro, Joshua Tree, and Organ Pipe Cactus national monuments; Canyonlands, Arches, Zion, and Guadalupe national parks; Glen Canyon and Lake Meade national recreation areas, and many other areas of the national park system. In addition, the deserts include numerous state parks, historical monuments, and other recognized points of interest.

Several federal agencies control portions of desert terrain. The largest federal holder of such land is the Bureau of Land Management. In fact, most of its holdings are desert or

In some locations the elements have formed natural enriching wonders. (National Park Service, photo by Jack Boucher)

semidesert terrain. A large portion of the desert land is in private ownership of individuals or companies for the purpose of livestock grazing and mineral exploration. States in the West also own a fair share of desert land, as do Indian tribes.

With the recent onslaught of recreational use of our desert areas, several problems have developed that require efforts toward control:

1.   the indiscriminate use of off-road vehicles that damage the terrain,
2.   the disturbance of wildlife and the destruction of habitat by the many visitors,
3.   the sale of certain desert plants that are delicate and slow to regenerate.

Tundra

Tundra, a natural ecosystem found in arctic and alpine zones, is characterized by a lack of trees and a predominance of grasses, sedges, herbs and dwarf shrubs. It generally has long, harsh winters and cool summers. Types of tundra range from the dry and barren to the very moist, each hosting different kinds of plants and animals.

A broad plain of arctic tundra stretches across the northernmost portion of the continent. Alaska accounts for most of the tundra within the United States. But the Rocky Mountains, the Sierra Nevada, the Cascades, and other western ranges contain several small regions of alpine tundra. Tundra also occurs on a few eastern peaks in the Adirondacks of New York and the White Mountains in New England.

Beautiful wild flowers, breathtaking vistas, and interesting ecological features make some tundra areas attractive places for hiking, camping, nature study, and sightseeing. However, the severe winter conditions which create the tundra and the tundra's inaccessibility and fragility limit its use for recreation.

Northern tundra is especially important to certain forms of wildlife, including moose, caribou, musk oxen and several species of waterfowl.

Most of the vegetation in tundra regions is delicate, and the soil in which it grows is unstable and easily deformed. These conditions result in easy destruction and slow recovery. Despite this, protection of the tundra environment has not been a major problem because it has been used sparingly. However, more hunting, fishing, and mineral developments in tundra areas spell environmental difficulties.

Practically all of the tundra in the United States is in government ownership, with the great majority owned by federal agencies, primarily the Bureau of Land Management, Forest Service, and National Park Service.

LIVING RESOURCES

Hunting provides a healthy outdoor recreation activity for more than 27 million Americans annually, according to the U.S. Fish and Wildlife Service. Millions more enjoy wildlife in nonconsumptive ways, such as wildlife watching, nature study, and outdoor photography.

More Americans fish than hunt. The freshwater and saltwater sports fisheries provide recreation to 36 million anglers in the United States.

Data from the Fish and Wildlife Service show there are about 3,700 species of vertebrates in the continental United States and its coastal waters. These birds, mammals, fish, reptiles, and amphibians traditionally have been categorized as game or nongame species. Game species are those which are hunted, fished, or trapped for sporting purposes. There is much more about wildlife as a form of outdoor recreation in Chapter 10, which deals specifically with that topic.

"That wildlife is merely something to shoot at or look at is the grossest of fallacies. It often represents the difference between rich country and mere land."–**Aldo Leopold,** *A Sand County Almanac,* **Ballantine Books, New York, p. 178. (U.S. Fish and Wildlife Service, photo by Frank R. Martin)**

Plant life relates to outdoor recreation because of its particular contribution to the attractiveness of the environment. Also, plant life is basic to the food chain of wildlife and to the control of soil erosion and to the building of soil.

RESOURCES BY CLASSIFICATION

In Chapter 1 a description was given of a classification plan that categorizes outdoor recreation into user-oriented, intermediate, and resource-oriented activities. A meaningful appraisal of the supply of recreation resources can be made by applying these classifications.

User-Oriented Areas

The National Recreation and Park Association estimates there are 2 million acres (0.8 million ha) of city and county parks and playfields in the United States. These acres comprise most of our user-oriented outdoor recreation areas. According to the standards recommended by the National Recreation and Park Association, there should be about 500,000 additional acres (200,000 ha) of such areas. This means that we might already be well behind in meeting the needs of the public as interpreted by recreation and park professionals. Based on predicted trends in population, it is calculated that a minimum of 1.5 million acres (600,000 ha) of user-oriented areas ought to be added by the year 2000, bringing the total to 3.5 million acres (1.4 million ha). If this is accurate, then a significant increase in the rate of acquisition will be required if the future needs are to be met.

One of the encouraging factors about user-oriented areas is that the potential supply is relatively unlimited, because such areas generally do not require land with hard-to-find features. Practically any piece of real estate can be developed into a desirable user-oriented recreation area. But, two questions are (1) whether the public can afford sufficient areas, and (2) whether the prime locations will remain protected from other development.

Intermediate Areas

Intermediate areas are neither fully user oriented nor fully resource oriented. In this category there are most of the state parks in the United States, comprising more than 11 million acres (4.5 million ha). Also, there are several million acres of state forests and an estimated 5 million acres (2 million ha) of federally owned reservoirs and other resources that fall into the intermediate category. Furthermore, there are some city and county parks and forests that are intermediate in nature. There are also privately owned intermediate areas available for public use. In all, it is estimated that intermediate areas now include more than 30 million acres (12 million ha).

Even though some parts of the country have an adequate supply of intermediate areas for the present, other parts, particularly the Eastern Seaboard, already have a large deficiency. An additional 5 million acres (2 million ha) of these areas could be justified at the present time to fully meet the public's needs. Experts agree that by the year 2000 an additional 10 million acres (4 million ha) of intermediate areas beyond what we now have would be desirable.

Although scenic beauty and other natural characteristics are desirable, attractive intermediate areas can be created on land that is rather common in type, by making some limited improvements. Often the construction of a boat-launching ramp on a lake, an access road into a scenic region, or picnic and camp facilities in desirable locations can greatly enhance the usefulness of potential intermediate areas. Such areas can often be developed from land that has low value for agriculture, forestry, or industry.

Because there is so much flexibility in location of intermediate areas, the cost of acquisition per acre can usually be kept within reason. Early planning and action are required if public officials are to keep ahead of the rapidly increasing demand.

For more information about areas such as state parks or state forests, refer to Chapter 11. More information about federal reservoirs appears in Chapter 9.

Resource-Based Areas

Resource-based areas provide unique recreational opportunities not available in other settings. These great outdoor areas are where people encounter nature in its relatively unmodified state. Generally, resource-based areas are remote. Therefore, most people visit these areas less frequently. Yet, in terms of total number of visits, certain resource-based areas (national parks, for example) are receiving very heavy use.

In terms of total acres, the supply of resource-based land seems sufficient. We have about 187 million acres (75.7 million ha) of national forests, 85 million acres (34 million ha) in our national park system, and many millions of additional acres in the form of large reservoirs, wildlife refuges, and public domain. Most of this land is "resource-based." Further, there is a considerable amount of nonfederal land that falls into this category.

Not all of the resource-based land is high in recreation value, particularly the public domain. Only some national and state forestland has high recreational potential. Of the 187 million acres (75.7 million ha) in the national forest reserve, the U.S. Forest Service has identified about 16 million acres (6.5 million ha) for outdoor recreation, of which about 80,000 acres (32,000 ha) are improved camp and picnic sites; the rest are unimproved wilderness. The remaining 171 million acres (6.9 million ha) of national forests are used for recreation on a very limited basis.

High-country wilderness can be inspiring for both the recreationists and the guide. (National Park Service)

Despite the many acres of resource-based land, there are some serious problems. Among the more difficult are the following:

1. Prospects for increasing the present total acreage are virtually nonexistent. No matter how hard we try it is not conceivable that more than a few million acres can be added to our present supply of public land.
2. Much of the best land is already under heavy recreational use. As the demand increases, people will have to use areas that are less appealing. The first-rate areas can accommodate only a certain amount of human traffic and still retain their quality.
3. As the high-quality areas become more crowded, there will be additional restrictions. This means that the users will have to adjust to increased regimentation, shorter visits, and less privacy.
4. People will have to accept new kinds of activities to substitute for some of the more traditional ones. For example, the supply of game and fish will not continue to meet the increasing demands at a level acceptable to many sports enthusiasts. This will cause some would-be hunters and fishers to pursue other activities that furnish greater satisfaction. Similar trends will occur in such activities as boating, camping, and even sightseeing as the areas for these activities become more congested.

Resource-based areas are the areas most likely to suffer from overcrowding, because their unique natural qualities are easily destroyed. While overuse destroys the physical features of a natural area, it also destroys the intellectual and emotional experiences that people seek. The serenity, the sense of being close to nature, and the scenic beauty can all quickly vanish in the presence of extensive roads, trodden vegetation, and large numbers of people. In the past, outdoor-recreation enthusiasts have jealously guarded against commercial exploitation of high-potential recreation areas by interests such as mining and agriculture. In the future, however, the greatest threat to these areas will come from overuse by recreationists themselves. For more information about the supply of resource-based areas, refer to Chapters 7, 8, and 9.

DISTRIBUTION OF RESOURCES

The total amount of recreation space is only one aspect of supply. Another aspect is the distribution of the space. Actually, the distribution of areas for user-oriented activities corresponds rather well with the population. The amount of such areas per capita varies little from one region to another. However, there is great variation among individual cities and counties within regions.

Intermediate areas correspond less to population distribution than user-oriented areas do; yet in a general sense the intermediate areas are located close to the population. For example, the heavily populated states have the most extensive state park and state forest systems—New York and California are examples. Heavily populated states have more water areas that are developed for recreational use, and intermediate areas of other kinds are more prevalent near populated regions.

The distribution of most resource-based land is poor, because most of the choice areas are not near the people. Let us review some of the important facts in regard to this matter:

1. More than 80% of the federally owned resource-based land is in the western states, where only 16% of the people live. People in these states have come to depend on the use of federal land to the extent they have neglected the development of user-oriented and intermediate areas.
2. The majority of our large cities are in the four great population centers of our nation: the Eastern Seaboard, the Great Lakes region, the Gulf area, and the Pacific Coast. Of these regions the Pacific Coast is the only one that has anywhere near its share of publicly owned resource-based areas. The other three regions are practically void of any large tracts of such land. This means that, for a large segment of those living in big cities, resource-based areas are out of convenient reach.
3. The trend in population is slightly west and southwest, but it still is not away from the four great population centers. This means that those who have much in the way of resource-based areas will continue to have much, although less than previously, while in the future those who have little will have even less per capita.
4. The distribution of recreation land has great significance for present and future planning. It means that the people in the areas of great population and little resource-based land must recognize that state, county, and city governments, in cooperation with private landowners, must carry the burden of providing close-to-home recreation areas.

Discussion Questions

1. Coastal zones provide various forms of recreation. What are the more prominent forms, and what are some of the problems and threats related to man's recreational use of these areas?
2. Why have recreationists and resource managers recently become concerned about the condition and uses of our rivers?
3. It is often claimed that our outdoor recreation resources are unequally distributed as related to the distribution of population. Explain this statement in terms of distribution of user-oriented, intermediate, and resource-based areas.
4. Some believe our natural environment is deteriorating rapidly while others do not. How do you feel about this? What are the most recent trends? What do you anticipate for the future?
5. About 34% of the land in the United States is in government ownership (federal, state, or local). Much of the government land is suitable and available for various forms of outdoor recreation. As a recreationist, would you support more or less government ownership and control? Why?
6. There are a large number of cases where river corridors have been dammed to generate hydropower. The Glen Canyon Dam on the Colorado is a prominent example. Many believe that this kind of project destroys the scenic and recreational values of the river. Do you agree or disagree? What are the advantages and disadvantages of such projects?

Recommended Readings

Bureau of Land Management. *Public Land Statistics.* Washington, D.C.: U.S. Department of the Interior, 1984.

Chubb, Michael, and Holly R. Chubb. *One-Third of Our Time.* New York: John Wiley & Sons, 1981. Chapter 9.

Citizens Advisory Committee on Environmental Quality. *From Rails to Trails.* Washington, D.C.: Superintendent of Documents, 1975.

Espeseth, Robert D. "Linear Recreation Ways." *Park and Recreation,* Vol. 26, No. 27, p. 38.

Heritage Conservation and Recreation Service. *Protection of Outdoor Recreation Values of Rivers: Task Force Report.* Washington, D.C.: U.S. Department of the Interior, 1978.

Knudson, Douglas M. *Outdoor Recreation.* New York: Macmillan Publishing Co., 1984. Chapters 8, 28, 29.

Land Use Planning, Management, and Control: Issues and Problems. Washington, D.C.: U.S. General Accounting Office, 1977.

"More Precious Than Oil: Conserving Water in America." *The Futurists,* August 1980, pp. 61–63.

Soil Conservation Service. *America's Soil and Water: Condition and Trends.* Washington, D.C.: U.S. Department of Agriculture, 1980.

Sutton, Ann, and Myron Sutton. *Wilderness Areas of North America.* New York: Funk and Wagnalls, 1974.

U.S. Army Corps of Engineers. *Wetland Values: Interim Assessment and Evaluation Methodology.* Washington, D.C.: 1977.

U.S. Fish and Wildlife Service. *National Survey of Hunting, Fishing, and Wildlife Associated Recreation.* Washington, D.C.: U.S. Department of the Interior, 1977.

U.S. Forest Service. *1980 RPA Assessment.* Washington, D.C.: U.S. Department of Agriculture, 1980.

"Who Owns This Land?" *Changing Times,* July 1981, pp. 31–32.

Wunderlich, Gene. *Facts About U.S. Land Ownership.* Washington, D.C.: U.S. Department of Agriculture, Information Bulletin No. 422, 1978.

CHAPTER 7

Natural Resources of Critical Concern

Is it possible to have technological progress and at the same time have clean beaches and rivers, unpolluted lakes, stretches of natural beauty, spots of wilderness, and places where people can find privacy and serenity not ordinarily available in daily living? We must believe that it is possible and work toward continued realization of such conditions. Some of the areas that are crucially involved with this kind of question are discussed here.

WILDERNESS AREAS

The Wilderness Preservation Act was passed by Congress in 1964 to establish a national wilderness system. The act immediately gave national wilderness status to 14 million acres (5.7 million ha) of forestland that had already been classified as wilderness by the U.S. Forest Service, and 2.2 million additional acres (900,000 ha) of national park land. Since that time many other areas have been added to the wilderness system, and new areas are being considered on a continuing basis (Table 7.1).

Table 7.1. Agency Jurisdiction Over Areas of the National Wilderness System, 1983

Agency	Number of Areas	Millions of Acres (ha)	
U.S. Forest Service	118	18.4	(7.45)
National Park Service	31	3.6	(1.46)
Fish and Wildlife Service	54	1.1	(0.45)
Bureau of Land Management	5	0.2	(0.08)
Total	208	23.3	(9.44)

Source: National Park Service Map of the National Wilderness System, 1982.

There are many Americans who think that the preservationists have moved too far toward promoting extensive wilderness. But there are others who think that we still lag behind in this regard, and that 20 to 30 years will prove a lack of insight and foresight by those who resisted the movement.

Actually, the wilderness concept among influential Americans is not new, even though the establishment of a national wilderness system is recent. Among the early promoters of the wilderness idea were Henry Thoreau, Theodore Roosevelt, John Muir, Aldo Leopold, and Robert Marshall.

In the 1964 Wilderness Act, wilderness is described as "an area where the earth and its community of life are untrammeled by man, where man himself is a visitor who does not remain." However, from the practical point of view, wilderness is a relative term. There is not an absolute division between wilderness and nonwilderness. This is illustrated in the writings of Thoreau, whose wilderness was the unexplored lakes and meadows around Concord, Massachusetts. In further travels he was amazed by the forests of Maine, finding them even more rugged and wild than anticipated. Having never traveled outside the northeastern United States, Thoreau had not experienced the great expanses of wilderness in the West, Northwest, Canada, or Alaska.

There must always be wilderness, a lovely someplace for the young spirits to discover the wonders of nature and the dependence of man on other living things.
  –U.S. Department of the Interior, *In Touch With People,* Conservation Yearbook Series No. 9, Washington, D.C., 1973, p. 47.

Wilderness as a recreation resource probably will always be highly controversial for two reasons: (1) because of its low-density use, and (2) because it precludes developments and modifications. The very nature of wilderness dictates that many acres are required in its natural state for each user. Too much use is incompatible with the wilderness concept because it dilutes the unique experience that people seek in wilderness. Advocates of wilderness justify it on the basis that it provides personal experiences that are necessary to the sanity of a segment of the population, and further, that it is good for everyone–even those who do not have direct contact with it but have only indirect experiences. Also, wilderness areas are valuable as natural museums so that man will never lose sight of what the environment was like before the human alterations occurred. Further, wilderness serves as a shelter for certain wildlife and plants that could not survive without it. It is also a valuable reference point for biological research and study.

One of the fast-shrinking categories of wilderness is coastlines. Cottages and tourist roads have all but annihilated wild coasts on both oceans, and Lake Superior is now losing the last large remnant of wild shoreline on the Great Lakes. No single kind of wilderness is more intimately interwoven with history, and none is nearer the point of complete disappearance.

There is no doubt that in the future the wilderness concept will be challenged repeatedly by people who consider it impractical in the face of increasing demands on our natural resources. Probably the concept of wilderness preservation will need to be modified from time to time, and each wilderness area will go through its own evolution of change in function.

In the meantime, the wilderness areas will serve their purposes to the small percentage of the population able to spend time there, and these areas will be altered from their present state for whatever uses future generations decide are best.

Figure 7.1 shows the locations of wilderness areas in the United States. Additional information about wilderness appears in Chapters 8 and 19.

BEACHES AND SHORELINES

Alaska's coast, 99% of which is in public ownership, includes 56% of the nation's coastline. The coastline of Alaska, however, is relatively useless for traditional forms of recreation, and it is inaccessible to most people.

Excluding Alaska, only 30% of the shoreline in the United States is controlled by public agencies, and only 10% is available for public recreation. Most of the heavily used beaches are controlled by local government. Federal and state-owned coastal areas are generally more remote, although there are some exceptions to this rule.

One of the great outdoor catastrophes of America is that most of our beaches are now in private ownership and lost to public use forever. This fact may seem relatively unimportant except in densely populated coastal areas. But as the population increases along other areas of the coast and across the country as a whole, the problem of insufficient publicly owned beaches will become greatly magnified. It will be financially prohibitive to reclaim the beach land needed for public use in the future. In view of the present circumstances it is imperative that the beaches presently in public ownership remain so, and that public agencies be ever watchful for opportunities to acquire additional beach space.

WILD AND SCENIC RIVERS

From the earliest colonial days, America's rivers have played a never-ending role in the nation's history. Today, these rivers continue to nourish our growth, irrigate our farms, provide electric power, and serve as avenues of commerce. But in the course of time and development, many of the streams that Americans cherished in their natural state have become either polluted or altered. Of the 3.25 million miles (5.24 million km) of rivers and tributaries in the United States that pour water into the sea, only a few major stretches remain unpolluted or unaltered. There has been a tremendous number of river-modification projects, such as the construction of dams, rechanneling, and dredging. Homes, factories, and entire cities have been built along the rivers, and in many cases the rivers have become dumping grounds for used and unwanted materials. It is an alarming fact that virtually all of the major waterways in our nation have become polluted.

Only recently have we begun to reverse this trend. A 1963 study by the Department of the Interior and Department of Agriculture led to the passage of the Wild and Scenic Rivers Act in 1968. In recommending the law the secretaries of the departments declared:

America's rivers flow deep through our national consciousness. Their courses beckoned us to explore a new continent and build a Nation, and we have come to know, depend upon, and love the rivers that water our land.

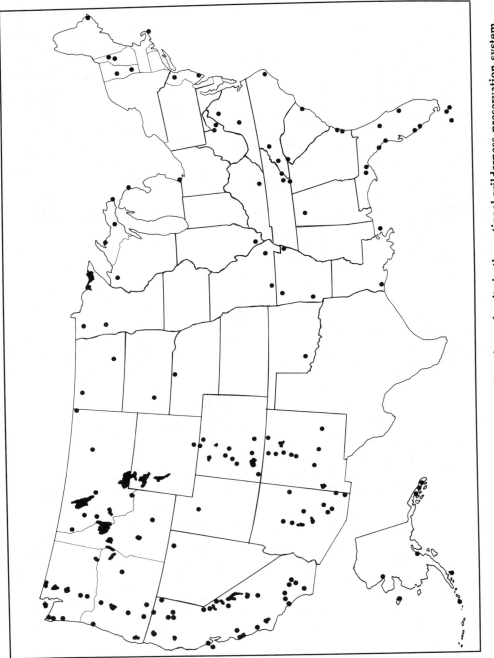

Figure 7.1. Map of the United States showing locations of units in the national wilderness preservation system. (Source: National Park Service)

A day filled with only me and the sand and the sea. (National Park Service)

We have harnessed many of our rivers, dedicating some to navigation, others to power, water supply, and disposal of wastes. But we have not yet made adequate provision to keep at least a small stock of our rivers as we first knew them: wild and freeflowing. In a Nation as bountifully endowed with rivers as ours, it is time to do so.

The act has helped to bring about a balance by designating certain segments of rivers as free flowing. The result will be that some rivers, or segments of rivers, will be permitted to flow wild and free indefinitely–largely unaltered by human handiwork.

The Wild and Scenic Rivers Act declares:

Certain selected rivers of the Nation which, with their immediate environments, possess outstandingly remarkable scenic, recreational, geologic, fish and wildlife, historic, cultural or other similar values, shall be preserved in free-flowing condition, and that they and their immediate environments shall be protected for the benefit and enjoyment of present and future generations. The Congress declares that the established national policy of dam and other construction at appropriate sections of the rivers of the United States needs to be complemented by a policy that would preserve other selected rivers or sections thereof in their free-flowing condition to protect the water quality of such rivers and to fulfill other vital national conservation purposes.

Congress designated all or portions of eight rivers as the initial components of the national wild and scenic rivers system, each to be administered by the Department of the Interior or the Department of Agriculture.

The 1968 Act also designated 27 additional rivers for detailed study as potential additions to the national system. Since 1968 the Wild and Scenic Rivers Act has been amended several times to add new components to the national system and to designate additional rivers for study.

All rivers in the national system must be substantially free flowing and have water of high quality or water that could be restored to that condition. Therefore, the Environmental Protection Agency, in cooperation with state pollution-control agencies, is involved in the study and selection of rivers for the system. The rivers and adjacent lands also must be in a natural or aesthetically pleasing condition and possess outstanding scenic, recreational, geologic, historic, cultural, or other natural values.

Rivers are diverse, and man's use of them and their watersheds has altered them to varying degrees. The Wild and Scenic Rivers Act therefore established three classifications for rivers of the system: *wild, scenic,* and *recreational.*

There are rational arguments for altering the environment which appeal to a sense of enlightened self-interest. But, there are other arguments that speak even more eloquently to the human heart.
—U.S. Department of the Interior, *Our Living Land*,
Conservation Yearbook Series No. 7,Washington, D.C., 1971, p. 34.

Wild rivers are unpolluted rivers or segments that are free of impoundments, generally inaccessible except by trail, and have essentially primitive shorelines and watersheds. They are vestiges of primitive America, and their management emphasizes preservation and the enhancement of primitive characteristics. Structures or other improvements are prohibited.

Scenic rivers are rivers or segments that are free of impoundments, are accessible in places by roads, but still have shorelines and watersheds that are largely undeveloped and primitive. The management objectives of these rivers focus on maintenance of the river's natural and scenic features. Modest recreation facilities are permitted if they are carefully designed and properly placed. These rivers may be accessible in places by road.

Recreational rivers are rivers or segments with high recreational potential that are readily accessible by road. They may have recreational developments and certain other development as well along the shorelines. Management procedures emphasize maintaining the environment while at the same time accommodating the needs and interests of the recreationists.

It is possible for a segment of a river to be divided into a combination of wild, scenic, and recreational designations. For example, there might be a 35-mile (56-km) stretch of a river with 15 miles (24km) designated wild, 10 miles (16 km) scenic, and 10 miles recreational. The entire segment must be at least 25 miles (40 km) long to meet the criteria.

"All the rivers run into the sea, yet the sea is not full; unto the place from whence the rivers come, thither they return again."–Ecclesiastes 1:7 **(National Park Service)**

The act specifies that wild rivers must be unpolluted, but it provides no specific guidance on water quality for scenic and recreational rivers. Nonetheless, the Water Quality Act of 1965 has made it a national goal that all rivers of the United States be made fishable and swimmable and provides the legal means for upgrading water quality in any river that otherwise would be suitable for inclusion in the wild and scenic rivers system. Therefore, rivers will not necessarily be excluded from the system because of poor water quality at the time, provided a water-quality improvement plan exists.

Table 7.2 lists some of the criteria used in classifying a river as wild, scenic, or recreational.

The Wild and Scenic Rivers Act provides two methods for adding a river to the system. The first method is by an act of Congress. Congress can designate a river directly, or it can authorize a river for study as a potential wild, scenic, or recreational river. After completion of the study, a report is prepared and transmitted to the president who, in turn, forwards it with a recommendation to Congress for action.

The second method for inclusion of a river in the system is through the authority granted to the secretary of the interior in the language of the act: "Upon application by the governor or governors of the state or states involved, the Secretary can designate a river as a component of the national system provided that the river has been designated as a wild, scenic, or recreational river by or pursuant to an act of the legislature of the state or states through which it flows...."

Table 7.2. Classification Criteria for Wild and Scenic Rivers

Attribute	Wild	Scenic	Recreational
Dams, reservoirs	Free of impoundment.	Free of impoundment.	Some existing impoundment for diversion. The existence of low dams, diversions or other modifications of the waterway is acceptable, provided the waterway remains generally natural.
Shoreline development	Essentially primitive. Little or no evidence of human activity. The presence of a few inconspicuous structures, particularly those of historic or cultural value, is acceptable. A limited amount of domestic livestock grazing or hay production is acceptable. Little or no evidence of past timber harvest. No ongoing timber harvest.	Largely primitive and undeveloped. No substantial evidence of human activity. The presence of small communities or dispersed dwellings or farm structures is acceptable. The presence of grazing, hay production or row crops is acceptable. Evidence of past or ongoing timber harvest is acceptable, provided the forest appears natural from the riverbank.	Some development. Substantial evidence of human activity. The presence of extensive residential development and a few commercial structures is acceptable. Lands may have been developed for the full range of agricultural and forestry uses. May show evidence of past and ongoing timber harvest.
Accessibility	Generally inaccessible except by trail. No roads, railroads or other provision for vehicular travel within the river area. A few existing roads leading to the boundary of the river area are acceptable.	Accessible in places by road. Roads may occasionally reach or bridge the river. The existence of the short stretches of conspicuous or longer stretches of inconspicuous roads or railroads is acceptable.	Readily accessible by road or railroad. The existence of parallel roads or railroads on one or both banks as well as bridge crossings and other river access points is acceptable.
Water quality	Meets or exceeds federal criteria or federally approved state standards for aesthetics, for propagation of fish and wildlife normally adapted to the habitat of the river, and for primary contact recreation (swimming) except where exceeded by natural conditions.	No criteria prescribed by the Wild and Scenic Rivers Act. The Federal Water Pollution Control Act Amendments of 1972 have made it a national goal that all waters of the United States be made fishable and swimmable. Therefore, rivers will not be precluded from scenic or recreational classification because of poor water quality at the time of their study, provided a water-quality improvement plan exists and is being developed in compliance with applicable federal and state laws.	

U.S. Department of the Interior, *National Wild and Scenic Rivers System: Revised Guidelines for Eligibility, Classification, and Management of River Areas*, Washington, D.C., 1982.

The Department of the Interior and the Department of Agriculture have encouraged state participation in the program. In addition, the act provides for technical assistance to the states, to their political subdivisions, and to private organizations in their efforts to identify and help establish wild and scenic rivers.

State comprehensive outdoor-recreation plans, which are required under the Land and Water Conservation Fund program, consider the need for preserving segments of free-flowing rivers. Financial assistance through the program is available on a 50-50 matching basis to plan, acquire, and develop state and local wild, scenic, and recreational rivers.

Table 7.3 indicates the administering agencies of the wild and scenic rivers system, the number of rivers, and total miles. Further, Figures 7.2 and 7.3 show the units of rivers in the system. Additional information about the Wild and Scenic River Act appears in Chapter 11.

LAKES AND RESERVOIRS

There are rather few large *natural* lakes in the United States. There are only 256 lakes of 10 square miles (26 km²) or more, and these are concentrated in two geographic areas. A total of 103 of these large lakes are in Alaska, and 106 are in the Great Lakes region (Wisconsin, Minnesota, Michigan, New York, and Maine). This leaves only 47 such lakes scattered throughout the remainder of the nation.

Encroachment and pollution have already seriously detracted from the beauty of the lakes in the lower 48 states. Good examples are the Great Lakes. An equally good example in the West is Lake Tahoe, located high in the mountains near Reno, Nevada. Fortunately, with many of the lakes, water quality has improved in recent years, but much more still needs to be done in this regard.

Further, on some lakes public access is a problem. First, there is the question of public welcome on lakes with privately owned shorelines, and there is also the problem of access right-of-ways.

**Table 7.3. Agency Jurisdiction Over
Wild and Scenic Rivers in the United States, 1983**

Agency	Number of Rivers	Miles	(km)
U.S. Forest Service	12	780	(1254)
USFS, NPS	3	456	(733)
National Park Service	6	405	(651)
USFS, BLM	4	204	(328)
Bureau of Land Management	1	180	(289)
Corps of Engineers	2	198	(318)
States	7	286	(460)
State, NPS	2	85	(137)
Total	37	2594	(4170)

Source: Federal Register, Vol. 47, No. 173, 7 September 1982, p. 3.

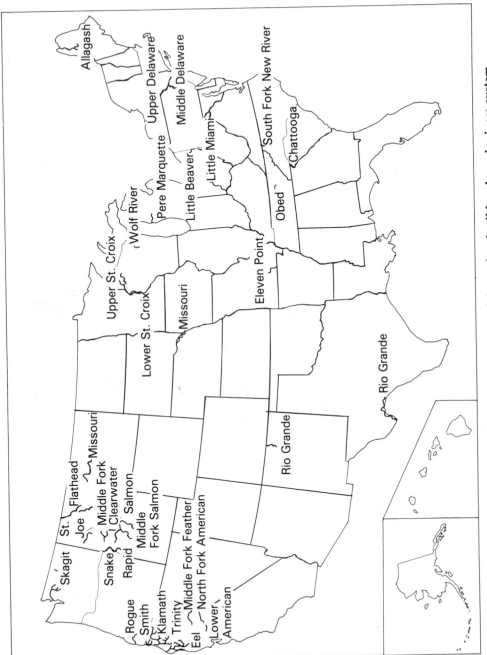
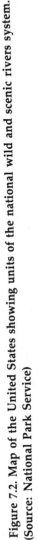

Figure 7.2. Map of the United States showing units of the national wild and scenic rivers system. (Source: National Park Service)

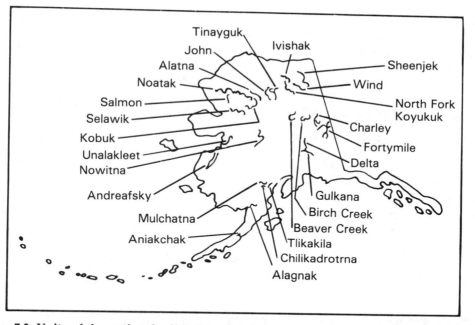

Figure 7.3. Units of the national wild and scenic rivers system in Alaska. (Source: National Park Service)

There are thousands of *artificial* lakes in the United States, and most of them have potential for recreation. Nonetheless, very few of the larger ones have come into existence without a struggle.

The most notable of the early projects were the lakes constructed by the Tennessee Valley Authority (TVA) in the 1930s. Many Americans considered that project a curse rather than a blessing. But now it is apparent that with 10,000 miles (16,000 km) of shoreline and more than 60 million visitors annually the TVA reservoirs are a great recreational asset.

Among the most vocal opponents of artificial lakes have been public officials deploring the loss of land from the tax rolls. But for these people time and experience have brought a happy surprise–the profitable recreation industry that has flourished in most areas where lakes have been developed.

Most of the large lakes have been constructed by the Army Corps of Engineers, Bureau of Reclamation, or Tennessee Valley Authority. Many smaller lakes have been developed by private agencies under the license of the Federal Power Commission.

The federal government now requires the Corps of Engineers and the Bureau of Reclamation to prepare a complete recreation development plan for all of their projects. Further, the Federal Power Commission requires a plan for public recreational use to be filed as part of all applications for hydroelectric projects. The plan must show the location of the areas and access roads proposed for camping, picnicking, swimming, boat launching, and sanitary facilities. Thus, virtually every new artificial lake of any size can be expected to give the American people a bonus in the form of recreational opportunities.

In some cases artificial lakes are in conflict with the wild and scenic rivers concept, and in many situations the choice is difficult. In this regard each proposed project must be considered on its own merits. There is more about lakes in Chapter 9.

THE NATION'S TRAILS

Despite the existence of about 310,000 miles (500,000 km) of identified federal, state, local, and private trails, there is still an inadequacy of trials in the United States as compared to the standards of many other countries, particularly countries of Europe. Unfortunately, complex problems of easements and rights-of-way, along with high costs, plague efforts to establish new trails.

There are about 125,000 miles (201,000 km) of identified hiking trails on the federal estate. Most of these are on lands managed by the Forest Service, National Park Service, and Bureau of Land Management. Further, there are about 70,000 miles (113,000 km) of trails that have been inventoried on state, country, and local government properties. The Soil Conservation Service has determined that more than 120,000 miles (193,000 km) of trails exist on private lands.

"The health of the eye demands a horizon."–Ralph Waldo Emerson. (National Park Service, photo by Richard Frear)

National Trails System

The National Trails System was established by the Congress through enactment of the National Trails System Act of 1968. The act, as amended in 1978, set forth the following policy:

> In order to provide for the ever-increasing outdoor recreation needs of an expanding population and in order to promote public access to, travel within, and enjoyment and appreciation of the open-air, outdoor areas and historic resources of the Nation, trails should be established (a) primarily near the urban areas of the nation, and (b) secondarily, within scenic areas and along historic travel routes of the Nation, which are often more remotely located.

The act defines the following categories of trails, which make up the national trails system:

1. National *scenic* trails, which are long trails that provide recreation in a nationally significant scenic or natural area.
2. National *historic* trails, which are long trails that follow as closely as possible historic and significant routes of travel. The purpose of national historic trails is to identify and protect the historic route and its remnants and artifacts.
3. National *recreation* trails, which will provide a variety of outdoor recreation near cities.
4. *Connecting* or *side* trails, which will join other national trails.

The 1968 act established the Appalachian Trail and Pacific Crest Trail as the initial components of the national trails system and prescribed the methods and standards by which additional components may be added.

The Appalachian Trail was first established in 1921 through the efforts of clubs that were organized to promote hiking. A large number of these clubs joined together to form the Appalachian Trail Conference. It is through this organization that the trail has been maintained and improved over the years. The Appalachian Trail runs 2050 miles (3300 km) through plush scenery and over rolling hills and high eastern mountains. It is ideally located because it is within a four-hour driving distance of about 60% of the nation's population. Because of this, it is by far the most heavily used major trail in the United States. (A map of the trail appears in Chapter 15.)

The Pacific Crest Trail had its beginning in 1932 when action was taken to form a conference in support of a trail that would run along the Pacific Crest from Mexico to the Canadian border–2313 miles (3719 km). This is more rugged than the Appalachian Trail, and it takes hikers through some of the most spectacular desert and mountain scenery in the United States. Fortunately, it passes close to the populated areas of California, Oregon, and Washington.

Since the system was initiated with two national trails, others have been added (Figure 7.4). There are now five scenic trails and five historic trails. The national scenic trails include the Appalachian Trail, Pacific Crest Trail, Continental Divide Trail, North Country Trail, and Ice Age Trail. The national historic trails are the Lewis and Clark Trail, Oregon Trail, Mormon Trail, Iditarod Trail, and Polar Mountain Victory Trail. Of these ten trails, six are administered

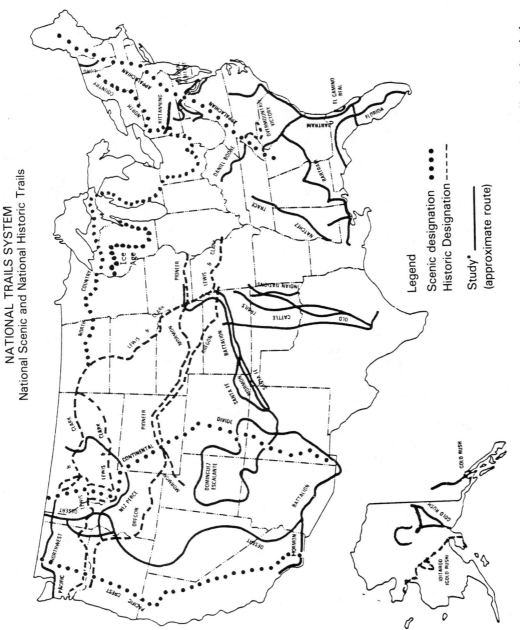

Figure 7.4. Map of the United States showing the national scenic and historic trails, including both existing trails and trails under study. (Source: National Park Service)

by the National Park Service, two by the Forest Service, one by the Bureau of Land Management, and one by the state of Wisconsin.

In addition to the scenic and historic trails listed above, there are more than 700 national recreation trails throughout the country. These trails total over 7200 miles (11,600 km) and are located in all 50 states, the District of Columbia, and Puerto Rico. The federal government administers 485 recreation trails; 10 are jointly administered by federal, state, and local governments; 75 are administered by states; 130 by local governments; and 23 by private organizations.

Other trails are under study for possible inclusion in each of the three categories. However, despite the progress that has been made, the trail system has not led to the development of new trails to the degree that many people had anticipated. This is especially true in the categories of scenic and historic trails. There are several problems that account for this: (1) the long-range goals of the trails system have never been clearly defined, (2) additions to the scenic and the historic categories have been time consuming and costly, and the final decisions have been slow, and (3) rights-of-way and easements have been a major barrier to expansion of the system. Many trail enthusiasts feel that with cutbacks in government programs, the trail system will develop even more slowly. Additional information about national trails appears in Chapter 11.

Other Alternatives

In addition to the need to further develop the national trails system, there is clearly a need for more trails close to urban areas for hiking, cycling, and jogging. The most useful trails are those near cities. In reviewing the potential for additional trails, the following possibilities ought to be considered:

1. Abandoned railroad rights-of-way. There are thousands of miles of abandoned railroads, many of which would be suitable for hiking and horseback riding.
2. Utility corridors. Many utility rights-of-way lie near metropolitan areas. Some would be good for hiking.
3. Stream valleys. Stream valleys provide ideal trail routes because these corridors are often scenic and have interesting features.
4. Lake and reservoir shorelines. Trails around lakes and reservoirs offer considerably more potential than has been developed thus far.
5. Scenic road and parkway routes. These are ideal for the development of trails for both hiking and cycling. The routes are already set with the needed rights-of-way, and the scenery along such routes would be attractive for trail users.

PARKWAYS AND SCENIC ROADS

There are numerous parkways in the United States, most of which are short routes or only segments of longer routes. Many of the parkways function as intended. Unfortunately, some parkways are now used as regular highways; the growth of the population has caused them to become crowded as people use them as commuter routes.

In addition to the short parkways there are two major parkways in the United States. They are the Blue Ridge Parkway (including the Skyline Drive) and the Natchez Trace—each exceeding 500 miles (800 km) in length. Both of these routes are designed for relatively slow and leisurely travel, and they take full advantage of the scenic characteristics. The rights-of-way are wide and well maintained, and along the way there are frequent areas for camping, picnicking, hiking, nature study, scenic views, lodging, and eating. Incompatible uses are prohibited.

Additional scenic roads and parkways could well serve outdoor recreation; however, there is an overriding resistance to the encouragement of too much pleasure driving because of the worldwide oil shortage and the cost of gasoline. Also, there has developed some resistance to using tax dollars for adding frills to motor routes. How much of this should be done relates to a question of philosophy about the relative importance of an attractive environment and the opportunity for people to enjoy everyday scenery.

NATIONAL RECREATION AREAS

The idea of having national recreation areas gained status in 1963 when the President's Recreation Advisory Council released its *Guidelines for National Recreation Areas.* The policy stated that areas suitable for this status should have "natural character above average in quality and recreation appeal transcending that normally associated with state and local park and recreation properties, but of lesser significance than the outstanding scenic and historic elements of the National Park System." It was recommended that special attention be given to locating such areas where recreation demand is not being met through other programs. Also, it was recommended that a national recreation area be no less than 20,000 acres (8100 ha) except in certain cases close to heavily populated areas or along rivers or coastlines. Outdoor recreation is to be the dominant or primary purpose of areas given national recreation area status.

National recreation areas may be managed by either the National Park Service or the Forest Service, and the areas may be either land-based or water-based. Table 7.4 provides a representative sample of national recreation areas.

Table 7.4. Representative National Recreation Areas

Name	Type of Area	Location	Managing Agency
Glen Canyon	Water	Arizona, Utah	NPS
Flaming Gorge	Water	Utah, Wyoming	USFS
Lake Mead	Water	Nevada	NPS
Spruce Knob, Seneca Rocks	Land	West Virginia	USFS
Gateway	Land, Water	New York	NPS
Golden Gate	Land, Water	California	NPS
Cuyahoga Valley	Land	Ohio	NPS
Ross Lake	Water	Washington	NPS
Chickasaw	Land, Water	Oklahoma	NPS

It is not anticipated that the system of national recreation areas will expand much. Areas that are added will likely result from combining smaller areas, which is how Gateway, Chickasaw, and Golden Gate national recreation areas recently were formed. Also, in the selection of new national recreation areas, special attention will probably be given to areas near cities. For additional information on national recreation areas, refer to Chapter 8.

URBAN OPEN SPACES

Outdoor areas of particular concern in urban settings include large city parks with a variety of natural and scenic features, golf courses, beaches and marinas, forests, groves, rivers and streams, and environments that support birds, fish, and other small animals. Trails for hiking, jogging, and cycling are especially important. America's cities have many such facilities, but in most urban areas they are heavily used.

People minus space equals poverty. This is true whether that space is a slum dwelling, a college classroom, a job opportunity, or a national park.

–Marya Mannes

Through many cities pass rivers and streams that have not been well developed in terms of their scenic and recreational potential. There are abandoned industrial sites that could be converted to nature areas, abandoned railroads that could serve as trails for hiking, jogging, and cycling, and in some places scenic trails could be developed along power and phone lines. For most people open space and attractive scenery close to home is the most valuable kind. More is said about this topic in later chapters.

HISTORIC PLACES

Our nation's resources include a vast number of buildings and areas that are historically significant for their architecture, archeology, or cultural heritage. Examples range from magnificent old buildings to inconspicuous but equally important ancient Indian dwellings. Such things as private homes, churches, schools, libraries, lighthouses, ships, and war relics are included in the long list of historic places.

The Historic Preservation Act of 1966 has stimulated the preservation of historic sites by private groups and local, state, and federal agencies. The protection of such sites helps to preserve our heritage, but these sites also can provide opportunities for outdoor recreation. This is especially true of such properties as historic trails, gardens, parks, and scenic vistas. The National Park Service has identified nine major themes that are used to categorize historic resources in the national park system. These themes are the following:

1. The original inhabitants–Indian cultures
2. European exploration and settlements
3. Development of the English colonies
4. Major American wars

Open space near cities for hiking, biking, and jogging is a necessity for good urban living. (Bicycle Manufacturer's Association of America, Inc.)

5. Political and military affairs
6. Westward expansion
7. America at work
8. The contemporary society—education, intellectual events, and the arts
9. Society and social conscience—American ways of life and social, humanitarian, and other movements

The National Register of Historic Places is the official list of the nation's historic properties worthy of preservation. It currently includes more than 20,000 listings. About 17,000 of the properties have been designated as National Historic Landmarks because they meet the stated criteria for national significance. Since many of the listings encompass entire districts or streets, the total number of buildings and specific sites is much higher.

Historic places may be of national, state, or local significance, and the distinction is sometimes a matter of opinion. Historic properties are unique and nonrenewable, and they are often intimately linked with their surroundings. Thorough study is required to determine their significance and how they can best be preserved.

Discussion Questions

1. When a river is included in the wild and scenic rivers system, it is classified and managed under one of three categories. What are the categories and what are the criteria for each?

The preservation of the site of Lincoln's boyhood has both historical and cultural significance. (National Park Service, photo by Richard Frear)

2.   What are the three classifications of trails that come under the National Trails System Act of 1968? Briefly describe each category and the status of its development.
3.   Explain when and how the national wilderness system was officially established. Comment about its growth since its origination.
4.   Why is the preservation of wilderness always a controversial matter?
5.   What seem to be the attitudes toward wilderness of current high-ranking government officials, such as the secretary of the interior, the director of the U.S. Forest Service, and the director of the National Park Service?
6.   Why is it correct to say that historic properties are generally *unique* and nonrenewable? Explain.

Recommended Readings

Dubro, Alec. "Wilderness on Trial." *Outside,* February–March 1982, p. 31.

Dwyer, John. "Wilderness in Century III." *Park and Recreation,* January 1981, p. 61.

"Hard Times Come to Environmentalists." *U.S. News and World Report,* 10 March 1980, p. 41.

Heinrichs, Jay. "Wilderness: Can We Have It and Use It Too?" *American Forests,* March 1980, p. 16.

Hooper, John. "Privatization: The Reagan Administration's Master Plan for Government Giveaways." *Sierra Club Bulletin,* November–December 1982, pp. 33–37.

Knudson, Douglas M. *Outdoor Recreation.* New York: Macmillan Publishing Co., 1984. Chapters 28, 29.

Mapes, Alan. "Trails for Enjoying Nature." *The Conservationist*, July–August 1982, pp. 23–29.

Miller, Pam. "Regulating the Last Slices of Wilderness." *Adventure Travel*, February–March 1981, p. 86.

"95,000-Mile Battle Line: America's Coasts." *U.S. News and World Report*. 4 August 1980, p. 62.

Norgaard, Judith King, and Steve Waterman. "Wilderness Tragedy." *American Forests*, June 1980, p. 21.

Painter, Bill. *Saving Our Last Free Rivers*. From William McGinn, *Whitewater Rafting*. New York: Time Books, 1980.

Schreyer, Richard. "Where Have All the Wildlands Gone?" *Western Wildlands*, spring 1981, p. 7.

"Three-Wheelers Cut a Swath: Whooppeedo for Riders, Headaches for Conservationists." *Time*, 9 November 1981, p. 111.

Tiedt, Glenn F. "From Rails to Trails and Back Again: A Look at the Conversion Program." *Parks and Recreation*, April 1980, p. 43.

"20th-Century Battle of the Wilderness." 14 July 1980, p. 56.

U.S. Department of the Interior. *Index: National Park System and Related Areas, 1984*. Washington, D.C.: U.S. Government Printing Office, 1984.

PART II

Involvement of Government Agencies

CHAPTER 8

Federal Land-Managing Agencies

As explained in Chapter 6, the federal government owns approximately 34% of the land and water area of the United States; about 98% of the federal estate is land and 2% is water. This chapter is concerned with the land-managing agencies (although the land includes many lakes); Chapter 9 is devoted to the agencies that construct and manage water projects.

Most federal land is managed by a few agencies in the Department of the Interior and the Department of Agriculture—namely the National Park Service, U.S. Forest Service, Bureau of Land Management, Bureau of Indian Affairs, and the Federal Highway Agency. Because of the resources these agencies manage, they have a significant impact on outdoor recreation.

The Bureau of Land Management is responsible for the largest acreage of any federal agency, and its land is located in the western portion of the continental United States and Alaska. The Forest Service manages the second-largest acreage, and its areas constitute the national forests and national grasslands. The National Park Service controls a relatively small portion of the federal estate, but much of its land is truly unique and highly attractive for recreation. Its land includes all of the areas in the national park system. The land under the jurisdiction of the Bureau of Indian Affairs belongs to the Indian tribes, and it is mostly reservations.

These agencies are all divisions of the Department of the Interior, except for the Forest Service, which is the largest and most diversified division of the Department of Agriculture. (Later in this chapter is a section about the Federal Highway Agency, which is part of the Department of Transportation. This agency administers a large amount of land in the form of transportation corridors.)

NATIONAL PARK SYSTEM

The areas in our national park system provide a rich display of our nation's most significant natural features. These areas make up a kaleidoscope of unspoiled regions rich in wildlife, desert scenes, alpine peaks, seashores, and a host of other natural and scenic splendors. Scenes from the national parks are as diverse as fountains of molten lava bubbling in the sunset at Hawaii's Volcano National Park, or a technician whisking away milleniums of rock dust from fossilized bones of a monster in Dinosaur National Monument, or giant Sequoias in Yosemite, or the grandeur of fog over the Great Smoky Mountains National Park, or the chorus sung by wetland birds of the Everglades.

As areas for recreation and exhibits of nature, our national parks and monuments are unequaled on any continent. They cover some 79 million acres (32 million ha) in 49 states, the District of Columbia, Guam, Puerto Rico, and the Virgin Islands. These areas are of such national significance as to justify special recognition and protection under various acts of Congress.

One of the best writers on the parks, Freeman Tilden, referred to an ancient Greek concept of a "fifth essence beyond fire, air, earth, and water." Tilden wrote:

> Any thoughtful person may find and meditate upon this fifth essence in his own backyard ... but the fifth essence is more available in our national parks than anywhere else. Many a man has gone there merely for serenity or scenery and has unexpectedly found a renewal and affirmation of himself.

The United States was the first nation to establish a national park, and our park system is far more extensive than any of the others. We now possess more than 330 of these national treasures–both large and small–48 of which are national parks; the rest fall into the various other categories within the park system (Table 8.1). It seems almost incredible how much America has made of the national park concept.

Historical Development

During the first half of the 19th century thoughtful men like Emerson, Thoreau, and Muir called for setting aside scenic nature preserves, but it was not until 19 September 1870, at a campfire in Yellowstone, Wyoming, that the idea of a national park came to fruition. While the flames danced under the starry sky, a group of future-oriented men discussed what should be done with the unique wilderness that they had been exploring for nearly five weeks. Some argued convincingly about the wisdom of staking personal claims, but Cornelius Hedges, later a judge in the Montana Territory, advocated that Yellowstone's unique beauty ought to belong to all the people as a national park. The others were persuaded, and two years later Congress passed a bill, which President Ulysses S. Grant signed, making Yellowstone the world's first national park. The act stated that Yellowstone was established "as a public park or a pleasuring ground for the benefit and enjoyment of the people." The park idea soon became a success, and before the turn of the century Sequoia, Yosemite, General Grant Grove, and Mount Rainier were added to the new national park system.

The Antiquities Act of 1906 gave the president the power to establish national monuments on public lands by proclamation, whereas action by Congress continued to be required for the establishment of national parks. This important law, first conceived to protect Indian ruins of the Southwest from souvenir hunters, has done much to preserve the history of man on this continent.

Table 8.1. Units of National Park System, Including Number and Acreage in Each Category, 1983

Classification	Number	Acres (Ha)
National parks	48	46,862,406 (18,964,955)
National monuments	78	4,693,988 (1,899,630)
National preserves	12	21,993,219 (8,900,533)
National lakeshores	4	197,907 (80,092)
National rivers (includes wild and scenic rivers)	10	525,747 (212,767)
National seashores	11	601,839 (243,561)
National historic sites	62	17,380 (7033)
National memorials	23	8228 (3329)
National military parks	10	34,668 (14,030)
National battlefield parks	3	8166 (3305)
National battlefields	11	11,038 (4466)
National historical parks	26	150,254 (60,807)
National recreation areas	17	3,659,040 (1,480,793)
National parkways	4	163,442 (66,144)
National scenic trail	1	52,034 (21,058)
Parks (other)	10	32,026 (12,960)
National capital parks	1	6468 (2619)
White House	1	18 (7)
National Mall	1	146 (59)
Total	333	79,018,014 (31,978,148)

Source: National Park Service, *National Park System Index*, U.S. Government Printing Office, Washington, D.C., 1983, p. 10.

During the early years most of the nation's parks and monuments were administered by the Department of the Interior; however, a few historical and natural areas were administered as separate units by the War Department and the Forest Service. No single agency provided unified management of the parks until 1916 when Congress created the National Park Service as a bureau of the Department of the Interior. The act creating the agency states:

> The service thus established shall promote and regulate the use of the Federal areas known as national parks, monuments and reservations ... by such means and measures as conform to the fundamental purpose of the said parks, monuments, and reservations, which purpose is to conserve the scenery and the natural and historic objects and the wildlife therein and to provide for the enjoyment of the same in such manner and by such means as will leave them unimpaired for the enjoyment of future generations.

When the National Park Service was created in 1916, the park system had only 37 areas. An executive order in 1933 transferred 63 national monuments and military sites from the Forest Service and the War Department to the Park Service. The agency also assumed control of federal park lands in Washington, D.C. This action was a major step in the consolidation of today's national park system. By 1956, at the start of the Mission 66 Project, the system included 182 areas. Mission 66 was a ten-year program to bring the national park system up to the standards that Congress felt were needed–the standards that ought to exist by 1966, the 50th anniversary of the Park Service. During that ten-year period nearly 100 areas were added to the park system and many of the existing areas were improved.

A favorite view of the Grand Canyon on the Colorado River. (National Park Service, photo by Fred Mang, Jr.)

Despite certain pressures against expansion during recent years, the national park system is still growing. In 1978 it more than doubled in acreage when the president exercised his authority under the Antiquities Act of 1906 to proclaim as units of the national park system 11 new national monuments in Alaska, and to make substantial additions to two existing monuments. The Alaska lands include pristine tundra at the Bering Strait, where it is believed people first set foot on the New World from Asia; the Noatak River's undisturbed drainage basin; and habitats of whales, sea lions, sea otters, wolves, brown bears, and the nesting sites of a great variety of northern and migratory birds.

Subsequently, the Alaska National Interest Lands Conservation Act of 1980 altered boundaries of the units established in 1978 and redesignated most of the units as national parks and national preserves. After that enactment, the National Park System stood at approximately 79 million acres (32 million ha), with 59% of the acreage in Alaska. A few other areas have been added since the great Alaska expansion, but these additions have been small in comparison.

Legislative Acts

The basic legislative acts that have given the national park system legal structure are the following:

1. Antiquities Act of 1906, which made it possible for the president to declare national monuments by proclamation.
2. The National Park Service Act of 1916, establishing the National Park Service as the agency to administer the park system.
3. The Historic Sites Act of 1935, which broadened the president's power to establish historic sites as areas in the national park system.
4. The separate acts of Congress and presidential proclamations pertaining to the establishment of the different national park areas.

Nomenclature of Park Areas

The diversity of the Park Service lands is reflected in the variety of titles given to them. These include such designations as national park, national preserve, national monument, national memorial, national historic site, national seashore, and national battlefield park.

Although some titles are self-explanatory, others are used in several different ways. For example, the title "national monument" has been given to natural reserves, historic military fortifications, prehistoric ruins, fossil sites, and the Statue of Liberty.

In recent years Congress and the National Park Service have attempted, with some success, to simplify the nomenclature and to establish clear criteria for use of the different official titles. Brief definitions of the most common titles follow.

Generally, a *national park* covers a large area. It contains a variety of resources and encompasses sufficient land or water to ensure adequate protection of the resources.

A *national monument* is intended to preserve at least one nationally significant resource. It is usually smaller than a national park and has less diversity of attractions.

In 1974 Big Cypress and Big Thicket were authorized as the first *national preserves*. This category is primarily for the protection of fragile resources. Activities such as hunting and fishing or the extraction of minerals and fuels may be permitted if they do not jeopardize the natural values.

For the preservation of shoreline areas and offshore islands, *national lakeshores* and *national seashores* focus on protecting natural values while at the same time providing water-oriented recreation. Although national lakeshores can be established on any natural freshwater lake, the existing four are all located on the Great Lakes. The national seashores are on the Atlantic, Gulf, and Pacific coasts.

National wild and scenic riverways preserve ribbons of terrain bordering free-flowing streams. Besides preserving rivers in their natural state, these areas provide opportunities for outdoor activities such as hiking, canoeing, fishing, and hunting.

In recent years, *national historic site* has been the title most commonly applied by Congress in authorizing the addition of areas that have national historic significance. Many titles—national military park, national battlefield park, national battlefield site, and national battlefield—have been used for areas associated with American military history. But other

Cross-country touring into the backcountry during winter can be a rewarding experience. (Photo by Douglas Nelson)

areas, such as national monuments and historic parks, may include features associated with military history. *National historical parks* are areas of greater physical extent and complexity than national historic sites, but otherwise are similar.

The title *national memorial* is most often used for areas that are primarily commemorative. But they need not include sites or structures historically associated with their subjects. For example, the home of Abraham Lincoln in Springfield, Illinois, is a national historic site, but the Lincoln Memorial in the District of Columbia is a national memorial. Several areas whose titles do not include the words *national memorial* are nevertheless classified as memorials. These are the John F. Kennedy Center for the Performing Arts, Lincoln Memorial, Lyndon Baines Johnson Memorial Grove on the Potomac, Theodore Roosevelt Island, Thomas Jefferson Memorial, and the Washington Monument–all in the District of Columbia.

Originally *national recreation areas* in the Park System were units surrounding reservoirs impounded by dams built by federal agencies. The National Park Service manages many of these areas under cooperative agreements. The concept of recreation areas has grown to encompass other lands and waters set aside for recreational use by acts of Congress and now includes several major areas in urban centers. There are also some national recreation areas outside the national park system that are administered by the Forest Service.

National parkways encompass roadways that offer an opportunity for leisurely driving through areas of scenic interest. They are not designed for high-speed point-to-point travel.

Two areas of the national park system have been set aside primarily as sites for the performing arts. These are Wolf Trap Farm Park for the Performing Arts, Virginia, and the John F. Kennedy Center for the Performing Arts, Washington, D.C. Two historical areas, Ford's Theatre National Historic Site, Washington, D.C., and Chamizal National Memorial, Texas, also provide facilities for the performing arts.

Designation of Wilderness Areas

In the Wilderness Act of 1964, Congress directed three federal agencies, including the National Park Service, to study certain lands within their jurisdiction to determine the suitability of these lands for inclusion in the national wilderness preservation system.

By subsequent legislation, Congress has designated wilderness areas in many units of the national park system. This designation does not remove wilderness lands from the parks. But it does ensure that they will be managed "to retain their primeval character and influence, without permanent improvements or human habitation . . . ."

The act provides that "there shall be no commercial enterprise and no permanent road within any wilderness area . . . and (except for emergency uses) no temporary road, no use of motor vehicles, motorized equipment or motorboats, no landing of aircraft, no other form of mechanical transport, and no structure or installation." Wilderness areas are open to hiking and in some cases, horseback riding, primitive camping, and similar pursuits. In 1984 there were 35 wilderness areas totaling 35.4 million acres (14.3 million ha) in the national park system.

Philosophy and Management Policy

Part of the philosophy of the National Park Service is that national park areas have meaning—a *common denominator*—for a great many people. This is why the Statue of Liberty is now preserved as a national monument and the Tuskegee Institute has become a national historic site. Further, for many the battlegrounds of Gettysburg, Vicksburg, and Shiloh have intense significance. Also, there is special reason that more than 2 million people gather in a season to watch the magnificent eruption of Old Faithful and that thousands gaze up at the mountain climbers scaling the 3000-foot (915 m) granite face of Yosemite's El Capitan.

The idea that parks are for people is often stressed in the argument that the National Park Service imposes too many restrictions pertaining to the use of the national parks. To see this criticism in perspective a person must recognize that national parks are places of national significance, either because of scenic beauty, unique characteristics, or their history. They are not meant to serve as children's playgrounds, athletic areas, or places where the public can participate in uncontrolled uses. Uses must be controlled to preserve the features that made the area worth designating as a national park. Fortunately, most of us sense the crucial importance of keeping our treasures intact.

Designated wilderness areas within national parks are managed to be preserved. More and more visitors seek experiences that bring them close to nature in the solitude of

Montezuma Castle, built by the Sinagua Indians in 1250, stands as one of the best-preserved prehistoric Indian structures in the Southwest. (National Park Service)

wilderness, and so the dilemma: How can multitudes enjoy together what is best enjoyed alone? This is one of the philosophical problems that the Park Service must cope with in its management procedures. The specific approach varies from park to park, depending on the characteristics of the particular natural area and the demand for its use. More is said about the preservation concept in Chapter 19.

For the most part, national park areas are administered under the *single-use* concept, as opposed to the *multiple-use* policy of the Forest Service and Bureau of Land Management. The single use is for people to experience the unique features of the parks, but not to take anything away except the memories.

The concept of single use relates closely to both the preservation concept and the wilderness concept, and all three of these are deeply integrated into national-park policy.

The size of a park is directly related to the manner in which you use it. If you are in a canoe traveling at three miles an hour, the lake on which you are paddling is ten times as long as it is to the man in a speedboat going thirty. . . . Every road that replaces a footpath, every outboard motor that replaces a canoe paddle, shrinks the area of the park.
—Paul Brooks, U.S. Department of the Interior, *The River of Life,*
Conservation Yearbook Series, Vol. 6, p. 29.

Wildlife in the Parks

Largely because of the preservation policy of the National Park Service, there is an abundance of wildlife in the parks. Within the parks, natural habitat is protected, and hunting is prohibited or strictly controlled. Consequently, mule deer, coyotes, mountain lions, black bears, grizzlies, bighorn sheep, elk, antelope, moose, wolverines, buffaloes, wolves, goats, and many other species are found in various national parks. Of 26 choice birding places cited by the Fish and Wildlife Service, 11 are National Park Service areas.

Sportfishing is popular in national parks. Dozens of areas have brook, rainbow and cutthroat trout, and a few areas have lake trout. Also, certain waters are known for bass fishing, such as Lake Mead and Lake Powell on the Colorado River. Several species of salmon frequent Olympic National Park, Glacier National Park, Coulee Dam National Recreation Area, and Crater Lake National Park. The national park waters of Alaska provide salmon, grayling and trout fishing. Acadia National Park has landlocked Atlantic salmon in its lakes and saltwater fishing on its coastline. Further, several national seashores–Cape Cod, Cape Hatteras, and Point Reyes–offer both freshwater and saltwater fishing.

Innovative Approaches

During the past decade the Park Service has been innovative in experimenting with new approaches. Some think, however, the agency is trying too hard to do all things for all people.

Plans for Yosemite.   Some innovative changes are planned for Yosemite National Park, and these changes may be signaling the future of other parks affected by overcrowding. The proposed master plan for Yosemite–a draft in which the public participated widely–aims to restore the natural scene as much as possible by closer controls on certain aspects of visitor use. The plan excludes private vehicles from the central areas and requires visitors to travel by bus. Limits on use of the areas and facilities have been established, and these limits will be enforced through the use of permits and reservations. Further, to restore the natural environment, the plan transfers some employee housing and other structures to locations outside the park. Also to be moved outside the park are car-rental and car-service firms, sportswear and gift shops, the ice rink, the golf course, tennis courts, and swimming pools. The park itself will be reserved for enjoyment of the natural scenery for which the park was established in the first place.

Urban National Park Areas.   Cityscapes recently have been added to the national park system. In San Francisco citizen groups worked for years to save dwindling open spaces before Congress established the Golden Gate National Recreation Area in 1972. The area now includes the infamous Alcatraz Island, the city's historic waterfront and ocean beach, Fort Point, Marin Headlands, Muir Woods National Monument, Audubon Canyon Ranch, and Point Reyes National Seashore.

Gateway National Recreation area in New York and New Jersey is a patchwork park composed of 26,000 acres (10,500 ha) divided into four main units scattered throughout the New York Harbor: Breezy Point on the Rockaway Peninsula, Jamaica Bay, the southeastern shore of Staten Island, and Sandy Hook on the New Jersey side. Together these areas offer beaches for swimming and fishing, abandoned military installations to explore, and one of the most successful bird sanctuaries on the East Coast–a paradise for bird watchers and city children.

Despite Gateway's 10 million annual visitors, both the National Park Service and many minority groups are pressing for more public transportation to its facilities. Without this the 57% of New Yorkers without cars have limited opportunity to visit the park. Although Gateway has only 1% of Yellowstone's acreage, its visitors outnumber Yellowstone's four to one. This is understandable because Gateway serves a population of more than 20 million people in the greater New York area. This does not mean to imply that the number of visits is indicative of relative importance. The significance and length of visits may be far greater in one park than another, even though the number may be less.

Subsequent to the establishment of the Golden Gate and Gateway national recreation areas, similar areas have been created in the vicinity of Los Angeles, Atlanta, and Cleveland. All told, the urban park concept is proving so successful that several other such areas are presently under consideration.

Transportation Innovations.   Park your car, use the bus, ride a bike, rent a horse, hike–all these things are being encouraged by the Park Service. They are signs of the 1980s and beyond.

Touring in buses has become a popular mode of travel in certain national parks, particularly in Washington, D.C., and Yosemite. Bus transportation is also available within numerous other parks, including the Everglades in Florida, Mount McKinley in Alaska, Grand Canyon in Arizona, Glacier National Park in Montana, and a host of others.

The rationale for discouraging automobile use in certain parks is based on the belief that mass transportation is better for the visitors, for the park employees, for the environment, and for the pocketbook of the visitors and the Park Service. The Park Service claims that the advantages of tourmobiles can be summed up with the "four e's": *environmental* protection, *enjoyment* of visitors, *efficiency* in terms of energy and personnel, and *economy*.

The increasing demand of Americans for water recreation has added scores of lakes and other water bodies to the national park system. Furthermore, the Park Service owns about 2000 miles (3200 km) of seashore and more than 500 miles (800 km) on the Great Lakes. To manage these areas the Park Service has a fleet of boats cruising the waters from Glacier Bay National Park in Alaska to Virgin Island National Park in the Caribbean.

Boats are the only practical method of visiting such areas as the Statue of Liberty, Fort Jefferson (Florida), and Fort Sumter (South Carolina). In the Everglades, one of every five visitors enters the park by boat.

The Park Service is providing public transportation of the various kinds discussed above by three methods: (1) completely or partially subsidizing concession operations, (2) granting permits to concessionaires to provide transportation in the parks, or (3) direct use of government vehicles.

Art in the Parks.   From its earliest days the talents of artists and craftsworkers have been essential to the fulfillment of the national park mission. Architects, designers, sculptors, writers, illustrators, and photographers have all helped shape our national parks. With the great expansion of the park system during the last three decades, there also has been an escalation of the cultural programs, including art and folk crafts.

One example of this is a kind of interpretive program known as *living history*. This program now enriches the visitors in more than 150 areas of the park system. Living history involves putting people in costumes and activities typical of the time when the site flourished. They may, for example, demonstrate the operation of a grist mill, the firing of cannons and muskets, the weaving of Indian baskets and rugs, or the making of pottery.

Another aspect of art in the parks is the encouragement given by the Park Service for selected artists to do their work while visitors stroll the walkways and watch. This effort has been more prominent in the national park areas of Washington, D.C., than elsewhere.

The Jefferson National Expansion Memorial in downtown St. Louis has been the place of dozens of artistic concerts over the past decade, and the New York City units of the national park system present more than 100 performing arts programs each year. Other sites that cater almost exclusively to the performing arts are Ford's Theatre and the John F. Kennedy Center for the Performing Arts in Washington, D.C.

In Vienna, Virginia, the Wolf Trap Farm Park for the Performing Arts continues to offer premiere entertainment for summer audiences. The emphasis is on folk art, but the total program is not limited to this, and a season of the performing arts at Wolf Trap will include a great variety of artistic productions.

The Park Service has been aided in its efforts through the National Endowment for the Arts and the Artists in Residence program. With the precedent that has been set over a long period and the recent emphasis that the Park Service has placed on parks near urban areas, it seems likely that art in the parks will continue to increase.

National Parks in Other Countries

The national-park idea originated in the United States with the establishment of Yellowstone, and it has flourished here more than anywhere else. But, fortunately, the national-park concept has spread to more than 100 other countries throughout the world, and more than 1400 such areas have been established outside the United States.

The first national parks outside of this country were the Royal Mountain Parks in New South Wales, Australia. However, Canada was the first country outside the United States to

An example of living history is this scene from the Booker T. Washington National Monument. (National Park Service, photo by Richard Frear)

inaugurate an extensive national park system. Canada now has the second largest park system in the world, made up of more than 50 areas of which 30 are large national parks and the others are historical monuments and sites (Figure 8.1).

In 1885 Canada set aside a small portion of what is now Banff National Park. Originally the Banff area became popular for its hot springs surrounded by majestic mountains. In 1887 the Parliament expanded the small Banff Park to include 260 square miles (673 km²) and changed its name to Rocky Mountain National Park. Later, the name was changed again and has since been known as Banff National Park. It has gained the recognition of being one of the world's most beautiful mountain areas.

In addition to the park systems of the United States and Canada, England has been quite aggressive in developing national parks (Figure 8.2).

U.S. FOREST SERVICE

People rightfully think of timber production as the paramount purpose of forests. Our forests provide the raw materials for lumber, plywood, laminated beams, fabricated boards, packaging materials, newspapers, and insulation. Other useful products that forests provide

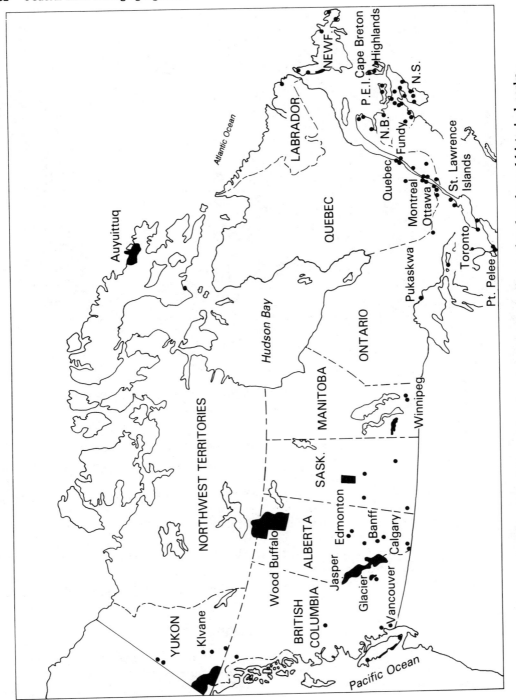

Figure 8.1. Map of the Canadian national park system, including national parks and historical parks. (Source: Parks Canada Information Division)

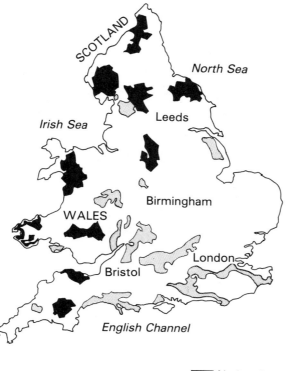

SCOTLAND

North Sea

Irish Sea

Leeds

Birmingham

WALES

London

Bristol

English Channel

■ National parks
☐ Areas of outstanding natural beauty

Figure 8.2. National parks and scenic areas of England and Wales. (Source: National Park Society of England)

are evergreen shrubs, poles, posts, moss and bark for landscaping, Christmas trees, and fuel wood for a crackling fireplace on a cold night. Also, forests enhance the outdoor environment by regulating the flow of water for domestic, industrial, agricultural, and recreational use, and the forests provide habitat and forage for various forms of wildlife.

In addition to their material contributions forests are scenic and have for a long time provided places of enjoyment for the people. Some visitors absorb the scenery from an automobile on a paved highway, while others prefer backpacking on a remote trail for a more penetrating experience. Outdoor recreation of various kinds attracts increasing numbers of forest visitors, many of whom are genuinely interested in the natural environment and the well-being of forests, and who consider forests a favorite place for recreation.

The Forest Service, the principal managing agency of the nation's forests but certainly not the only one, provides an abundance of outdoor recreation opportunities. It is the guardian of the national forest reserve, which includes 154 national forests and 19 national grasslands comprising 187 million acres (75.7 million ha) in 41 states and Puerto Rico (Figure 8.3). These

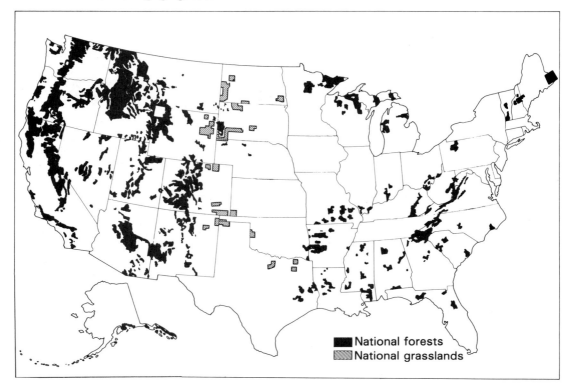

Figure 8.3. U.S. national forest reserve. (Source: U.S. Forest Service)

forests are often referred to as the nation's playgrounds, and rightfully so, because they host well over 400 million recreation visits annually. As part of its effort to enhance recreation opportunities, the Forest Service is the nation's largest provider of public camp areas.

National Forest Reserve

Under the Creation Act of 1891 the president was authorized to create the U.S. forest reserve. In part, the act states:

> The President of the United States may from time to time set apart and reserve, in any State or Territory having public lands, wholly or in part covered with timber or undergrowth, whether of commercial value or not, as public reservations, and the President shall, by public proclamation, declare the establishment of such reservations and the limits thereof.

Additional protection and development of the forest reserve was made possible under the Organic Act of 1897. Subsequently, numerous other acts have enhanced the management of our national forests.

Most of the land presently in the forest reserve has been taken parcel by parcel from the public domain. The original parcel, set aside in 1891, was known as the Yellowstone Park Timberland Reserve. It was later named the Shoshone National Forest (Wyoming). After this initial action the forest reserve grew rapidly, and within two years after the passage of the Creation Act, more than 13 million acres (5.3 million ha) of forestland had been placed in reserve. Through the years additional land has been added to the system, and now there are more than 187 million acres (75.7 million ha) in the reserve.

Establishment of the Forest Service

The Forest Service, the largest and most diverse division of the Department of Agriculture, has been the administrator of the national forests since the service was created by Congress in 1905. (The forest reserve was administered under the General Land Office of the U.S. Department of Interior before 1905). When the 1905 act became effective, the Secretary of Agriculture, James "Tama" Wilson, issued instructions that have served as the basis for Forest Service policy since. Among these instructions were:

Mountain wilderness is an important part of the national forest reserve. (U.S. Forest Service, photo by Daniel O. Todd)

(a) All the resources of forest reserves are for use and this use must be brought about . . . under such restrictions only as will assure the permanence of these resources . . . ; (b) In the management of each reserve local questions will be decided upon local grounds . . . ; (c) . . . the dominant industry will be decided first, but with as little restrictions to minor industries as possible. . . . Where conflicting interests must be reconciled the question will always be decided from the standpoint of the greatest good to the greatest number in the long run.

The concepts of *conservative use, multiple use,* and *decentralized administration* still form the foundation of the Forest Service policy.

The top administrator in the Forest Service is the director, or chief forester, and he is accountable to the secretary of agriculture. The agency is divided into nine geographical regions, each administered by a regional forester who reports to the chief forester. Within each region is a supervisor over each of the national forests, and working under each supervisor are several district rangers. In total there are 154 national forests and 666 ranger districts. Each Forest Service officer is responsible for a specific geographic territory. Information about the recreation resources and the opportunities within a particular region may be obtained from the regional office.

The Forest Service has identified for itself three major functions, and these functions apply to outdoor recreation as well as the other responsibilities of the agency.

Cooperation.   The Forest Service cooperates with the states and territories and with a large number of private landowners to meet the various forest needs of an expanding population. These cooperative efforts involve (1) reforestration projects, (2) efforts to increase forest yields, (3) better use of forest products, (4) reducing wood waste, (5) conserving soil and water, (6) providing outdoor recreation, (7) enhancing natural beauty, and (8) increasing fish and wildlife habitat. In regard to outdoor recreation, the Forest Service cooperates with private interests, local and state governments, and federal agencies by sharing its knowledge and capabilities.

Land Planning and Management.   The forests are managed with recreation being one of the five major uses, along with timber production, water management, range management, and wildlife and fish habitat. These lands include 3.5 million big-game animals, 60 endangered wildlife species, a large number and variety of developed recreation facilities, thousands of miles of trails–most of which are useful for recreation, many lakes and streams that are used extensively for recreation activities, and extensive growths of timber and grasslands.

Research and Information.   The Forest Service does extensive research through its forest experiment stations and land-use projects to determine better methods of serving the public. It is especially concerned about discovering improved methods of protecting the forests from fire, insects, disease, and pollution. Much research has been done to aid recreation management of forests and to provide information to enhance visitor enjoyment.

Recreational Use of Forests

Considering the extent and variety of outdoor recreation on forestlands, it is no wonder that the national forests often are called the nation's playground. The activities include: picnicking and camping; water sports such as boating, sailing, waterskiing, and swimming; fishing and hunting; winter sports, particularly alpine and cross-country skiing, and snowmobiling; driving, cycling, or hiking; visiting well-developed tourist resorts or cultural or historic sites; and participating in nature study, photography, painting, and many other hobbies.

Each year Forest Service lands receive more than 400 million visitor-days of recreation use. About two-thirds of these visits involve dispersed use, away from the developed facilities. The other one-third are in such places as ski areas, waterfront resorts, campgrounds, picnic areas, visitor centers, and museums. Table 8.2 shows the percentage of use by activity.

Developed recreation areas in national forests have a capacity of 1.5 million people. This figure does not include the vast potential for recreation in the forests separate from the developed areas. To receive a better idea of the extent of resources and facilities available for recreation, study the following list of special areas and facilities on Forest Service land:

1.8 million acres (729,000 ha) of natural lakes
880,000 acres (356,000 ha) of man-made reservoirs
83,000 miles (133,000 km) of streams
98,000 miles (158,000 km) of hiking and riding trails
154,000 miles (275,000 km) of scenic roads
115 designated wilderness areas
11 national wild and scenic rivers (or river segments)
7 national recreation areas
15,000 miles (24,000 km) of marked snowmobile trails
One third of the big-game animals in the United States, including four fifths of the moose, elk, and grizzly bears, and two thirds of the mule deer, black bears, and bighorn sheep
80,000 developed family camp units

Table 8.2. Use of National Forests by Activity

Activity	Percent of Total Annual Use
Camping	27
Touring and sightseeing	24
Fishing	9
Hunting	8
Winter sports	7
Hiking and climbing	5
Boating, sailing, and waterskiing	5
Picnicking	4
Vacation-home use	3
Swimming activities	3
Resort use	2
Horseback riding	2
Nature study	1
Total	100

Source: Unpublished data, U.S. Forest Service, Washington, D.C., 1984.

24,000 picnic units
23,000 identified cultural, historical, and archeological sites
420 recreation resorts
255 winter sport sites
950 boating sites
325 swimming sites
470 interpretative sites
19,000 summer homes
41 visitor centers or museums

The great increase in recreation visits to national forests has created problems in fire control, clean water supply, sanitary facilities, protecting recreationists from hazards, and protecting the resources themselves from destruction by users.

In addition to the other recreation benefits of forestlands, the Forest Service is extensively involved with wildlife habitat. It cooperates with the state fish and game departments to balance wildlife populations with available habitat. The national forests provide sportsmen and sportswomen, bird-watchers, photographers, and students with opportunities to enjoy a variety of wildlife activities.

For each creature, there is a time and a place. This magnificent bull elk resides on U.S. Forest Service land. (U.S. Fish and Wildlife Service, photo by Chuck Sowards)

While the national forest system constitutes less than one fifth of the country's total area, it is the home of about 35% of the nation's big game, and hosts more than half of the nation's annual big-game hunters. Further, the numerous streams, lakes, and reservoirs on Forest Service land accommodate much of the nation's freshwater fishing.

Management Policies

In the early days of the Forest Service, its personnel managed recreation to protect the forest environment from damage and abuse. Gradually the Forest Service adapted a more positive and aggressive approach. Eventually, the official policy of the Forest Service became one of encouraging recreational use of the forests.

To effectively accomplish its objectives for outdoor recreation, the Forest Service has established these important guidelines:

1. Recreation resources are to be made available to the public in a manner consistent with overall management of the forests.
2. Within reason, all measures are taken to assure the safety of users.
3. Care is taken to prevent unsanitary conditions, pollution, and forest fires.
4. Provision is made for the best possible wildlife habitat and best possible hunting and fishing consistent with all other uses.
5. Only those facilities suitable to the forest environment are provided.
6. The operation of service facilities, such as resorts, motels, ski lifts, filling stations, and the like, by concessionaires is under the supervision of the Forest Service.
7. Lands that are mainly valuable for their wilderness qualities are protected.
8. Preferential private uses, for example, summer homes, are allowed only where lands are not needed for the public.

As a matter of policy the Forest Service coordinates with other government agencies and the private sector to guard against unwanted duplication and to make sure that the efforts are complimentary. Further, private enterprise is permitted to develop certain kinds of public recreation facilities on forestlands, provided the long-term public interest is perpetuated.

Legislation.   Several legislative acts have significantly influenced national-forest policy. Acts that have had particular influence are the following:

1. The Creation Act of 1891 authorized the president to establish the National Forest Reserve. Most of the land in the reserve has been set aside under this law.
2. The Organic Act of 1897 established the governing principles for the protection and development of forest reserves.
3. The Weeks Act of 1911 opened the door for the purchase of lands to protect navigable streams. Most of the forest reserve in the eastern states was acquired under this act.
4. The Term Lease Law, passed in 1915, authorized the Forest Service to issue long-term permits for summer homes, hotels, concessions, and other types of resort facilities.
5. The Multiple-Use Standard-Yield Act of 1960 reemphasized the basic concept that the national forests are to be administered on a multiple-use basis with five primary

The U.S. Forest Service becomes involved in a variety of outdoor recreation, as illustrated by this directional sign. (U.S. Forest Service)

uses: outdoor recreation, watershed protection, grazing, timber production, and the propagation of fish and wildlife.

6. The Wilderness Act of 1964 established the national wilderness preservation system, the nucleus of which was the 9 million acres (3.6 million ha) of wilderness that had been designated by the Forest Service beginning as early as 1924.

7. The Land and Water Conservation Fund Act of 1965 established an additional method of financing outdoor recreation, and the Forest Service, along with many other agencies, profited from this.

8. The National Trail System Act of 1968 was important to the Forest Service because the majority of the trails are on Forest Service land.

9. The Wild and Scenic Rivers Act of 1968 designated 11 rivers, or sections of rivers, to be retained in a free-flowing condition. At least a portion of each of these rivers is on Forest Service land. Several other streams have since been added.

10. The Forest and Rangeland Renewable Resources Planning Act of 1974 established guidelines and support for better planning for the management of Forest Service areas.

11. The National Forest Management Act of 1976 provided revised guidelines for management priorities and procedures for our national forests.

Multiple Use. One of the most significant policies in terms of outdoor recreation has been the policy of *multiple use*. The Forest Service has generally applied the multiple-use concept since 1905 when Secretary of Agriculture Wilson directed that "all the resources of forest reserves are for use," and "the dominant industry will be decided first but with as little restrictions to minor industries as may be possible." The Multiple-Use Sustained-Yield Act of 1960 bestowed congressional approval on the multiple-use policy. The intended meaning of multiple use is shown in this quotation from the 1960 act:

"Multiple Use" means: The management of all the various renewable surface resources of the national forests so that they are utilized in the combination that will best meet the needs of the American people; making the most judicious use of the land for some or all of these resources or related services over areas large enough to provide sufficient latitude for periodic adjustments in use to conform to changing needs and conditions; that some land will be used for less than all of the resources; and harmonious and coordinated management of the various resources, each with the other, without impairment of the productivity of the land, with consideration being given to the relative values of the various resources, and not necessarily the combination of uses that will give the greatest dollar return or the greatest unit output.

The act further provides "that it is the policy of the Congress that the national forests are established and shall be administered for outdoor recreation, timber, range, watersheds, and wildlife and fish purposes." These five basic uses are supposedly of equal importance, although any one of them may be emphasized over the others in a particular area. Some specific areas may be administered primarily for timber production or grazing, while others may be used primarily for outdoor recreation.

Wilderness Preservation. Another very important aspect of the involvement of the Forest Service in recreation is the designation of *wilderness areas.* The Forest Service pioneered the establishment of wilderness in 1924 with the nation's first such area–the Gila Wilderness in New Mexico. Now increasing numbers of visitors are using the 15 million acres (6.1 million ha) of designated wilderness included in 115 wilderness units within the national forest system. Additional proposals for wilderness units await congressional approval.

During the 40 years between 1924 and 1964, the Forest Service established some 88 areas to be managed in their natural state. These were classified by the Forest Service as *wilderness* areas, *wild* areas, *primitive* areas, and one *canoe* area in Minnesota. In 1964 the Congress passed the Wilderness Act, which created a national wilderness preservation system. Soon after, all of the Forest Service wilderness, wild, and primitive areas that met the criteria described in the Wilderness Act were placed in the national wilderness system. Subsequently, other Forest Service areas were added to bring the total to 115 wilderness areas on Forest Service lands.

We need the tonic of wilderness–to wade sometimes in marshes where the bittern and the meadow-hen lurk, and hear the booming of the snipe; to smell the whispering sedge where only some wilder and more solitary fowl builds her nest.

–Henry David Thoreau

For the participant, wilderness experiences provide challenge and adventure in an environment of solitude and serenity. Such experiences are becoming increasingly popular. This, of course, contributes to the problem of overuse and possible abuse of these ecologically sensitive areas. Wilderness is an example where popular use can be destructive to the very characteristics which attract the users—the environment in its unaltered state and the accompanying peace, quiet, and solitude. In addition to their recreational appeal, wilderness areas have significant scientific value because they are islands in a developed world where man can observe nature in its unaltered state. This provides a useful standard of comparison for nonwilderness areas, which are used and altered regularly by people.

The Forest Service is especially concerned about encouraging dispersed recreation to get a better balance of recreational use of forests. A noteworthy effort relating to this was the 1978 Roadless Area Review and Evaluation (RARE II), through which more than 60 million acres (24 million ha) of the national forests were studied to determine potential dispersed use. Also, the study was used to identify areas that have potential for inclusion in the national wilderness system.

Additional information pertinent to the recreation involvement of the Forest Service can be found in the preceding chapter under the sections on wilderness, wild and scenic rivers, national trails, and national recreation areas. Also, in Chapter 19 is information pertaining to selected management concepts of forests and other resources. Further, certain legislative acts in Appendix A pertain to the management of the national forests.

BUREAU OF LAND MANAGEMENT

The Bureau of Land Management was created within the Department of the Interior in 1946. It resulted from the combining of two agencies, the General Land Office and the Grazing Service.

The lands managed by the Bureau of Land Management are the remainder of the original *public domain,* an expanse that once stretched from the Ohio River all the way to the Pacific and across most of Alaska. Over the years the public domain has provided lands for transfer from the federal government for state school systems, land-grant colleges, transcontinental railroads, national forests, national parks, wildlife refuges, Indian reservations, and military installations. Further, the public domain has provided homesteads for more than a million settlers, plus several thousand who earned land for military service, and for miners who discovered and developed mineral resources. Of the original 1.8 billion acres (730 million ha) of public domain, most of it has been transferred or sold. The amount that remains constitutes the 343 million acres (139 million ha) presently managed by the Bureau of Land Management (46% of the federal estate). Of these lands, 145 million acres (59 million ha) are in Alaska, and 175 million acres (71 million ha) are in the ten western states (Figure 8.4).

Much of the area managed by the bureau is arid or semiarid, supporting a fragile cover of vegetation which controls the delicate balance between soil stability and deterioration. Almost 100 years of unregulated livestock use, coupled with brush fires and drought, has caused severe depreciation of the protective cover.

Because of these circumstances, the conservation and rehabilitation of public lands are high priorities with the bureau. Escalated conservation efforts have become necessary to: (1) prevent and control unnatural erosion, (2) enhance water quality and flood control, and (3) improve the usefulness of the land for fisheries and wildlife habitat, livestock forage, and outdoor recreation.

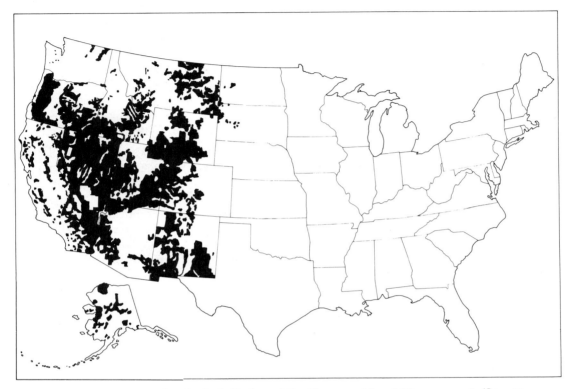

Figure 8.4. Areas under the jurisdiction of the Bureau of Land Management. (Source: Department of the Interior)

Legal Authority

The Bureau of Land Management manages public lands under the conditions of several pieces of legislation. The most relevant is the Federal Land Policy and Management Act of 1976 (sometimes called the Organic Act). This act officially ended the policy of transferring public lands to private ownership. It established the intent of the federal government to retain essentially all of the lands under the control of the Bureau of Land Management or other federal agencies. The act also clarified that the lands were to be managed in accordance with the multiple-use and sustained-yield concept. This concept provides for controlled use while giving ample protection for the scientific, scenic, historical, ecological, and archeological values.

The Organic Act finally gave the bureau the authority and definition needed to manage its lands in a much-improved fashion. It both enabled and directed the Department of the Interior to proceed with developing sound and complete regulations.

The Organic Act also made it possible for the Bureau of Land Management to participate under the conditions of the Wilderness Act of 1964, the Wild and Scenic Rivers Act of 1968, and the National Trails System Act of 1968. (Refer to Appendix A for additional information about the acts mentioned.)

Further, the Bureau of Land Management now is able to participate along with several other federal agencies under the terms of the Land and Water Conservation Fund Act of 1965. Funding under the terms of this act has been helpful to the development of the recreation potential of bureau areas.

Other acts that affect the programs of the bureau include the following:

1.   The Recreation and Public Purposes Act of 1926 (as amended in 1954) has allowed the bureau to transfer parcels of land to state and local agencies for recreation purposes, and to issue long-term leases to state, local, and voluntary agencies for recreation developments.
2.   The Federal Water Projects Recreation Act of 1965 has had significant impact on the development of recreation potential of numerous bureau water-development projects.
3.   The National Environmental Policy Act of 1969 furnishes applicable guidelines and requirements concerning various aspects of environmental protection of lands administered by the bureau.

Other acts that have had limited influence on the recreational use of Bureau of Land Management lands include the Taylor Grazing Act of 1934, the Oregon and California Grant Lands Act of 1937, the Sykes Act of 1938, and the Alaska National Interest Lands Conservation Act of 1980. (Refer to Appendix A.)

Recreation Policy

The Bureau of Land Management's primary recreation role is to provide dispersed and resource-dependent types of outdoor recreation (for example, fishing, hunting, rockhounding, four-wheeling) and to deal with the limited number of situations where special or more intensive types of recreation management are required. More intensive recreation is provided where recreation of that kind is not available elsewhere in the area, or where there is a significant need for bureau management because of resource damage or visitor health and safety problems.

> To those devoid of imagination, a blank place on the map is a useless waste. To others, it is the most valuable part.
> —Aldo Leopold, *A Sand County Almanac*,
> Ballantine Books, New York, 1978, p. 294

The bureau's long-term recreation objectives are (1) to provide the maximum variety and amount of recreation on the public lands commensurate with public needs and resource potentials, and (2) to preserve and protect significant natural historic and cultural resources and provide for their public use and enjoyment where consistent with preservation goals.

Recreation Involvement

Because of its extensive and diverse holdings, the Bureau of Land Management is involved in a variety of outdoor recreation. Most of the bureau's land is in a natural state. But in recent years the bureau has enhanced the use of some of its areas by making improvements to accommodate recreationists.

For specific examples of recreational opportunities on bureau lands, consider the Rogue River in Oregon, which offers some of the best white-water boating in the United States, or the public lands of Royal Grand Gorge in New Mexico, which provide excellent terrain for backpacking and camping. Loon Lake in Oregon is an outstanding example of recreational development around a reservoir that offers boating, waterskiing, and swimming, as well as such shoreline activities as camping and picnicking.

Camp and picnic sites were first constructed on bureau land in 1960. Since then, the number has increased to more than 350 areas involving about 45,000 acres (18,000 ha). The sites include more than 11,000 family units. Moreover, the bureau has developed more than 8000 trailer spaces and many other facilities, such as boat-launching ramps and swimming facilities.

Further, to help promote the best recreational use of the lands for long-term public benefit, the Bureau of Land Management encourages state and local governments to lease suitable tracts of land and develop them for outdoor recreation. In 1954 Congress amended the Recreation and Public Purposes Act of 1926 to authorize the secretary of the interior, under specified conditions, to sell or lease public land to state and local governments and nonprofit organizations for recreation and other public purposes. This act still applies to all lands administered by the bureau. Leases in force for recreation and wildlife purposes include 62 leases for about 11,000 acres (4500 ha) to states, 225 leases for more than 21,000 acres (8500 ha) to cities and counties, and 66 leases for 7900 acres (3200 ha) to nonprofit organizations. In addition, the bureau cooperates with other federal agencies and with state governments in a program designed to achieve coordinated planning for all management activities on substantial portions of the public lands.

Because of the arid condition of most of its land, the Bureau of Land Management is vitally concerned with water management. Consequently, the agency has become involved in many water-development projects on rivers and streams. For the most part the projects have a positive impact on recreation, and they require additional recreation management by the bureau. Also figured into watershed management is the preservation of wildlife habitat. The preservation of environmental aesthetics is still another aspect that receives attention. All of this contributes to better outdoor recreation. For example, a reservoir designed primarily for flood prevention and stream stabilization also furnishes water for wildlife, creates habitat for fish, provides water for boating and waterskiing, and creates shorelines for camping, picnicking, and swimming.

The Federal Water Projects Recreation Act of 1965 authorizes the Bureau of Land Management to respond to recreation needs around new impoundments. When such projects are developed by other government agencies, the law provides a framework for cooperative arrangements with the bureau.

If the bureau's ambitious conservation plan succeeds, there will be marked improvement in the development of water resources over the next two decades. This will substantially increase the fish and wildlife population and expand other kinds of recreational opportunities. About 2 million big-game animals (including 234,000 antelope, 37,000 bear, 89,000 moose, 1.2 million deer) and a large population of small-game animals now live on bureau lands. Among these are 19 species of rare animals and 21 endangered species.

Also, there are extensive fishing opportunities on bureau holdings. In the Rocky Mountain and West Coast states the bureau has more than 25,000 man-made impoundments, all of which have fishery potential. In addition, there is a large number of natural lakes on the bureau's Alaska lands. Also, the agency has 52,000 miles (84,000 km) of fishable streams (85% in Alaska), and about 23 million acres (9.3 million ha) of wetlands, mostly in Alaska.

Central to the program is cooperation with state and federal agencies engaged in the conservation and management of fish and wildlife and their habitats. State wildlife agencies are primarily responsible for the management of wildlife. The primary concern of the bureau is for development and management of wildlife habitat. Policies and procedures for cooperation are defined in memorandums of understanding between each bureau state office and state wildlife agencies.

In 1982 Bureau of Land Management lands received more than 65 million visitor-days of use by recreationists. The highest number of visits was recorded for sightseeing, followed in order by hunting, fishing, camping, and picnicking.

The Bureau of Land Management provides habitat for a large number of wildlife, including these Dall Sheep (ewe and lamb) on Alaska lands. (U.S. Fish and Wildlife Service)

Because of the multiple-use mandate in the Federal Land Policy and Management Act of 1976, it is almost certain that bureau lands will play an expanded public recreation role in the future while still meeting the need for energy, minerals, forage, timber and other traditional resource uses.

BUREAU OF INDIAN AFFAIRS

Most of the 3 million annual visitors to Indian lands go there for tourism and outdoor recreation. These lands total some 51 million acres (20 million ha)–an area slightly larger than Kansas–about 2% of the nation's total land area (Figure 8.5). The lands are held in trust or restricted status for the Indians and are, therefore, in a sense private property. The lands are administered jointly by the Indian tribes and the Bureau of Indian Affairs, a branch of the Department of the Interior.

Many present-day Indian holdings were acquired by treaty or other agreements with the federal government, beginning in the early 19th century, when the population boom in the

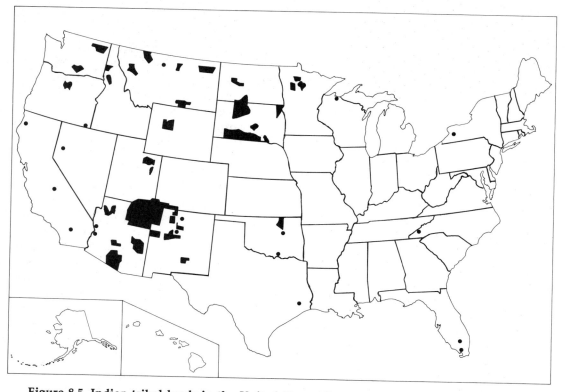

Figure 8.5. Indian tribal lands in the United States. (Source: Department of the Interior)

East precipitated forcible movement of the Indians westward. Subsequently, the Gold Rush and movement of pioneers westward brought about confrontations with the tribes west of the Mississippi and all the way to the Pacific.

Today, most Indian lands are located in the western half of the nation, though there are reservations of considerable size in Minnesota and Wisconsin and smaller reservations in Florida, Louisiana, Maine, Michigan, Mississippi, New York, North Carolina, and South Carolina. Arizona contains the most Indian land, 21.5 million acres (8.7 million ha); then New Mexico with 6.4 million acres (2.6 million ha); Montana with 5.2 million (2.1 million ha); and South Dakota with 4.9 million (2 million ha).

Much of the land awarded the Indians following the 19th-century Indian wars was barren, remote, and scarcely productive enough to support the tribal populations. Today, however, some of the once-isolated areas are in the path of heavy tourist traffic, and forest, water, and mineral reserves offer potential for economic improvement. Among the leading areas of economic potential are outdoor recreation and tourism.

Indian reservations contain more than 3600 ponds and lakes with a water area of approximately 750,000 acres (304,000 ha). There are 6600 miles (10,600 km) of rivers and streams—some of which have great fishing. About half of the Indian lands have been classified as hunting areas. Each year more than 800,000 visitor-days are spent in fishing and about 300,000 visitor-days in hunting on Indian reservations. Recreation visits for all purposes, including ceremonials and museum visits, exceeds 3 million visitor-days annually.

Commercial recreation developments have been encouraged by the Bureau of Indian Affairs because of the economic potential. In this connection the bureau is aided by other federal agencies in helping the Indians to build lakes, create wildlife refuges, stock ponds and streams, and develop recreation resorts. At the same time, Indian tribes are investing income from other sources (forests and minerals) in tourist-oriented enterprises.

One of the most successful Indian-owned undertakings is Kah-Nee-Ta, a mineral-springs resort on the Warm Springs Reservation in Oregon. The project could serve well as a model for similar developments of Indian lands.

Sports, fishing, and hunting have greatly enhanced tourism on tribal lands. On the Mescalero Apache Reservation in south-central New Mexico, for example, a visitor at the tribe's luxurious Inn of the Mountain Gods can enjoy unequaled deer, elk, or bear hunting, ski the 12,000-foot (3700-m) Sierra Blanca Mountain, fish the mountain lakes, play golf or tennis, or just enjoy the scenery.

As a general rule, even in the absence of treaty provisions, Indians may hunt or fish on the Indian reservations in accordance with their own tribal regulations, and are not subject to state laws. Non-Indians may not hunt or fish on Indian reservations without the permission of Indians, regardless of the state's fish and game laws. Other recreational uses of Indian lands are also dependent upon permission from the Indians.

Before the last two decades Indians were generally reluctant to share the recreation potential of the reservations with non-Indians, especially with respect to hunting and fishing. But recently many of the Indian tribes have recognized the income potential of recreational use of their resources. This is exemplified by the numerous tourist and recreational projects that have been developed. Further, more than 100 tribes are now members of the American Indian

Travel Commission as operators of hotels, motels, campgrounds, parks, and recreation centers.

The Bureau of Indian Affairs encourages recreation and tourism through the administration of financial assistance programs. In addition, many of the tribes obtain technical assistance from the U.S. Fish and Wildlife Service to improve hunting and fishing. Also cooperative programs with state conservation agencies have included joint studies of major watersheds, reservoirs, and streams.

FEDERAL HIGHWAY ADMINISTRATION

The Federal Highway Administration, which is within the Department of Transportation, has three principal functions: (1) the administration of federal aid to the states for highway construction, (2) highway planning and research, and (3) road building on federal domain.

As the road-building agency for the federal government, the Federal Highway Administration administers funds for roads on federal lands or directly handles the engineering and construction. These roads include forest highways, park roads and parkways, logging and development roads for the Forest Service and Bureau of Land Management, and access roads to national fish hatcheries and game-management areas.

The tremendous increase in the use of federal recreation areas during the past years has been possible because of their accessibility via public roads. It is estimated that more than 95% of the visitors to Yellowstone, Glacier, Grand Canyon, and Great Smoky Mountains national parks come by private automobile.

While they are usually considered as a means to an end, highways also provide opportunities for recreational experience in and of themselves in the form of traveling. More information about this topic appears in Chapter 11, in the section pertaining to the Department of Transportation.

Discussion Questions

1. List the different kinds of National Park Service areas and explain the differences among the areas.
2. What is meant by *single use*, and how is this concept applied in the administration of our national parks?
3. The U.S. Forest Service has identified for itself three major functions. Describe each function.
4. What are the five major uses of our forests under the Multiple-Use and Sustained-Yield Act of 1964? How compatible do you think these uses are with each other? How much do they conflict?
5. When was the Bureau of Land Management established and for what purpose? How and why did it become involved in outdoor recreation?
6. The Federal Highway Administration has three principal functions. What are they and what impact do these functions have on outdoor recreation?
7. It has been stated that the National Park Service advocates that "the parks should be used for the good of the people now while preserving them in their natural state for future generations." Is this actually possible? Do you agree with this philosophy? Is it being effectively carried out?

8. It has been proposed that some parks and wilderness areas be restricted to experienced outdoor recreationists. One's qualifications to use such areas would be determined by written examination. Do you support this proposal? Why or why not?

9. James Wilson, former secretary of agriculture, stated that where conflicting interests occur, U.S. forestlands should be used to serve "the greatest good for the greatest number in the long run." Do you agree with this policy? Why? What does it really mean in terms of application?

Recommended Readings

"America's Federal Lands." *National Geographic*, September 1982, p. 37.

Brockman, Frank, et al. *Recreation Use of Wildlands*, 3rd ed. New York: McGraw Hill, 1979. Chapters 8, 9.

Bureau of Land Management. *Public Land Statistics–1984*. Washington, D.C.: U.S. Government Printing Office, 1984.

Cahn, Robert. "Forgotten Values." *Audubon*, July 1982, p. 32.

Chubb, Michael, and Holly R. Chubb. *One-Third of Our Time*. New York: John Wiley & Sons, 1981. Chapter 15.

"Crisis Ahead in Our National Parks." *U.S. News and World Report*, 27 September 1982, p. 74.

"Dodging the Crowds at National Parks." *U.S. News and World Report*, 3 May 1982, p. 47.

Frome, Michael. "Will Politics Destroy Our National Parks?" *National Parks*, February 1981, p. 15.

Goldman, Don. "Land Use: The Multiple-Use Concept." *Environment*, October 1981, p. 4.

Knudson, Douglas M. *Outdoor Recreation*. New York: Macmillan Publishing Co., 1984. Chapters 14, 15, 17, 18.

National Park Service. *Federal Recreation Fee Report–1984*. Washington, D.C.: U.S. Department of the Interior, 1984.

National Park Service. *Index of the National Park System and Related Areas–1984*. Washington, D.C.: U.S. Government Printing Office, 1984.

National Park Service. *National Park Statistics*. Washington, D.C.: Department of the Interior, 1984.

"The Parks Are In Trouble." *Newsweek*, 29 June 1981, p. 34.

Schroeder, Herbert, and Terry C. Daniel. "Progress in Predicting the Perceived Scenic Beauty of Forest Landscapes." *Forest Science*, March 1981, p. 71.

Soil Conservation Service. *For the Fun of It–and Then Some!* U.S. Department of Agriculture, Program Aid 1060. Washington, D.C.: U.S. Government Printing Office, 1974.

U.S. Department of Agriculture. *National Forest Vacations*. Washington, D.C.: 1979.

U.S. Department of the Interior. *Index: National Park System and Related Areas–1984*. Washington, D.C.: U.S. Government Printing Office, 1984.

U.S. Department of the Interior. *The Third Nationwide Outdoor Recreation Plan: The Assessment*. Washington, D.C.: 1979.

U.S. Department of the Interior. *The Third Nationwide Outdoor Recreation Plan: The Executive Report*. Washington, D.C.: 1979.

U.S. Forest Service. *The Forest Service Roles in Outdoor Recreation: Program Aid 1205*. Washington, D.C.: U.S. Government Printing Office, 1978.

CHAPTER 9

Federal Reservoir Providers

Including reservoirs, natural lakes, and streams, there are almost 100 million acres (40.5 million ha) of surface water in the United States. About one fourth of this is usable and accessible for recreation. The rest is inaccessible, badly polluted, or restricted from public use.

There are almost 50,000 man-made dams and reservoirs in the United States. Most of these are small, built by individuals or local agencies. A large number of medium-sized structures were planned with the help of the Soil Conservation Service, while virtually all of the large reservoirs were built under the direction of the Bureau of Reclamation, U.S. Army Corps of Engineers, or the Tennessee Valley Authority.

The recreation and fish and wildlife benefits of reservoir projects have been apparent to the public for a long time. The impoundment of water in canyons and channels behind storage dams has provided habitat for fish, resting and nesting areas for birds, and water and shorelines for a variety of recreational activities. In most cases, as soon as the reservoirs have filled, they have become popular recreation sites for boating, waterskiing, fishing, sightseeing, camping, picnicking, hiking, and a variety of other activities. Despite the recreational attractions of the reservoirs, the agencies that developed them had no official responsibilities for recreation planning and management before the early 1960s.

In 1962 President John F. Kennedy approved Senate Document 97, which was prepared to give additional direction to federal agencies engaged in water-resources development. It specified that full consideration be given to the opportunity and need for outdoor recreation and fish and wildlife enhancement in planning for water projects.

In 1965 recreation took another major step forward when Congress passed the Federal Water Projects Recreation Act. Among other elements, the act provided that "full consideration shall be given to recreation and fish and wildlife enhancement as purposes in federal water resource projects...."

This act specifies that planning for the recreational potential of the projects is to be coordinated with existing and planned federal, state, and local public recreation developments, and that nonfederal administration is to be encouraged for the recreational aspects of the projects.

With the implementation of the Water Projects Recreation Act, the federal government has clearly become the nation's largest provider of inland water-recreation opportunities. This is evident in the following information about water project developments of the Army Corps of Engineers, Bureau of Reclamation, Tennessee Valley Authority, and Soil Conservation Service.

BUREAU OF RECLAMATION

Much of the prime water recreation in the West is the result of the reservoirs constructed by the Bureau of Reclamation. The Reclamation Act of 1902 authorized the secretary of the interior to locate, construct, operate and maintain projects for the storage, diversion, and development of waters for the reclamation of arid and semiarid lands in the 17 westernmost states. This function was first established within the U.S. Geological Survey in 1902 and remained there for five years. In 1907 the Reclamation Service was formed within the Department of the Interior, and in 1923 the agency was named the Bureau of Reclamation.

Bureau of Reclamation lakes have provided water access to some of the nation's most scenic areas. (Bureau of Reclamation, photo by Mel Davis)

The Reclamation Act of 1902 was the beginning of an extensive dam-building program that has extended over eight decades and has had a significant impact on the development of the western United States through delivering water and power to thousands of farm areas and communities. Practically all of the reclamation projects have had some favorable impact on outdoor recreation, and some of them have become national attractions, such as Hoover Dam, Glen Canyon Dam, Flaming Gorge Dam, and Grand Coulee Dam.

In addition to its original function of providing water for arid and semiarid lands, the bureau now has the authority to develop water resources for recreation, fish and wildlife enhancement, water-quality control, municipal and industrial water supplies, and hydroelectric power. In this way it assists local governments, states, and other federal agencies to stabilize and stimulate local and regional economics and enhance and protect the environment. (By virtue of the legislation which established the bureau, the functions are limited to the 17 contiguous western states.)

The first five pioneering reclamation projects, all authorized in 1903, were the Salt River project in Arizona, the Truckee (now Newlands) project in Nevada, the Gunnison (now Uncompahgre) project in Colorado, the Sweetwater (now North Platte) project in Wyoming and Nebraska, and the Milk River project in Montana. These were all highly successful irrigation enterprises, and subsequently, they have all become valuable providers of recreation opportunities.

One of the most dramatic reclamation projects is Glen Canyon Dam on the Colorado River, which created Lake Powell. This massive lake, combined with its unique desert and canyon scenery, soon became a tourist and recreation attraction of national and international significance. The lake has 1960 miles of scenic shoreline, and it offers a variety of recreation opportunities. Other reclamation projects of unusual recreation prominence include Grand Coulee Dam in Washington with more than 100,000 acres (40,500 ha) of water surface and adjacent land; Blue Mesa Reservoir in the Colorado Rockies, now the largest lake in Colorado; San Luis reservoir, the largest lake in California's San Joaquin Valley; and Lake Meredith in Sanford, Texas, the largest body of water in the Texas Panhandle.

It is true, however, that though reclamation projects have created some recreation opportunities, they have impaired others. For example, the Gunnison project destroyed a portion of one of the finest trout streams in the country, and the Glen Canyon project has inundated one of America's unique and most beautiful canyons.

Authority to Provide Recreation

More than 330 reclamation storage dams are now in existence, and they provide a total reservoir capacity of 1.8 million acres (730,000 ha) of water surface. These projects provide 12,500 miles (200,100 km) of reservoir shoreline—most of it accessible to the public and available for recreation. Figure 9.1 is a map of the United States showing the locations of these projects.

During the early years of reclamation, recreation was not considered important in the planning of water projects. However, it was found that as soon as reservoirs filled, they became recreational focal points, and some of the initial reclamation projects established excellent reputations as recreation areas. One example was the Theodore Roosevelt Dam, the

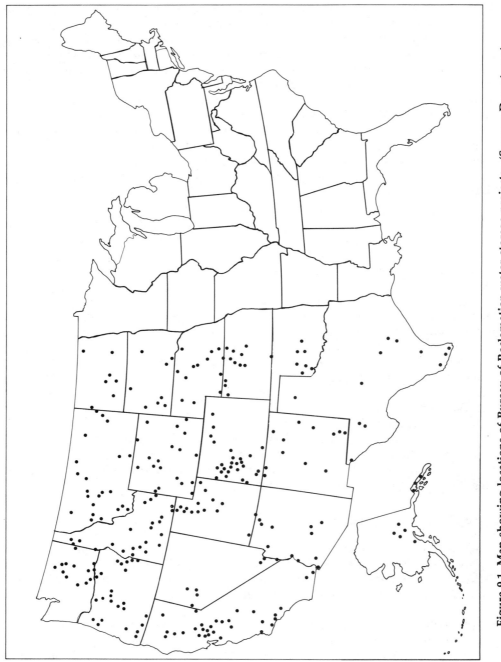

Figure 9.1. Map showing locations of Bureau of Reclamation water-storage projects. (Source: Department of the Interior)

first major construction undertaken by the Bureau of Reclamation on the Salt River Project and completed in 1911. The reservoir soon became one of the main attractions along the route between Globe and Phoenix, and it drew many visitors each year. A large hotel was built along the shore near the dam to accommodate the increasing crowds. Thousands of visitors enjoyed the horseback trails each summer, as well as boating and swimming at the reservoir.

In 1936 the Bureau of Reclamation entered agreements with the National Park Service to provide tourist facilities at Hoover Dam's Lake Mead and Grand Coulee Dam's Roosevelt Lake. Since that time, the bureau traditionally has established agreements that transfer responsibility for managing recreation areas to other federal agencies or to local organizations, such as state and county governments and water-use organizations.

More recently, Congress has recognized the need for basic recreation facilities at federally constructed reservoirs. For example, in 1949 the Weber Basin (Utah) Project Act prescribed facilities for recreationists, including access roads, parking areas, picnic sites, water supplies, sanitation, and boat-launching ramps. Further, the Colorado River Storage Act of 1956 directed the secretary of the interior to "investigate, plan, construct, operate, and maintain (a) public recreational facilities on lands acquired for the development of that project, to conserve the scenery, the natural, historic, and archeologic objects, and the wildlife on said lands, and to provide for public use and enjoyment of the same and of waters created by these projects by such means as are consistent with the primary purposes of said projects; and (b) facilities to mitigate losses of, and improve conditions for the propagation of fish and wildlife."

It gradually became apparent that general statutory authority was needed to provide for planning and construction of recreational facilities at all reclamation projects. Such authority was granted under the Federal Water Projects Recreation Act of 1965, which was described earlier in this chapter. This act requires that a nonfederal agency share the costs of developing recreation facilities with the federal government and accept full responsibility for the operation and maintenance of those facilities. Nonetheless, recreation facilities may be developed solely at federal expense when the area is appropriate for management by a federal agency.

Benefits to Wildlife

The benefit to fish and wildlife habitat has become one of the most important environmental results of reclamation projects. Some of the best fishing in the West is found in these reservoirs. A notable example is the recently built Flaming Gorge Reservoir; it has become a major attraction for anglers, who catch approximately 1 million fish annually from its depths. Further, the 35-mile (56 km) stretch of Green River below the dam, which previously provided very limited fishing because of siltation, is now recognized as one of the top trout fisheries of the nation. It yields more than 25,000 trout annually. The controlled release of clear, cold, oxygenated water from the reservoir created this fabulous fishing stream.

The benefits to fishing are not limited to the reservoirs and the regulated streams below the dams. One of the Bureau of Reclamation's latest innovations to improve fishing is the creation of artificial spawning beds for chinook salmon on the Tehama-Colusa Canal in California. Other fish habitat innovations have been implemented, such as multilevel outlets in dams

Some Bureau of Reclamation areas have greatly enhanced fishing opportunities.

for temperature-controlled releases, barriers for drainage of the salt flows which are toxic to fish, and directional louvers used during migration.

In the lower Colorado River channel below Lake Mead the bureau is involved extensively with the dozen or more federal, state, and county recreation areas and wildlife refuges located along the river. The marshland in the area actually owes its existence to the reclamation project and the regulating facilities on the river. There were almost no marshes in the lower Colorado basin before 1935 when Hoover Dam was completed. This was the case because the streams in the area would dry up in late summer each year. Now marshes with their fish and waterfowl populations occupy between 10,000 and 20,000 acres (4000–8000 ha) along the river below the dam.

The initial phase of the Garrison Diversion unit in North Dakota provides for 147,000 acres (59,500 ha) for fish and wildlife habitat. This area is on the nation's most heavily used waterfowl flyway. It will be the largest single federal wildlife conservation project, except for certain projects in the waterfowl restoration program of the Fish and Wildlife Service. In total, 18 national wildlife refuges comprising about 250,000 acres (101,000 ha) have been established in connection with reclamation projects. This is in addition to the many smaller wildlife projects not of national refuge status. In addition to the effects on waterfowl and fish, irrigated fields resulting from reclamation projects are responsible for a phenomenal rise in the pheasant population in the Dakotas and Rocky Mountain states.

Recreation Policy

It is the Bureau of Reclamation's policy to transfer the responsibilities for recreation development and management to local and state agencies or to other federal agencies whenever possible. For this reason, the state agencies have developed recreation sites on 108 of the

Table 9.1. Number of Reclamation Projects

Agency	Projects
State agencies	108
U.S. Forest Service	51
Water-user organizations	14
U.S. Fish and Wildlife Service	15
Counties	31
National Park Service	10
Local recreation districts	4
Bureau of Land Management	3
Bureau of Reclamation	50
Total	286

reclamation projects, and county governments have taken the recreation responsibility on 31 projects. Of the federal agencies, the U.S. Forest Service is the most active in the development of recreation sites on reclamation projects (51 sites). Other agencies that are involved and the number of projects taken on by each agency are indicated in Table 9.1. The total is less than the total number of reclamation projects, because some projects do not involve recreation.

If an area has national recreation significance, it might be designated by Congress as a national recreation area, in which case it would be administered by the National Park Service, unless it is located within or adjacent to a forest reserve; then it would be administered by the Forest Service. If a reservoir area has less than national significance, its recreational aspects are administered by some other agency. In some cases the Bureau of Reclamation administers the recreation aspect itself—at least for a time until suitable arrangements can be worked out with another agency.

Bureau reservoir areas now receive over 75 million recreation visitor-days per year. This represents a significant increase over past years; there were 6.6 million visitor-days in 1950, 24.3 million in 1960, 54.2 million in 1970, and 66.5 million in 1980. The future offers little hope of relief from the demands placed on the agency by recreationists. In fact, it seems certain that recreation on these projects will continue to increase at about the same rate as in the past.

THE CORPS OF ENGINEERS

The U.S. Army Corps of Engineers administers 11 million acres (4.5 million ha) of land and water in 442 lakes and reservoirs, providing over 460 million recreational visits of use each year. The proximity of many of the Corps' areas to cities results in a high rate of repeat visitors (Figure 9.2).

The Corps of Engineers' involvement in recreation has evolved out of an interesting history of an organization that was originally strictly military. Being part of the U.S. Army, the Corps traces its beginning to 1775, when a group of engineers fortified the colonies' positions for the Battle of Bunker Hill. In 1776 the Continental Congress authorized Gen. George Washington to create a regular Corps of Engineers to be employed to build fortifications and to fight as infantry during the remainder of the Revolutionary War.

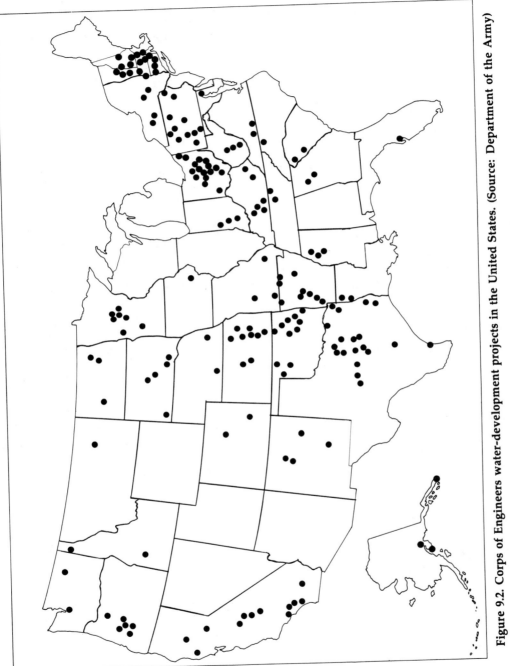

Figure 9.2. Corps of Engineers water-development projects in the United States. (Source: Department of the Army)

In 1783, as part of the general reduction of the army, the Corps of Engineers was disbanded and its companies of "sappers and miners" were mustered out. In 1794 Congress provided for a corps of artillerists and engineers to be raised for a period of three years and established an engineer school at West Point. Subsequent acts of Congress (1795 and 1796) provided that the Corps of Artillerists and Engineers be continued indefinitely and that it become a permanent part of the military establishment. In 1802 Congress divided the Artillerists and Engineers into separate corps.

Civil Works Responsibilities

The evolution of the mission of the Corps of Engineers from its strictly military function to one including civil works began in 1824 with the passage of the first river and harbor act. Civil works is a collective title for nonmilitary functions that relate to planning, design, construction, operation, and maintenance in connection with America's water resources. It includes the improvement of rivers, harbors, and other water areas for water supply, navigation, flood control, hydroelectric power, fish and wildlife, shore protection, and recreation. These functions are separate from the military activities. The following is a summary of the events that have shaped the present civil works activities of the Corps of Engineers.

In 1824, under authority of the commerce clause of the Constitution, Congress formalized the civil works function of the Corps of Engineers and authorized studies of canals, roads, and river and harbor improvements.

The Mississippi River Commission was created in 1879 to supervise the program for controlling the river and developing its alluvial valley.

In 1893 participation by the Corps in the regulation of hydraulic mining and flood control in the Central Valley of California extended the Corps' interests west of the Mississippi River.

In 1917 Congress adopted the first major flood-control legislation, which authorized Corps of Engineers improvements on the Mississippi and Sacramento rivers. Ten years later Congress directed the Corps of Engineers to make comprehensive surveys of United States rivers for navigation, flood control, hydroelectric power, and irrigation. Basic data were collected and analyzed and plans of development prepared for 191 rivers.

The authority of the Corps of Engineers was extended in 1932 to provide for consideration of recreational boating as well as commercial waterborne commerce in planning navigational improvements.

The 1936 Flood-Control Act established a national flood-control policy and assigned responsibility for planning and construction of flood-control projects to the Corps of Engineers.

The Flood-Control Act of 1944 greatly expanded the Corps of Engineers' responsibilities in providing recreational facilities at civil works projects.

The 1965 Land and Water Conservation Fund Act made funds available to agencies at the various levels of government to finance recreation development. The Federal Projects Recreation Act, also passed in 1965, officially recognized the public benefit of recreation planning and development in connection with reservoir projects.

The reservoir-construction agencies of the federal government have created thousands of bodies of water and greatly expanded our water-recreation opportunities. (Soil Conservation Service, photo by Berlyn Brixner)

Recreation Involvement

The 1944 Flood-Control Act authorized the Corps of Engineers "to construct, maintain, and operate public park and recreational facilities in reservoir areas" as part of multiple-purpose projects. The act also specified that the water areas of all such reservoirs shall be open to public use, generally without charge.

The Corps interprets the 1944 act as authority to install basic facilities for recreation. These facilities include overlook stations, public sanitary facilities, parking areas, access roads, guardrails, fences, informational signs, camp and picnic facilities, and boat-launching ramps. The Corps encourages state and local governments to assume responsibility for additional construction and maintenance of recreation facilities.

Under Senate Document 97 (1962) and the Federal Water Projects Recreation Act of 1965, both described earlier, the Corps took on additional responsibilities for recreation and fish and wildlife. Further the Land and Water Conservation Fund Act authorized the establishment of entrance, admission, and user fees at designated federal recreation areas, and some Corps of Engineer sites are among the designated user-fee areas.

The recreational use of Corps of Engineer projects has experienced a phenomenal increase since World War II. In 1946 visits to these areas totaled only 5 million. By 1959 the number of visits exceeded 100 million, and in 1964 it exceeded 155 million. Now there are over 460 million visits of use recorded on Corps of Engineers projects each year, mostly for boating, fishing, picnicking, and sightseeing.

The provision of the basic visitor facilities gradually became inadequate as the Corps was confronted with the task of accommodating ever-increasing numbers. Therefore, in addition to the millions of acres of water and thousands of miles of shoreline within the Corps of Engineer projects, the following special facilities and areas are now provided on many of the projects, either by the Corps or by concessionaires: camping areas, swimming beaches, rental units, boat rentals, stores, and restaurants. Figure 9.3 shows the wildlife and public use areas on a Corps of Engineers project in Missouri.

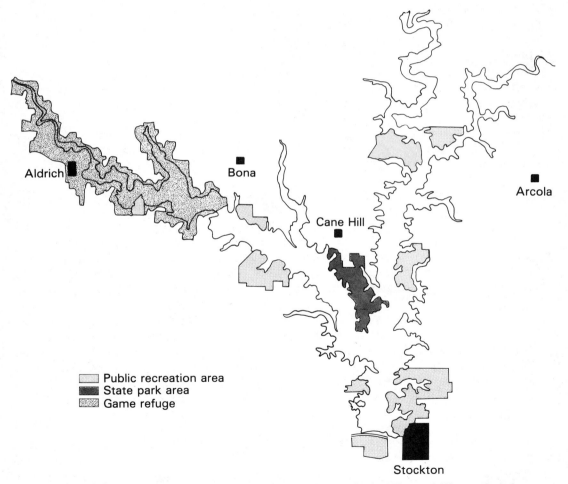

Figure 9.3. A Corps of Engineers project on Stockton Lake in Missouri illustrating the recreation areas that have been designated or developed. (Source: Corps of Engineers)

The Flood-Control Act of 1944 authorized the Corps to issue licenses to federal, state and local agencies without monetary consideration to develop and maintain recreational areas. Leases may be granted for commercial concession developments and to nonprofit organizations such as the Izaak Walton League, Boy Scouts of America, and church organizations at reduced or nominal rates. Under certain conditions, and when land is available, the Corps may lease sites for private recreational developments or for cottages.

Recreation Policy

The current Corps of Engineers' policy on recreation is to consider it a project purpose when the project is expected to produce a significant increase in recreation. However, to ensure against overemphasis of recreation, the Corps of Engineers does not recommend federal construction of projects primarily for recreation. Further, in plan formulation, each purpose (including recreation) must produce benefits approximately equal to the incremental cost of adding that purpose to the plan.

The Corps of Engineers' increasing involvement in outdoor recreation has caused it to play host to more visitors each year than any other federal agency, except possibly the Forest Service, and the rate of increase during the past two decades has been extraordinary. The fact that many of its projects are close to cities has proven to be of great benefit to outdoor recreation. The Corps is committed to continue its efforts to accommodate the public's increasing recreational needs. In so doing, it will have to critically evaluate how recreation will fit in with its other major responsibilities.

TENNESSEE VALLEY AUTHORITY

The Tennessee Valley Authority (TVA) is a U.S. government corporation created by the TVA Act in 1933, as a regional resource-development agency. The act was based on the concept that all the resources of a river basin are interrelated and should be developed under one unified plan for maximum effectiveness. To put the Tennessee River to work, the TVA built a system of multipurpose dams with primary goals of flood control, navigation, and hydropower.

The original act made no specific reference to recreation. It did authorize surveys, plans, and demonstrations for fostering an orderly and proper physical, economic, and social development of the Tennessee basin and adjoining territory. TVA officials apparently interpreted this to include planning and development for recreation, because recreation sites have been included in the planning process since the beginning of the agency.

Recreation Areas

Early recognition of the lakes' recreation potential resulted in a decision to acquire lands that might be necessary to guarantee public access to the project areas. The TVA has never departed from the principle of including public access. The several lakes created by TVA cover more than 500,000 acres and have shorelines totalling more than 11,000 miles (17,700 km). These man-made lakes attract more than 70 million recreation visits annually.

Sailing on a lake resulting from a Corp of Engineers project adds a new recreational dimension to this locale. (Corps of Engineers)

Much of the popularity of the TVA projects can be attributed to their combination of scenic beauty and water resources. The weather is suitable for outdoor recreation most of the year. TVA sites are within two days of automobile travel to more than half the people in the United States.

More than 500 public accesses, 20 state parks, and about 100 county and municipal parks have been created on the shores of TVA lakes. In addition, the TVA has transferred about 117,000 acres (47,400 ha) to the National Park Service, the Fish and Wildlife Service, and the Forest Service. Some 335 fishing camps, boat docks, and resorts are operated by private businesses on TVA lakeshores, and about 20,000 privately owned vacation cabins and homes have been built on lakefront sites. TVA lands have also been sold or leased to private clubs and to service organizations such as the YMCA and the Boy Scouts. Properties sold for recreation are subject to repossession by TVA should use for recreational purposes cease.

The TVA has set aside 25 "natural areas" which include ecological study areas, small wild areas, and habitat protection areas ranging in size from 10 to 500 acres (4–200 ha). These areas have been established to preserve such natural features as scenic views, interesting plant life, special wildlife habitat, waterfalls, and caves. In addition, the TVA has developed some 25 trails for hiking and interpretation in conjunction with small wild areas and recreation sites. Figure 9.4 shows numerous lakes that have resulted from projects the TVA has completed.

Recreation Policy

The TVA was the first water-resource agency to aggressively plan for recreational use of impounded waters and shorelines, and other agencies have benefited from this leadership. Recreation policies of the TVA have thus far enjoyed great success, but increasing recreation pressure will call for more attention to recreation planning on a broader scale than in the past.

TVA's concern with recreation, as with other resources of the Tennessee Valley, is not limited to its lakes. Its responsibility is *regional* resource development, and in recreation it operates through a program of direct action as well as providing technical assistance to other agencies and organizations throughout the region.

In addition to providing occasional special water releases from some of its dams to accommodate fishing and boating on the rivers, TVA has purchased land to provide public access to scenic rivers and streams. The agency also works with state organizations to purchase and protect natural and scenic sites not associated with the reservoirs, and it sets aside on its own land small areas of natural or scenic significance.

Land Between the Lakes

At the Land Between the Lakes in western Kentucky and Tennessee the TVA is developing a national demonstration program in outdoor recreation, environmental education and resource management. The 170,000 acres (69,000 ha) of wooded peninsula is located between Kentucky Lake and Lake Barkley, two of the largest man-made reservoirs in America. It includes about 300 miles (480 km) of shoreline.

Land Between the Lakes is being managed under a multiple-use concept to show how marginal land can be utilized to provide recreational and educational benefits to the public while also providing greater wildlife benefits. Land Between the Lakes is managed as a year-round public-use area where people can enjoy wholesome recreation and gain an appreciation of the natural environment and the importance of proper conservation of natural resources. Camping, fishing, boating, hiking, hunting, and nature study are among the favorite activities.

Trails on the property vary from sparsely marked paths to paved nature trails and two national recreation trails. There is a special area of 2500 acres (1000 ha) for off-road vehicles, and there are horse trails and scenic tour routes. A well-developed environmental-education facility located on 4500 acres (1800 ha) of land near Lake Barkley, accommodates various youth and adult-education programs.

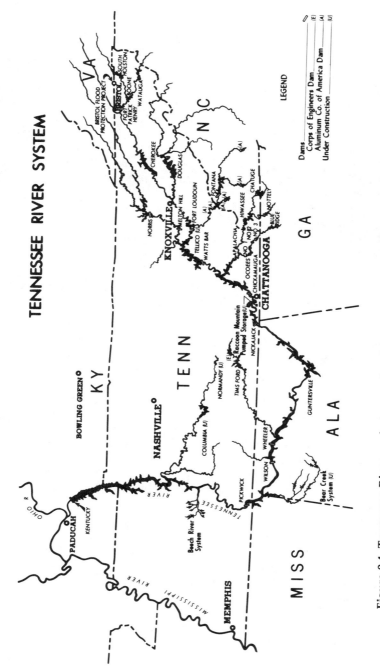

Figure 9.4. Tennessee River projects completed by the TVA. (Source: Tennessee Valley Authority)

Many reservoir projects have enhanced wildlife habitat, especially for fish and waterfowl. (U.S. Fish and Wildlife Service, photo by Hans Stuart)

A significant component of the Land Between the Lakes mission is the enhancement of economic developments. In this context the projects serve as the focal point for a multimillion dollar tourism industry in western Kentucky and Tennessee.

SOIL CONSERVATION SERVICE

The Soil Conservation Service, a division of the Department of Agriculture, exists primarily to promote and coordinate programs which both conserve and rehabilitate surface soil and which enhance soil productivity.

The Soil Conservation Service is involved in reservoir recreation through its *small watershed projects* program. This program comes under the Watershed-Protection and Flood-Prevention Act of 1954. The law specifies that the Soil Conservation Service may share with state and local government agencies up to half the cost of construction and land acquisition needed for public recreation and fish and wildlife development on small water projects.

State park departments and fish and game agencies are eligible to sponsor watershed projects. Also eligible are counties, municipalities and special-purpose districts. The sponsoring unit of the watershed project owns the structures and facilities that are built and is responsible for their operation and maintenance. The Soil Conservation Service participates in planning the project and helping to finance it.

In addition to watershed projects, the Soil Conservation Service offers *technical assistance* to landowners and outdoor recreation operators. The assistance relates to planning and developing commercial recreation enterprises. The agency also provides technical assistance to local units of government and nonprofit organizations in the planning and use of soil and water resources for outdoor recreation. These services are made available through the soil and water conservation districts, more than 3000 of which blanket the nation.

Discussion Questions

1. In terms of outdoor recreation, what are the ramifications of the Federal Water Projects Recreation Act of 1965?
2. What is the policy of the Bureau of Reclamation in regard to recreational developments and the administration of its projects? What is the bureau's preference in terms of its involvement in recreation management?
3. Of what significance was the Flood-Control Act of 1944 to the Corps of Engineers' involvement in outdoor recreation?
4. What are the major factors contributing to the high use of Corps of Engineers projects by recreationists?
5. For what purpose was the Tennessee Valley Authority formed? How did it become extensively involved in outdoor recreation?
6. What is the Land Between the Lakes project and why is it an excellent example of an outdoor recreation project? What economic benefits have resulted from it?
7. What is the Soil Conservation Service's involvement in outdoor recreation and how does this relate to the basic purposes of the agency?

Recommended Readings

Knudson, Douglas M. *Outdoor Recreation.* New York: Macmillan Publishing Co., 1984. Chapter 19.

National Park Service. *Federal Recreation Fee Report–1984.* Washington, D.C.: U.S. Department of the Interior.

Tennessee Valley Authority. *Tennessee Valley Authority Annual Report–1984.* Washington, D.C.: U.S. Government Printing Office.

U.S. Army Corps of Engineers. *Corps of Engineers Annual Report–1984.* Washington, D.C.: U.S. Government Printing Office.

U.S. Department of the Interior. *Bureau of Reclamation Annual Report–1984.* Washington, D.C.: U.S. Government Printing Office.

U.S. Department of the Interior. *The Third Nationwide Outdoor Recreation Plan: The Assessment.* Washington, D.C.: 1979.

U.S. Department of the Interior. *The Third Nationwide Outdoor Recreation Plan: The Executive Report.* Washington, D.C.: 1979.

CHAPTER 10

Federal Wildlife Conservation

Wildlife means different things to different people. To a city dweller the sight of a coyote trotting across the back country could be a highlight of a summer trip. To a sheep rancher the same coyote is a destructive predator. For some individuals geese are valuable to observe and study, or to photograph and paint. To others, geese are only for hunting. Despite one's view of a particular animal species, it seems that generally humans favor the protection, at some reasonable level, of other life forms. The extinction and near extinction of several species have brought this to light. For example, snowy egrets are no longer killed by the thousands for the sake of stylish hats. The wearing of alligator shoes in public has become uncomfortable if not embarrassing. Celebrities have been chided for wearing wraps made of tiger skin, and there are many other examples of human concern for animal species that have become scarce.

Probably one reason for this is that the presence of wildlife indicates that the earth's natural processes are still intact–that water is drinkable and food chains remain undestroyed. Animals are a barometer of environmental balance and well-being. Their abundance or diversity is a favorable sign.

> That wildlife is merely something to shoot at or look at is the grossest of all fallacies. It often represents the difference between rich country and poor land.
>
> –Aldo Leopold, *A Sand County Almanac*,
> Ballantine Books, New York, 1978, p. 178.

Another reason for the appreciation of wildlife is that it represents a chance for man's encounter with animals in their natural habitat–a first-hand experience undiluted, irreducible, and extraordinarily real. There are few events that stir the emotion of a person more consistently than the unexpected view of a wild creature–the sudden flush of a pheasant or quail

"You will find angling to be like the virtue of humility, which has a calmness of spirit and a world of other blessings attending upon it."–Izaak Walton (U.S. Forest Service)

from the underbrush, the sketchy sight of a deer darting through the trees, honking geese over the marshlands, or a busy squirrel gathering pine nuts.

For this reason, and other reasons as well, effective wildlife management is an absolute necessity. Wildlife management is in essence people management–when and where to allow hunting, how great a kill to allow, which regulations to enforce, and how much habitat to sacrifice. With the human impact properly controlled, wild species usually do quite well on their own.

WILDLIFE CONSERVATION DEVELOPMENT

The management of wildlife is almost as ancient as recorded history. There are accounts of it in the literature about the early Romans and the ancient Sumerians and Thebians. Even the Bible includes references to wildlife management.

In the United States there were sketchy efforts toward wildlife management during the colonial period but nothing of much significance. A bounty was placed on wolves in 1799 in the northwestern United States to help protect other species, especially valuable fur-bearing animals. During the mid-1800s lawmakers in Oregon, Washington, Idaho, and Montana began to enact seasons for the hunting of big game. Also about that time, it became apparent that the existence of some species was being seriously threatened. Subsequently, certain measures were taken for the protection of endangered species. However, this came too late to save some species. Aside from these measures, little occurred in the United States relative to wildlife management before the beginning of the present century.

In 1903 wildlife conservation received a large boost when President Theodore Roosevelt started the vast system of national wildlife refuges and hatcheries. He proclaimed tiny Pelican Island off Florida's east coast as the first refuge. The president followed this by transferring several other public lands into the refuge system. Subsequently, several reservoirs created by federally built dams were made into sanctuaries for migratory birds. At about this same time the National Bison Range in Montana was established to save the few remaining buffalo. Later, under other administrations, game refuges were added to preserve remnant herds of elk, sheep, bighorns, and pronghorn antelope.

During the early decades of the 1900s some state wildlife agencies became well established and initiated effective management programs. Since then many states, as well as private conservation organizations, have made significant contributions to the preservation of wildlife and its habitat. This has been a rear-guard action against a growing national obsession with industrial and agricultural progress.

The survival of wildlife in a fast-changing world serves as a barometer of the health of man. If wild creatures can thrive, it is a good bet that human-kind will find the environment livable too.
                                    –Preface to the Endangered Species Act of 1973

Despite the earlier conservation efforts, wildlife continued to decline as habitat was converted into farmland and then put to urban and industrial uses. Waterfowl in particular suffered as more and more marshlands were drained. Then more catastrophy: the worst drought in modern history struck the Great Plains during the 1930s, causing much of the shrinking wetlands to become dust bowls. Because of these unfavorable circumstances, some very important measures toward the long-term conservation of native wildlife were taken during the middle to late 1930s, and these actions have had a positive influence on American wildlife ever since.

The epic story of wildlife conservation has confirmed that it is necessary for conservationists to think nationally or internationally while acting locally. To be sound, conservation concepts must be applicable over a broad span of space and time, but they must be applied in specific ways because most of the effective conservation programs are at the grassroots level. Conservation efforts are led by people who understand and truly believe in the protection of a balanced environment.

U.S. FISH AND WILDLIFE SERVICE

The U.S. Fish and Wildlife Service, a bureau in the Department of the Interior, is the agency through which the federal government carries out its responsibilities for the conservation and management of the nation's wildlife resources. Certain elements of the agency reach back more than 100 years to the establishment in 1871 of its predecessor, the Bureau of Fisheries. A second predecessor, the Bureau of Biological Survey, was established in 1885. These two agencies were consolidated in 1940. In addition, other modifications have been made along the way, and all of this has finally evolved into the agency presently known as the U.S. Fish and Wildlife Service.

The major responsibilities of the Fish and Wildlife Service include (1) managing the federal wildlife refuges and fish hatcheries, (2) controlling predators and rodents, (3) studying federal water-development projects, (4) saving rare and endangered species, (5) managing the nation's migratory bird programs, and (6) promoting research on a wide variety of subjects related to wildlife. These efforts of the Fish and Wildlife Service involve much cooperation and coordination with the state wildlife agencies.

In its efforts to enhance outdoor recreation, the Fish and Wildlife Service (along with state wildlife agencies) faces the following problems:

1. Preservation of adequate wildlife habitat.
2. Provisions for public access to water and wildlife areas.
3. Prevention of water pollution.
4. Control of the use of damaging insecticides.
5. Provisions for adequate visitor facilities at refuges and hatcheries.
6. Control of predators that seriously threaten wildlife.
7. Coordination of the various agencies interested and involved in wildlife.
8. Enhancement of public hunting and fishing on private lands.

The U.S. Fish and Wildlife Service manages over 300 wildlife refuges. (U.S. Fish and Wildlife Service, photo by W. F. Kubichek)

FEDERAL LEGISLATION

Several acts of Congress have formed the basic legal structure for the programs of the Fish and Wildlife Service.

The Lacey Act of 1900 designated the Department of the Interior as the agency that has the responsibility and authority for the federal government's role in the management of wildlife. This act clarified and expanded the official involvement at the federal level. The act also controlled interstate shipment of game and thus put a big dent in market hunting.

The Migratory Bird Treaty Act of 1918 provided protection for migratory birds by controlling the possession, sale, transportation, and importation of migratory birds.

The Migratory Bird Conservation Act of 1929 (amended in 1976) had several important effects, among which was the appointment of a commission to approve recommended areas for migratory-bird refuges. The act also authorized land acquisition and refuge development and maintenance.

The Fish and Wildlife Coordination Act of 1934 (amended in 1958) provided that "wildlife conservation shall receive equal consideration and be coordinated with other features of water-resource development programs." It requires that federal agencies constructing or licensing water-development projects shall consult with the Fish and Wildlife Service and the comparable state agency before the construction or licensing of such projects. The purpose of this requirement is to protect wildlife habitat and resources. In carrying out this requirement, the licensing agencies study all federal water-development projects (as well as nonfederal projects requiring a federal license) to: (1) determine the effects of the projects on fish and wildlife resources, (2) formulate measures to mitigate adverse effects on these resources, and (3) to take advantage of the construction to enhance wildlife.

The Migratory Bird Hunting Stamp Act (often called the Duck Stamp Act) of 1934 requires a fee for all persons over age 16 who hunt ducks, geese, and other waterfowl. Proceeds from the fee are used to acquire refuge properties for migratory birds. The law has substantially helped the expansion of refuges.

Under the Pittman-Robertson Act of 1937 an excise tax was levied on sporting arms and ammunition, the proceeds going to state wildlife agencies as grants-in-aid to help with wildlife management.

The Dingell-Johnson Act of 1950 provided benefits to states for fisheries management from revenues derived from an excise tax on fishing equipment.

The Refuge Recreation Act of 1952 allowed for the purchase, development, and management of lands adjacent to refuges and hatcheries for recreational use, provided it does not interfere with the more basic purposes of the particular refuge or hatchery.

The Fish and Wildlife Act of 1956 clarified certain national policies relative to wildlife, and established the Fish and Wildlife Service in approximately its present form. The act bolstered research and enhanced the acquisition and development of refuge lands.

The National Wildlife Refuge System Administration Act of 1956 described and refined the policies of Congress in connection with the national wildlife refuge system. The act provided guidelines and directives for the acquisition, development, and management of refuge areas.

The Endangered Species Act of 1973 authorized the listing of endangered and threatened species and prohibited the possession, sale, and transport of endangered species. Further it authorized expanded habitat acquisition and a cooperative program with states to protect and propagate these species.

In addition to the aforementioned federal legislation, there are several international treaties pertaining to wildlife protection and management, with particular emphasis on selected species. Also, there are numerous state laws concerning wildlife. It should be noted that wildlife management is primarily the responsibility of the states, not the federal government.

NATIONAL REFUGE SYSTEM

The main reason for having refuges is to provide wildlife with sanctuaries–places where some of the wildlife can survive relatively unmolested by people. The wildlife preservation concept is strongly interwoven into the management of refuges.

Even though refuges are not established to accommodate visitors, these areas do have recreation value, and the managing agencies usually give consideration to this potential. Because refuges are areas of relatively undisturbed nature and especially attractive to certain forms of wildlife, people can go there and see wild animals in their native habitat. Most refuges are not especially scenic, except to a naturalist with particular appreciation for that kind of environment. Further, viewing elk inside a large compound, or seeing ducks and geese at their stopover points on migratory flights, are not wildlife experiences that attract visitors in large numbers. Yet, refuges do offer a unique recreational dimension, and their total recreation visits annually is quite significant. As a result, at least minimal visitor arrangements are provided at many of the refuges.

Interestingly, on many refuges recreation activities extend well beyond wildlife watching. Hunting, fishing, and fur trapping often occur within proper controls. Nonconsumptive recreational activities include nature study, bird watching, and dog training for hunting. Also some refuges provide opportunities for horseback riding, cycling, backpacking, picnicking, and camping, along with water-oriented activities such as waterskiing, sailing, canoeing, and ice-skating. A recent study of California wildlife refuges showed that 80% of the recreational use was by nonconsumptive recreationists rather than by hunters, fishers, and trappers.

There are presently about 400 national wildlife refuges in the United States (plus a large number of state-owned refuges). The first national refuge was established in 1903 at Pelican Island off the coast of Florida. The refuge system expanded slowly for the first five decades; then during a 20-year period from 1955 to 1975, the system tripled to reach a total area of more than 33 million acres (13 million ha). During the next five years, from 1975 to 1980, it doubled again, largely because of extensive additions in Alaska. Subsequently, other areas have been added, and now the national refuge system includes more than 70 million acres (28 million ha), with a little over half of the acreage being in Alaska (Figure 10.1).

Consider the development of the refuge system from the standpoint of a whooping crane, whose population diminished to almost zero during the 1930s. Fortunately, by this time the crane spotted a few refuges along the migratory flyways. When the crane arrived in the autumn of 1938 at Medicine Lake in Montana, it saw ditches being dug and dikes being built to restore the drained alkali flats to lush marshlands. As it moved across the Great Plains, the

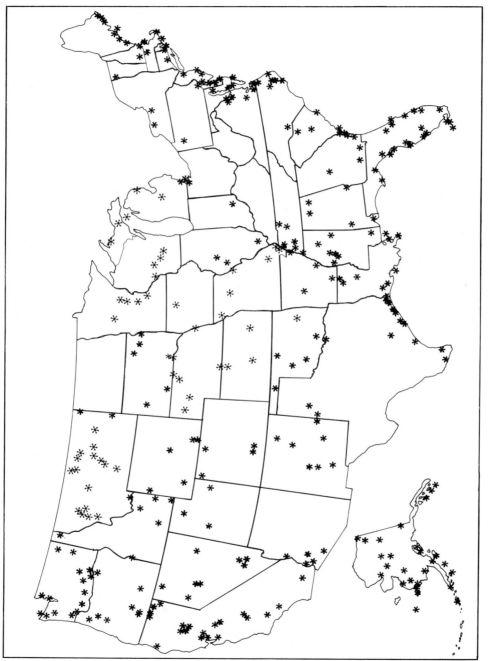

Figure 10.1. Locations of refuges in the national wildlife refuge system. (Source: U.S. Fish and Wildlife Service)

crane found similar work in progress at Lacreek Refuge in South Dakota, at Crescent Lake Refuge in Nebraska, at the Salt Plains Refuge in Oklahoma, and at Aransan near the Gulf Coast of Texas. Finally, it and other whooping cranes could spend the winter in the protection of a wildlife refuge. The next spring, when it returned north for nesting, the crane used some of the same refuges, and also found that safe nesting grounds were being preserved in the Northwest Territories of Canada.

By showing appreciation and respect for all forms of life, we will ulti-mately contribute better toward a livable environment for ourselves.

During the next 40 years the crane saw numerous other refuges added along the flyways–Lostwood, Audubon, Lamesteer, Kirwin, and Quivira–each one providing additional bits of wilderness that would help the species survive. The crane saw ducks and geese and many other migratory birds return by hundreds of thousands, and it observed its own numbers increase gradually so that by the mid-1980s–if this crane still were making the annual flight–it would be 1 of approximately 80 whooping cranes in existence.

The migrating crane would see only a narrow corridor of the total refuge system. It would not know that elsewhere refuges have been developed for other forms of wildlife. It wouldn't recognize that what it had seen is only a small part of the refuge program that has caused

Hunting is permitted in season on many of the refuges. (U.S. Fish and Wildlife Service, photo by David B. Marshall)

America to achieve the greatest refuge system in the world. But then it wouldn't care about all of that. It would care only that there are now a few places for its species to winter in the south and nest in the north and spots of sanctuary to rest in between. These small islands of hope will enable its species, and many others, to survive indefinitely.

According to the U.S. Fish and Wildlife Service the purpose of the national refuge system is to "provide, manage, and safeguard a national network of lands and waters sufficient in size, density, and location to make available, now and in the future, public benefits that are associated with wildlife over which the federal government has responsibility, particularly migratory birds and endangered species."

In another portion of the mission statement the Fish and Wildlife Service gives emphasis to the recreational value of refuges, which are "to provide understanding and appreciation of fish and wildlife ecology and man's role in his environment, and to provide visitors at service installations with high quality, safe, wholesome, and enjoyable recreational experiences oriented toward wildlife."

Most of the land in the refuge system is owned by the federal government; however, there are some exceptions. In the total system there are three classifications of jurisdiction:

1. A few areas are managed by private owners through agreements with the Fish and Wildlife Service. The landowner agrees to protect the specified wildlife environment in exchange for cash or other compensation. Most of these arrangements involve wetlands for migratory birds.
2. Some refuges result from cooperative agreements between the Fish and Wildlife Service and other federal agencies or state agencies. These interagency agreements with the Fish and Wildlife Service are fairly common, especially with the Bureau of Land Management. Other cooperators include the Tennessee Valley Authority, Water and Power Resources Service, Corps of Engineers, Defense Department, Bureau of Indian Affairs, and several state agencies.
3. Most refuge land is federally owned and under the singular management of the Fish and Wildlife Service.

There has been an effort to have at least one refuge in each state and this has been accomplished except in West Virginia and Kentucky. There are six kinds of refuges according to the Fish and Wildlife Service classification plan: (1) migratory-bird refuges (general), (2) migratory-bird refuges (waterfowl), (3) waterfowl production areas in wetlands management districts, (4) big-game refuges, (5) wildlife ranges and game ranges, and (6) wildlife coordination management areas. In addition to its 400 refuges, the Fish and Wildlife Service administers 20 research centers, more than 90 national fish hatcheries, and 11 fish research stations.

WILDLIFE HABITAT CONSERVATION

Unspoiled land and water is what usually is meant by natural wildlife habitat. Habitat includes food, cover, water and space. This kind of resource has been disappearing rapidly during recent decades, and the reduction of the animal population is only a symptom of the more basic problem. Therefore, the major thrust of current wildlife conservation efforts is toward saving enough natural living space for the animals. If this is accomplished, the animals can pretty well take care of themselves.

To help preserve livable habitat, the construction projects of dams and bridges on the nation's streams are being carefully monitored by conservation agencies to ensure that the needs of wildlife are taken into account. The same is true of coastal swamps and wetlands as domestic developments around these choice wildlife areas threaten numerous animal species. Further, the control of pollutants and the use of insecticides are receiving much attention by conservationists.

In the past it was easy to see the economic benefits of dredging rivers for navigation, damming streams for irrigation, draining wetlands to provide more farmland, and constructing sprawling residential areas around cities. But what has not been so obvious is the great toll that these actions were taking on wildlife and wildlife habitat. Although a few individuals of exceptional vision have warned of the detrimental effects of these activities, it was not until recently that a general awareness developed about the importance of treating the earth with more respect.

Experience has confirmed that it is only through the protection of the full spectrum of plant and animal life that we are able to afford protection to any particular species. If we are to preserve the bald eagle, the peregrine falcon, and the grizzly bear, we must conserve the network of life on which those species depend.

Estuaries

Estuaries, those sprawling aquatic areas where the fresh waters of the rivers meet the salt waters of the sea, are scattered throughout the various coastlines of our nation and territories. Estuaries go by several other names–bays, harbors, sounds, lagoons, tidal marshes, inshore waters, and channels. They are generally fertile and productive of plant and animal life–often more productive, in fact, than either the land on the one side or the sea on the other.

Nowhere else do wild creatures and cities occur in closer relationship than in some of our estuaries, and nowhere are environmental problems more acute. Estuary marshlands often serve as meccas for waterfowl and marshland animals, and these areas also provide man with an array of recreational opportunities. Yet, marine scientists have generally characterized estuaries as the septic tanks of urban America, and the estuaries are gradually diminishing in size and quality. In the past 30 years approximately 10% of the wildlife habitat in estuaries has been destroyed by dredging and filling alone. During that same period pollution and domestic development have further reduced the natural use of estuaries.

Two thirds of all coastal-supported fish are dependent on estuaries, for these areas are spawning grounds, nurseries, and feeding places for fish. Some species migrate in and out of estuaries and others spend their entire lives there.

In addition to providing fish habitat, estuaries are important to the survival of ducks, geese, various wading birds and shorebirds, and a variety of other animals. For waterfowl, estuaries provide vital nesting and winter habitat as well as resting and feeding places during migration.

Because of the increasing encroachment on estuary terrain, Congress passed the Estuary Protection Act in 1968. Since then, measures taken under the act have helped to control, but

Estuaries and wetlands are the most ecologically productive areas in our environment. (Florida State Bureau of Tourism)

have not eliminated, the destruction of estuaries. The Fish and Wildlife Service has made an important contribution by establishing several large wildlife refuges on estuaries. Yet, the battle to preserve valuable estuary terrain goes on, and it is gradually being lost.

There are certain other areas similar to estuaries but not entirely fitting the description. One interesting example is the Everglades region, where the fluctuating water level has seriously endangered the delicate balance of the plant and animal life. Ecologists say that this environment (the only one of its kind in the world) will cease to exist if the water level is not strictly controlled.

Even though the alligator is considered obnoxious by people in general, it is crucial to the survival of the Everglades environment. (Unfortunately, the alligator population has dropped drastically in the past half-century, though it has made a partial recovery during the past decade.) Alligators create and maintain "'gator holes," which hold water and sustain life–fishes of various sizes and numerous lesser aquatic organisms–and permits these organisms to repopulate the Everglades when summer rains again flood the area. Many of the rare and beautiful birds of the Everglades depend greatly on these holes to sustain them and their young during the dry winter and early spring. Also, the alligators, by pushing up muck around the survival holes, create a high ground on which plants and trees become established. These provide nesting places for the birds close to a food source; thus, the alligator is essential to the basic productivity of the Everglades and is instrumental in maintaining stable year-round conditions for various wildlife.

This level of dependence of almost all other species on the alligator is a simple but clear lesson about the interrelationship of the different aspects of nature. It especially points out how important a particular species can be to the total ecological balance.

Wetlands

Wetlands are as important as estuaries in the propagation of wildlife. These are the waterlogged spaces given such names as meadows, marshes, sloughs, swamps, bogs, and ponds. Wetlands have been shrinking as a result of industrial development, urbanization, and agricultural drainage. Most wetlands can be drained, diked, or filled for conversion to dry land—and this is the crux of the wetland dilemma. A large percentage of the nation's wetlands have been destroyed or modified to make way for new croplands, buildings, airports, highways, industrial sites, and dumping areas. Land statistics from the Fish and Wildlife Service show that since colonial times nearly half of America's wetlands have been drained or filled. Even now 200,000 to 300,000 acres (80,000 to 120,000 ha) of wetlands are destroyed each year in the United States.

To give an example of the effects on wildlife, consider that at one time, the "prairie pothole" region of Minnesota and the Dakotas produced about 15 million ducks a year. Today, because of reduction and modification, these wetlands produce only about 5 million ducks. Waterfowl production is crucial to the size of autumn flights across the middle region of the nation; thus, it has direct effects on waterfowl-related recreation activities.

A boon to wetland preservation came in 1958 when the Fish and Wildlife Coordination Act Amendment was passed. One of the purposes of the amendment was "to provide that fish and wildlife conservation shall receive equal consideration . . . with other features of water-resource development programs." Under the act the Fish and Wildlife Service is required to study and comment on the effects to fish and wildlife habitat of federal projects or projects requiring federal permits. This includes permits for dredging and filling issued by the Corps of Engineers, and the water-resources development projects of all other federal agencies, such as the Bureau of Reclamation, the Water and Power Resources Service, and the Soil Conservation Service. This protective measure has had a significant benefit.

Large expanses of wetlands have been preserved through the national wildlife refuge program, which was discussed earlier in this chapter. Also, there is a large number of state-owned refuges and wildlife management areas that encompass thousands of wetlands. But wetlands not under refuge protection, many of which are small areas on private lands, still are vanishing steadily.

Big-Game Habitat

In managing the number of big-game animals of any particular region, the emphasis is placed on three aspects: (1) the number of animals allowed for harvest by hunters, (2) predator control, and (3) habitat conditions, especially winter range. In all areas of the United States there are now strict controls placed on the number of permits available each year to big-game hunters, and strong efforts are being made to control poaching. The number of permits

"In dire necessity, somebody might write another *Iliad*, or paint an 'Angelus,' but fashion a goose?"–Aldo Leopold, *A Sand County Almanac*, Ballantine Books, New York, p. 229. (U.S. Fish and Wildlife Service, photo by Ray C. Erickson)

fluctuates from year to year, depending on the animal population and the ability of the habitat to sustain the animals.

Also, predator control programs are carefully planned and monitored to keep the predator population at the optimum. Predators are an important element in the control of the other wildlife species.

In most areas of the United States the provision of adequate range, particularly winter range, has become the most crucial problem of big-game management. With our continuing domestication of land, it has become increasingly difficult to maintain a sufficient amount of habitat to sustain the big-game herds.

State and federal wildlife agencies are struggling to retain natural habitat. Large tracts of land have been purchased by these agencies or acquired through cooperative agreements with private landowners. Also, measures are being taken to cause the range to be more productive.

Efforts are also being made to improve wildlife habitat in forest regions. This involves the control of timber harvest and the provision of forest openings where natural clearings are inadequate. Spot thinning of forests so that sunlight can reach the forest floor encourages grasses and shrubs, which offer food and cover to wildlife. Also, timber harvest patterns are distributed in time and area to enhance habitat variety. Further, prescribed burning is used in pine forests for stimulating tree regeneration.

A deer's natural habitat requires no fence lines or ditches; it is open space calmly aloof to these devices of alleged owners. (U.S. Fish and Wildlife Service, photo by Phillip K. White)

There is value in any experience that exercises those ethical restraints collectively called "sportsmanship." Our tools for the pursuit of wildlife improve faster than we do, and sportsmanship is a voluntary limitation in the use of these armaments. It is aimed to augment the role of skill and shrink the role of gadgets in the pursuit of wild things.
–Aldo Leopold, *A Sand County Almanac*,
Ballantine Books, New York, 1978, p. 212.

Grassland management is aimed at spreading wildlife grazing over the entire range so as to not deplete portions of the range. Special attention is given to plant composition, and this often involves artificial seeding of the more desirable plants.

Birds and Small Game

The natural habitat of small game and game birds consists of a variety of terrain and cover. Such spaces have diminished significantly because of the vast expansion of cities, industrial complexes, and agriculture, and the continuation of this trend seems inevitable. Fortunately, croplands with sufficient areas of natural cover are an effective substitute for the natural habitat. Many small-game species thrive on such foods as corn, barley, sorghum, rye, wheat, soybeans, rice, alfalfa, and clover. Further, these forms of wildlife are rather easily replenished as improvements in habitat make it possible to sustain larger numbers.

Most game birds and small animals now exist on privately owned lands. In light of this, it would appear that the best solution for the future will depend on increased cooperation with landowners to improve habitat conditions. Wildlife agencies have been somewhat successful in convincing farmers and ranchers to leave relatively unproductive areas in a seminatural state and to leave strips of cover for wildlife along fence lines and creeks.

Endangered and Threatened Species

Because of the persistent efforts of conservationists, we can still see a bald eagle soar and witness the return of whooping cranes to Texas after their long migration from Canada. Tiny key deer still roam a few islands off southern Florida, and Puerto Rican parrots still exist.

These irreplacable living resources are among the 236 native animals and plants included in the U.S. list of endangered and threatened species (Table 10.1). In addition, 468 foreign wildlife and plant species are also listed for protection under the Endangered Species Act of 1973.

By definition, an *endangered* species is one on the brink of extinction throughout all or a significant portion of its range. A *threatened* species is one likely to become endangered within the foreseeable future. Restoring these listed creatures to the point where they are again viable is the main goal of the endangered-species program. The program is the responsibility of the Fish and Wildlife Service.

The endangered-species program is somewhat controversial, because many people feel that certain species are obnoxious, worthless, or even damaging and ought to become extinct. There is a natural resistance to expensive efforts meant to save insects, bats, reptiles, and rodents. Conversely, there are other endangered species that almost everyone would agree ought to be saved: bald eagles, blue whales, peregrine falcons, and whooping cranes.

Table 10.1. Endangered and Threatened Species of Animals and Plants

Species	Endangered	Threatened
Mammals	33	3
Birds	67	3
Reptiles	11	10
Amphibians	5	2
Fish	29	12
Snails	2	5
Clams	23	0
Crustaceans	1	0
Insects	6	2
Plants	20	2
Total	197	39

Source: Department of the Interior, U.S. Fish and Wildlife Service, *Endangered and Threatened Wildlife and Plants*, 1982, pp. 1–13.

There are various reasons for a species' decline. For example, the peregrine falcon disappeared from the eastern United States after its food sources were contaminated by pesticides. In other cases, the decline of a species is caused when habitat is destroyed by human developments (as with the bison) or when an ecosystem is disrupted by the introduction of nonnative (exotic) animals or plants (as with the greenback cutthroat trout).

When a species is listed as threatened or endangered, it becomes protected by federal law. This alone is sometimes enough to save it from extinction and start it on the road to recovery. The comeback of the American alligator is a good example. During the 1950s and 1960s market hunting for its prized leather nearly eliminated the alligator from the southeastern United States. The states in that area recognized the problem and halted the hunting for this animal. In 1966 the federal government listed the species as endangered and later prohibited both the killing of alligators and the sale of products made from them. With this form of protection the population of alligators rapidly increased, and by 1984 there were nearly 1 million in existence.

To help reach the goals of the Endangered Species Act, the Fish and Wildlife Service systematically develops recovery plans for various species on the list. A recovery plan is a guide that identifies, describes, and schedules the actions necessary to restore the particular species to a more secure biological condition.

A major problem for most wildlife is destruction of habitat, usually the result of industrial, agricultural, residential, or recreational developments. Recovery plans, therefore, call for preservation of the land and water conditions needed for a species to survive. Critical habitat can be protected in a number of ways, including working with private landowners, negotiating cooperative agreements with land-managing agencies, and acquiring easements to ensure existing use while guarding against harmful future developments.

When the habitat cannot be maintained any other way, it is sometimes purchased by the Fish and Wildlife Service. Most of the money for such land acquisition comes from the Land and Water Conservation Fund. In some cases, however, the land is donated by individuals or corporations. Further, habitat protection often is assisted by such private organizations as the Nature Conservancy, which can move quickly to acquire land for later repurchase by the government. Habitat purchased by the Fish and Wildlife Service usually becomes part of the national wildlife refuge system.

Sometimes the solution is to clean up the habitat from harmful chemicals. The key factor in the recovery of the bald eagle, peregrine falcon, and brown pelican has been legal restrictions on the use of DDT and other long-life pesticides. Such contaminants can enter the food chain and accumulate in the animal's body tissues, eventually having destructive results.

A creature is sometimes crowded out of its habitat by competing species. When this happened to the greenback cutthroat trout, biologists cleared its native Colorado streams of exotic fish species and reintroduced hatchery-raised greenbacks.

Some species have become so depleted that captive propagation is considered necessary to ensure their survival. This is the case with the California condor, North America's largest bird, whose numbers have dropped to fewer than 30. A recovery plan that calls for captive breeding to increase the condor population is being implemented.

One of the more encouraging efforts has been the reintroduction to Arizona of captive-reared, masked bobwhites. This species had been eliminated from the United States by 1900 after overgrazing destroyed its habitat, although a few of the birds remained in northern Mex-

This magnificent polar-bear skin is a confiscated product of an endangered species. (U.S. Fish and Wildlife Service, photo by Steve Hillebrand)

ico. Biologists have been quite successful in breeding this species in captivity and replenishing its population in its original Arizona habitat.

Perhaps the most dramatic success story involves the whooping crane. The population of this bird was reduced to a mere 20 by the late 1930s. In 1954, after years of searching, the whooping crane's breeding grounds were found in the marshes of the northern Canadian wilderness. It was a crucial discovery. U.S. and Canadian wildlife officials cooperated on a recovery plan that involved not only preservation of the breeding grounds but also key stop-overpoints on the bird's 2600-mile (4200-km) migratory route to its wintering habitat on the Texas coast. With habitat preservation underway, wildlife biologists set out to increase the whooping crane's numbers. After three decades of intensive effort involving a combination of strict protection, public education, and innovative propagation techniques, the number of whooping cranes has increased to more than 100. With cooperation and support from the public, wildlife specialists are working toward similar successes with other endangered species.

The severity of the extinction of a species is expressed in the following anonymous quote: "Once the last of a species can be no more, a heaven and earth must pass before such one can be again."

Discussion Questions

1. What are the major responsibilities of the U.S. Fish and Wildlife Service as contrasted to the state fish and wildlife agencies?
2. What contributions do wildlife refuges, sanctuaries, and preserves make to outdoor recreation?
3. In managing the number of big-game animals of any particular region, the emphasis is placed on three aspects. What are they? What is the most crucial problem of big-game management?
4. It is sometimes claimed that the most effective conservation efforts are at the grass roots. What does this mean? Do you agree? What particular efforts of this kind are you acquainted with?
5. Is it possible for man to overprotect a particular species of wildlife? If so, give examples. What are the possible results?
6. Should the preservation of wildlife and their habitat in any form be given preference over domestic animals and industrial development? Should all endangered species be given protection?

Recommended Readings

"Bad News for the Birds." *Time,* 5 October 1981, p. 52.

"Endangered Species: States Take a Hand." *U.S. News and World Report,* 18 August 1980, p. 70.

Knudson, Douglas M. *Outdoor Recreation.* New York: Macmillan Publishing Co., 1984. Chapter 16.

Kostka, Donna. "Our Wildlife: Wild or Weird?" *Park and Recreation,* April 1981, p. 45.

National Wildlife Federation. "1981 Environmental Quality Index." *National Wildlife,* February–March 1981, p. 29.

Sansom, Jack. "Ronald Reagan's Thoughts on Guns, Hunting, and Conservation." *Field and Stream,* October 1980, p. 27.

Soil Conservation Service. *More Wildlife Through Soil and Water Conservation.* U.S. Department of Agriculture Bulletin No. 175. Washington, D.C.: 1977.

Soil Conservation Service. *Trout Ponds for Recreation.* Washington, D.C.: U.S. Department of Agriculture, 1976.

Thompson, Larry S. "Wildlife and Land-Use Change: Some Considerations in Assessing Impact Risk." *Western Wildlands,* spring 1977, pp. 10–28.

Towell, William E. "The Hunter as a Conservationist." *American Forests,* October 1980, p. 46.

U.S. Department of Agriculture. *Making Land Produce Useful Wildlife.* Farmers' Bulletin No. 2035. Washington, D.C.: 1975.

U.S. Department of Agriculture. *Ponds and Marshes for Wild Ducks on Farms and Ranches in the Northern Plains.* Farmers' Bulletin No. 2234. Washington, D.C.: 1973.

U.S. Department of Agriculture. *Warm-Water Fishponds.* Farmers' Bulletin No. 2250. Washington, D.C.: 1977.

U.S. Department of the Interior. *The Third Nationwide Outdoor Recreation Plan: The Assessment.* Washington, D.C.: 1979.

U.S. Fish and Wildlife Service. *Endangered and Threatened Wildlife and Plants.* Washington, D.C.: U.S. Government Printing Office, 1984.

U.S. Fish and Wildlife Service. *Endangered Species: The Road to Recovery.* Washington, D.C.: U.S. Government Printing Office, 1981.

U.S. Fish and Wildlife Service. *1984 Refuge List.* Washington, D.C.: U.S. Department of the Interior, 1984.

U.S. Fish and Wildlife Service. *Wetlands Values and Management.* Washington, D.C.: U.S. Government Printing Office, 1981.

"Wildlife Habitat in Managed Forests: The Blue Mountains of Oregon and Washington." *Forest Science,* September 1981, p. 602.

CHAPTER 11

Financial and Technical Assistance Programs

Not only do federal agencies develop recreation sites and manage recreation areas directly; they also administer numerous financial- and technical-assistance programs. This chapter presents the various opportunities for assistance and the agencies through which these programs are administered.

NATIONAL PARK SERVICE RESPONSIBILITIES

The traditional role of the National Park Service has been the management of the national park system. That role was discussed in Chapter 8. Recently, however, the Park Service's role has been expanded to include several important functions that do not involve land management.

On 9 February 1981 the secretary of the interior issued a consolidation order that placed the major functions of the Heritage Conservation and Recreation Service within the National Park Service. These new functions are quite different from the traditional responsibilities of the Park Service.

Section 1 of the consolidation order states the following:

The purpose of this order is to achieve economies in the utilization of funds, personnel, and equipment and to improve program services by: (1) Effecting the transfer and consolidation of the major functions of the Heritage Conservation and Recreation Service into the National Park Service, (2) Terminating the residual functions of HCRS, and (3) Abolishing HCRS as a separate entity of the Department of the Interior.

The Heritage Conservation and Recreation Service was created within the Department of the Interior in 1978 by combining the former Bureau of Outdoor Recreation (which originated in 1968), the Office of Archeology and Historic Preservation, and the Natural Landmarks

Program. The Heritage Conservation and Recreation Service took on a long list of major outdoor-recreation responsibilities which it conducted for three years. The following sections explain the responsibilities transferred to the National Park Service.

Land and Water Conservation Fund

The Land and Water Conservation Fund grant program provides matching grants to state and local governments to plan, acquire, and develop outdoor recreation areas and facilities. The fund also provides financial assistance to federal agencies for the development of outdoor recreation. Established by the Land and Water Conservation Fund Act of 1965, the fund has provided over $2.7 billion to state and local governments to acquire some 2 million acres (810,000 ha) of land and develop facilities at 29,500 park and recreation projects. The projects have a broad range that includes neighborhood playgrounds, large parks with outdoor sports facilities, and extensive natural areas.

Approximately 60% of the annual appropriation for the fund is apportioned by the secretary of the interior among the 50 states and 5 territories. About 38% is divided among principal federal land-managing agencies for land acquisition. A small portion of the total appropriation may be set aside by Congress for the secretary's discretionary fund to be used for special demonstration projects or to meet emergency acquisition needs of states.

State and local governments submit proposals to the state outdoor recreation liaison officer, who is designated by the governor as the state's Land and Water Conservation Fund contact. Projects selected for funding must be in accordance with priorities stated in the statewide comprehensive outdoor-recreation plan. Project proposals are then sent to the National Park Service for final approval.

The Land and Water Conservation Fund is financed primarily by revenues from federal leasing of the outer continental shelf for oil and gas exploration and drilling. Additional funds come from federal surplus-land sales and the federal tax on motorboat fuel.

Between 80% and 90% of the new areas acquired for recreation purposes by use of the fund are within three hours' driving time of heavily populated areas. This has particular significance for people living in crowded places who are in great need of nearby outdoor recreation.

Urban Park and Recreation Recovery Program

The Urban Park and Recreation Recovery Program provides matching grants to local governments for rehabilitating existing recreation facilities and for demonstrating innovative ways of providing better services and management. Grants are also available to support the revitalization of community recreation sites.

This program was established under the Urban Park and Recreation Recovery Act of 1978. During the first five years, $127 million in grants were awarded. Projects have included basic structural repairs of older neighborhood recreation centers, the redesign and remodeling of facilities, and the rehabilitation of deteriorated community parks and sports facilities such as swimming pools, tennis courts, and game fields. Also, grants have covered a variety of local initiatives, including new programs for the handicapped and elderly, public-private partnerships to operate and maintain parks, new uses of abandoned schools and industrial sites, methods of increasing nontax revenues to support recreation programs, and numerous other creative approaches.

The Urban Park and Recreation Recovery program in several ways has complemented the Land and Water Conservation Fund. While the conservation fund grants are aimed at land acquisition and park development, urban park grants pay for improvements in existing resources, indoor and outdoor.

Nationwide Recreation Planning

The National Park Service is now responsible for the nationwide outdoor recreation plan, which is designed to guide government agencies at all levels and the private sector in managing recreation resources to meet present and future needs. Nationwide plans have been prepared on approximately five-year cycles since 1969 (1969, 1973, 1979).

Further, each state maintains a current statewide plan which coincides in a general sense with the nationwide plan. A state plan must be approved by the Park Service before the state can receive apportionments under the Land and Water Conservation Fund. The Park Service provides technical and financial assistance to help states prepare their plans. More is said about statewide and nationwide planning in Chapter 18.

Trails and Wild and Scenic Rivers

The national trails and national wild and scenic rivers programs were described in detail in Chapter 7, and the same information will not be repeated here.

The National Park Service coordinates the national wild and scenic rivers program, which was established in 1968. Also, the Park Service manages or cooperates in the management of a few of the rivers. Typically, a river is managed by the agency that controls the nearby land.

The Park Service also manages the national trails system, which was started under the National Trails Act of 1968. Many kinds of trails are included, ranging from lengthy scenic and historic hiking routes to short recreation trails near urban areas.

Technical Assistance and Information Exchange

The law requires the secretary of the interior to assure adequate outdoor-recreation resources for the present and future generations through prompt, coordinated action by all levels of government. Among other functions prescribed by the Congress to achieve this national objective, the Park Service is responsible for technical assistance to federal, state, and local government agencies and the private sector. Through technical publications and training programs, the Park Service provides state and local agencies and private interests with information on park and recreation problems, trends, and management techniques. Also, the Park Service sponsors or fosters nationwide surveys to provide data for analyzing issues and making plans. As an outgrowth of this effort, the Park Service maintains information on the current status and future trends of recreation and prepares special reports on topical recreation issues.

Interagency Coordination

The combination of responsibilities that have been given to the Park Service causes it to be the focal point of federal government outdoor-recreation involvement. Also, these responsibilities give the Park Service reasons to work closely with the other federal agencies. As a result, the Park Service is now responsible for monitoring federal activities and new legislation that has the potential of influencing the quality and availability of recreation services and facilities.

Federal Real Property

The Surplus Property Act calls for the identification and transfer of federal surplus land to state and local governments for recreation, wilderness, wildlife and conservation purposes. The Park Service helps meet this public need by:

1. Identifying potential access of surplus properties and notifying the appropriate public agency of those lands which appear to have wilderness, wildlife, conservation, or recreation value.
2. Providing state and local agencies with assistance in planning for the use of lands to be transferred and assisting in the transfer.
3. Providing technical assistance to the president's Economic Adjustment Committee to determine recreation potentials when military-base closures are being considered.

Federal Recreation Fee Program

The Park Service is required by Congress to prepare an annual report relative to compliance with the prescribed entrance fees charged at federal recreation areas. The main objective is to achieve uniformity and consistency with respect to recreation fees charged by federal agencies. Specifically, the Park Service does the following under this responsibility:

1. Coordinates the collection of the recreation fee and the reporting of visitation data.
2. Produces and sells to the public the annual access permits, such as the Golden Eagle passport sold to the general public, and the Golden Age passport sold at a reduced rate to the elderly.
3. Analyzes fee policies and recommends changes.

Natural Landmarks

Natural areas with national significance are designated by the secretary of the interior as national landmarks. The areas are significant because they include important examples of America's natural history in the form of plant and animal communities, landforms, or geologic features. More than 548 national natural landmarks have been designated since the program was established in 1963.

Landmarks are located on both public and private land. Landmark designation does not affect ownership or tax status, but is meant to encourage the area's owner to preserve its significant qualities, and to enhance the area's educational and scientific value.

A unique form of recreation is illustrated here on the Oregon Dunes. (National Park Service)

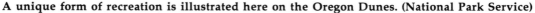

State Natural Heritage

The Park Service helps states establish and maintain natural-heritage programs that describe the state's significant natural features. A state's natural-heritage program includes information on important plant and animal communities, land formations, and geologic features. The Park Service is able to provide both technical and financial assistance for the development of such programs. State natural-heritage programs are not required, but more than half the states have chosen to participate in this effort with the Park Service.

Cultural Programs

The cultural programs of the Park Service help to preserve the nation's historic and cultural resources. There are six specific branches under this group of Park Service responsibilities.

The *National Register of Historic Places* lists the nation's buildings, sites, districts, structures, and objects significant in American history, architecture, archeology, and culture. The register includes more than 26,000 listings, and new ones are being added each year. The National Register was established by the National Historic Preservation Act of 1966. Although the Antiquities Act of 1906 and the Historic Sites Act of 1935 had already authorized the federal government to recognize historic resources of national significance, the 1966 Act expanded this responsibility by establishing the National Register to recognize properties of state and local significance.

The *national historic landmarks* include properties of national historic significance. More than 1500 landmarks have been designated, including places such as Mount Vernon and Pearl Harbor. Owners of national historic landmarks who sign an agreement with the Park Service to preserve the landmarks are eligible to receive a certificate and a bronze plaque indicating the property is a registered national historic landmark.

The *Historic Preservation Fund*, administered by the Park Service, provides matching grants to identify, preserve, and protect historic properties. Established by the National Historic Preservation Act of 1966, the fund has provided financial assistance for more than 6000 historic preservation projects. Projects range from private homes to commercial blocks in

Chesapeake and Ohio Canal park interpreters conduct guided tours aboard an old-fashioned mule-drawn barge. (National Park Service)

historic districts to lighthouses and covered bridges. Matching grants are available for state-wide surveys to identify properties with historic significance and for state plans to preserve and protect historic properties. Grants for the protection of historic properties are also available to local governments, private organizations, and individuals for up to 50% of the project's cost. Applications must be channeled through the state historic preservation officer.

Technical preservation services include (1) interpretation of the tax benefits of property rehabilitation, (2) the preparation of a variety of technical publications on the repair, maintenance, and preservation of historic properties, and (3) the transfer of federal surplus properties listed in the National Register of Historic Places to state and local governments at no cost upon request channeled through the state historic preservation offices.

The *National Architectural and Engineering Record* includes buildings and structures significant in American architecture, engineering, and industry. The Park Service documents these historic properties, and the records are kept in the Library of Congress for public viewing and reproduction. They are used in planning preservation projects and for historical information. The American Institute of Architects and the American Society of Civil Engineers cooperate with the Park Service in this effort.

The *interagency archeological services program* oversees the protection and recovery of the nation's archeological resources by (1) issuing permits for archeological explorations on federal lands, (2) contracting with scientific and educational institutions to perform archeological surveys and excavations, and (3) providing guidance and technical assistance on the identification and evaluation of archeological resources.

Environmental and Compliance Review

The Park Service reviews and comments annually on approximately 2000 federal regulations and environmental-impact statements to assess their effects on recreation and natural and cultural resources. The Park Service also assesses the environmental effects of projects assisted by Park Service grants and technical services. Further, approximately 600 U.S. Department of Transportation projects are reviewed by the Park Service annually in accordance with the Transportation Act of 1966. The act prohibits the approval of projects that will adversely affect public parks, wildlife refuges, recreation areas, or historic sites, unless there is no reasonable alternative to the project.

Miscellaneous

The Park Service also has the responsibility to enhance the use of military lands for public recreation and wildlife activities in the following ways:

1. By promoting the sharing of recreation and wildlife resources through cooperative arrangements between state and local governments and military installations.
2. By providing assistance to military installations for outdoor-recreation planning and development.

DEPARTMENT OF AGRICULTURE

The two major land-management divisions of the Department of Agriculture were discussed in Chapter 8 (Forest Service and Bureau of Land Management). Further, the Soil Conservation Service, also part of the Department of Agriculture, was discussed in Chapter 9. In addition, the department has certain other programs that contribute to outdoor recreation.

The *Agricultural Stabilization and Conservation Service* helps meet some of the pressing farm-related conservation and environmental problems through the encouragement of long-range preservation of the environment and increased forest production. It accomplishes these things through three particular programs:

1. The agriculture conservation program is designed to encourage and assist farmers with improving wildlife habitat. About 3000 farmers participate annually. Many of the ponds built by farmers are funded through this program, and most of the ponds provide either direct or indirect recreational opportunities.
2. The forestry incentive program promotes timber improvement on private lands.
3. The Water Bank program helps to preserve, restore, and improve wetlands for waterfowl and other wildlife.

The *Farmers Home Administration* relates to recreation opportunities by providing financial and management assistance to those in rural areas who are unable to get loans from other sources on reasonable terms. It operates principally under the Consolidated Farm and Rural Development Act, and Title V of the Housing Act. Some of the loans are for recreation-related enterprises.

The *Soil Conservation Service* assists local groups and individuals in planning and developing land and water resources. Projects frequently involve water development for recreation, conservation, and scenic attractions. This agency also assists in agricultural pollution control, environmental improvement, and rural community development.

The *Soil and Water Conservation Program* of the Soil Conservation Service provides technical assistance to about 3000 locally organized and operated conservation districts. Most of these districts carry on some projects each year that contribute to recreational developments and opportunities.

The *Agricultural Extension Service* (also called Cooperative Extension Service) has become the main educational arm of the Department of Agriculture. This agency cooperates closely with state land-grant universities and county governments. The Extension Service is actually focused at the state level, and the majority of the states employ at least one recreation and park specialist to help individuals and communities better plan and manage recreation enterprises, facilities, and services. The Extension Service is particularly interested in assisting with private recreation developments in rural areas.

DEPARTMENT OF TRANSPORTATION

The nation's transportation system is a vast and intricate network of streets, roads, highways, skyways, railways, sealanes, and inland waterways. Since 1967 the Department of Transportation has been helping to keep this system running to ensure fast, safe, reliable, and convenient transportation. A number of the department's highway programs are specifically designed to protect the natural environment and preserve the country's historical, archeological, and paleontological assets, as well as promote and enhance citizens' enjoyment of travel, vacation, and outdoor recreation opportunities.

The *Federal Highway Administration*, an agency of the Department of Transportation, is concerned with the total operation of the highway system. The Highway Administration, working in cooperation with the states, administers the multibillion dollar federal-aid highway program for planning, developing, and building the nation's 800,000 miles (1.3 million km) of primary and secondary highways, and the 45,000-mile (73,000-km) limited-access interstate system. The Highway Administration also assists the Forest Service, the National Park Service, and other federal agencies in designing and building principal roads in national forests, national parks, and similar areas.

Important considerations under the Highway Administration's highway beautification program are the protection and preservation of the highway's natural environment–scenic beauty; public parks and recreation areas; wildlife habitats; and historic, archeological, and paleontological sites. Also important is the enhancement of highway travel as a pleasurable driving experience and a ready means of access to outdoor activities.

The Highway Administration provides money to the states to help finance protective measures for vulnerable natural environments, such as wetlands and wildlife refuges adjacent to federal-aid highway projects. Also, funds are provided for historic markers and signs, tourist information centers, scenic overlooks, hiking paths and bikeways, access roads to public boat-launching areas, public campgrounds and other recreational areas.

The secretary of transportation oversees the nine divisions of the department, which include the Federal Aviation Administration, Highway Administration, Maritime Administration, St. Lawrence Seaway Authority, Urban Mass Transportation Administration, U.S. Coast Guard, Railroad Administration, and Highway Traffic Safety Administration.

The Highway Administration also administers Section 4 (F) of the Transportation Act, which provides that federally aided highways shall not impinge upon public recreation areas, wildlife refuges, or historic sites without sufficient reason as described in the law.

DEPARTMENT OF HOUSING AND URBAN DEVELOPMENT

Besides administering the housing-assistance programs of the federal government, the Department of Housing and Urban Development handles programs that aid neighborhood rehabilitation and economic development, and assists with urban planning and design.

In terms of parks and recreation, the law permits department assistance programs to include acquisition, construction, reconstruction, and installation of public parks, playgrounds, and recreation facilities. Funds may also be used where justified for community special services, including recreation programs, if such funding is not available from other sources.

DEPARTMENT OF LABOR

Recreation agencies are among the beneficiaries of federal employment and job-training programs administered through the Department of Labor. In the 1930s the Civilian Conservation Corps (CCC) developed trails, roads, and camping and picnic areas in the national parks and forests. Many of these facilities remain in use today. Several similar but more limited programs, which are having benefits for recreation, began in the 1970s.

Many local park and recreation departments have used grant money under the Comprehensive Employment and Training Act, and some departments have employed up to 50% of their seasonal personnel with money from this source. Similar benefits have accrued for recreation and park departments through the Young Adult Conservation Corps, which is a conservation works program sponsored through the Department of Labor.

DEPARTMENT OF COMMERCE

This department has several divisions that have limited but sometimes significant involvement with recreation. One such division is the *National Oceanic and Atmospheric Administration*. It has major responsibilities for the management of ocean resources through the Coastal-Zone Management Act. The agency provides matching grants to states for managing their coasts. The provision of public access to the shores is among the major benefits of this program. Also, the National Oceanic and Atmospheric Administration supports numerous research projects related to marine recreation.

As a natural outgrowth of its census function, the *Bureau of the Census* publishes a wide variety of data about the population and social and economic conditions. The bureau provides census information that has application in terms of recreation trends, recreation expenditures, recreation product and service markets, and public access to recreation areas.

During 1983 the Demographic Surveys Division of the bureau conducted a nationwide recreation survey. The purpose was to provide measures of participation in various outdoor recreation activities. The information is being used to determine recreation trends, barriers to participation, and expenditures on recreation at the national level and by regions.

The *Economic Development Administration*, a branch of the Department of Commerce, is responsible for fostering the long-range economic development of areas with severe unemployment and low family income. The Economic Development Administration aids the development of public facilities and private enterprise, including recreation, to help create new jobs. Among the kinds of programs administered by the agency are public-works grants and loans, business loans for industrial and commercial facilities, and technical planning and research assistance for area redevelopment projects.

The *U.S. Travel and Tourism Administration* is a division of the Department of Commerce that develops, plans, and carries out a comprehensive program to stimulate travel to the United States by residents of foreign countries. Recently, this agency has also been given the authority to encourage, promote, and develop travel within the United States and its territories. The agency cooperates with state and local tourism agencies as well as other federal agencies to improve tourist attractions and opportunities. The efforts of the agency make a significant contribution toward the number of people who travel from abroad and within the United States as a form of outdoor recreation.

SMALL BUSINESS ADMINISTRATION

The Small Business Administration provides loans to small businesses to help finance their operations. Some of these businesses are involved with recreation. With the increasing need for private enterprises in outdoor recreation, the SBA has the potential of playing a greater role in its contribution to this field.

ENVIRONMENTAL PROTECTION AGENCY

Established in 1970 as a result of the public concern over environmental quality, the Environmental Protection Agency at once became the federal regulator of these matters and the banker for federal funds as well. The Environmental Protection Agency generally improves recreation opportunities and experiences through its nationwide efforts to clean up and protect the environment. The agency's programs and standards are directly related to water recreation in at least two respects: (1) water-quality planning and (2) wastewater treatment.

As explained in Section 201 and Section 208 of the Federal Water Pollution Control Act amendment of 1972, water-quality planning for the nation must include consideration of water recreation. Another involvement with recreation lies with the multibillion dollar program for wastewater-treatment plants, which include considerable open space in urban areas. The act requires consideration of recreation benefits in all wastewater-treatment facility projects and water-quality management plans. Guidelines for accomplishing this have been prepared by the Environmental Protection Agency.

MILITARY LANDS

More than 30 million acres (12 million ha) of military bases, airfields, and training camps were acquired by the Army, Navy, and Marines during World War II. Over the years some of these lands have been declared surplus and transferred to federal, state, and local agencies, often for use as recreation sites. The remaining military acreage frequently affords recreation opportunities equal to those on other public lands. However, access is limited, depending on the use of the particular area. On military lands, the military requirements rank ahead of other uses.

Recreation resources on these lands play a significant role in providing on-base recreation for military personnel, their dependents, and civilian employees. This relieves the impact on state and local facilities.

The Sykes Act provides authority and limited funding to the Fish and Wildlife Service and the National Park Service to provide technical and financial assistance to stimulate and help military personnel do a better job with recreation resources, primarily for the benefit of military personnel and their dependents. Many improvement programs have been initiated under the provisions of this act.

U.S. COAST GUARD

The Coast Guard is officially a branch of the Armed Forces, but it operates during peacetime within the Department of Transportation. During war it becomes a part of the U.S. Navy.

The Coast Guard maintains a system of rescue vessels, aircraft, and communications facilities to carry out its functions of saving life and property in and over the high seas and the navigable waters of the United States. This function includes providing flood relief and removing hazards to navigation. The Coast Guard has made over 900 acres available for public recreation through cooperative arrangements with the National Park Service. Also, the Coast Guard auxiliary provides classes about boating safety, and voluntary boat-safety inspections are available to the public.

GENERAL SERVICES ADMINISTRATION

The General Services Administration enhances recreation opportunities in two ways: as the disposal agency for surplus property, and as the manager of a multitude of government buildings and other properties. About 1000 properties totaling more than 100,000 acres (40, 000 ha) have been conveyed to states and localities during the last two decades. Under the former Legacy of Parks program during the early 1970s, instead of selling such properties, the agency emphasized the transfer of these lands to states and localities for recreation purposes. Recently, the emphasis has turned to the sale of surplus properties with the revenue used to reduce the national debt.

The National Parks and Recreation Act of 1978 (Section 303) declares that it is the policy of the Congress to conserve wilderness and enhance wildlife conservation and recreation on federal lands. Further, the act emphasizes that unused and underused federal properties be studied as to the suitability for the above uses. This process is focused within the General Services Administration and the National Park Service. The General Services Administration identifies unneeded federal properties and the Park Service studies their suitability for the purposes described in the act.

COUNCIL ON ENVIRONMENTAL QUALITY

Although the Council on Environmental Quality has no direct responsibility for recreation planning or program administration, it is charged with monitoring the quality of the environment in all aspects. There are several trends in land use and air and water quality that have obvious implications for recreation. The council develops and recommends to the president national policies to promote the improvement of environmental quality to meet the conservation and health goals of the nation.

COMMUNITY SERVICES ADMINISTRATION

The Community Services Administration came into existence in 1975 as the successor to the Office of Economic Opportunity. The agency operates various programs, including youth work projects in connection with recreation and park programs through local agencies and state job-opportunity offices. The agency's *community action program* seeks solutions to the social and economic problems related to poverty. In some cases this results in recreation planning and development.

FEDERAL ENERGY REGULATORY COMMISSION

The Federal Energy Regulatory Commission has a large impact on recreation because it is responsible for regulating the interstate aspects of power and natural-gas industries. The commission requires a plan from each new licensee (or license-renewal applicant) regarding the steps that will be taken to provide public recreation in conjunction with the project being licensed. Thus, many projects provide recreation opportunities to the public along with the generation of power.

Discussion Questions

1. In 1981 the secretary of the interior consolidated the functions of the Heritage Conservation and Recreation Service with the National Park Service. What added responsibilities did this give to the Park Service?
2. The Land and Water Conservation Fund provides money to what kinds of agencies and for what purposes?
3. In what significant ways has the Urban Park and Recovery Act of 1978 affected recreation in urban areas?
4. In what ways and to what extent has the Department of Labor become involved in outdoor recreation?
5. What kinds of valuable information concerning recreation does the Bureau of Census provide? How can this information be effectively used by management personnel?
6. How has the Environmental Protection Agency affected recreation opportunities? What do you perceive the effect of this agency will be in the future?
7. Do you agree with the various ways the federal government is involved in financial and technical assistance for outdoor recreation? Which particular assistance programs do you think are clearly justified and which are marginal or unjustified?

Recommended Readings

U.S. Department of the Interior. *Index: National Park System and Related Areas*. Washington, D.C.: U.S. Government Printing Office, 1984.

U.S. Department of the Interior. *Third Nationwide Outdoor Recreation Plan: The Assessment*. Washington, D.C.: 1979.

U.S. Department of the Interior. *Third Nationwide Outdoor Recreation Plan: The Executive Report*. Washington, D.C.: 1979.

CHAPTER 12

The Roles of State Agencies

A century ago state government was relatively simple and was concerned with only a few functions. Many of the present services, such as education, health, and welfare, were initiated and carried on for a long time by private agencies. As their need and value became more recognized, the services were gradually taken over by government, and special agencies were created to administer them.

For a long time, recreation was of little public concern, and the early attempts to provide recreation opportunities were carried on by private initiative and funds. Over the past century, however, recreation has changed from solely private support to an accepted responsibility of government. Today certain aspects of recreation are—in fact, in law, and in public opinion—a recognized function of the state.

The 50 states collectively own nearly 78 million acres (32 million ha) of land and water, approximately 5% of the nation's total. Much of this land is high in recreation value, with large acreages being in the form of state forests, fish and wildlife areas, and parks. Table 12.1 shows the distribution of state-owned land by regions of the nation and how this compares to population. Table 12.2 shows the use classification of state-owned land and the acreage in

Table 12.1. State-Owned Land Distribution
by Region and Percentages of Land and Population in Regions

Region	Total Acres (ha) of State-Owned Land	Percent of State-Owned Land	Percent of U.S. Population in Region
West	51,225,102 (33,670,834)	65	17
North-central	12,492,490 (5,055,641)	16	28
Northeast	9,524,583 (3,854,545)	12	24
South	4,595,583 (1,859,806)	6	31

U.S. Department of the Interior, Bureau of Land Management, *Public Land Statistics,* 1983.

each category. The great majority of the state land is in the western part of the nation, and this region has the smallest population.

AUTHORITY TO PROVIDE RECREATION

"The powers not delegated to the United States by the Constitution, nor prohibited by it to the States, are reserved to the States respectively, or to the people."

The Tenth Amendment to the Constitution of the United States gives the separate states authority to provide recreational services. Commonly referred to as "the states' rights," the amendment is also the authority by which state governments provide public education, welfare, health services, and numerous other functions.

In view of this right, every state has seen fit to become involved in selected recreational services. These services are not consistent throughout the states, and neither are the types of organizations for administering the services consistent. Each state is unique in the services it offers and in its methods of administering them. Thus, the reader should keep in mind that, as a general rule, the information herein is common to most of the states, but not specific to any particular one.

> The state is created to enable people to do collectively what they could not accomplish individually. It is an instrument of the people and for the people.
>
> *—Case Studies in Parks and Recreation,*
> National Association of County Officials, Washington, D.C., 1969, p. 4.

STATE RECREATION SERVICES

The state is a governmental institution that enables people to do collectively what they would be unable to accomplish individually. It is the principal organization through which people are able to promote education and health, improve living and working conditions, expand ways and means of communication and transportation, and achieve many other acts that contribute to an orderly society.

Table 12.2. State Lands by Use Classification and Acreage

Use Classification	Acres (ha)
Forests	26,503,389 (10,725,774)
Fish and Wildlife Areas	9,005,445 (3,644,453)
Parks	5,528,030 (2,237,163)
School land	430,807 (174,345)
Unclassified	36,400,000 (14,730,878)
Total	77,867,671 (31,512,613)

U.S. Department of the Interior, Bureau of Land Management, *Public Land Statistics,* 1983.

A busy day at a state beach illustrates an attractive intermediate-use area (New Jersey State Parks Department)

The first significant involvement of a state in the field of recreation was in 1864 when Congress granted to California a large portion of public domain that included Yosemite Valley and the Mariposa Big Tree Grove. The land was transferred on the condition that the areas would be held for public use and recreational benefit for all time. In essence this became the first state park, even though it did not carry such a title. Unfortunately, California at the time was unable to manage those resources; so in 1884 the federal government repossessed the areas, eventually including them in the establishment of Yosemite National Park in 1891.

In 1872 the federal government declared Yellowstone a national park, providing 25,000 square miles (65,000 km²) of land, which was placed under the supervision of the territory of Wyoming. This proved unsuccessful and subsequently Yellowstone was managed under the supervision of the military for 32 years before finally being assigned to the Department of the Interior.

New York was the first state to make a clearly successful effort related to outdoor recreation. In 1885 New York established a state forest reserve in what is now Adirondack State Park. Also in 1885 Fort Mackinac was given to Michigan. It has since developed into a significant recreational attraction.

In 1894 the New York Constitution was amended to provide funds to purchase forestland under the Forest Preservation Act of 1885. This enlarged the areas known today as the Adirondack and the Catskill reserves. In 1898 Pennsylvania followed New York's lead and took measures to protect forest areas.

In the 1890s the beautiful Palisades of the Hudson River were recognized for their utility as raw material for concrete, and their defacement began to proceed rapidly. Women's groups can claim the initial credit for halting this destructive action, because in 1899 the New Jersey Federation of Women's Clubs convinced the New Jersey Legislature to pass a bill allowing the governor to study the situation. Subsequently, on Christmas Eve of 1900 an interstate agreement between New York and New Jersey was signed to save the scenic value of the Palisades.

In 1919 the Illinois Division of Parks and Memorials was established within the Department of Public Works and Buildings. That same year Indiana followed Illinois' lead by establishing a Division of State Parks within the Department of Conservation.

During the decade after World War II, both federal and state governments made positive moves to improve their park and recreation services. The Surplus Property Act of 1944 was amended in 1948 to allow certain federal lands to be converted to state park and recreation areas. Under this act surplus property could be transferred at 50% of its appraised value to states and local governments for recreation.

In 1960 New York became the first state to go to the public with a bond issue to support the development of state parks, and the voters supported the issue by a good majority. In that same year California published a two-volume state recreation plan.

The Open-Space Program, authorized in 1961 under the Housing and Home Finance Agency, provided for financial assistance to state and local governments to acquire and improve open areas. Since the inauguration in 1965 of the Land and Water Conservation Fund, federal grants for the acquisition and development of recreation areas have greatly accelerated. In connection with the use of these funds, every state has been required to complete and keep updated a comprehensive state outdoor-recreation plan.

Each of the 50 states has one or more agencies with a principal responsibility for outdoor recreation, and several other departments in each state contribute to recreation on a more limited basis. Appendix C contains a list for each state of the government agencies that have recognized outdoor recreation responsibilities. The agencies are classified two ways: those with principal responsibilities, and those with limited responsibilities. Some agencies that are not listed make supporting contributions to recreation, but their involvement is more difficult to define. In addition, Appendix D is a list of the state outdoor-recreation liaison offices for the 50 states.

ENABLING LEGISLATION

Legal powers are needed for the acquisition, development, and maintenance of recreation areas; for the construction and operation of buildings and facilities; for the purchase of supplies; and for the employment of personnel for leadership and other services. Through enabling legislation, states permit local governments to conduct recreation programs under the prescribed administrative arrangements.

The first enabling act of this kind was passed in 1915 in New Jersey, and by 1947, 34 states had such laws. The other states have passed recreation enabling acts since that year. Now all of the states allow local governments to sponsor recreation programs and manage areas and facilities. However, in many of the states enabling legislation is still inadequate.

STATE PARK SYSTEM

State parks rank high in the recreation concerns of the states. In practically all of the states the size of the state park system has grown tremendously during the past two decades. By the mid-1980s public visits to the 4600 state parks in the nation totaled more than 700 million annually.[1] Their total patronage ranked second only to municipal areas (Figure 12.1).

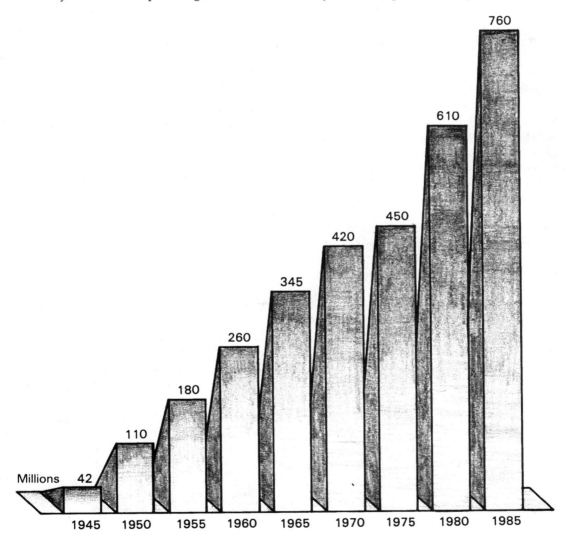

Figure 12.1. Trends in the number of visits to state parks in the United States. (Source: National Park Service, *Annual State Parks Statistics,* **1983)**

1. National Association of State Park Directors, *Annual Information Exchange,* St. Paul, Minnesota, 1983.

Illinois is credited with establishing the first state agency for managing state parks. In 1903 Illinois acquired Fort Massac as a state park. In 1909 the legislature appointed a commission to investigate the best method of managing state parks. In 1911 the nation's first state park system was established under the Illinois Park Commission. In 1919 the Illinois Division of Parks and Memorials was permanently established.

At the time of the first national conference on state parks in 1921 at Des Moines, Iowa, 19 states had at least one park. This conference marked the beginning of an organized park movement. National parks were proving successful, and the public was asking the first director of the National Park System, Stephen T. Mather, for more parks. Mather saw state administration as an alternative to protecting some of the prize areas until he could gather political and financial support to bring them into the national park system. As a result, Mather became a dynamic influence in organizing the 1921 state park conference.

Since its inception, the National Conference on State Parks (changed in 1974 to National Society for Park Resources) has been the foremost professional group in the advancement of our state park systems. This organization encourages states to seek suitable lands and adequate funds to improve their parks. It also encourages cooperation among the states and with the National Park Service.

A few states have found wealthy philanthropists to help finance their park systems. Some states have taken unique approaches, such as Colorado, where lottery money is used for state parks. Also, the federal government has been helpful by enabling states to acquire selected sites of public domain at a very low cost. Further, federal assistance programs have helped in the direct financing of areas and facilities.

Despite these forms of assistance, financing has been a traditional problem for state parks. Nonetheless, a few states have found bonding to be a solution. In 1960 New York passed a bond issue for $75 million to acquire state park and recreation lands. In succeeding years the totals grew in other states. California in 1964 approved bonds for $150 million, Michigan in 1968 for $100 million, and New Jersey in 1974 for $200 million. More recently, several other states, including Nevada, Nebraska, Kansas, and Minnesota, have passed park bond issues.

All of the 50 states now have state park systems. In some states the park agency is a separate department of government, whereas in other states it is a division within a larger department, usually the Department of Natural Resources.

State parks are most prevalent in states with large populations. Examples are Illinois, 276 parks; California, 245; and New York, 231. Alaska has the most space in its system with 3.3 million acres (1.3 million ha) in 92 separate areas. Figures 12.2 and 12.3 show the distributions of state park areas in California and Michigan, both of which have extensive park systems.

Following is a list of the kinds of areas and number of each kind in all of the states combined.[2]

2. National Association of State Park Directors, statistics provided to the National Park Service, 1983.

Kinds of Areas	Number
State parks	1,906
State natural areas	336
State recreation areas	754
State historic areas	551
Water-use areas	548
Environmental education areas	19
State trail systems	23
Miscellaneous areas	314
	4451

It is enlightening to note the many improved recreational facilities in the state parks:

Modern campsites	123,500
Primitive campsites	36,000
Lodge rooms	4600
Cabins and cottages	3900

Even though there are many systems that continue to provide only the "traditional" activities such as sightseeing, camping, hiking, and picnicking, several states now provide diverse opportunities for park patrons. Cultural arts, equestrian opportunities, areas for motorcyclists or snowmobilers, and resort areas are all facilities or program ideas that are no longer foreign to the state parks.

For the most part state parks are *intermediate* areas, as contrasted to wild areas and municipal areas. The parks take a variety of forms even within the same state, and they vary immensely among states. The particular kind of terrain that a state has, the extent of its scenery, and the significant cultural and historical sites strongly influence the size and characteristics of its park system.

More and more state park agencies are developing facilities and programs that cater to their own residents, and are finding that this approach attracts more visitors. Another factor contributing to this trend has been the increase in travel costs, which has caused many people to rediscover the beauties and wonders of their home state.

State park agencies are incurring the same financial difficulties that have hit other government programs. With continued reduction of general tax support it appears inevitable that fees and charges will play an increasing role in the operation of the state parks. Of the 50 states, 34 charge entrance fees. Financial pressure will surely cause some of the remaining states to inaugurate entrance fees.

STATE FISH AND WILDLIFE AGENCIES

Each of the 50 states has created either a separate department or a major division within a department for the management of fish and wildlife. The responsibilities of these agencies generally include: (1) propagating, protecting, and distributing game fish and game animals, (2) issuing licenses for hunting, fishing, and trapping, and enforcing the laws and regulations

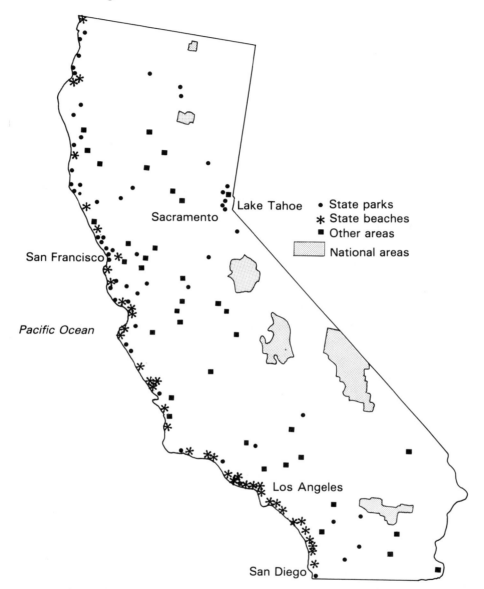

Figure 12.2. Locations of state parks, state beaches, and other areas in California's park system. The major national parks also are indicated. (Source: California State Parks Department)

pertaining to these activities, (3) managing a variety of wildlife areas, including reserves, sanctuaries, game farms, hatcheries, and special shooting grounds, and (4) assisting landowners, both private and public, with habitat management.

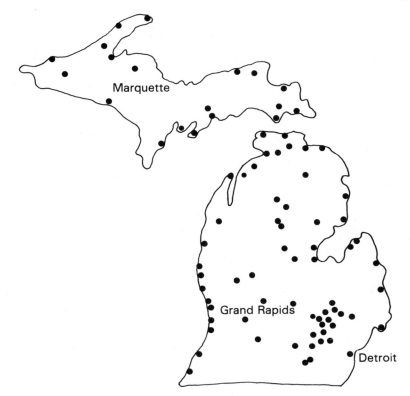

Figure 12.3. Locations of Michigan's state parks. (Source: Michigan State Park Department)

Each year more than 80 million people participate in hunting or fishing in the United States. Many others reap enjoyment from nonconsumptive wildlife activities such as photographers, artists, hikers, and sightseers. The states take in over $350 million annually for hunting and fishing licenses, and they reap another $80 million in excise taxes on hunting and fishing gear and ammunition. These sources provide the majority of the financing for state fish and wildlife management.[3]

Fish and wildlife agencies are faced with a number of difficult problems that will get worse instead of better and that will surely test the ability of management personnel. Among these problems are: (1) the steady reduction of natural habitat due to our increasing population and land development, (2) more participants in hunting and fishing due largely to greater population and more leisure time, (3) increased controversy between private landowners and sporting participants, (4) continued increases in the cost of fishing and hunting licenses and the resistance to this by the sporting participants, (5) the dilution of hunting and fishing experiences caused by the inability of the fish and wildlife base to meet the expectations of the increasing number of sporting participants.

3. Unpublished data provided by the U.S. Fish and Wildlife Service, 1984.

Suitable habitat for the natural reproduction of wildlife is absolutely essential to sound management. (U.S. Fish and Wildlife Service)

Additional information about fish and wildlife as a source of recreation appears in Chapter 10.

STATE FORESTS

State forest systems exist in practically all of the states, and there are more than 1000 state forest units with more than 24 million acres (9.7 million ha). Forests usually are administered by a separate state forest agency (department or division). However, in a few cases the forests are managed in combination with state parks or other state lands. State forest systems take on vastly different characteristics in the various states, and these differences are often influenced by: (1) the kind and abundance of forestland, (2) the extent to which the forestland of the state has been included in the national forest reserve, and (3) the philosophy of the particular state government toward state forests and how they should be used.

Typically, state forest systems are better developed in the eastern, southern, and midwestern states where the forests are of high quality and where a small amount of forestland is in the national forest reserve. Examples of the better state forest systems are Maine, Pennsylvania, Michigan, and Minnesota. In the western states, the great majority of the good forestland belongs to the U.S. Forest Service or a private landowner. In these states the forest systems are less prominent and are less developed for all forms of use, including recreation. The Great Plains states and the states in the southwest are very short on all kinds of forestland; therefore, state forests in these regions are meager or nonexistent. Table 12.3 provides information about selected state forest systems in the different regions of the United States.

This state-owned hardwood forest in Kentucky is an attractive area for both people and wildlife. (U.S. Fish and Wildlife Service)

Alaska has the largest forest program, with more than 5 million acres (2 million ha) followed by Michigan with 3.8 million acres (1.5 million ha), Minnesota with 3 million acres (1.2 million ha), and Pennsylvania and Washington with about 2 million acres (800,000 ha) each.[4]

In the future the amount of land in the state forest systems will likely remain nearly constant, because the states will not want to lose control of the forests they already have, and there will be very little opportunity to expand. As the nation continues to develop, these forest reserves will come under heavier demand for all uses, including recreation.

4. Unpublished data provided by the U.S. Forest Service, 1984.

**Table 12.3. Distribution of Selected State
Forestland in the United States by Region and State**

Region	State	Thousands of Acres (ha)		Percent of National Total
New England	Maine	912	(369)	4.8
Middle Atlantic	Pennsylvania	2000	(809)	10.6
	New York	724	(292)	3.8
South Atlantic	Florida	307	(124)	1.6
	Maryland	130	(53)	0.7
East South Central	Tennessee	164	(66)	0.9
East North Central	Michigan	3772	(1526)	20.0
	Wisconsin	446	(180)	2.4
West South Central	Arkansas	19	(8)	0.1
West North Central	Minnesota	3000	(1214)	15.9
	Missouri	195	(79)	1.0
Mountain	Utah	1440	(587)	7.6
	Idaho	491	(198)	2.6
	Montana	199	(80)	1.1
Pacific	Washington	1992	(806)	10.6
	Hawaii	808	(327)	4.3
	Oregon	785	(318)	4.2

Unpublished data from the U.S. Forest Service, 1983.

TOURISM

Every state and territory is actively involved in the development of tourist attractions and the promotion of tourism. In some localities tourism has become a significant industry with ever-greater potential for the future. From the states' point of view, there are two reasons for promoting tourism: (1) increased revenue from taxes, and (2) more jobs for the state's residents.

It has been calculated that on the average tourists in the United States spend $40 per person per day. Figuring a 5% sales tax, this would amount to about $2 per tourist per day in the form of tax revenue to the state. An additional tax benefit is that tourist developments improve property values and thereby increase the property tax base. New jobs grow out of the promotion and management of the tourist industry, and also the development of areas and facilities to accommodate the tourists.

Several states have a separate department of tourism, whereas in other states tourism is a division within a department, such as the Department of Commerce, the Department of Natural Resources, or the Department of Highways. In addition to the central office of tourism, states typically have regional offices and often local offices in outlying communities.

The states vary greatly in their emphasis on tourism and their tourist attractions. The state of Virginia, for example, has capitalized on its colonial history and early American culture. Utah emphasizes its diverse scenery. Minnesota has placed great emphasis on its 10,000 lakes and the water activities that these lakes accommodate. Florida has appealed to tourists on the basis of its warm climate and extensive coastline. Every state is unique in its philosophy toward tourism and its potential. Across the nation tourism is certainly a significant part of the total outdoor recreation scene, and it is one that outdoor recreation specialists should be vitally concerned with. (Also refer to Chapter 5.)

PUBLIC EDUCATION

There are several ways that the state education system becomes involved in outdoor recreation. Some information about the involvement is condensed here, but much more is said about the topic in Chapter 21. Also, there are sections about education in Chapters 4 and 16.

It used to be that education for leisure was largely unplanned and not considered a responsibility of the public schools. In light of vast changes in living conditions during recent decades, education for leisure has been recognized as an important function of education. "Worthy use of leisure" was one of the seven cardinal principles of education stated by the National Education Policies Commission as early as 1917. It was sometime later, however, before the schools showed much response. Nonetheless, eventually the development of skills, attitudes, and abilities in desirable recreation become accepted as important to modern education.

Another area of education involvement is the professional preparation of recreation and park leaders. More than 320 colleges and universities in the United States now offer curricula in the different specialized areas of recreation leadership. Also, many of the institutions conduct recreation surveys of various kinds, and some of the professors become involved in consultation work with communities and private enterprise.

The Cooperative Extension Services of the land-grant universities were among the first state agencies to provide leadership in recreation. The Extension Service has for a long time conducted recreation training courses, sponsored statewide conferences, provided consultation, and published resource materials. This agency also sponsors the 4-H program in each state.

STATE CONSULTATION SERVICES

Numerous states, including North Carolina, New Jersey, Michigan, and California, provide consultation to local governmental units and to nonprofit organizations and private individuals. The purpose is to help these organizations and individuals be more successful in their efforts to provide park and recreation services to the public. In addition, as mentioned above, consultation services are provided in many of the states through the Extension Service and by some university professors.

Also, every state has a specialist in the area of health, physical education, and recreation on the staff of the state department of education. Most states have more than one such staff member. Practically all of the work of these specialists is in connection with the public school programs.

STATE HIGHWAY AGENCY

Travel has become a popular recreational activity. In fact, travel for pleasure accounts for the greatest single recreation expenditure in America. Roads built and maintained under the authority of state highway agencies accommodate a significant portion of this travel.

In addition to the use of roads for pleasurable travel, many roads are built and maintained specifically for recreation access. Among these are roads to winter sports areas, water-recreation sites, hunting and fishing areas, and scenic drives. Also, the state highway agency is often involved in the construction of roads on state-owned lands—state parks, forests, and wildlife refuges. Further, many roadside parks are built and maintained in conjunction with state highways. Bike trails are also a responsibility of some highway agencies.

OTHER OUTDOOR RECREATION FUNCTIONS

In addition to the more paramount functions that have already been explained, other agencies of state government become involved in recreation in an indirect or secondary manner. Following are explanations of some of these functions.

Health Department

State health departments are required to establish and enforce health regulations in the various facilities and areas used by the public. These regulations cover such aspects as water quality, the licensing and monitoring of swimming pools, inspection of restaurants, and monitoring of commercial camp areas. The health department's functions with respect to recreation are only in the form of health controls.

Certain agencies of government have responsibilities for applying safe controls. (Utah State Department of Health)

Land Bank

Most states have a land-reserve system commonly called the state land bank. These are state-owned lands that have not been designated for particular uses. Such parcels are often leased to private individuals for grazing or other commercial use until such time that they are designated for public use. Much of the land bank serves an outdoor recreation function in the form of hunting and fishing, hiking, camping, or sightseeing. Its usefulness for recreation is determined largely by its natural characteristics and accessibility to the public.

Nature Preserves

A few states have nature preserves. Since they are *preserves*, the preservation concept is paramount in their management. This means rather strict controls and sometimes limited visitation. In some states the preserves are part of the state park system, whereas in other states they are attached to the fish and wildlife agency, or the state forest system.

Several states have undertaken an ecological inventory under the auspices of the heritage program of the Nature Conservancy (a nongovernment organization). The inventory helps to identify areas of unusual natural features and encourages the protection of these areas for either immediate or future use as nature preserves for the benefit of the public. Nature preserves are generally closed to camping, picnicking, horseback riding, or motor-vehicle use. Further, most of the preserves are relatively small areas containing fragile features of unusual significance.

State Historical Features

Memorials, museums, and identified historical sites are usually under the jurisdiction of an agency responsible for the state's heritage programs and the preservation of events and places of historical significance. The National Park Service, through its heritage preservation program, cooperates with states in this kind of effort, and usually the state's historical society also provides much assistance and support.

Trails, Rivers, and Parkways

Some states have become involved on a limited basis in the development of hiking trails, designated scenic rivers, and scenic parkways. These corridors are managed by a variety of agencies within the several states. Many recreation corridors offer much potential for additional development and use as the population increases and the recreation demand escalates.

LAND ACQUISITION METHODS

Before the middle of the 20th century, most state parks, forests, wildlife reserves, and related areas were acquired from one of the following sources: (1) original state holdings (lands of the colonies or territories that never belonged to the federal government), (2) tax-delinquent lands, (3) lands acquired by the state from the federal government, and (4) gifts of land or land purchased with gifts.

Some of these same methods are still used, but recently it has become more common to acquire such lands with funds from bonding, taxation, or federal matching grants. Numerous states have passed large bond issues, and others have designated special taxes as sources of capital in support of parks and related areas. Examples are the gasoline tax, alcoholic-beverage tax, and cigarette tax.

Several federal laws have enabled states as well as local governments to benefit from federal matching grants. The most prominent of these has been the Land and Water Conservation Fund, which originated in 1965 and has functioned continuously ever since. Many state and local recreation areas have been acquired and developed through this source of financial assistance.

In connection with outright purchases, there are several methods that should be considered. A *purchase leaseback* is a method by which a government agency can gain ownership of property, and then receive income by leasing it back to the seller or someone else. For example, the state might purchase land, and then lease back to the seller the mineral rights or the grazing rights. *Donations* of various kinds from philanthropists and corporations have helped state and local governments with the purchase of much land, whose cost otherwise would have been prohibitive. *Bargain sales* of distressed properties and tax-delinquent properties can sometimes help government agencies gain ownership at a low price. *Condemnation* (right of eminent domain) is a method that government agencies sometimes find necessary to purchase property the owner does not want to sell. Condemnation procedures enable the government to acquire the property at fair market value.

Even though outright purchase and clear ownership of land is usually preferred, there are other methods that are sometimes more feasible, even though they are restrictive in terms of long-range development and independent decision making. Among the alternatives are the following:

1. Several states are involved in the long-term leasing of private or federal land, and some of these lands are for recreational use. Louisiana, Georgia, and Mississippi, for example, lease much of their state-controlled fishing and hunting lands from forest-products companies. Also, the timber states of the Northeast and Northwest lease land from forest companies for scenic routes, campgrounds, and hunting and fishing rights-of-way.
2. Public-use easements allow states to maintain public access over private lands to land and water that otherwise would be inaccessible. In such cases, the state either makes a cash payment or performs services in return, such as maintaining fences, building and maintaining roads, and financing flood-control measures.
3. Scenic easements, in which the landowner conveys some or all development rights, are sold to the states by private individuals and companies. Sometimes they are given as public relations gestures and without remuneration.

It is a fact that the acquisition of land by states has become increasingly difficult and will be even more so in the future. This is because most of the unproductive lands are already in public ownership or under public use through an ownership alternative, while the more productive land is under heavy demand for other uses and is producing a profit. The cost has escalated to the point that it has become almost prohibitive for the states to buy additional land. This points out the importance of managers being both alert and thorough in their efforts to retain lands that are especially suited for recreation. (The information in the preceding section also applies to the local government level.)

SAMPLE ORGANIZATIONAL PLANS

Figure 12.4 shows the organizational diagram for the state agency in Michigan that has the principal responsibility for outdoor recreation. Figure 12.5 shows the same information for California. The following narrative is a description of the organization plan for Utah.

Utah has three governmental units that are primarily concerned with outdoor recreation at the state level. They are the Division of Parks and Recreation, the Division of Wildlife Resources, and the Outdoor Recreation Agency. These units function as divisions of the state Department of Natural Resources.

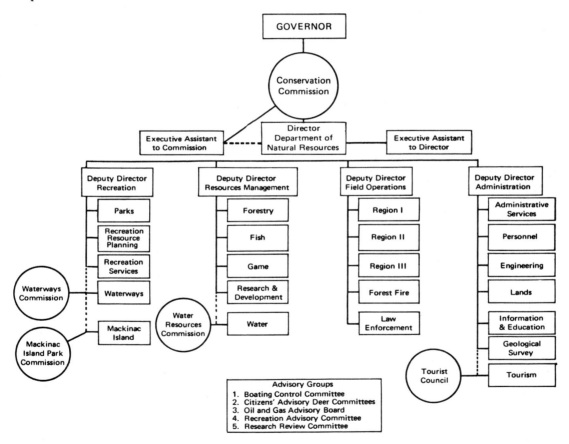

Figure 12.4. State organization chart for the Michigan Department of Natural Resources. (Source: Michigan Department of Natural Resources)

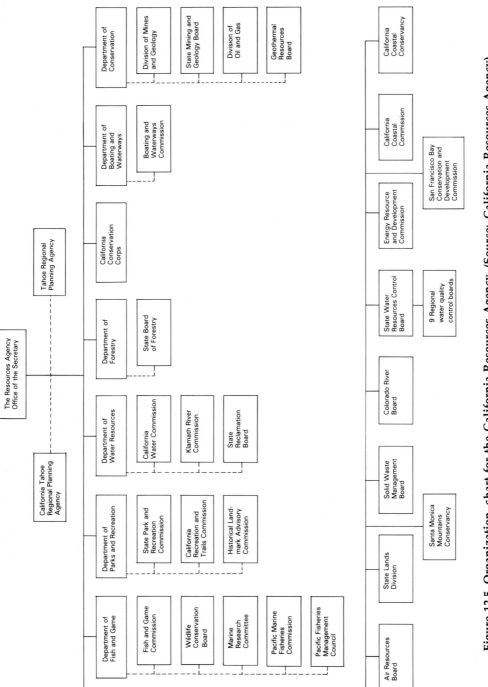

Figure 12.5. Organization chart for the California Resources Agency. (Source: California Resources Agency)

There are several state agencies that make a secondary contribution in outdoor recreation, including the Division of State Lands, the Utah Travel Council, and the state Department of Transportation.

The Division of Parks and Recreation functions under the direction of the Board of Parks and Recreation. It has responsibility for the acquisition, planning, protection, development, operation, and maintenance of park areas and facilities in such manner as may be authorized by the policies and regulations of the board. It is also responsible for the administration of the 1959 Boating Act and the Off-Road Vehicle Act.

The board receives its income from a state appropriation and from user and entrance fees to state parks. The board has developed a long-range program with the full cooperation of all 29 counties, many independent organizations, and federal and state agencies. The plan includes historical sites and trails, areas of important scientific interest, and areas of unusual scenery and topography. These areas range from alpine peaks in the north to semidesert in the south.

The Division of Wildlife Resources is charged with the responsibility to protect, propagate, manage, and distribute game animals, game birds, and game fish. It manages game land and fisheries and issues licenses for hunting, fishing, and trapping. Policies of the division are developed by the Wildlife Board and the Board of Big-Game Control. The division is supported by fees, fines, sales (principally of beaver furs), state appropriations, and federal grants. The Wildlife Board has the power to enter into cooperative agreements with federal agencies, other states, educational institutions, municipalities, corporations, clubs, landowners, associations, and private individuals in the interest of fish or game management. The division owns 12 developed waterfowl marshes and 4 undeveloped areas in addition to several tracts maintained for upland game and big game. There are 12 state fish hatcheries and 2 game-bird farms. The division owns or otherwise controls approximately 350,000 acres (140,000 ha).

The Utah Outdoor Recreation Agency, established in 1968, directs the state's outdoor-recreation planning and administers the provisions of the Federal Land and Water Conservation Fund Act at the state level. An eight-member committee provides advisory services to the agency. The committee is composed of the state planning coordinator, the executive director of the Utah Association of Cities, the executive director of the Utah State Association of Counties, and the directors of the Division of Wildlife Resources, Division of Parks and Recreation, Division of Industrial Promotion, Division of Travel Development, and State Department of Highways.

The Division of State Lands has responsibility for the direction, management, and control of all state land, except land used or set apart for specific public purposes or occupied by public buildings. It may sell or lease state land for the best interests of the state. It has the power to acquire land, which it may transfer to the State Board of Parks and Recreation. There is reserved to the public the right to hunt, trap, and fish on state land.

The Utah Travel Council encourages and assists in the coordination of activities of persons, firms, associations, corporations, and governmental agencies engaged in publicizing, developing, and promoting tourism.

The State Road Commission is authorized to build and maintain roads and parking spaces to serve areas used for salt-flat races, ski meets, and other activities, when such areas are near a designated highway. Roadside parks, scenic turnouts, and highway-rest facilities are maintained by the commission along interstate and primary road systems throughout the state.

Discussion Questions

1.   How does the Tenth Amendment of the Constitution affect the sponsorship and management of outdoor recreation at the state level?
2.   More states are emphasizing state park facilities and programs that cater to their own residents. What has caused this and what are the results?
3.   Each of the 50 states has an agency for the management of fish and wildlife. What are the basic responsibilities of such an agency?
4.   Today, federal, state, and local governments are extensively involved in outdoor recreation. Originally this was a function of private initiative. In your opinion, who should be the major sponsor of public recreation—the private sector or government agencies? Support your point of view.
5.   How do you feel about user fees in state parks? If user fees are required, do you feel there may come a time when state parks will be limited primarily to the rich and middle class? Support your position.
6.   What are the more crucial problems presently facing the state fish and wildlife agencies? What are the possible solutions to these problems?
7.   What will be the main problems the state forest systems will face in the future, and what are some of the possible solutions?

Recommended Readings

Brockman, Frank, et al. *Recreation Use of Wild Lands.* New York: McGraw Hill, 1979. Chapter 11.

Bureau of Land Management. *Public Land Statistics–1984.* Washington, D.C.: U.S. Department of the Interior.

Chubb, Michael, and Holly R. Chubb. *One-Third of Our Time.* New York: John Wiley & Sons, 1981. Chapter 14.

Jensen, Clayne R. "Roles of State Agencies in Outdoor Recreation." Brigham Young University, 1984.

Knudson, Douglas M. *Outdoor Recreation.* New York: Macmillan Publishing Co., 1984. Chapters 12, 13.

National Park Service. *State Recreation Fee Report–1983.* Washington, D.C.: U.S. Department of the Interior. Includes statistics about state park systems in the U.S.

"States Rights and Other Myths." *Time,* 9 February 1981, p. 94.

U.S. Department of the Interior. *National Urban Recreation Study: Executive Report.* Washington, D.C.: 1978.

Walters, William C. "State Park Systems." *Park and Recreation,* August 1980, p. 44.

CHAPTER 13

Local Government Participation

Municipal recreation areas and programs have a long but spotty history in America. The Pilgrims brought with them the concept of the commons (or village green), and fortunately, this was not one of the many Old World customs that was rejected by the colonists. Initially, the village commons was multifunctional and served important purposes for social, economic, and military activities. The Boston Commons, established in 1634, is recognized as the first city park in the United States.

William Penn's plan for Philadelphia, presented in 1682, provided for five community squares to be used for public affairs. It also included provisions for timber reserves to be maintained within the city. For every 5 acres (2 ha) of timber cut, 1 acre (0.4 ha) was to remain.

In 1839 Fort Dearborne park was developed in Chicago, and in 1853, New York City acquired 700 acres (280 ha) for Central Park. A decade later Philadelphia acquired the site for Fairmont Park, and before 1890 numerous other park sites were purchased by the larger cities.

The first municipal park-management agency was established in 1882 to administer the Boston Metropolitan Park System. In 1895 the first recorded county park system was begun in Essex County, New Jersey. In 1903, in Chicago, a $5 million bond issue for the support of parks passed with an overwhelming 83% of the vote. The money was used for developing small parks in the crowded neighborhoods of South Chicago.

By the turn of the century, eastern cities had become innovative in the development of parks and recreation, and in 1904 the innovation moved west when Los Angeles established a Board of Playground Commissioners. The commissioners immediately took an aggressive approach toward developing a system of city parks and playgrounds. Another important milestone occurred in 1906 when New Jersey passed the first enabling legislation authorizing local governments to provide recreation programs under a variety of organizational structures. As an outgrowth of these early developments, the municipal park and recreation movement continued to gain momentum until eventually thousands of local governments were providing public recreation services.

Fortunately, the National Association of Counties strongly supports adequate parks and open spaces in and near cities, as indicated by this quote from the association:

> We cannot afford to abuse our natural environment, scar our scenic wonders, and destroy our historic sites. Densely populated metropolitan areas should not be devoid of open spaces and parks. If all Americans are to enjoy their precious heritage, every community must initiate a park and recreation program.

The League of Cities is equally supportive, and it has stressed that the responsibility for providing local park and recreation opportunities must be fixed, and the essential tools—money, leadership, facilities, equipment, and supplies—must be provided systematically and continuously. It further stresses that a citizens' council representing the various interested groups should be active, and that a board or commission officially responsible for direction of a public recreation and park system should be established. As part of the complete community plan, voluntary and private agencies can provide additional opportunities for individual and group recreation.

RECREATIONAL GROUPS

Numerous groups and agencies participate in meeting the various recreational interests of the people in a community. These groups and agencies generally can be classified as private, voluntary, commercial, or public.

Private groups, such as clubs and fraternal, social, and church organizations, are ordinarily financed by the membership. In every community of much size a variety of clubs offer recreational opportunities, usually restricted to members of the private group. They include golf clubs, tennis clubs, yacht or sailing clubs, chess and bridge groups, athletic or sports clubs, and a host of others. These organizations serve a valuable purpose in rounding out the recreational opportunities and serving special interests.

Voluntary agencies are usually service oriented, and in many cases they are geared toward serving youth. Ordinarily they are supported by membership fees, which sometimes are supplemented by community funds and donations. Included in this group are the Boy Scouts, Girl Scouts, YMCA and YWCA, and certain church-sponsored programs. Usually recreational service is only one of the purposes of these organizations, while education and social adjustment programs are also important.

Commercial recreation is sponsored primarily for gaining a profit. Unfortunately, some commercial forms of leisure activities are undesirable to the development of individuals and to the welfare of the community, but they continue because people support them and they are profitable. On the other hand, there are many commercial enterprises that offer desirable forms of recreation and contribute to the overall balance of recreational opportunities.

Public programs are usually under the sponsorship of the municipal recreation and park department. The kinds of areas ordinarily managed by the local recreation agency include parks, playgrounds, athletic fields, recreation buildings, golf courses, community centers, cultural centers, aquatic facilities, and sometimes zoos, gardens, museums, camp areas, waterfront areas, and winter-sport areas.

Activities sponsored by local recreation agencies make an important contribution to outdoor recreation. (National Park Service, photo by Jack Rottier)

LEGAL ASPECTS

The legal basis for local-government participation in the field of parks, recreation, and open-space preservation is provided by state enabling laws, local charters, and ordinances. These legal instruments authorize local governments to establish agencies to operate park and recreation systems. They also permit local governments to acquire land and spend funds for buildings and programs.

Enabling Legislation

Before a local government may provide recreation services it must be empowered by the state to do so. State enabling laws authorize localities to establish, maintain, and operate park and recreation systems. These laws specifically empower local governments to acquire and develop necessary land and facilities, to create an agency to administer parks and recreation, and to finance the system. In some states, such as Utah and California, the state law specifies the exact organization that must administer the program. Other states allow great flexibility on this matter. For example, the North Carolina enabling statute, applicable to cities, counties, and towns, provides that local park and recreation systems may be conducted just as any other function of the local government. However, local elected officials are authorized to create recreation boards or commissions by ordinance or resolution if such appears to be in the best interest of the people.

Some state enabling laws empower school districts, municipalities, counties, and other units of local government to join with one another to establish, own, operate, and maintain park and recreation systems. For example, the Michigan law permits any two or more units of local government to join forces in providing recreation. The expenses of the joint operation are apportioned among the participating agencies. The laws of Idaho, Oregon and several other states permit the same arrangements. The Iowa law authorizes the creation of county conservation boards and permits them to cooperate with appropriate state and federal agencies, as well as cities, towns, villages, or other county conservation boards to establish and maintain park and recreation systems.

It is essential that local government officials be familiar with the state recreation and park enabling laws so that they may effectively operate local programs within the provisions of the law.

Charters and Ordinances

Cities and counties operating under *home-rule charters* have the authority to establish and operate park and recreation programs under their general power to promote the welfare, safety, health, peace, and morals of citizens (in other words, the police power). Charter provisions related to parks and recreation usually call for the creation of a park and recreation department and provide for the appointment of a director and often for the formation of an advisory board. The charter usually outlines the duties of both the director and the board.

A local government not acting under home rule may, by use of an ordinance, create a park and recreation department and an administrative board. The ordinance usually indicates the manner in which the park and recreation director and the administrative board are selected and outlines their duties.

The following are specific features that are essential in an ordinance or charter used to establish a recreation and parks department:

1. Name of the department
2. Designation of the managing authority (board, commission, council)
3. Outline of the powers, responsibilities, and duties of the managing authority
4. Authorization and provisions for hiring and supervising personnel
5. Authorization for cooperative agreements and relationships with other agencies
6. Authorization for the acquisition and management of areas and facilities
7. Authorization for methods of financing the department
8. Description of limitations in programming, if any
9. Description of the nature of records and reports to be kept by the department

MANAGING AUTHORITY

There are several kinds of managing authority for parks and recreation at the local level. Most often these functions are administered under a single department–a department of parks and recreation. But sometimes they are administered separately–a recreation department and a parks department. In certain cases the county government is the administering agency, and in a few areas special recreation and parks districts have been formed. Occasionally school districts manage local recreation programs as a function supplementary to public education.

According to the National Recreation and Park Association about 75% of the local recreation and park programs are sponsored by city (or town) governments. Counties sponsor about 10%, special districts 8%, schools 2%, and multijurisdiction and other arrangements are involved in 5%.

No one authority is the best suited in all cases. The circumstances of the particular locality influence which administrative arrangement is best. At least the following should be considered: (1) which options are available under the state's enabling legislation, (2) which managing authority would result in the best financial support, (3) which organizational option would be preferred by the public, and (4) which arrangement would be the best in terms of the availability of areas and facilities.

Combined Department

As stated earlier, this is by far the most common of the different forms of organization, and it is increasing the fastest. This approach is especially popular among small and medium-sized communities. Perhaps the strongest points in favor of a combined department are: (1) efficiency, (2) coordination of the use of areas and facilities, and (3) less potential conflict between park management and recreation programming. Overall, the combined department usually results in financial savings and better services. Communities that have combined departments are Fresno, California; Lincoln, Nebraska; Ashville, North Carolina; Provo, Utah; Syracuse, New York; and Fort Worth, Texas.

Separate Departments

A few cities maintain separate park and recreation departments, each with its own administrator and separate but related responsibilities. In some cases the two departments are under the control of the same governing board, and sometimes they have separate boards. The advocates of separation claim that (1) more direct and expedient attention will be given to both aspects by having separate administrators reporting directly to the municipal officials, and (2) a combined system in a large city is too unwieldy to be administered by one department.

The disadvantages of separate departments are (1) they generally compete for budgetary support, (2) the leaders of the two departments are sometimes unwilling or unable to coordinate effectively, and (3) the departments are often (but not always) more expensive to operate because of some duplication of equipment and personnel.

In the early development of the recreation movement, city parks preceded government interest in recreation programming. When recreation programs did develop, this function was usually added to either the parks department or the school system. A few separate departments for this purpose were established, however, and some of them have continued to exist. In Cincinnati, Ohio, for example, the officials believe that the duties of each department are sufficiently diverse to justify separation.

Another kind of separation is illustrated in Monroe County, New York, where the county coordinates major land purchases and leaves programming, which varies considerably in different localities, in the hands of the communities. This approach would require close cooperation between the county and the cities.

County Administration

The most frequent involvement of county government is in the provision of physical facilities such as parks, golf courses, playgrounds, athletic fields, and recreation centers. In counties where many people live outside the boundaries of the incorporated communities (a large rural or semirural population) it is important that the county government provide recreation opportunities.

In Iowa the legislature has delegated to the board of supervisors of each county the responsibility for appointing a five-member conservation board to handle land purchases and development. The board of supervisors can levy a tax of not more than 1 mill annually on the assessed valuation of taxable real and personal property. Almost all of Iowa's 99 counties have been involved in the purchase and development of parklands under the authority of this state law.

Special Districts

In some states special park districts are legal political subdivisions and consequently are separate from any city or county government. Such special districts are regional complements to local recreation and park systems. They are permitted to levy taxes and issue bonds. Special districts have some unique characteristics:

1. They are usually organized to perform a single function.
2. They can enter into contracts and own and dispose of property.
3. They have fiscal and administrative independence from other political subdivisions.
4. They are frequently exempt from the tax and debt limits imposed on city and county governments.

One example of such a district is the North Jefco Metropolitan Recreation and Park District, an 84-square-mile (218-km²) rural area in the northeast corner of Jefferson County, Colorado. This agency is the sole sponsor of the public recreation and park program in that area. The Cleveland Metropolitan Park District carries on a different kind of function. It is concerned primarily with land acquisition, development and maintenance, and not with recreation programming.

School Administration of Recreation

School systems usually have extensive indoor and outdoor facilities. By putting these facilities to effective use, they need not be duplicated in the form of community centers, playgrounds, and athletic fields. Further, school personnel represent a valuable source of leadership that can be available during the summer, and on a limited basis during the school year.

School districts, however, usually are not able to sponsor a balanced recreation and park program because, in addition to the recreation facilities and activities that are closely related to the school program, a complete recreation program involves nonschool facilities–golf courses, aquatic areas, picnic facilities, and sometimes such specialized accommodations as boat-launching ramps, winter-sports areas, zoos, aquariums, and museums. In other words, even though many aspects of recreation are closely aligned with the school functions, some are not. A school district dedicated to doing a good job of sponsoring recreation can make a significant contribution, and this can be an effective approach, provided that local agencies supplement the school's recreation efforts.

Community-school cooperation is generally encouraged by planners, and this approach has been advanced under the *park-school* and *community-school* concepts. The park-school is a facility that consists of one or more school buildings constructed in conjunction with a park site. The community-school is a modern concept in which the school is conceived of as an agency that makes maximum use of its facilities and other resources to serve the expanded needs of the community, including recreational activities.

The concept of community-school cooperation was given impetus in 1911 when the National Education Association formally approved the use of schools and grounds for recreation. Also in 1911, Wisconsin authorized a tax by school districts for recreation facilities and programs. Milwaukee quickly took advantage of this authorization and began building a successful school-related recreation program. Fortunately, the concept of community-school cooperation has spread across the county, but as yet, this approach has nowhere near reached its potential.

Joint planning is necessary for cooperative school and community use of areas and facilities to be effective. This means that each recreation and education facility or area should be planned and constructed for joint use by the two agencies. Further, a detailed cooperative management agreement is essential to the success of such an approach.

Richmond Case Study on Organization

Richmond, Virginia, covers 62 square miles (161 km²) and has a population of 278,000. The Richmond Department of Recreation and Parks has an annual operating budget of about $6 million and a capital budget of about $1 million. The department employs 232 full-time and 72 seasonal maintenance people, 29 professional administrators, 149 full-time recreation leaders, and 432 seasonal recreation leaders. The park system contains 26 parks with 1247 acres (505 ha), 62 playfields with 340 acres (137 ha) and 539 acres (218 ha) of parks on school sites. In addition, the department administers 7 cemeteries, 33 gymnasiums, and 37 community centers.

The director of the Department of Recreation and Parks is appointed by the city manager. The department staff, regulated by civil service, is divided into four units (Figure 13.1 shows the organizational pattern in detail):

1. The Administrative Division maintains all records and controls pertaining to the budget, payroll, personnel, purchases and contracts, inventories, public information, and services to the operating bureaus.
2. The Bureau of Recreation is responsible for planning, organizing, promoting, and conducting recreation programs. It also provides services and coordination to civic groups and organizations.

People need attractive open spaces close to home where nature can provide refreshment and renewal. (National Park Service)

3. The Bureau of Parks maintains, constructs, and polices all recreation areas and facilities and has charge of the street-tree program. It also schedules the use of areas and facilities for which permits are issued.
4. The Bureau of Cemeteries maintains, operates, and polices municipal cemeteries.

To assist the department in its service to the community, the city charter specifies the establishment of a Recreation and Parks Advisory Board. It consists of nine members, of whom one must be a member of the school board appointed by the school board and one must be a member of the Planning Commission appointed by the commission. The remaining seven are appointed by the City Council for terms of three years.

Maricopa County Case Study on Organization

Maricopa County, located in southwestern Arizona, has a population of approximately 1.5 million and a land area of 9226 square miles (23,902 km²). Phoenix, with a population of

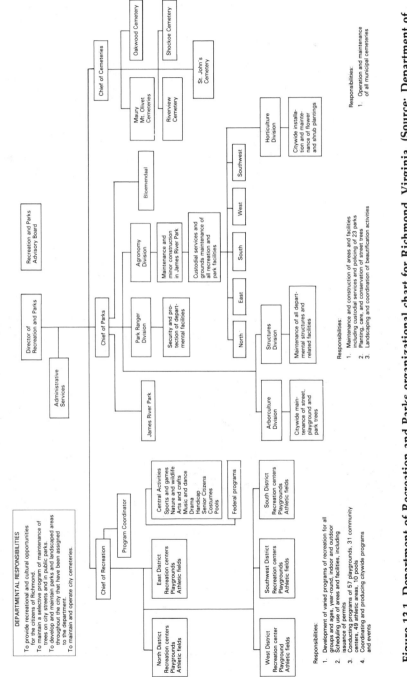

Figure 13.1. Department of Recreation and Parks organizational chart for Richmond, Virginia. (Source: Department of Recreation and Parks, Richmond, Virginia)

about 1 million, is the county seat and the largest incorporated area. The Maricopa County Park and Recreation Department is responsible for the management of 93,546 acres (37,858 ha) of parkland consisting of nine regional and five community park sites, plus approximately 10,000 acres (4,000 ha) of land within the various flood-detention basins.

The department operates golf courses, lake programs, shooting ranges (including one of the largest range facilities in the country), archery ranges and field courses, a nature center, hiking and horse trails, picnic areas, horse arenas, a community center, and other park-related facilities. In addition, a wide variety of recreation programs are offered at 22 sites throughout the county, 9 of which are year-round.

The annual operating budget for the 1982–83 fiscal year was $3.89 million, and there is a full-time staff of 109 employees. The department is presently in an active park-development phase and is cooperating with various city, county, state, and federal agencies in an effort to expand the open space and recreation opportunities available to the residents of Maricopa County (Figure 13.2).

FINANCING

To a large degree the availability of funds determines the scope and quality of the recreation opportunities that can be offered. Funds are needed to acquire areas and facilities, employ qualified leaders, purchase supplies and equipment, and maintain the parks, community centers, and other sites that are essential for a well-rounded program.

Financial needs are normally of two kinds: *current operating costs* and *capital outlay*. Current operating funds usually come from appropriations, special recreation taxes, and user fees. Many of the funds for capital outlay are provided from bond issues, special assessments, donations, and government grants.

Appropriated Funds

Tax funds may be appropriated for the support of recreation and parks on the same basis as other services of local government. Decisions about the allocation of such funds are made by the elected government officials and are not voted on directly by members of the public. This is the most widely used method of financing local park and recreation systems, and other methods are usually considered supplementary to it.

The amount of appropriated funds obtained each year depends to a large extent on the ability of the administrator to win approval of a program by those who determine the allocation of funds. If the budget proposal is well prepared and justified, and if the proper groundwork is laid with the governing authorities, the budget proposal will likely succeed. How well the funds are used in providing important services will usually have a strong influence on the amount of funding in the future.

Special Taxes

In accordance with the enabling legislation in some states a local government can levy a special property tax for the financing of parks and recreation. Certain states allow municipal officials to decide whether to levy such a tax, whereas in other states it must be approved by

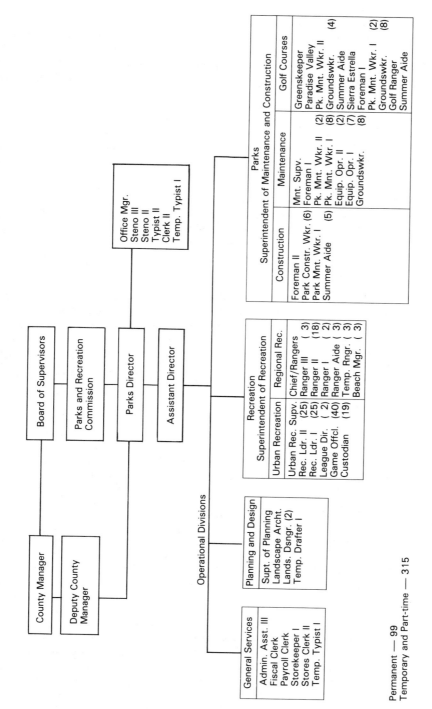

Figure 13.2. Maricopa County Parks and Recreation Department organizational chart. (Source: Maricopa County [Arizona] Parks and Recreation Department)

the local voters. Money obtained by this method can be spent only for the purposes for which it is raised. The special tax is expressed in terms of a number of mills per dollar, or cents per $100 of assessed valuation of real property. In some states the legislation places a ceiling on the tax, whereas in other states this is left to the discretion of local officials.

There are numerous examples where special taxes are levied on the sale of particular products. Examples include a cigarette tax, alcoholic beverage tax, or local excise tax.

Fees and Charges

Two approaches can be taken on fees and charges: (1) the use of special fees not related to recreation, such as revenue from parking meters, or from rented or leased property; (2) admission fees from recreation facilities such as golf courses, swimming pools, museums, zoos, and aquariums, and profits from concessions.

It is important to realize that public park and recreation programs can no more be self-supporting than can public education. But the collection of certain fees can be justified, and this reduces the amount needed from other sources.

Bond Issues

Local governments have the authority to bond to finance capital acquisitions and improvements, including park areas and recreation facilities. The issuing of bonds must be approved by the voters of the municipality, and a limit to bond indebtedness is placed by state law. The issuing of bonds is actually a form of borrowing, and it is not a substitute for appropriated funds or revenue. The bonds must be paid off over a period of years, much the same as a mortgage on a home. The sale of bonds is often used in connection with the acquisition and development of large park areas and the construction of such facilities as swimming pools, community centers, and golf courses.

Special Assessments

Special assessments are sometimes used to finance improvements. This amounts to a special fee assessed against property owners in the area who benefit from the improvements. This method is not used frequently, but under certain circumstances it is a desirable approach. The positive feature is that it places the cost on those who benefit. If this becomes a common method of financing, however, the poor areas of the community, which often need facilities and improvements, are generally neglected.

Land dedication assessments (a form of special assessment) are sometimes used in connection with new residential developments. This approach is explained later in this chapter in the section on planning and zoning.

Donations and Gifts

Donations, gifts, and bequests can be important forms of income. Philanthropic organizations and civic-minded individuals have, in some cases, been generous with park and recreation departments. In most communities, however, this is not a significant source of funding, and it is usually not a regular source. This form of financing is often in the form of real property gifted for a park or a historic or cultural site, or funds for a community center or a boys' or girls' club. In their long-range plans, recreation leaders should be alert to the possibility of this source of financial assistance.

Government Grants

The federal government, and in some cases state agencies, can grant money to local governments for approved park and recreation projects. By far the most prominent source of grant money in recent years has been the Land and Water Conservation Fund, which is now administered by the National Park Service. This source was instituted in 1965, and since then a large number of local sites have been purchased and developed with government aid that could never have been acquired otherwise. In recent years, however, funding from this source has been reduced significantly because of reductions in government spending.

Milwaukee County Case Study on Finance

The 242 square miles (627 km²) of Milwaukee County are totally incorporated into 19 cities and villages with a population of about 1 million. The Milwaukee County Park System provides facilities in all 19 municipalities except Milwaukee itself.

The Parks Department has an annual budget that exceeds $40 million, with approximately 41.5% of the budget derived from revenues from fees and concession receipts, and a minor amount from federal and state grants. The principal source of financing for the department, however, is the annual appropriation by the County Board of Supervisors.

It is an established policy of the county to avail itself of grants, either federal or state, for capital improvements. Because these sources of funding have diminished, the county has had to rely more on its own tax base. In recent years, greater emphasis has been given to user fees to obtain revenue to meet operating costs. Few facilities are self-sustaining, the exceptions being the major golf courses, the Lake Michigan Marina and the Milwaukee County Stadium. Collectively, these facilities return approximately $6 million annually.

Cleveland Metropolitan Park District Case Study on Finance

The funds available to the Cleveland Metropolitan Park District consist of receipts from taxes levied on all real estate within the district and miscellaneous receipts from district operations. These funds are paid into the office of the Cuyahoga County Treasurer, who acts as treasurer for the Park District. Approximately 70% of Park District funds are derived from taxes and 30% from golf course fees, concessions, the Metropark Zoo, property rentals, and state sales tax returned for local-government use.

The law permits the district to levy a general tax, not in excess of 0.05 mill, with the exact amount to be determined by the Budget Commission. Any additional tax funds requested by the district must be approved by a majority of the votes cast in the district at a general election.

For several years the Budget Commission has allocated 0.05 mill of general taxes to the district. But, this tax yield has not been adequate to acquire, develop, and maintain the park system. Consequently, the Park District has asked and received voter approval for additional tax funds. The currently approved levy rates are 0.35 mill until 31 December 1984, then 0.41

Providing an adequate recreation environment near large cities will be a tremendous challenge in the future. (National Park Service)

mill until 31 December 1988, and 0.50 mill until 31 December 1990. These levies are for land acquisition, capital development, and continued maintenance and operation of the parks. Approximately $14 million per year is produced by the tax levies, and about $4 million per year from fees, concessions, and rentals.

Financial Curtailment

Local governments vary greatly in expenditure per capita for recreation. Many such agencies have experienced economic cutbacks during the past decade. A high percentage have experienced hiring freezes and temporary moratoriums on land acquisition and development. Also, surveys have indicated that the urgency to provide leisure services has declined with greater competition now for city tax dollars. The tax rebellion, spearheaded by Proposition 13 in California, has caused a general trimming of budgets among tax-supported agencies.

The most obvious negative result of financial curtailment is a reduction in recreation opportunities as measured by quantitative indicators; however, the quality of the supply may also be diluted, and this is less obvious. It is not the amount of open space per se that determines the recreational health of a community. Where that space is located, the programs conducted on it, the responsiveness of personnel who manage it, and the physical conditions of the space itself are more significant factors. It may be generalized that qualitatively, public recreation and park facilities are less well maintained, less well supervised, and less used under conditions of financial restraint.

PROVIDING AREAS AND FACILITIES

One of the major responsibilities of a park and recreation department, and one that has long-term impact, is the planning and development of areas and facilities. In a large system the following are usually planned and developed:

Large multipurpose parks
Small neighborhood parks and playgrounds
Community centers and clubhouses
Athletic and playfields
Golf courses
Forest or nature reserves
Zoos, aquariums and gardens
Museums and galleries
Street and area beautification
Facilities for the performing arts
Swimming facilities and waterfront areas

Contrary to the beliefs of many, American cities and towns are not blessed with an abundance of park and recreation space. By European standards, where numerous cities are

Too much living in too little space always results in poverty of one kind or another. (National Recreation and Park Association)

spotted with attractive parks and beautiful city squares, many American cities are impoverished in this regard. The land-acquisition programs of the faster-growing cities–Los Angeles, Orlando, Salt Lake City, Dallas, Denver, Houston, and Phoenix–are not keeping pace with their rapid growth.

Land is being consumed for subdivisions at an alarming rate. For example, the open-space report published by Fairfax County, Virginia, indicates that if the present rate of space consumption of 188 acres (76 ha) per 1000 new residents continues for two more decades, the entire county will be consumed by urban sprawl. Many other areas across the nation are in the same fix.

The price of land, especially that of attractive sites, increases each year. The Department of the Interior publication *Recreation Land Price Escalation* reports that values generally are rising throughout the nation at the rate of 5% to 10% annually, and the value of land suitable for recreation is increasing at a higher rate.

Riding trails in nearby localities provide one kind of attractive recreational opportunity. (National Park Service)

Land for public use is obtained in a variety of ways, and resourceful public officials will thoroughly explore the various possibilities. The most successful and frequent method is negotiation with the owner on outright *purchase*. In some cases payments can be spread over several years on a real-estate contract.

Occasionally it is necessary for local governments to exercise the right of *eminent domain*, which is a provision in the law allowing agencies of government to condemn privately owned land and acquire it for the public use at the appraised market value. This right is usually viewed as a last resort, but sometimes it is needed as a protective measure on behalf of the public.

The *donation* of land is another form by which local governments acquire land that is particularly suitable for park and recreation developments. Some departments have been able to acquire a large portion of their parkland by this method. Where the enabling laws permit, local officials have sometimes enacted subdivision regulations demanding dedication of park sites in new subdivisions, or a cash payment per lot in lieu thereof.

In addition to acquiring complete title to a tract of land, some local officials have experimented with buying less than full title rights through the use of *scenic easements, right-of-way accesses*, and *conservation easements*. Also, property and facilities are sometimes *leased* by local governments on long-term agreements. In the final section of the preceding chapter, additional information is provided about the different methods of acquiring the use of outdoor-recreation lands. Much of that information applies to municipalities and counties as well as states.

Westchester County Case Study on Land Acquisition

Westchester County, New York, has developed a land-acquisition policy worthy of note. The policy is based on (1) anticipated population and characteristics by the year 2000, (2) the number of acres required to meet the recreational needs according to a standard of 12 acres (4.9 ha) per 1000 projected population; and (3) general recognition of areas of great need. The land-acquisition policy is composed of the following elements:

1. Recognition that the management of lands, facilities, and programs to serve recreational interests and cultural needs is a governmental responsibility.
2. Recognition that all four levels of government–municipal, county, state, and federal– must cooperate to serve recreational interests.
3. Division of responsibility among all four levels of government according to types of resources and programs. Municipalities and school districts are responsible for acquiring lands, developing facilities, and operating programs at neighborhood and community levels. Tot lots, horticultural displays, and local passive parks are also provided by this level of government. The county supplements local actions by providing large parks for visitors from throughout the country.

By the year 2000, 18,000 acres (7300 ha) will be needed to provide recreation for an anticipated population of 1.5 million in the county. This will be an increase of about 5000 acres (2000 ha) over the amount available in 1984. Because 80% of the people will live in the southern part of the county, emphasis will be placed on acquiring lands conveniently accessible to this population concentration. The policy stresses the need to buy land early, before it is developed for other uses. In addition to user-oriented facilities to serve the southern half of the county, prime targets of purchase include waterfront lands, natural conservation areas, and scenic areas throughout the county.

Discrepancies in Supply

There is considerable evidence that the recreation supply in *inner-city areas* is inferior in regard to safety, maintenance, accessibility, pollution, and qualifications of its staff. Further, the historic gap in federal funding for capital outlay (acquiring and developing areas) but not for operating expenses (staffing and maintaining) has contributed toward local recreation systems being overbuilt but undermaintained and understaffed.

Along this same line, it's important to recognize that acreage statistics can be misleading. Not all acreage within a community counts the same in terms of meeting recreational needs. Several factors influence this, such as terrain, location as related to neighborhood population, quality of development and maintenance, placement of facilities, and programmed activities offered for the public.

Another matter pertaining to the supply of recreational resources concerns the *information gap*. Often there is not a systematic source of information concerning the availability of recreation opportunities. This means that a recreation area goes unused.

This is an example of a well-developed waterway through a city. (San Antonio Convention and Visitors Bureau)

Special Outdoor Areas

There are certain kinds of outdoor recreation opportunities that have not been developed to anywhere near their potential. Among these are the following:

1. *Rivers and streams through cities.* The recreational development and beautification of streams often have far more potential than the present level of development.
2. *Waterfront facilities.* Many cities are located on the banks of lakes or large rivers. This offers the potential for the development of recreational sites along the waterfront. In many cases more could be done in this regard.
3. *Nature paths.* Many people like to walk for exercise and pleasure. Walking can be even more pleasurable along a scenic route with interesting natural features.
4. *Jogging and bike trails.* Both jogging and cycling are excellent for physical fitness. Safety, attractiveness and convenience are important characteristics of jogging and bike paths.
5. *Skating ponds.* Skating is often feasible on lakes in or near city parks. Also, many communities have diked areas in city parks to be flooded for skating in the winter.
6. *Cross-country ski routes.* Routes for skiing close to city parks are likely possibilities in many locations where the snow depth is sufficient.

These kinds of areas (in addition to those traditionally provided by cities—golf courses, tennis courts, swimming pools, athletic fields, and playgrounds) can round out the outdoor recreational opportunities that ought to be available at the local level.

Discussion Questions

1. List the different kinds of managing authority for parks and recreation at the local level. What are the merits of each one?
2. How can a school system aid in the sponsorship of a park and recreation program? What are its limitations?
3. Explain the park-school and community-school concepts and how they can contribute to recreation.
4. What are bond issues and how have they been useful in the development of community park and recreation facilities? Do you know of a community that has recently approved bonding for parks and recreation?
5. What federal fund is the most prominent source of assistance for community parks and recreation areas? How can a community obtain financial assistance from this source?
6. What is the right of eminent domain? How has it been applied on occasions for acquiring park and recreational areas?
7. What are some examples of special taxes assessed for financing local parks and recreation? Are there any special taxes levied in your community for this purpose? What are they?
8. Do you feel community recreation centers should be financed through user fees rather than appropriated funds? Why or why not?

Recommended Readings

"Applications of Park Management: Information Systems." *Leisure Sciences*, Vol. 3, No. 1, p. 25.

Bloomfield, Howard. "Green Survival: A Program for Our Cities." *American Forests*, February 1980, p. 47.

Chubb, Michael, and Holly R. Chubb. *One-Third of Our Time*. New York: John Wiley & Sons, 1981. Chapter 13.

"Comeback for Cities, Woes for Suburbs." *U.S. News and World Report*, 24 March 1980, p. 54.

"Dimensions of Municipal Leisure Service Delivery." *Leisure Sciences*, Vol. 2, No. 1, p. 39.

Doell, Charles E., and Louis F. Twardzik. *Elements of Park and Recreation Administration*, 4th ed. Minneapolis, Minnesota: Burgess Publishing Co., 1979.

Howard, Dennis R., and John L. Compton. *Financing, Managing, and Marketing Recreation and Park Resources*. Philadelphia: William C. Brown Publishers, 1980. Chapter 2.

Kershow, Warren W. *Land Acquisition*. Reston, Virginia: National Recreation and Park Association, 1975.

Kraus, Richard. "The Changing Face of Urban Recreation and Parks: Implications for Professional Preparation." *Journal of Physical Education, Recreation and Dance*, March 1981, p. 20.

Meyer, Ann. "Revitalizing Urban Parks: It's Time to Restore Our Older City Parks." *Sierra Club Bulletin*, November–December 1982, p. 38.

Miller, Tyler. *Living in the Environment*, 2nd ed. Belmont, California: Wadsworth Publishing Co., 1979. Chapter 11.

"Municipal Recreation and Park Standards in the U.S., Central Cities, and Suburbs." *Leisure Sciences*, Vol. 2, No. 3, p. 277.

National League of Cities. *Case Studies in Urban Recreation: A Policy Guide for Local Officials*. Washington, D.C.: 1980.

Stark, Stephen L., and Bobby E. Parker, "A Viable Partnership: Community Education and Parks and Recreation." *Journal of Physical Education, Recreation and Dance*, March 1981, p. 17.

"Urban Recreation Research: An Overview." *Leisure Sciences*, Vol. 3, No. 1, p. 25.

U.S. Department of the Interior. *Handbook for Recreation Planning and Activity*. Washington, D.C.: 1980.

U.S. Department of the Interior. *National Urban Recreation Study: Summary Report*. Washington, D.C.: 1978.

U.S. Department of the Interior. *National Urban Recreation Study: Technical Reports* (TR1–13). Washington, D.C.: 1978.

PART III

The Private Sector

CHAPTER 14

Private, Commercial, and Industrial Recreation

Of the 2.3 billion acres (930 million ha) in the United States about 60% is in private ownership. Some of the privately owned lands are managed as outdoor recreation enterprises, but most are managed for the production of commodities of one sort or another. Often the land serves secondary uses, of which one is recreation.

As a general pattern, privately owned resources are close to cities, whereas large government expanses are far away from cities. Therefore, the distribution of the privately owned resources contributes significantly to the geographic balance of available recreation opportunities.

There is more recreation by members of the public on privately owned areas than on federal and state lands combined. Municipal recreation areas rank second to privately owned resources in recreational use.

Recreation on private land is a privilege, not a legal right. In the future this source of recreation will be ever more essential if the needs of the people are to be met.

Private individuals or families own the majority of the guest ranches, campgrounds, shooting preserves, hunting and fishing camps, equestrian areas, boating facilities, and vacation farms and ranches. Companies or corporations own most of the recreation resorts, resort hotels, commercial beaches, ski areas, theme parks and private forestlands. Membership clubs or quasi-public agencies own most of the yacht and boating clubs, golf and tennis clubs, and organization camps and waterfront areas.

Most private recreation facilities are located totally on privately owned lands. Some areas, such as many ski resorts, are partly on private lands and partly on lands leased from government agencies. A few of the enterprises are completely on acreage that is leased.

Even though much information is unavailable about private-sector outdoor recreation, the following is clear: (1) the private sector makes a significant contribution to the recreation opportunities of the American people, (2) the demand for recreation on private resources is increasing at a steady rate, and (3) private landowners are becoming more aware of opportunities to increase their income and at the same time provide a public service by developing the recreational potential.

Recreation on private lands can be logically divided into two general categories: (1) that occurring on areas that are unimproved for recreation, where recreation is a secondary use (such as agricultural and grazing areas that are used for hunting and fishing in season), and (2) that occurring on areas especially improved to accommodate recreationists.

PRIVATE LANDS UNIMPROVED FOR RECREATION

Examples of privately owned lands unimproved for recreation are forestlands owned by individuals or companies, private lakes and streams, and farms or grazing lands where people hunt, fish, or ride horses.

Of the 1.4 billion acres (570 million ha) in private ownership it is estimated that more than 50% has some recreation value, and most of it is available to the public for recreation under prescribed conditions. Probably small-game hunting is the most frequent activity on unimproved private areas, and the majority of this kind of hunting is done on private lands. Also a great amount of fishing is done on private unimproved resources.

The main problem associated with recreational use of private lands is maintaining good relations between landowners and recreationists. As the demand for recreation increases, people should become more and more cognizant of the landowners' problem, which derives from public use of the land.

RECREATION ON PRIVATELY OWNED IMPROVED AREAS

Many private areas are designed and managed primarily for recreationists. Some of these are *commercial* enterprises operated to produce profit. Examples include commercial camps and picnic grounds, resorts, dude ranches, commercial beaches, golf courses, ski areas, shooting preserves, riding stables, outfitting and excursion services, and theme parks.

Another group of privately owned operations is noncommercial. This group includes *private clubs* where the facilities and services are available primarily to club members, but sometimes to others for a fee. It also includes facilities and services available through *voluntary and quasi-public organizations* such as the YMCA, YWCA, Boy Scouts of America, and other agencies that own facilities and perform services for a segment of the public. Charges often are involved, but profit making is not the main reason for the organization's existence.

There is still a third category of nonpublic sponsorship that involves *corporations* or *companies*. Many industrial organizations own property available for public recreation. Perhaps the best example is industrial tree farms. Some wood and paper companies own large tracts of forestlands that are used extensively by the public under regulated conditions. The water

When one looks across open space, it is not only the boundaries that disappear, but also the thought of being bounded. (U.S. Department of the Interior, photo by Richard Frear)

resources of many hydroelectric power plants are available for public recreation. Many industrial organizations provide recreational areas, facilities, and programs for their employees, and sometimes these facilities are available to other segments of the public, either free or at a nominal fee. Further, large corporations and companies sometimes donate land for public use, and the use often involves recreation.

When comparing outdoor recreation on private land to that on public land, there are both advantages and disadvantages to be considered. Among the advantages of private areas are these:

1. Recreation areas provided by private enterprise handle relatively large numbers of people on small acreage. They receive high-intensity use by recreationists.
2. Private recreation can meet needs of targeted audiences instead of having to serve the general public.
3. Private recreation providers may be able to adapt to trends faster than public agencies.
4. Private recreation contributes to the tax base instead of depleting it.
5. Private recreation contributes to employment from sources not involving government funds.

Some of the disadvantages of private enterprise include these:

1. Private agencies may be too concerned with profit at the expense of recreation experiences.
2. Private agencies may discriminate economically by charging higher fees than many members of the public can afford.
3. Liability often discourages private owners.
4. Problems such as regulations, vandalism, trespassing and liability sometimes discourage private owners.

There is additional information in Chapters 5, 16, and 20 on the issues related to privately sponsored outdoor recreation.

INDUSTRIAL ORGANIZATIONS

It is often thought that industries and large companies are incompatible with the conservation of natural resources and the provision of outdoor opportunities. Such is not always the case. There are many corporations and companies that use their land and financial resources to enhance public opportunities. Often, there are benefits for the companies as well, such as improved public relations and tax savings. This section includes only a sampling of the kinds of corporations and companies involved in outdoor recreation.

Industrial or Private Forestlands

According to the U.S. Forest Service an estimated 7.8 million private forest landowners hold 333 million acres (135 million ha) of forestland in the United States. These owners are diverse in legal status (individuals, families, corporations) and economic circumstance.

Privately owned timberlands serve as an important recreational outlet for thousands of Americans each year. These forests are fine examples of private enterprise serving the expanding recreational need of the public. In such forests there is rarely a waiting line for picnic tables, fireplaces, and campsites. Most of the facilities are free or cost very little, and some of the forests are located within a short driving distance of cities.

Private groups and industrial organizations own some of the finest forests in our land, and many of them are available for public use. (U.S. Department of Agriculture, photo by Sherm Finch)

Interesting facts concerning recreation facilities on private forestlands were uncovered in a 1982 survey by the American Forest Institute:

1. A total of 61.4 million acres (24.9 million ha) of privately owned forestland is open to the public for recreation.
2. Within these lands there are more than 86,000 miles (139,000 km) of privately owned roads open to visitors.
3. An additional 700,000 acres (280,000 ha) of natural and artificial lakes are available to the public.

This willingness to welcome the public is not new. Hunters have enjoyed these privileges for many years. However, the corporate owners of these lands seem to have sensed the pressing demands being made on municipalities and other public agencies for more parks; consequently, recreational opportunities on privately owned forests have been greatly expanded in recent years. In effect, the actions of the owners have reduced the burdens on tax-supported park and recreation agencies.

A recent survey report from the American Forest Products Industry shows that each year nearly 2 million people use industrial forestlands for various forms of recreation. It was found that more than 90% of the forestland owned by companies is open for certain forms of public recreation. The most frequent recreational activities are hunting and fishing, but picnicking, camping, backpacking and skiing are also popular.

Company-owned forests contain many free public parks. Most of the parks are equipped with campsites, picnic grounds, water, sanitary facilities, and playgrounds. Some have covered shelters, boat ramps, and swimming areas. A few have provisions for skiing and ice-skating. About 20% of the companies included in the survey had plans to develop additional recreational accommodations soon. The following are a few examples:

Bullwater's Southern Paper Corporation has set aside several outstanding scenic areas for public enjoyment and some small "pocket" wilderness areas. Four trails totaling 29 miles (47 km) in the pocket wilderness areas of Tennessee and North Carolina have been placed in the national trails system.

The Texas Forestry Association, working with six forest product companies and several individual landowners, established a system of woodland trails throughout eastern Texas.

St. Regis Paper Company, which has large forest holdings, makes almost all of its forestland available to recreationists for dispersed activities including hunting, fishing, hiking, and camping.

Weyerhaeuser Corporation claims that 90% of its extensive tree-farm lands are open to the public for a variety of recreational pursuits. It hires a staff of wildlife and conservation specialists to help manage the resources. Also, this corporation leases large tracts of land to hunting clubs, owns a ski resort in Vermont, and maintains hiking and cross-country ski trails in many of its locations.

The International Paper Company has as one of its five goals the enhancement of recreational opportunities and an increase in the production of game and other wildlife. It controls more than 15 million acres (6.1 million ha) of forestland.

One might wonder why companies, corporations, and individual landowners would make their areas available for public recreation. Perhaps the main reason is a spirit of public service, but there are also some concrete benefits to the landowners, such as the following:

1. Protection from the right of eminent domain is one advantage. Forestland is often prime property, and sometimes it needs to be transferred from private to public ownership to serve the broad interests of the public. Under the right of eminent domain, public agencies can do this. In fact, it has been done in numerous cases. For example, the 65,000-acre (26,000-ha) Redwood National Park was purchased from corporate landowners under the provisions of eminent domain. Also, 40,000-acre (16,000-ha) Voyageurs National Park in Minnesota was acquired from corporate owners in the early 1970s. The same is true of much of the property presently in the Allagash Scenic Riverway, and there are numerous other examples. When the forestlands are already serving the public, they are less likely to be condemned and acquired for public use.
2. Forestland owners generally feel that people will take better care of the property if they are permitted to use it in a positive atmosphere, and if they are welcome guests of a company that cares about the public. This helps with fire control, litter, theft, damage to equipment, and other such problems.
3. There is at least a small economic factor, because in some cases fees are charged and this is another source of revenue.

Construction, maintenance, and repairs cost when the public uses an area. Legal liability is also a problem. Landowners never seem to be totally free of possible liability suits in case of injury or damage to a visitor. To avoid the liability, some companies lease the recreational right of their land to a government agency. For example, the states of Vermont, Maine, and New Hampshire have leased public snowmobiling rights from forest companies that own large tracts of land. This shifts the burden of possible liability from the private landowners to the state, and the state is less susceptible to liability suits. This arrangement also has been successful in other states and with activities other than snowmobiling.

Hydroelectric Projects

All privately owned hydroelectric projects must be licensed by the Federal Energy Regulatory Commission. This commission now requires that public recreation opportunities be made available on these projects. This requirement has significantly increased recreational opportunities, because it has caused the development of a variety of water-related public recreation facilities on privately owned lands. Often, activities on these lands are free, but sometimes minimal fees are charged to help offset the cost of developing and maintaining the recreational facilities.

There are now almost 600 private hydroelectric projects that provide recreation. In addition, the development of these sites has sometimes fostered the growth of recreational facilities on adjacent properties, and this has further expanded the overall supply of public recreation. Boating of different varieties, waterskiing, picnicking, and fishing are the major forms of recreation on hydroelectric projects.

Fishing on privately owned lakes is becoming more prevalent. It offers improved opportunities for both sports enthusiasts and landowners. (Soil Conservation Service, photo by P.N. Jensen)

The recreational requirements of the Energy Regulatory Commission are unlikely to change. Therefore, this source of recreation will steadily increase with the development of additional hydroelectric facilities. Several such facilities are completed in the United States each year.

Industrial Employee Recreation

Many industrial firms provide recreational areas for their employees. Sometimes the areas are adjacent to the industrial plant, and in other cases they are far from the plant location. The areas vary considerably in size, ranging from only a few acres to more than 1000 acres (400 ha). According to the National Employee Services Recreation Association, the most popular activity on industrial recreation sites is picnicking, followed by outdoor games, swimming, fishing, hunting, camping, and golf. Employee recreation is one of the fringe benefits offered by many industrial establishments.

The National Employee Services Recreation Association (see description in Chapter 15) is a professional service organization that has a membership of about 1900 companies. The membership consists of a variety of enterprises, including some of the largest corporations in the nation, and also some small ones. The association is primarily a resource organization to enhance recreation opportunities for company employees. It emphasizes the advantages of increased productivity and reduced absenteeism, along with better employee-employer relations and improved community relations.

Land Donations

During the past decade the Nature Conservancy (see Chapter 15) has received more than 250,000 acres (101,000 ha) of land donated by companies, corporations, and individuals for the purpose of preservation and conservation of natural areas. The largest of these gifts was 49,000 acres (19,800 ha) of the Great Dismal Swamp in Virginia, which was donated by the Union Camp Corporation to be used as a national wildlife refuge. Weyerhauser Corporation donated another 11,000 acres (4500 ha) of the swamp. Also, the International Paper Company donated Genesis Point in Georgia (26,000 acres, or 11,000 ha).

The most prominent motivating factor behind gifts of this kind is to save taxes–income tax or capital-gains tax or both. Charitable gifts such as these sometimes actually save the donor money because of the impact of the tax write-off. But in most cases such gifts are made for a combination of reasons, two of which are public benefit and tax savings.

COMMERCIAL ENTERPRISES

Commercial enterprises originate and continue primarily for profit. This does not mean that profit is the only benefit or the only reason for their existence. In the field of recreation, commercial enterprise offers a dimension that is truly important to the public.

Commercial Campgrounds

Camp areas are of several kinds, many publicly owned and free of charge. The particular camp areas discussed here are privately owned commercial campgrounds, where travelers can pitch tents or park trailers and campers for a fee. These commercial areas vary from small roadside camping spaces to large and elaborate camping resorts. The well-developed areas offer such extras as swimming, tennis, children's play equipment and horseback riding. A few include adjacent waterfront areas for boating, canoeing, and waterskiing. Also, private campgrounds often have concessions, such as a general store, game room, snack bar or family restaurant, and a stock of outdoor supplies for sale. Many of the campgrounds are franchised with such companies as Kampgrounds of America (KOA), United Camps, Safari Camps, Kamp Dakota, and Yogi Bear's Jellystone Parks.

Recently, the National Campground Owners Association completed a national economic survey that reveals a basically healthy camping industry. The survey convincingly shows that private enterprise is providing this form of outdoor recreation for Americans in a cost-efficient way. The association estimates that the private campground industry satisfies about 75% of the nation's camping needs. The private campgrounds now provide the public with more than 1.2 million individual campsites in about 13,000 campground areas. (There are 5500 public campgrounds, which provide 350,000 individual campsites).

The privately owned campgrounds have gained rapidly in size, as indicated by the fact that during the past ten years the average number of campsites per campground has increased from 41 to 98. Further, the survey showed that in 1982, 32% of the existing private campgrounds planned to expand within the next 12 months. Private campgrounds have been the fastest growing and the most profitable segment of private outdoor recreation during recent years, and the future still looks bright.

Ski Areas

Snow skiing, one of the most fascinating of outdoor sports, has grown tremendously during the last two decades. Formerly considered a sport for only the young and the daring, it is now enjoyed increasingly by adults and many older folks. An estimated 10 million people ski in the United States, according to the National Ski Association of America, and this number is increasing by 12% to 15% annually. There are more than 700 ski areas in the nation. Of these, 25% are rather limited and are situated on less than 50 acres (20 ha); however, 20% of the areas are on large tracts of more than 500 acres (200 ha). Though the most popular activity is skiing, other activities are tobogganing, sledding, cross-country touring, sightseeing, snowmobiling, ice-skating, and swimming (where heated pools are available). Many ski areas have become year-round resorts, providing different activities each season of the year.

Ski slopes in the United States vary greatly in terms of terrain. Most of the ski areas in the West are in the high country of the Rocky Mountains, the Cascade Range, or the Sierra Nevada. The slopes of the East and Midwest are on gentler terrain and at lower elevations. Many of our ski slopes are on Forest Service land and are subject to Forest Service policies and supervision.

Even though skiing has become very popular and is increasing relatively fast, ski areas have traditionally not been good financial investments for people who need a quick return. Most ski areas require a large capital outlay, and they have provided little, if any, financial return for the investors during the early years of operation. The operating costs are high, including very expensive liability insurance. But generally the well-located and well-managed areas have been sound financial ventures over the long term.

Resorts

Recreation resorts are among the most widespread of all privately owned recreation enterprises. They range from waterfront hotels, cottages, and motels, usually situated on small sites and providing such activities as swimming and sunbathing, to huge sprawling complexes on sites of 1000 acres (390 ha) or more, where even the most difficult-to-please guest can find interesting activities.

More than 50% of the resorts in the U.S. are owned by companies or corporations. About 40% are owned by individuals or families, and the remaining resorts are owned by private clubs, partnerships, or nonprofit groups. They range in size from less than 1 acre (0.4 ha) to more than 30,000 acres (12,000 ha). Two-thirds of them are 50 acres (20 ha) or more. According to the Department of the Interior, about three-fourths of the land included in resorts is managed especially for recreational purposes. Water sports are by far the most popular activities at resorts, with swimming being the favorite single activity. Fishing, boating, golf, and waterskiing follow in that order.

The resort movement in the United States started in the 1920s when continental travel began to boom. The movement has gradually gained momentum since then, even though there have been some irregularities in the upward trend. Because of the greater mobility and

"Give me health and a day. He is only rich who owns the day."–**Ralph Waldo Emerson**
(Sundance Ski Corporation, Provo, Utah)

the increased income of the American people, recreation resorts are still gaining in popularity.
The success of resorts relates closely to tourism, and the future of tourism seems bright.

Theme Parks

There are over 30 major theme parks and many smaller ones, virtually all of which have
been developed since World War II. The first famous one was Disneyland in Los Angeles,

which opened in 1955. Since then a number of other major parks have been developed, including Six Flags, which has three locations in the Southwest; Sea World in San Diego and Orlando, Florida; Cedar Point in Sandusky, Ohio; King's Island in Cincinnati; Disneyworld in Orlando; King's Dominion in Richmond, Virginia; and Safari Land near San Diego.

Many of the major theme parks and some of the others, including some zoos, are being developed on large expanses of land, with open spaces and natural features included in the overall design. This contributes to more of an outdoor-recreation experience instead of purely entertainment. Some of the parks have a tremendous number of visitors. The greatest number is at Disneyworld—more than 15 million annually.

Commercial Beaches

In many sections of the United States most of the shoreline has been developed with private homes and thus is not available for public recreation. In other sections, hotels, motels, and private clubs have acquired long stretches of private waterfront. State, national, and local parks are the major providers of opportunities for the general public to enjoy the unique qualities of shorelines.

Fortunately, there are many commercial beaches that supplement the opportunities provided on public beaches. This source of recreation will find little room for expansion in the future, however, because practically all of the desirable beach property is already committed. Where such property is available, competition is keen and the price of ownership high.

The majority of the commercial beaches are located on the coastlines of our surrounding oceans, but there are some beaches on the shores of rivers, lakes, and bays. Commercial beaches vary greatly in size and quality—from less than 1 acre (0.4 ha) to more than 1600 acres (650 ha). Most commercial beaches are in the East and Midwest, though a few are in the Southwest and West Coast.

Guest Ranches and Vacation Farms

A number of ranches in the United States provide vacation facilities for guests. Many of the ranches are primarily working ranches where the guests (dudes) provide additional revenue and their entertainment is closely related to the work of the ranch. Conversely, at some ranches the fees paid by the guests are the major source of income. Here the care of ranch livestock and the production of crops are of secondary interest. Nearly half of the identified dude ranches in the United States consist of 1000 acres (400 ha) or more. Some are less than 100 acres (40 ha), while others approach 100,000 acres (40,000 ha) in size. The most popular activity on dude ranches is horseback riding, followed by fishing, swimming, and hunting. Other popular activities are cookouts, hiking, camping, boating, pack trips and trail rides. Most dude ranches are in the West, and most of them are especially designed to have a western atmosphere.

Many city dwellers are sampling another very different way of life through farm vacations. A number of farm families are making their homes and their meadows, woods, streams, and ponds available to paying guests. These guests often bring with them new interests and new ideas welcomed by the farm families. Guests benefit from the fresh air, from the country scenery, from being free to walk virtually wherever they choose with no restrictions, and from helping with farm chores. Among the more popular activities are fishing, swimming, boating, hunting, hiking, horseback riding, picnicking, camping, cookouts, and lawn games. Some vacation farms include golf courses, swimming pools, and other specialized facilities. Vacation farms are on the increase and are becoming more popular among city dwellers.

Many rural landowners permit public access (sometimes for a fee) to farm ponds and lakes for fishing and other water-based activities. Further, hunting is often permitted for a fee on croplands, pasture, and woodlands.

Ranch and farm vacations, as well as hunting and fishing on private lands, will probably increase at a steady rate as we become more urbanized and people try to keep in touch with nature and with our agrarian heritage.

Outfitting and Excursion Services

Specialized camps for hunters and anglers are provided in various localities throughout the nation. Naturally these camps are concentrated in the areas where game and fish are abundant. Typically, the camps consist of a relatively small acreage where living accommodations and certain recreational facilities are provided and are located next to large tracts of public or private land open to hunting and fishing. Usually the services provided include outfitting and guided trips. In the case of guided hunts, the game is often guaranteed. In addition to hunting and fishing, some outfitters and guides provide river float trips, canoe trips, and wilderness pack trips on horseback for those interested in unusual scenery and high adventure.

Outfitting for hunting and fishing has built-in limitations for the future, due to expanding urbanization, diminishing wildlife, and more regulatory controls. Conversely, sightseeing and adventure excursions have a bright future, because these activities do not depend on the consumption of natural resources.

PRIVATE CLUBS

Private clubs are often overlooked in the analysis of recreation opportunities. Yet private clubs provide recreation for a large portion of the population. Private clubs range from hobby groups or special-interest organizations to membership clubs available only to the affluent. Only three kinds of recreation clubs are discussed here.

Golf Courses

There are thousands of golf courses in the United States, and more are built each year. Many of the courses are public, but most are privately owned. Most of the private courses are available only to members of the club, though others are managed as commercial operations–open to the public for a fee. Even though golf courses are everywhere and golf receives much exposure, still only 1 of every 12 people in the United States play golf. Even so, golf is among the fastest-growing outdoor sports, increasing about 10% annually. Overall, golf courses provide a significant amount of recreation opportunity.

The future for private and commercial golf courses seems promising because (1) golf courses are outdoor areas that can be constructed as needed on sites close to the population,

Many wilderness guides now offer air travel into the backcountry. (U.S. Fish and Wildlife Service, photo by J. Malcolm Greany)

and (2) trends are favorable toward increased participation in golf—more leisure time, more urbanization and higher per capita income.

Boating Clubs

Pleasure boats are no longer solely the playthings of the well-to-do. The greater ability of people to own boats of all kinds is reflected in the increasing number of yacht, sailing, and boating clubs and in their growing memberships.

There are more than 1350 identified yacht and sailing clubs in the United States. These clubs vary from the long-established ones to those so new they are still seeking sites on which to build docks and clubhouses. Typically, yacht and sailing clubs do not occupy large acreages. Approximately 65% of the clubs occupy 5 acres (2 ha) or less, and only 15% occupy 15 acres (6 ha) or more. The most popular activities at these clubs are boating and boat racing, including sailing. Other popular activities are swimming, fishing, tennis, and social activities. Many of the clubs are commercial operations, where their facilities are available to nonmembers at established fees. Yacht clubs, along with boating in general, continue to increase, and many new clubs are being added each year. One of the great restricting factors in the establishment of new clubs is the declining availability of suitable areas.

Boat clubs differ from yacht clubs chiefly in the kind of boats that the members own. Outboard-motor boats of various sizes and the small inboard boats are the principal types found in boat clubs, while large sailboats and inboard cruisers are typical at yacht clubs. There are more than 600 identified boat clubs in the United States. Like yacht clubs, these organizations are located on small acreages. They serve primarily their own members, but in many cases services are available to nonmembers at a fee. Popular activities at boat clubs in addition to boating are waterskiing, swimming, camping, and picnicking.

An exclusive yacht club on the Florida coast. (Miami Recreation and Park Department)

Shooting Preserves

There are more than 1600 shooting preserves in the United States. Not all of these are operated on a commercial basis. Many are private clubs, while others function solely for the personal pleasure of the landowners and invited guests.

No two shooting preserves are alike. Some are resorts with many attractive features and comforts. Other preserves simply provide daily fee hunting with no frills. Charges vary, depending on the facilities and services offered. Some preserves charge by the number of birds or game animals bagged, others by the hour or day, and others by still different methods.

More than half of the shooting preserves are owned by individuals or families. About 20% are owned by private clubs and 20% by companies or corporations. The remaining preserves are owned by partnerships or through some other arrangement. Numerous preserves offer a wide variety of both land-based and water-based recreation. Though hunting is the predominant activity, it is often combined with fishing. Other activities are camping, hiking, horseback riding, trap, skeet and target shooting, and dog training.

"In terms of conventional physics, the grouse represents only a millionth of either the mass or the energy of an acre. Yet subtract grouse and the acre loses much of its character."–Aldo Leopold, *A Sand County Almanac,* Ballantine Books, New York, p. 146. (U.S. Fish and Wildlife Service, photo by Daniel H. Chapman)

TECHNICAL AND FINANCIAL ASSISTANCE

Various sources provide private citizens and enterprises with technical or financial assistance. At the state level, technical assistance may be obtained from faculty members of many state universities and colleges, and from some private universities. Such faculty members are typically assigned to the university's department of recreation, but in certain cases assistance might be sought from specialists in business, economics, or site planning. The land-grant university in each state includes the Extension Service. In a number of states, the Extension Service has on its staff one or more recreation specialists who work for the promotion and planning of better recreation opportunities. The park and recreation departments of some states provide consultation services to private enterprise.

Besides the assistance available at the state level, federal agencies provide certain kinds of assistance. The Small Business Administration will provide low-interest loans for private projects that qualify. The Area Redevelopment Administration will provide low-interest loans and, in some cases, grants of money for private projects located in designated districts. Through the Rural Area Development program (administered through the Extension Service) technical assistance is available on any approved project that contributes to rural development. Programs of the Agricultural Stabilization and Conservation Service and the Soil Conservation Service provide technical and financial assistance for approved projects.

The best source of information within each state is the state outdoor recreation liaison officer (each state has one), who is responsible for coordinating federal and state programs in outdoor recreation. A list of the liaison offices appears in Appendix D.

ASSOCIATIONS AND SOCIETIES

There are numerous associations and societies (private groups) that influence the use of resources. In general, the wise use of natural resources is the rallying point of groups such as the American Rivers Conservation Council, Boone and Crockett Club, Conservation Foundation, Izaak Walton League of America, National Wildlife Federation, Sierra Club, and Friends of the Earth. Groups such as these play important roles in educating the public about land-use priorities and conservation.

Other organizations representing millions of recreation enthusiasts frequently appeal to more specific interests like hiking, boating, or camping. It is within these groups that pressures for trails, wild and scenic rivers, or better campgrounds arise and eventually influence decisions and policies. Active in this area are groups such as the Appalachian Mountain Club, Brooks Bird Club, Bass Anglers Society, Sport Fishing Institute, and the American Camping Association. Specific information is given about many of these organizations in Chapter 15.

Discussion Questions

1. How have privately owned recreation areas reduced the recreation load of municipalities and other public agencies? How has it affected the tax burden of communities?
2. How do the various associations and societies, such as the Sierra Club and the American Camping Association, contribute to outdoor recreation?

3.   What kind of technical and financial assistance can a private citizen or enterprise find at the state and federal levels?

4.   What are some examples of privately owned (or commercial) outdoor-recreation enterprises in your community? Do you feel they are well managed? Do they serve a useful purpose? How could they be improved?

5.   The demand for recreation on private lands is increasing at a steady rate. What are some of the reasons for this and what are the potential problems associated with it?

6.   Recently the National Campground Owners Association completed a survey that showed that private enterprise is meeting approximately 75% of the nation's camping needs in a cost-efficient way. Considering the economic advantages of this to the public in general, should we promote the idea of turning over many of the government areas and facilities to the private sector? Why or why not?

Recommended Readings

Ball, Armand B., and Beverly H. Ball. *Basic Camp Management.* Bradford Woods, Indiana: American Camping Association, 1979.

Brockman, Frank, et al. *Recreation Use of Wild Lands,* 3rd ed. New York: McGraw Hill, 1979. Chapter 12.

Chubb, Michael, and Holly R. Chubb. *One-Third of Our Time.* New York: John Wiley & Sons, 1981. Chapter 12.

Epperson, Arlin F. *Private and Commercial Recreation.* New York: John Wiley & Sons, 1977.

Holecek, Donald F., and Richard D. Westfall. "Public Recreation on Private Lands: The Landowners Perspective." Ann Arbor: Michigan State University AES Research Report No. 335, 1981.

Howell, Richard L. "Complimentary Curricula: Tourism and Recreation." *Park and Recreation,* November 1982, p. 34.

Knudson, Douglas M. *Outdoor Recreation.* New York: Macmillan Publishing Co., 1984. Chapters 9, 10.

"Now, Disney World Isn't All Mickey Mouse, (EPCOT)." *U.S. News and World Report,* 13 September 1982, pp. 72–73.

Private Sector Campground Data–Section 3. Washington, D.C.: The National Campground Owners Association, 1982.

U.S. Department of the Interior. *The Third Nationwide Outdoor Recreation Plan: The Assessment.* Washington, D.C.: 1979.

U.S. Forest Service. *The Private Forest Landowners of the United States.* Resource Bulletin WO-1. Washington, D.C.: U.S. Government Printing Office, 1982.

Van Doren, Carlton S., George B. Priddle, and John E. Lewis. *Land and Leisure: Concepts and Methods in Outdoor Recreation.* Chicago: Maaroofa Press, Inc., 1979. Chapters 15, 16.

CHAPTER 15

Professional and Service Organizations

In addition to government agencies and private enterprise, there are many professional and service organizations that carry on various functions in outdoor recreation. To get a complete view of recreation involvement, it is necessary to become familiar with these citizen organizations, hereafter arranged alphabetically.

AMERICAN ALLIANCE FOR HEALTH, PHYSICAL EDUCATION, RECREATION, AND DANCE

AAHPERD was created for the purpose of promoting better programs in health, physical education, and recreation. Its major efforts are in connection with school and college programs. AAHPERD has one or more staff consultants in each of its several related areas. Its division of recreation provides professional leadership, including workshops and conferences devoted to the improvement of recreation personnel and school and college programs.

Through this group numerous books and pamphlets relating to recreation have been prepared. It also publishes the monthly *Journal of Physical Education, Recreation and Dance* and the *Research Quarterly*. It is financed mostly by fees from its 56,000 members, but it does receive some assistance through grants and gifts. It has affiliates in all states. The home office is located at 1900 Association Drive, Reston, VA 22091.

AMERICAN ASSOCIATION OF ZOOLOGICAL PARKS AND AQUARIUMS

The American Association of Zoological Parks and Aquariums was organized in 1966 as a branch affiliate of the National Recreation and Park Association. In 1971 it became an independent association. It currently represents virtually every zoological park, aquarium, wildlife park, and oceanarium in America.

The purpose of the group is to promote the welfare and betterment of zoological parks and aquariums and their advancement as instruments for public education, scientific observation, wildlife exhibition and conservation practices.

The association publishes a monthly newsletter for its members, and numerous pamphlets and manuals describing various aspects of zoo and aquarium management. Its office is located at Oglebay Park, Wheeling, WV 26003.

AMERICAN CAMPING ASSOCIATION

The American Camping Association was established in 1910 to further the welfare of children and adults of America through camping and to extend the recreation and education benefits of outdoor living. The association serves as the voice of camp leaders throughout the nation and stimulates high professional standards among camp leaders and camp agencies. It sponsors national conferences to improve camp leadership and programs.

The association publishes *Camping Magazine* eight times a year. It also distributes several books and pamphlets on camping and related activities. It is financed through membership dues. The home office address is Bradford Woods, Martinsville, IN 46151.

AMERICAN FORESTRY ASSOCIATION

This American Forestry Association was founded in 1875. Its purpose is to teach people about the importance of forest resources. It is the key organization concerned with improving the qualifications of forest-management personnel.

The association has published several booklets, and it prepares a monthly magazine entitled *American Forests*. The association also sponsors national and regional conferences devoted to the improvement of America's forests. Its home office address is 1319 18th Street NW, Washington, DC 20036.

AMERICAN WATER SKI ASSOCIATION

The American Water Ski Association was founded in 1939, and today it has a membership of more than 20,000. The group sanctions more than 275 major tournaments and hundreds of small tournaments annually. These competitions draw thousands of skiers.

Membership in the association is open to any individual interested in the sport of waterskiing. The group has its own magazine, *The Water Skier*, published seven times yearly. Information on the sport of waterskiing and the group can be obtained from: American Water Ski Association, 799 Overlook Drive, Box 191, Winter Haven, FL 33880.

AMERICAN YOUTH HOSTELS, INC.

Youth hostels were first established in 1909 in Germany by Richard Schirrmann, a young German schoolteacher. He envisioned hostels as places where young city dwellers could stay inexpensively overnight while on walking or cycling trips in the country. Soon the movement spread to other nations, and in 1934 the first American Youth Hostel was established in Northfield, Massachusetts, by Isabel and Monroe Smith, two American schoolteachers.

The present purpose of youth hostels in America is to provide overnight housing to young people who cannot afford to stay at more expensive accommodations while traveling throughout the country "under their own steam"–hiking, biking, canoeing, on horseback, or skiing.

The organization is made up of 31 area councils throughout the United States with membership and support from individuals and organizations of the various communities. It publishes various pamphlets and booklets designed especially for hostelers. It is financed through membership and program fees paid by participants. For information write for a free folder: American Youth Hostels, Inc., National Campus, Delayslane, VA 22025.

APPALACHIAN MOUNTAIN CLUB

The Appalachian Mountain Club was founded in 1926, for the purpose of enjoying and protecting the beauty of the mountains, forests, and natural areas of the Northeast. Members are organized into 11 chapters from Maine to the Delaware Valley.

The club provides guidebooks and maps for recreational use. The group also maintains more than 1000 miles (1600 km) of foot trails in the Northeast, 20 shelters, and a unique system of huts for use by the public in the White Mountains. It also sponsors instruction in such outdoor activities as showshoeing, ski touring, canoeing, mountain climbing, trip leadership, and safety.

The club is financed by membership dues and donations. It publishes a monthly magazine called *Appalachia Bulletin* and a semiannual journal, *Appalachia*. It maintains one of the most complete mountaineering libraries in the country. The home office is at 5 Joy Street, Boston, MA 02108.

APPALACHIAN TRAIL CONFERENCE, INC.

The Appalachian Trail Conference was established for the purpose of promoting, constructing, and maintaining a continuous trail extending from Maine to Georgia through the mountain country of the Atlantic Seaboard states (Figure 15.1). The trail is supplemented by primitive camps placed at intervals along the trails. The organization is devoted to conserving the primitive environment of the Appalachian Mountain regions.

Five times a year, the conference publishes the *Appalachian Trailway News*. It also publishes guidebooks, maps, and other information of interest to hikers. The mailing address is Box 236, Harpers Ferry, WV 25425.

ASSOCIATION OF INTERPRETIVE NATURALISTS

The Association of Interpretive Naturalists is a nonprofit organization organized in 1961 to encourage the development of natural and historical resource interpretation and related professional skills. Association members benefit from the monthly newsletter (*AIN News*), the *Journal of Interpretation* (published biannually), national workshops, regional newsletters and workshops, a variety of booklets and pamphlets, and many other services based on membership needs and requests. The membership is about 1500. The national office is located at 6700 Needwood Road, Derwood, MD 20855.

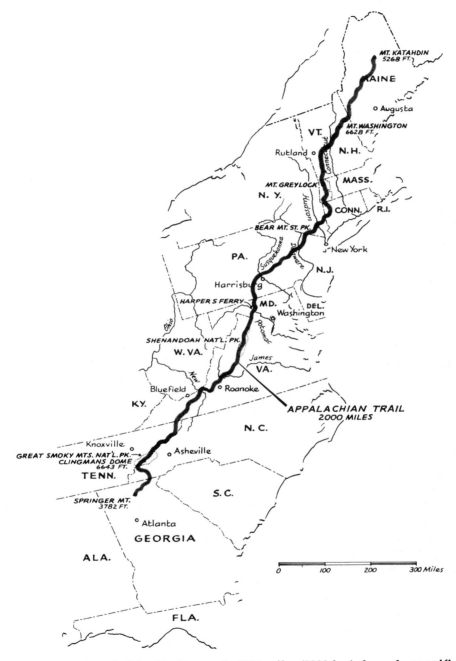

Figure 15.1. The Appalachian Trail extends 2000 miles (3200 km) through magnificent country from Georgia to Maine.

CONSERVATION FOUNDATION

The Conservation Foundation, started in 1948, is a nonprofit research and communications organization. Its primary purposes are to improve the quality of the environment and to promote the wise use of the earth's resources. Toward these ends, the foundation conducts interdisciplinary research and communicates its views and findings to policymakers, opinion leaders, and interested citizens. The foundation does not have members, is not a lobbying organization, and does not buy or sell land. The office address is 1717 Massachusetts Avenue NW, Washington, DC 20036.

IZAAK WALTON LEAGUE OF AMERICA

The Izaak Walton League of America is a 50,000-member citizen-action group founded in 1922 to promote the conservation and wise use of our nation's natural resources and the enjoyment of America's outdoors. Public education, policy research, citizen involvement, and legal action are fostered through the national, state, and local chapters.

Current priorities include supporting stricter air- and water-pollution controls, protecting wetlands, controlling acid rain, protecting our heritage of public lands and wildlife, and promoting ethical outdoor behavior by sports enthusiasts and recreationists.

The league publishes a bimonthly magazine entitled *Outdoor America*. The address of the national headquarters is 1800 North Kent Street, Suite 806, Arlington, VA 22209.

NATIONAL ARCHERY ASSOCIATION

The National Archery Association, founded in 1879, is one of the oldest sports organizations in the country. It is the only organization recognized by the Federation of International Target Archery and the United States Olympic Committee for the purpose of selecting and training archery teams to represent the United States in international competition.

Many state archery groups have organized and affiliated with the National Archery Association. The office address is 1750 East Boulder Street, Colorado Springs, CO 80909.

NATIONAL ASSOCIATION OF COUNTY PARK AND RECREATION OFFICIALS

The National Association of County Park and Recreation Officials is an independent organization affiliated with the National Association of Counties. Its membership consists of more than 500 county park and recreation professionals throughout the United States. By providing its membership a forum for discussing concerns and exchanging innovative ideas in park and recreation, the association encourages communication and cooperation among county park and recreation officials as well as with other park and recreation professional organizations. The group encourages well-planned parks, open space, quality recreation opportunities, and the education of park users. The address is: National Association of County Park and Recreation Officials, c/o National Association of Counties, 1735 New York Avenue NW, Washington, DC 20006.

NATIONAL AUDUBON SOCIETY

The National Audubon Society was established in America in 1905. It strives to advance public understanding of the value of natural resources.

Newly hatched American egrets in Florida's Everglades. (National Park Service, photo by Fred R. Bell)

The society sponsors several workshops each year, which are dedicated to developing an appreciation for nature and a sense of responsibility for the protection of natural resources. It offers lectures on nature subjects and assistance in the development of community nature centers. The society owns and operates a number of wildlife sanctuaries. It also conducts wildlife research, supplies educational materials, and operates model nature centers.

The society publishes *Audubon,* a bimonthly magazine. It also publishes a magazine entitled *American Birds* six times a year and distributes several pamphlets. The society is financed primarily by membership dues but has supplementary income from gifts, grants, foundations, film rentals, and lectures. Its home office is 950 Third Avenue, New York, NY 10022.

NATIONAL CAMPERS AND HIKERS ASSOCIATION

The National Campers and Hikers Association was established in 1954 to educate the public about the conservation of natural resources and especially about the use and values of the outdoors. It develops outdoor programs and facilities and publishes pamphlets on camping and outdoor living. Its monthly magazine is entitled *Camping Hotline.* The association is financed by membership dues, and its home address is 7172 Transit Road, Buffalo, NY 14221.

NATIONAL EMPLOYEE SERVICES AND RECREATION ASSOCIATION

The National Employee Services and Recreation Association was incorporated in 1941 in Illinois. Until 1980 it was named the National Industrial Recreation Association. It currently serves as a national clearinghouse for the dissemination of information and ideas on employee recreation for 2500 member companies in the United States and Canada. Its official publication is *Employee Services Management*, which reaches 5000 industries ten times a year. The association holds annual national and regional conferences and exhibits and five national tournaments. Its address is 20 North Wacker Drive, Chicago, IL 60606.

NATIONAL FIELD ARCHERY ASSOCIATION

In 1939 the National Field Archery Association was founded and had a membership of 1000 active archers. Today the association has 50 chartered state associations and more than 1000 affiliated clubs in the United States and abroad. These clubs have a membership of more than 100,000 archers. The work of the association over the past few years has resulted in bowhunting seasons in all 50 states, allowing over 500,000 archers to take to the field each year in search of big game. Membership is open to anyone interested in archery and bowhunting. Its address is Route 2, Box 514, Redlands, CA 92373.

NATIONAL GOLF FOUNDATION

The National Golf Foundation was founded in 1936 by the major manufacturers of golf equipment. Its purpose is to increase the opportunities to enjoy golf by assisting in the development of more and better golf facilities and golf instructional programs. It places special emphasis on (1) increasing participation in golf, (2) assisting in the design and development of golf facilities, (3) offering consultation workshops and seminars for teachers and coaches, and (4) conducting research.

The foundation is financed by manufacturers of golf equipment and facilities. It publishes and distributes numerous pamphlets and booklets on topics relative to golf facilities, equipment, and programs. The address of its home office is 804 Merchandise Mart, Chicago, IL 60654.

NATIONAL RECREATION AND PARK ASSOCIATION

The National Recreation and Park Association is a nonprofit service organization dedicated to the conservation of natural resources, the beautification of the environment, and the development, expansion, and improvement of park and recreation leadership, programs, facilities, and services. The association is the only independent national organization serving all aspects of the nation's park and recreation movement. Much of its income is raised through membership dues.

The National Recreation and Park Association was formed in 1966 by the merger of five pioneer organizations in the park and recreation field: the American Association of Zoological Parks and Aquariums, the American Institute of Park Executives, the American Recreation Society, the National Conference on State Parks, and the National Recreation Association. It has a professional staff located at the headquarters office. Additional professional personnel in five regional offices across the United States provide consultation to park and recreation agencies and related organizations at the municipal, county, and state levels.

The association sponsors conferences and workshops on national and regional levels. It produces the following periodicals: *Parks and Recreation* magazine (monthly); *Management Aids* (quarterly); *Newsletters* (monthly); *Washington Action Report* (biweekly); *Journal of Leisure Research* (quarterly); *Therapeutic Recreation Journal* (quarterly); and *Dateline* (monthly newsletter). The home office of the National Recreation and Park Association is at 3101 Park Center Drive, Alexandria, VA 22209.

NATIONAL WILDLIFE FEDERATION

The National Wildlife Federation was established in 1936 and today stands as America's largest private conservation education organization. Its purpose is to encourage the intelligent management of natural resources. It sponsors an extensive educational program and provides much educational material in the form of booklets and leaflets. It publishes *National Wildlife*

The Rocky Mountain bighorn sheep lives in high, secluded mountains, but once it lived even along river basins. Unfortunately, things wild and free are constantly being pushed farther back because of increased development and more visitors. (National Park Service, photo by William Keller)

and *International Wildlife* magazines (both bimonthly), *Ranger Rick's Nature Magazine* (monthly), *Conservation Report* (weekly while Congress is in session), and *Conservation Directory* (annually). The federation also grants a number of fellowships to graduate students in fields related to natural-resource conservation. It is financed by membership dues, contributions, and the sale of educational materials. The home office is at 1412 16th Street NW, Washington, DC 20036.

NATURE CONSERVANCY

The Nature Conservancy began its work in 1917 as a national committee of the Ecological Society of America. In 1946 this committee organized as an independent group and in 1950 adopted its present name. It promotes the preservation of natural areas of outstanding scientific or aesthetic significance through their actual acquisition by purchase or gift. The Conservancy (1) maintains and manages a system of preserves throughout the United States, (2) raises money to apply toward the acquisition of natural areas, (3) accepts gifts and bequests of land for conservation purposes, (4) assists universities in the acquisition of lands for biolog-

Powerboating and waterskiing have become popular activities that contribute much to the economics of outdoor recreation. (Bureau of Reclamation, photo by F. S. Finch)

ical research and field study, and (5) assists governmental agencies and local communities in establishing natural parks and open areas.

The group is financed through gifts from individuals, grants from foundations, and membership dues. It publishes a quarterly bulletin entitled *The Nature Conservancy News,* and it also publishes pamphlets relative to the conservation of natural resources. The home office is 1800 North Kent Street, Arlington, VA 22209.

OUTBOARD BOATING CLUB OF AMERICA

This club was organized in 1928 to promote better boating opportunities for Americans. It promotes boating safety, better boating laws, and improved boating facilities and equipment. It provides information to the public through pamphlets, booklets, and safety posters. It also provides the public with information about films related to boating, as well as booklets and other materials on how to organize and operate a successful boating club. The club has affiliates throughout the country, and in turn, is affiliated with the National Boating Federation. The club is financed by membership dues. It publishes a monthly newsletter entitled *Legislative Ledger.* It also publishes and distributes booklets on boating and boating facilities. Its home office is at 401 North Michigan Avenue, Chicago, IL 60611.

SIERRA CLUB

The Sierra Club was founded in 1892 by John Muir to help people explore, enjoy, and learn to protect parks, wilderness, waters, forests, and wildlife. It is based on the idea that wild lands can and should continue to exist, and that they will if people are intelligent in their use and care of such lands.

The Sierra Club organizes trips of various kinds into wilderness areas in the United States and abroad. Local chapters and groups run day-long and weekend trips. In addition, the club maintains several lodges in California and one in British Columbia, and publishes trail guidebooks–the Totebook series. The club has sponsored numerous high-quality books, and it publishes *Sierra Magazine* monthly. It also is an active lobbyist for the interests of environmentalists and outdoor enthusiasts. It is financed by membership dues, special grants, and the sale of publications. The address of the home office is 530 Bush Street, San Francisco, CA 94108.

SPORT FISHING INSTITUTE

The Sport Fishing Institute was organized in 1949 by a group of fishing-tackle manufacturers. The institute is organized around three major functions: (1) research in fishery biology, (2) fisheries conservation education, and (3) professional service to official agencies and citizen groups. It is financed by contributions from more than 150 manufacturers of fishing tackle and accessories, outboard boats and boat motors, and other sporting goods used directly or indirectly in fishing, as well as contributions from individuals.

The institute has prepared several booklets on conservation. It also publishes the monthly *SFI Bulletin.* Its home address is Suite 503, 719 13th Street NW, Washington, DC 20005.

SPORTS FOUNDATION, INC.

The Sports Foundation, Inc., was established in 1965 as a public nonprofit organization to receive and maintain funds exclusively for the promotion of all types of sports. Working under grants from the National Sporting Goods Association, the foundation sponsors the annual National Gold Medal and Special Recreation Awards programs. Through these programs it selects and honors the nation's outstanding recreation and park programs at the local and state levels. On occasion the foundation gives special recognition to other agencies that make significant contributions to sports and recreation.

It encourages participation and facility development in a wide range of recreation activities. The headquarters office is at 717 North Michigan Avenue, Chicago, IL 60611.

UNITED STATES GOLF ASSOCIATION

The United States Golf Association was established in 1894 to provide American golf with a governing body to administer the game, to conduct recognized national amateur and open championships, and to codify and interpret the rules of golf and the rules of amateur status. Besides sponsoring 12 national championships and 3 international competitions, the association actively carries out a multitude of programs for one purpose–to promote the game of golf. The group publishes *The Golf Journal* and *The Green Section Record*. It also maintains a museum and library (open to the public) at its headquarters. The association maintains regional offices throughout the country. Its home office is at the Golf House, Far Hills, NJ 07931.

WHEELMEN, INC.

The League of American Wheelmen, Inc., was established before 1880, and in 1893 its rolls showed 40,000 members. Its main objective is to encourage bicycling. It resists developments that make bicycling inconvenient or impossible. Because of the development of the automobile and a network of roads built only to accommodate auto traffic, the group declined drastically and struggled for survival. However, during recent years the group has been growing steadily. Its mailing address is Box 988, Baltimore, MD 21203.

WILDERNESS SOCIETY

The Wilderness Society has been in the forefront of major conservation battles for decades. Foremost among the society's achievements was its active role toward the enactment of the Wilderness Act of 1964, which established the National Wilderness Preservation System.

A nonprofit membership organization, the Wilderness Society has about 60,000 members. It organizes local citizens and conservation groups to assist government officials in making land and policy decisions, monitors federal actions affecting wilderness and land management, and testifies before Congress on a wide range of land-preservation issues.

The society is devoted to preserving wilderness, protecting America's forests, grasslands, wildlife, waters, and shorelands, and fostering an American land ethic to better harmonize people's relationships with the natural environment. It has six regional offices, and its headquarters is located at 1901 Pennsylvania Avenue NW, Washington, DC 20006.

Hiking the backcountry is both healthy and exciting. (National Park Service, photo by Richard Frear)

WILDLIFE MANAGEMENT INSTITUTE

The Wildlife Management Institute's main objective is to promote the restoration, improved management, and wise use of wildlife, soils, waters, forests, and other renewable natural resources. The institute provides consulting services at all levels–from the national level to private landowners. Its staff includes nationally recognized authorities on fish and wildlife administration, wildlife law enforcement, water conservation, and wetland ecology.

It is a nonprofit conservation organization supported by individuals and industries. The institute publishes a bimonthly newsletter, several authoritative books on wildlife, and many booklets and leaflets. Membership is open to individuals, corporations, or groups. The headquarters is at 1000 Vermont Avenue NW, 709 Wire Building, Washington, DC 20005.

WILDLIFE SOCIETY

The Wildlife Society, founded in 1937, is a professional, nonprofit organization composed of individuals active in research, management, education, and administration. Of primary interest is wildlife ecology. The principal objectives are (1) to develop and promote sound stewardship of wildlife and of the environments upon which wildlife and humans depend, (2) to undertake an active role in preventing human-induced environmental degradation, (3) to increase awareness and appreciation of wildlife values, and (4) to seek the highest standards in all activities of the wildlife profession.

The society has 8000 members in 40 countries. Its purposes are served through chapter, regional, national, and international meetings, and by the publication of *The Journal of Wildlife Management, Wildlife Monographs, Wildlife Society Bulletin,* and many books on scientific and professional subjects. The national office is at 5410 Grosvenor Lane, Bethesda, MD 20814.

ADDITIONAL ORGANIZATIONS

Many additional organizations are concerned with specialized phases of outdoor recreation. Following are the names and addresses of many of these organizations.

Amateur Trapshooting Association
601 West National Road
Vandalia, OH 45377

American Alpine Club
113 East 90th Street
New York, NY 10028

American Association of Botanical
Gardens and Arboreta, Inc.
New Mexico State University
Department of Horticulture
Las Cruces, NM 88003

American Association of Museums
1055 Thomas Jefferson Street NW
Washington, DC 20007

American Canoe Association
National Office
4260 East Evans Avenue
Denver, CO 80222

American Casting Association
Box 51
Nashville, TN 37202

American Cycling Association
107 Barron Street
Petal, MS 39465

American Duck Hunters Association,
Inc.
Box 27372
Memphis, TN 38127

American Fisheries Society
5410 Grosvenor Lane
Bethesda, MD 20814

American Forest Institute
1619 Massachusetts Avenue NW
Washington, DC 20036

American Geographical Society
Suite 1501
25 West 39th Street
New York, NY 10018

American Hiking Society
323 Pennsylvania Avenue SE
Washington, DC 20009

American Historical Trails
Box 810
Washington, DC 20036

American Lawn Bowling Association
10337 Cheryl Drive
Sun City, AZ 85351

American League of Anglers, Inc.
810 18th Street NW
Washington, DC 20006

American Power Boat Association
The Whittier
415 Burns Drive
Detroit, MI 48214

American Rivers Conservation
Council
323 Pennsylvania Avenue SE
Washington, DC 20003

American Snowmobile Association
13104 Crooked Lake Boulevard
Anoka, MN 55303

American Society of Landscape
  Architects
  1750 Old Meadow Road
  McLean, Virginia 22101
American Wilderness Alliance
  4260 East Evans, Suite 8
  Denver, CO 80222
Bicycle Institute of America
  122 East 42nd Street
  New York, NY 10017
Boone and Crockett Club
  Route 1, Box 468-A
  Hughsville, MD 20637
Center for Environmental Education,
  Inc.
  1925 K Street NW
  Washington, DC 20001
Conservation Education Association
  1250 Connecticut Avenue NW
  Washington, DC 20036
Conservation Services, Inc.
  South Great Road
  Lincoln, MS 01733
Defenders of Wildlife
  1244 19th Street NW
  Washington, DC 20036
Discover American Travel
  Organizations, Inc.
  1899 L Street NW
  Washington, DC 20036
Ducks Unlimited, Inc.
  Box 66300
  Chicago, IL 60666
Ecological Society of America
  c/o Dr. Lawrence C. Bliss
  Department of Botany
  University of Washington
  Seattle, WA 98195
Environmental Action Foundation
  346 Connecticut Avenue NW
  Washington, DC 20036
Federation of Western Outdoor Clubs
  c/o Florence W. Baldwin, president
  Box 548
  Bozeman, MT 59715

Garden Clubs of America
  598 Madison Avenue
  New York, NY 10022
Ice Skating Institute of America
  Drawer 2506
  Fort Myers, FL 33902
Industrial Forestry Association
  225 SW Broadway
  Portland, OR 97205
International Bicycle Touring Society
  846 Prospect Street
  LaJolla, CA 92037
International Recreation Association
  345 East 46th Street
  New York, NY 10017
Keep America Beautiful, Inc.
  99 Park Avenue
  New York, NY 10016
National Association for Environmen-
  tal Education
  Box 400
  Troy, OH 45373
National Council of State Garden
  Clubs, Inc.
  4401 Magnolia Avenue
  St. Louis, MO 63110
National Forest Recreation Association
  22841-A Medina Lane
  Cupertino, CA 95014
National Jogging Association
  2420 K Street NW
  Suite 202
  Washington, DC 20006
National Park Foundation
  1825 K Street NW
  Washington, DC 20037
National Parks and Conservation
  Association
  1701 18th Street NW
  Washington, DC 20009
National Rifle Association
  1600 Rhode Island Avenue NW
  Washington, DC 20036

National Skeet Shooting Association
212 Linwood Building
2608 Inwood Road
Dallas, TX 75235

National Trails Council
Box 1042
St. Charles, IL 60174

National Society for Park Resources
1601 North Kent Street
Arlington, VA 22215

National Trust for Historic
Preservation
Route 2, Box 352
Leesburg, VA 20075

National Wildlife Refuge Association
Box 124
Winona, MN 55987

Natural Areas Association
320 South Third Street
Rockford, IL 61108

Natural Resources Defense Council
1725 I Street NW
Suite 600
Washington, DC 20006

North America Family Campers
Association
Box 328
Concord, VT 05824

North America Trail Complex
Box 805
Bloomington, IN 47401

North American Wildlife Foundation
1101 14th Street NW
Suite 725
Washington, DC 20005

North American Yacht Racing Union
37 West 44th Street
New York, NY 10036

Outdoor Writers Association of
America, Inc.
3101 West Peoria Avenue
Suite A207
Phoenix, AZ 85029

Resources for the Future
1755 Massachusetts Avenue NW
Washington, DC 20036

Society of American Foresters
5400 Grosvenor Lane
Bethesda, MD 20814

Trout Unlimited
118 Park Street SE
Vienna, VA 22180

U.S. Parachute Association
Box 109
Monterey, CA 93940

U.S. Ski Association
1726 Champa Street
Suite 300
Denver, CO 80202

Western Interpreters Association
Box 28366
Sacramento, CA 95828

Wetlands for Wildlife, Inc.
39710 Mary Lane
Oconomowoc, WI 53066

World Leisure and Recreation
Association
345 East 46th Street
New York, NY 10017

Discussion Questions

1. For what purpose was the American Forestry Association founded? How does it contribute to outdoor recreation?
2. What is the major purpose of the Appalachian Mountain Club and what is its involvement in outdoor recreation?
3. What outdoor recreation purposes are served by the Conservation Foundation, the Izaak Walton League of America, the Nature Conservancy, and the Audubon Society?

4.   How and when was the National Recreation and Park Association created and what are its major functions?
5.   The Sierra Club was founded in 1892. Who was the founder? What does the club contribute to outdoor recreation?
6.   There are many professional and service organizations involved in the various aspects of recreation. Which ones do you align with? Which ones make the best overall contributions to outdoor recreation?

Recommended Readings

Jensen, Clayne R., and Jay H. Naylor. *Opportunities in Recreation and Leisure.* Skokie, Illinois: National Textbook Co., 1983.

Knudson, Douglas M. *Outdoor Recreation.* New York: Macmillan Publishing Co., 1984. Chapter 33.

National Wildlife Federation. *Conservation Directory–1983*, 28th ed. Washington, D.C.

PART IV

Management Practices and Considerations

CHAPTER 16

Demand and Participation Trends

Fifty years ago Sen. Robert LaFollette made a solemn plea: "It is urgently essential to save for the human race the things on which a peaceful, progressive, happy life can be founded." His reference was to the outdoor environment; his theme was preservation and conservation. With the passing of years the significance of this warning and its relevance have become more and more apparent.

Today we struggle with the questions of (1) how can we make outdoor opportunities more available to people who need them, and (2) how can we cause the resources to meet the ever-increasing demands of the public? We are coming to use the land, air, and water in every conceivable manner to pursue our interests and enrich our lives. On a single body of water some people boat, some water-ski, some canoe or sail, some fish, while still others swim on or under the surface. We participate in a large variety of activities on the surface of the earth. We dig for archeological relics or descend into caves, and we go aloft in gliders and planes.

Some of our pursuits are complex, elaborate, and expensive, but Americans seek the simple pleasures most often. The more popular activities require a small amount of preparation and little specialized equipment–walking, jogging, swimming, cycling, and driving for pleasure. Activities that call for special skills, conditions, and equipment, such as mountain climbing, scuba diving, sailing, and hang gliding, rank low in frequency. They do not, however, rank low in intensity of personal involvement. The participants in these specialized skills show great enthusiasm. Whether it is pride of skill, a sense of fraternity, or perhaps the thrill of danger, a powerful motivating force is at work, and one has only to listen to climbers or sailing enthusiasts "talk shop" to grasp how compelling these activities can be.

PARTICIPATION TRENDS

It is interesting that outdoor recreation has increased significantly faster than predicted. This fact is illustrated by a comparison between the actual 1976 participation level and the

When John Wesley Powell first conquered the turbulent Grand Canyon stretch of the Colorado, he never dreamed that thousands of recreationists would float the same stretch. (Photo by Douglas Nelson)

Outdoor Recreation Resource Review Commission projection for 1976 (made in 1962). The comparison appears in Table 16.1.

A. C. Nielson has monitored the participation levels of selected recreation activities on 3-year cycles over the past 12 years, with the most recent survey being in 1982. He found that between 1979 and 1982 the highest growth rates were in snow skiing (up 27%) and sailing (up 23%). The most popular of all activities monitored was swimming, which attracted an estimated 102 million participants–about 45% of our population. The average increase for all of the activities over the 3-year period was moderately higher than the increase in population during the same period. Table 16.2 summarizes Nielson's survey.

John Hof's extensive research on future participation is summarized in Table 16.3. This information appeared in the *Third Nationwide Outdoor Recreation Plan*, prepared by the Department of the Interior. The report indicates that some of the activities requiring extensive

**Table 16.1. Comparison of Actual 1976 Participation Level
of Persons 12 and Older in Selected Activities as Compared With the
Outdoor Recreation Resource Review Commission Projection for 1976 Made in 1962**

Activity	Projected by ORRRC (%)	Participating in 1976 Survey (%)
Driving for pleasure	56	69
Swimming	55	70
Walking for pleasure	37	68
Sightseeing	47	62
Picnicking	57	73
Fishing	32	55
Bicycling	11	47
Attending outdoor sports events	27	61
Boating (not canoeing or sailing)	28	35
Nature walks	16	49
Hunting	14	20
Camping	11	37
Horseback riding	8	15
Water-skiing	9	17
Hiking	8	28
Attending outdoor concerts, plays, etc.	12	40

From ORRRC "Study Report 26," p. 27.

Table 16.2 Ranking of Participation in Selected Activities

1982 Rank	Sport	Projected Partici- pants 1973 (millions)	Percent Change	Projected Partici- pants 1976 (millions)	Percent Change	Projected Partici- pants 1979 (millions)	Percent Change	Projected Partici- pants 1982 (millions)
1	Swimming	107.2	−3	103.5	+2	105.4	−3	102.3
2	Bicycling	65.6	+14	75.0	−7	70.0	+3	72.2
3	Fishing	61.2	+4	64.0	−7	59.2	+7	63.7
4	Camping	54.4	+7	58.1	+4	60.0	+2	61.2
5	Boating	32.6	+8	35.2	+8	38.0	+11	42.0
6	Jogging, running	*	*	*	*	36.0	−4	34.3
7	Snow skiing	7.8	+42	11.0	+40	15.4	+27	20.0
8	Hunting	20.0	+2	20.5	−4	20.0	−5	18.7
9	Ice-skating	24.9	+4	25.8	−26	19.0	−5	18.0
10	Waterskiing	14.0	+5	14.7	+15	17.0	+7	18.0
11	Golf	17.0	−3	16.6	−4	15.9	+9	17.3
12	Sailing	7.0	+4	7.3	+19	8.7	+2	10.7
13	Snowmobiling	7.7	+19	9.2	−6	8.6	−	8.6
14	Archery	5.8	−6	5.5	+1	5.5	*	*

A. C. Nielsen Co., Nielsen Plaza, Northbrook, Illinois, 60062.

Table 16.3. Projections in Number of Participants in Various Activities in the United States

Type of Activity	1977[a]	1985	1990	Year 2000	2010	2020	2030
Land based	100	107	111	122	136	150	163
Camping (developed)	100	116	126	150	181	214	245
Camping (dispersed)	100	110	116	133	157	182	205
Driving, off-road vehicle	100	105	108	118	129	139	148
Hiking	100	106	109	117	132	146	159
Horseback riding	100	106	109	118	139	159	181
Nature study	100	106	110	121	133	145	155
Picnicking	100	107	112	124	137	150	162
Pleasure walks	100	105	108	116	126	135	143
Sightseeing	100	107	112	123	136	150	163
Water	100	111	118	135	161	188	218
Canoeing	100	113	121	141	175	209	249
Sailing	100	127	145	185	239	298	367
Other boating	100	112	119	137	163	188	220
Swimming outdoors	100	109	115	127	145	168	190
Waterskiing	100	106	109	118	140	161	185
Snow and ice	100	114	123	144	177	212	250
Cross-country skiing	100	120	133	161	200	241	280
Downhill skiing	100	125	142	179	332	289	352
Ice-skating	100	114	123	144	177	212	250
Sledding	100	111	118	133	163	193	227
Snowmobiling	100	106	109	120	141	161	181

[a]1977 = 100. All other numbers compare to this base value.

Department of the Interior, *The Third Nationwide Outdoor Recreation Plan,* Appendix II, Survey Technical Report 4 (modified), 1979.

land and water areas will continue to be popular. The data also show that several of the fastest-growing activities are those which, given proper conditions, can occur close to home on rather ordinary areas and facilities.

The U.S. Forest Service recently completed a series of long-range estimates of recreation participation. The results indicate substantial growth in recreation participation for all activities studied. In terms of activity groups, however, *snow-based* recreation will show the most pronounced increases, followed closely by *water-based* recreation. Among individual activities there were strong trends toward increasing popularity for downhill skiing, sailing, cross-country skiing, developed and primitive camping, canoeing, and boating. The Forest Service indicates that expected increases in population, income, and education will all contribute to a rise in recreation participation. It noted, however, that the rate of increase will be less than the rapid growth during the 1960s and 1970s.

Deterrents to Participation

Included in the *Third Nationwide Outdoor Recreation Plan* was information about people's reasons for not using recreation areas. Of those surveyed, 52% cited *lack of time* as a reason for not using available recreation areas. Other reasons that were cited follow:

Lack of time	52%
Areas too crowded	43%
Lack of money	37%
Lack of information about opportunities	32%
Recreate mostly at residence	30%
Interesting areas not convenient	29%
Areas had pollution problems	25%
Lack of interest	22%
Personal health reasons	21%
Lack of transportation	20%
Areas poorly maintained	20%
Personal safety problems at areas	19%

FACTORS RELATING TO DEMAND

To a large degree we have established a leisure democracy in the United States, meaning that what a person does during his or her free time is determined less by status or station in life than by the individual's interests and preferred life-style. The leisure democracy has reduced the differences in leisure-time use that once existed between the affluent and the nonaffluent, the educated and the noneducated, and those who live in cities as opposed to rural areas. However, a few of these differences are still fairly prominent.

Geographic distribution and *age distribution* are two of the major factors that influence recreation demand. Other factors include *sex differences, family conditions, income level,* and *employment.*

Geographic Distribution of Population

Naturally, the distribution of people affects the amount of recreation participation in the various geographic areas. There are influencing trends on a national scale, and there are also population shifts within particular regions that need to be considered.

Over the past century there has been a migration of people from rural to urban and suburban areas. Further, during the past century there has been a steady shift of population westward. More recently, the pronounced shift has been from the north-central and northeastern states to the Southwest (and Florida)–the Sunbelt.

Despite the population shifts among regions, it is apparent that population shifts within regions are just as important in recreation planning. If there is an influx of people moving from suburbs to inner cities (as there is in some locales), then there need to be more recreation opportunities of all kinds available in the inner cities.

Also during the past decade there has been a trend toward people's establishing residence in or near a recreation resort. Some have found that living in the resort environment and commuting to work provide better conditions for the family. As a result, some resort areas have become surrounded with condominiums, apartments, and family homes.

Whether the population shift is on a national, regional, or local scale, it has implications for recreation planning and development, because people demand adequate recreation opportunities.

Age Distribution

Numerous studies have shown that recreation is linked to age, and in a general sense age correlates negatively with recreation participation. As people get older beyond age 17, they tend to participate less in active recreation and in fewer activities. The young have the most diverse interests, the highest frequency of participation in strenuous activities, and the greatest interest in beginning new activities.

These trends are important because the median age of Americans continues to increase. The median reached 30.2 by 1980, and the Bureau of the Census predicts it will reach 33.0 by 1990 and 35.5 by the year 2000. The Bureau of the Census also reports that the number of Americans 65 and older now exceeds 25 million, and the projection indicates that this age group will increase by 500,000 individuals per year over the next decade. Even though Americans are getting older, the following four trends will escalate the impact of the retirement group on the purchase of recreation goods and services, and their use of recreation areas:

1. Most workers are now covered by retirement plans–nearly 81%.
2. Retirement plans are providing the elderly with more disposable income.
3. Despite new laws allowing continued employment, the trend is still toward early retirement.
4. The number of couples retiring together is increasing.

Sex Differences in Participation

While the percentage of males participating in outdoor recreation is still higher than that of females, there is strong evidence that this historic gap is closing. The *Third Nationwide Outdoor Recreation Plan* showed that in 23 of the 30 activities included, there were more male than female participants (see Table 16.4). But, it also showed that females are at least as likely as males to begin new activities. Overall, the participation among males and females is more nearly equal than it used to be, and there is still a gradual narrowing of the gap. However, males are still five times more likely than females to hunt and twice as likely to participate in primitive camping, waterskiing, and golf. Females are slightly more likely than males to participate in pleasure walking or jogging and in nature walks. The gap between male and female participation is greater among older children than younger ones, and it is greater for those with lower levels of education than those with higher levels.

It is unclear whether the greater inequality in participation among older respondents is caused by the pressures of family responsibilities among females ages 21–30 or by other physiological and sociological factors. Despite this dip in female participation during young adulthood, recreation participation between the sexes is becoming more nearly equal, and this trend is continuing.

Family Influence

The Bureau of the Census reports that the average size of the American family is presently about 2.85–a considerable decline from the average size of 3.7 in 1965. Further, the bureau estimates that the average size will fall still more in years ahead. Almost half of the nation's

Table 16.4. Outdoor Recreation Activities Attracting Participation by Male or Female Respondents

Activity	11- to 20-Year-Olds Greater Male Participation	Greater Female Participation	21- to 30-Year-Olds Greater Male Participation	Greater Female Participation
Camping in a developed area	■		■	
Camping in a primitive area	■		■	
Canoeing, riverrunning	■		■	
Sailing		■	■	
Waterskiing	■		■	
Fishing	■		■	
Other boating	■			■
Outdoor pool swimming		■	■	
Beach swimming		■		■
Nature walks, birdwatching		■		■
Hiking or backpacking	■		■	■
Walking or jogging		■		■
Bicycling		■		■
Horseback riding		■	■	
Off-road vehicle use	■		■	
Hunting	■		■	■
Picnicking		■	■	
Golf	■		■	
Outdoor tennis		■	■	
Cross-country skiing		■	■	
Downhill skiing	□	□	■	
Outdoor ice-skating		■	■	■
Sledding	■		■	
Snowmobiling	■		■	
Other outdoor sports or games	■		■	
Sightseeing	□	□	■	
Driving for pleasure		■		■
Attending dances, concerts		■	■	
Visiting zoos, amusement parks		■		■
Attending outdoor sports events	■		■	

Key: Greater ■, equal □

Source: Department of the Interior, *Third Nationwide Outdoor Recreation Plan,* 1979.

60 million families consist of only two members. The fastest growing family type is the single-parent family, which accounts for approximately one of every five families with children. In addition, substantial changes are taking place in the social characteristics of families and in the role models.

Several studies confirm that the family organization plays a fundamental role in recreation, and the family has been identified as the single most important socializing influence on recreation. This would imply that these changes in the structure and nature of American families may influence recreation.

Effects of Income

Economic statistics show that expenditures for recreation are rising slightly faster than consumer spending as a whole. Consumer spending for all leisure activities now amounts to about $1 of every $8 spent.

As one's total income increases, the proportion of money available for recreation also increases. While income must first be applied to meet the basic needs, after a point its uses are discretionary. Thus, a rise in real income implies a rise in discretionary spending (spending for nonessentials).

People with higher incomes participate in more recreational activities than those with low incomes. In the *Third Nationwide Outdoor Recreation Plan* it was found that participation increased with income for 23 of the 30 activities studied. The lowest relationship between income and participation existed with hunting and fishing, while the level of income had the greatest influence on outdoor swimming, golf, sightseeing, and visiting aquariums, zoos, outdoor sports events, and other activities where admission fees are charged. It is interesting that tennis, walking and jogging were the more popular activities for new participants in both high- and low-income groups.

A study by John Robinson and Geoffrey Godbey[1] showed that the more affluent members of our society feel the most rushed. They spend more time on the job, in travel, in self-improvement, in formal organizations, and in recreation and entertainment away from home. And they spend less time resting.

Employment Conditions

Because of the shortened work year (as explained in Chapter 4), smaller families, time-saving technology, and other factors, Americans have more leisure time than ever before, and this time is available for discretionary uses, including recreation.

Leisure time has increased for every population subgroup regardless of whether the individuals are men or women, employed or housewives, married or single, young or old.

Robinson's and Godbey's research indicates that leisure time has increased the fastest for people between 18 and 25 (27.9% gain in ten years) and those between 55 and 65 (12.7% gain in ten years). Smaller but positive gains have been recorded for all other age groups.

Increases in available leisure time do not correlate directly with increased recreation, because people devote their leisure time to a wide range of activities. However, Robinson and Godbey found that for nearly all categories of respondents recreation increased as leisure time became more abundant.

There are other factors in employment patterns that are having a noticeable effect. An example is the increased number of mandated three-day weekends, which have increased recreation visitation to many outdoor areas on these holidays.

Also, more people in the labor force are now taking advantage of flexible work schedules that afford the opportunity of more daylight hours for recreation. Further, more and more

---

1. Robinson, John, and Geoffrey Godbey, "Work and Leisure in America: How We Spend Our Time," *Journal of Physical Education, Recreation and Dance,* October 1978, p. 6.

people are working a four-day week. Even though this has only a small effect on increased leisure, it does have an influence on recreation because it alters the pattern of available time.

Effects of Energy Costs

High energy prices reduce the purchase and use of large recreation vehicles, off-road vehicles, snowmobiles, and large powerboats. If gasoline prices continue to rise, the use of this equipment will probably be curbed even more. Nonetheless, many technologists believe that over the long term, technical advances will produce viable fuel alternatives and vehicles that are more fuel efficient.

Because large self-contained recreation vehicles consume a lot of gas, sales of these vehicles dipped sharply after the 1973 oil embargo. Nonetheless, the sales rebounded strongly during the mid-1970s. Since 1977 the sales of these vehicles gradually have fallen to a lower level.[2]

It has been suggested that off-road vehicles and snowmobiles be curtailed as an energy-saving measure. However, a recent study by the Council on Environmental Quality estimates that these motorized forms of recreation account for less than 1% of the nation's total gasoline consumption. This estimate, however, does not include the extra gasoline used in hauling the recreation vehicles to and from the sites of use.

Recent studies substantiate the idea that price increases in fuel do not cause a proportional reduction in recreation travel. People make other adaptations in their travel to compensate. It has been found that consumers actually modify their daily driving habits to protect their opportunities for weekend travel. Regardless of the adaptations that people are able to make, one adjustment that does seem certain is that fuel costs will have a long-term effect, curbing people's purchase and use of recreation vehicles that consume large amounts of fuel.

ADVENTURE AND RISK ACTIVITIES

There has been a tremendous growth of outdoor adventure activities, such as white-water canoeing, kayaking, rafting, rock and ice climbing, cross-country ski touring, hang gliding, skydiving, scuba diving, and other such activities. People of all ages are turning to programs that offer instruction and participation in adventurous pursuits. Further, the interest in these activities is evident by the popularity of a number of relatively new adventure periodicals, such as *Backpacker, Back Country, Mountain, Wilderness Camping, Nordic World, Cycling, Bike World, Camping Journal, Downriver, Adventure,* and *Summit.*

Paul W. Darst and George P. Armstrong[3] define adventure pursuits as follows:

Outdoor adventure activities include all pursuits that provide an inherently meaningful human experience that relates directly to a particular outdoor environment–air, wind, water, hills, mountains, rocks, woods, streams, rivers, lakes, ice, snow, or caves. A certain amount of risk, adventure, exploration, and travel are involved, depending on the skills of the participants and the nature of the activity. *Competition between individuals* and groups is minimal, whereas competition between people and their environment is the norm. The emphasis is not on winning or losing, but rather on facing the challenges of a natural environment.

2. U.S. Department of the Interior, *Third Nationwide Outdoor Recreation Plan,* Washington, D.C., 1979, p. 89.
3. Darst, Paul W., and George P. Armstrong, *Outdoor Adventure Activities for School and Recreation Programs,* Burgess Publishing Co., Minneapolis, 1980, p. 3.

These authors go on to point out that most outdoor adventure can be adapted or arranged to provide competition between people or groups. For example, cycling, cross-country skiing, or orienteering can be organized in the form of races. Even though this kind of competition may appeal to some and may prove worthwhile, such competition is not a necessary ingredient of adventure pursuits.

Adventure activities have different degrees of risk. It is helpful to think of the risk factor in terms of a simple classification system involving three categories: *low-risk, medium-risk,* and *high-risk* activities. It is possible for a particular activity to vary in risk. For example, kayaking or canoeing can range from high risk to low risk, depending on the water conditions. The same would be true with scuba diving, depending on the extensiveness and circumstances of the dive. Further, there can be varying degrees of risk with rock climbing, downhill skiing, skydiving, and practically every other adventure activity. In addition to being related to the conditions of participation, the risk factor is also influenced by the skill and experience of the participants.

Reasons for Popularity

There are *economic, sociological,* and *personal psychological* reasons why people enter particular adventure activities. In terms of economics, some people canoe, kayak, and wind surf because these are relatively inexpensive water activities as contrasted to yachting, powerboating, and waterskiing. Mountain climbing to places of height and scenic beauty is less expensive than skydiving or piloting one's own aircraft for pleasure. Cross-country skiing is less expensive than alpine skiing at a resort. Numerous other examples could be given to point out the economic advantage of certain activities as contrasted to the alternatives that might be chosen if one's finances would permit.

People engage in certain activities to develop a feeling of belonging to a group or class of people. That is the sociological reason for participation in a recreational activity. There is a social unity associated with skiing, for example, as there is with scuba diving, hang gliding, cycling, backpacking, and practically every other specialized activity. A large number of outdoor clubs have developed around common interests in outdoor adventure.

Among the personal psychological reasons for participation are the thrills that some people receive from being exposed to danger and risk. Also, there is the drive to overcome fear and gain self-confidence. Some want to become more self-sufficient. Many participants are looking for new experiences, excitement, and challenges. Their reasons are many: to escape the monotony or complexity of their life-styles, to release tension and anxiety, to obtain a feeling of success and achievement, to find out more about their limits and limitations, to become more knowledgeable about another dimension of life, to improve their physical or psychological fitness, or to test their current fitness levels.

Leslie Tompkins[4] provides additional reasons for adventure activities:

Many feel that adventure programs supply the needed emotional outlets for youth who might otherwise pursue less desirable activities–that the need for self-testing can be satisfied through

---

4. Tompkins, Leslie, "As We See It," *A Newsletter for the Exchange of Ideas on Outdoor Education,* Fall–Winter 1976–1977.

Wide open spaces are sanctuaries for the primitive arts of travel, especially backpacking, cross-country skiing, and canoeing. (Photo by Douglas Nelson)

adventure programs. Other goals sought by adventure programs are improvement in self-awareness, self-concept, judgment, decision making, compassion, increased potential, sensory perception, awareness of and respect for individual differences, endurance, cardiovascular improvement, strength, coordination, skills, and an understanding of and cooperation with nature—a motivation to learn—in and out of the formal educational system.

Richard M. Tapply[5] further explains the importance of high adventure:

We have need for challenge and risk taking in recreation programs. Such elements must be regulated to assure the penalties for failure are not too high. They can be graduated to all levels of skill and risk, but they are essential elements that have great relevance to self-discovery,

5. Tapply, Richard M., "High Adventure: Confronting the Essentials," *Parks and Recreation* 12(1977), p. 26, cited in Meier, Joel F., Talmage W. Morash, and George E. Welton, *High Adventure Outdoor Pursuits: Organization and Leadership*, Brighton Publishing Co., Salt Lake City, Utah, 1980, pp. 4–9.

self-development, and self-enhancement. Risk and challenge are not only present in physical activities; they can be ingredients in social activities also. Challenge is present in a broad range of pursuits, from skydiving to sailing and from acting to angling.

Sponsoring Agencies

Adventure activities have become popular elements in the programs of a variety of youth agencies, such as the Boy Scouts, YWCA, and YMCA. Further, it is not uncommon for schools to offer outdoor programs that involve low-risk adventure activities. Also, outdoor clubs of various kinds frequently exist at high schools and colleges, and there are classes involving such activities as skiing, canoeing and kayaking, rock climbing, and scuba diving.

Several colleges and universities have become interested in specialized adventure programs. Among these have been Brigham Young University, which has given emphasis to wilderness survival techniques, and the University of Montana and Colorado College, which offer adventurous excursions. Explaining how these activities fit into college curricula, Joel F. Meier[6] wrote the following:

Interest in risk-taking activities has increased tremendously over the past decade. This has produced demands on recreation curriculums throughout the country to train individuals to be equipped with the essential skills to serve as leaders of high-risk programs. The focus of the recreation curriculum of the University of Montana attempts to integrate recreational performance and risk activities with proper understanding of emotional prerequisites of risk-taking activities, individual's own capabilities, and how to cope with conflict situations. With the ever-increasing number of individuals pursuing risk recreation today, it is imperative that institutions of higher learning prepare adequately the future recreation professionals for such a challenge.

Outward Bound, National Outdoor Leadership School, Project Adventure, and Wilderness Encounter are examples of standardized adventure programs (packaged programs) that have become popular. There have been various spin-off projects or courses from these more standardized programs. Outward Bound is the best-known course of this kind. As it has spread across the country, the course has been adapted to the particular terrain and other circumstances. Outward Bound courses have been held in the Florida Everglades, Death Valley in California, the White Mountains of New Hampshire, the Cascades of Washington, the Boundary Waters Canoe Area in Minnesota, and the Alaskan tundra. According to Kurt Hahn,[7] the developer of Outward Bound,

The purpose of Outward Bound is to protect youth against a declining civilization; the decline of physical fitness due to methods of locomotions; the decline of skill and care due to the weakened tradition of craftsmanship; the decline of initiative due to spectatorities; the decline of discipline due to tranquilizers; and the decline of compassion which William Temple called spiritual death.

6. Meier, Joel F., Talmage W. Morash, and George E. Welton, *High Adventure Outdoor Pursuits: Organization and Leadership*, Brighton Publishing Co., Salt Lake City, Utah, 1980, p. 232.
7. Hahn, Kurt, *Outward Bound Bulletin* [brochure], 1983.

Is It Worth the Risk?

Accidents are the fourth-leading cause of death in the United States, with an annual fatality rate of 55.2 per 100,000 population. This data, however, includes all types of accidents and not just those that occur in recreation. The *New York Times* recently reported that "the number of deaths from the whole range of the new risk taking [recreation] is still low compared with the deaths each year on the nation's highways, household and industrial accidents, or deaths from natural causes." Americans die each year as a result of some avocation, and the figure is growing. One primary reason for the increasing number of accidents in these activities is the phenomenal growth of participation.

Intelligent risk assessment involves (1) defining goals, and (2) asking whether obtaining the goals is worth the danger. Development of a better self-concept and improved self-reliance might be reasonable goals; but whether these or any other goals justify the risk is a question to be carefully analyzed and correctly answered in each case.

There exists a possibility of legal liability by the sponsoring agency of risk activities. Therefore, agencies need to (1) make sure that their sponsorship is prudent in view of the potential for accomplishment as contrasted to the risk; and (2) be sure the activities are done in accordance with sound procedures and under well-qualified leadership. More is said about this in Chapter 20, which deals with legal considerations.

SPECIAL POPULATIONS

There are identifiable segments of our general population that are often referred to as *special populations*. This term describes subgroups that have needs different from those of the general population. Among them are the elderly, the handicapped and ethnic groups. Effective recreation planners take special populations into account and include their particular needs in the overall program.

Cultural Groups

America has long been known as the melting pot of nationalities and cultures. There are many cultural subgroups in our society. These groups have their own influencing characteristics–political, religious, and traditional. Such characteristics strongly affect the atmosphere in which recreation takes place. For example, a subculture with strong Protestant influence would resist recreation participation on Sunday. Subcultures that customarily have not favored government sponsorship of recreation may have very limited park and recreation systems. Some cultures and ethnic groups, such as Ukranians, have strong traditions regarding festivals. Others have certain holiday celebrations. Obviously, the presence of special populations such as these can have a significant influence on the overall recreation plan.

Consider, for example, the various cultural influences on recreation in areas where there are communities of immigrants from such places as the Orient, Polynesia, the Slavic countries, or India. Also, think of the marked influence on participation by religious groups such as the several denominations of Christianity, the Jewish faith, Islamic beliefs, and atheism.

Older People

It is easy for older people to become forgotten members of society. Yet their lives need to remain full and enriched. It is especially important that opportunities for older people be fully integrated into the planning of recreation areas and facilities and that these people be encouraged to participate in the particular pursuits that can add enjoyment and meaning to their lives.

Many older people are somewhat isolated by a lack of mobility. Their involvement often can be enhanced by making sure they receive information about recreational opportunities. The particular way to accomplish this varies with each local situation.

Further, many of these folks have very limited finances, and this further restricts their mobility. Recreation participation by older citizens can be greatly enhanced by the provision of needed transportation and the elimination of other barriers that restrict their involvement.

Too often the number of participants has been our only criteria for evaluation. We count numbers–and after a while only numbers count.

Handicapped Citizens

According to the White House Conference on Handicapped Individuals, there are now more than 35 million handicapped Americans, who constitute about 17% of the total population. The handicapped are generally divided into two main subgroups–physically handicapped and mentally handicapped. The physically handicapped include the visually impaired, the hearing impaired, and the orthopedically disabled. The mentally handicapped include the mentally retarded and the emotionally ill. The range in disabilities is tremendous.

Since many handicapped people are not able to work at regular jobs, they are deprived of some of the daily challenges that other members of the population regularly experience. The White House conference estimated that the nation's handicapped individuals accumulate more than 170 million hours of forced leisure time daily. Thus, recreation represents an important means of personal fulfillment and therapy for millions of employed and unemployed handicapped persons.

It is especially important for recreation managers to recognize that handicapped people have essentially the same desires and needs as the nonhandicapped. They are much more like others than most of us recognize. The main difference is in the difficulties that the handicapped encounter.

In meeting the recreational needs of the handicapped, there are two concerns that rank high: accessibility of facilities and accessibility of programs. The Architectural Barriers Act of 1968 and the Rehabilitation Act of 1973 require that all buildings and facilities built and programs and activities sponsored with federal funds or federal assistance be made accessible to the handicapped. To help meet this requirement, the Department of the Interior has prepared

The handicapped have essentially the same desires and needs as the nonhandicapped, and they deserve ample opportunities. (National Park Service, photo by Cecil W. Stoughton)

some useful guidelines that must be followed if an agency is to receive financial assistance from the Land and Water Conservation Fund. Further, the General Services Administration of the federal government has ordered that all new construction contracts permit easy access for the disabled, and the National Park Service and the Forest Service have moved forthrightly to make sure that the steps, curbs, doors, and other barriers of their hundreds of facilities are modified to permit entry by the handicapped. Agencies are now required to allow handicapped people to become involved at an early stage in state recreation planning.

The essential laws are in place, and some honest efforts toward compliance are being made. Much confusion exists about what actually is required under various circumstances, and information among planners and implementers about the real needs of handicapped people is generally lacking. Understanding how the law applies to a swimming pool, a fishing pier, a picnic area, a campground, a hiking trail, or a wilderness area is not easy. There is such a variety of outdoor-recreation resources that it is impossible to legislate all of the possibilities that should be considered in terms of access for the handicapped.

To bring together useful information for the handicapped and to serve as a base for the evaluation of its own areas, the Park Service has published *Access National Parks: A Guide for Handicapped Visitors*. The book describes each area in the national park system, providing information that would help a handicapped visitor understand the kinds of opportunities, conveniences, and difficulties at a particular site.

The Park Service also has established "sense trails" in certain places to accommodate the physically handicapped and to increase the acuteness of hearing, smelling, tasting, and touching. Further, many parks now have interpreters capable of communicating with visitors through sign language to accommodate those with speech and hearing handicaps.

Adventure or risk activities are favorites of many handicapped individuals. Just which activities can be done with reasonable safety depends on the person's handicap. It isn't unusual to see an amputee come down the ski slope on one leg, or a paraplegic participate in kayaking, or a retarded person engage in horseback riding. Handicapped people are attracted to risk activities for the same reasons as the nonhandicapped, and they achieve the same rewards.

Since most handicapped people are capable of a variety of recreational activities and since participation has great potential for enrichment among the handicapped, then education for leisure is at least as important for the handicapped as for the population in general. Unfortunately, society has not responded very well to this fact. However, in recent decades much progress has been made toward recognizing the potential of the handicapped, educating them for fuller and richer lives, and bringing them into the mainstream of society. Yet, there is much to be done, and recreation planners, managers, and educators should be especially sensitive to the particular needs of this segment of our population.

Discussion Questions

1. What is meant by "leisure democracy"? What influences does this concept have on recreation opportunities for various segments of the population?
2. Think of a handicapped person you know. Do the basic recreation needs of this person differ from the norm? What kind of outdoor recreation pattern does the person have? How could this be improved?
3. Review how the rate and kind of participation in outdoor recreation is influenced by such factors as age, sex, income, length of work week, and family structure.
4. Outdoor recreation is increasing faster than the population. What are some of the reasons for this? Will this trend likely continue? Why?
5. It has been found that people's rate of participation in recreation declines only slightly in times of economic difficulty. Why is this so?
6. What are some of the personal benefits to participating in a challenging, risk-oriented recreational activity? Can the same results be achieved in nonrisk activities?

Recommended Readings

"Activity Preferences and Participation." *Journal of Leisure Research*, March 1979, p. 92.
"Americans Get the Trail Blazing Urge." *U.S. News and World Report*, 11 August 1980, p. 52
"Americans Play–Even With Economy in Spin." *U.S. News and World Report*, 8 September 1980, p. 52.

Bury, Richard L. *Risk and Accidents in Outdoor Recreation Areas.* College Station, Texas: Texas Agricultural Experiment Station, Texas A&M University, 1981.

Chubb, Michael, and Holly R. Chubb. "Changing Human Elements." *Journal of Physical Education, Recreation and Dance,* October 1981, p. 12.

"The Four-Day Workweek: An Assessment of Its Effects on Leisure Participation." *Leisure Sciences,* Vol. 2, No. 1, p. 55.

Godbey, Goeffrey, Arthur Patterson, and Laura Brown. *Relationship of Crime and Fear of Crime Among the Aged to Leisure Behavior and Use of Public Leisure Services.* Washington, D.C.: American Association of Retired Persons, 1979.

Godbey, Geoffrey, and John P. Robinson. *Outdoor Recreation and Age: A Study of Demand and Supply.* University Park, Pennsylvania: Department of Parks and Recreation, 1980.

Jensen, Clayne R., and Craig Jensen. *Backpacking for Fun and Fitness.* New York: Leisure Press, 1981.

Kelley, John R. "Outdoor Recreation Participation: A Comparative Analysis." *Leisure Studies,* Vol. 3, No. 2, p. 129.

Miner, Joshua L., and Joe Boldt. *Outward Bound USA.* New York: William Morrow and Co., Inc., 1981.

National Recreation and Park Association. *Demand for Recreation in America: An Overview.* Arlington, Virginia: 1983.

"The Need for Leisure Education for Handicapped Children and Youth." *Journal of Physical Education, Recreation and Dance,* March 1976, p. 29.

Neilsen Study of Recreation Participation in the U.S. Northbrook, Illinois: A.C. Nielsen Co., 1982.

Nesbitt, John A., and Delores G. Nesbitt. "The Nonvisible Population." *Journal of Physical Education, Recreation and Dance,* October 1981, p. 61.

Rossman, J. Robert. "Evaluate Programs by Measuring Participant Satisfaction." *Park and Recreation,* June 1982, p. 33.

Twight, Ben W., and Kenneth L. Smith, and Gordon H. Wissinger. "Privacy and Camping: Closeness to the Self Vs. Closeness to Others." *Leisure Sciences,* Vol. 4, No. 4, p. 427.

Van Doren, Carlton S., Goerge B. Priddle, and John E. Lewis. *Land and Leisure: Concepts and Methods in Outdoor Recreation.* Chicago: Maaroofa Press, Inc., 1979. Chapter 7.

Van Doren, Carlton S. "Outdoor Recreation Trends in the 1980's: Implications for Society." *Journal of Travel Research,* winter 1981.

West, Patrick C. "Perceived Crowding and Attitudes Toward Limiting Use in Back-Country Recreation Areas." *Leisure Sciences,* Vol. 4, No. 4, p. 419.

"Why More Vacationers Rough It." *U.S. News and World Report,* July 1980, p. 71.

Witt, Peter A., and Thomas L. Goodale. "The Relationships Between Barriers to Leisure Enjoyment and Family Stages." *Leisure Sciences,* Vol. 4, No. 1.

CHAPTER 17

Environmental Quality

Perhaps the most important of all outdoor recreation is the kind found in everyday living. Whether such recreation opportunities exist depends on whether there is a proper environment. Are there convenient places to walk and ride bicycles? Are there attractive open spaces where nature can refresh the spirit? Are there attractive streams and lakes and wooded areas? Or have all of these been buried in culverts or under concrete and asphalt?

Our ancestors were privileged to start a nation on virtually an unspoiled continent–a landscape of mountains, valleys, and plains, drained by one of the world's most generous water systems. Here were resources for life, wealth, and enjoyment beyond measure, enough to meet our needs for all time. Yet within a few generations we have fouled the streams, marred the landscape, built sprawling and often unattractive cities, and generally degraded and polluted the resources that were willed to us.

It was roughly 350 years ago that an adventurous people confronted a virgin land on this continent. Any act that subdued the wilderness was considered good. Subjugation meant growth, and growth was next to godliness in the American scene. For a century or more every individual or group that conquered a native, felled a giant oak, hacked out a road, laid out a farm, or built a fence was an authentic agent of the American advance.

The pioneers either conquered or failed to find a foothold. Action was essential and raw courage counted the most. The people cut down forests, plowed up plains, rechanneled streams, killed off animal species, and segmented the nation with fence lines. Growth was progress and progress was growth.

At a later period in American history when this concept of growth was engrafted into the industrial revolution, the defilement and spoilage of the American environment really began. Whether it was mining, the cutting of timber, or the building of an industrial plant, we used the quantitive test to measure its worth. It seems that every engineering effort, however ill conceived, was applauded. As a result, in too many cases both our cities and our countryside have come to lack character.

In America we have the most automobiles and the worst junkyards. We use the most energy and have the foulest air. Our factories pour out the most products and our rivers carry some of the heaviest loads of pollution. We have the most goods to sell and the most unsightly signs to advertise them. We have rich cities but very few handsome ones.

This dilemma challenges the proposition that we can continue to progress while protecting our environment from further damage. Can we build the character into our land it deserves, but which we have thus far ignored?

Our fragmented power has outrun our methods of deciding how to use it. Unless we invent means of dealing with technology's side effects, they will bury us.

–Max Ways, *Living With the Environment*,
Conservation Yearbook, U.S. Department of the Interior,
1978–1979, p. 82.

THE BASIC PROBLEM OF POLLUTION

In the polluting sense, humans are the greatest offenders of all living beings, and the pollution we cause shows no preference. Like the common cold, pollution strikes the rich as well as the poor, the people in the cities and in the country, the young and the old.

What is happening to America the Beautiful? This recurring question reflects rising frustrations over the nation's polluted air, dirty streets, and filthy rivers. And the pollution, bad enough in itself, reflects something even worse: the dangerous illusion that industrial societies can grow bigger and bigger without regard for the eternal laws of nature.

More than 30 years ago Buckminster Fuller calculated that the total energy generated in the United States was equal to the muscular energy that would be generated if each American had 153 slaves. Today a similar calculation would indicate that each American has the equivalent of 500 slaves. These slaves enable us to increase our own mobility hundreds of times and to toss around incredible masses of materials, altering not only their location and external shapes but also their actual molecular composition. This abundance of energy available to each of us explains a lot of the environmental woes that are otherwise quite mysterious.

It has become ever more apparent that in dealing with the environment we must do less to master nature and more to master ourselves, our institutions, and our technology. We must achieve a better awareness of our dependence on our surroundings and on the natural systems that support all life. We must recognize that water, air, and land are no longer available for use in any manner one may choose. The right to use is not the right to pollute or destroy. The unintelligent and uncontrolled tampering with nature will have to be restricted at a much higher level in the future if we want to have any chance of maintaining a livable environment.

"When you defile the pleasant streams...you massacre a million dreams."–John Drinkwater (Utah State Department of Health)

The evil that men do lives after them.
                                        –Henry David Thoreau

LAND POLLUTION

Frequent sources of ugliness are garbage dumps, automobile salvage areas, unattractive billboards, abandoned railroads, utility lines, industrial and mining complexes, and eroded land. Control of these forms of ugliness is the official responsibility of certain city, county, state, and federal agencies. But such control is also dependent upon an attitude among the public that the prevention of ugliness is important–in fact, essential.

Probably our greatest problem with land pollution is trash and litter. Just one day's accumulation of trash nationwide is horrendous, and it contains large amounts of iron, glass, tin, plastics, and paper products. All of us suffer from our extravagant use of material, much of which becomes waste and litter. It contributes to a degrading of our environment.

In connection with pollution, the following comparisons are enlightening.[1] An orange peel decomposes in two weeks to five months, but a plastic bag lasts 10 to 20 years. An alumi-

1. Seed, Allen H., Jr., "Who Litters–and Why? *Journal of Environmental Education,* March 1970, pp. 93–94.

num can remains 80 to 100 years, and a glass bottle is expected to stay intact for up to 1 million years. Litter components along highways are 67% paper, 16% metal cans, 10% bottles, and 7% miscellaneous garbage.

Fortunately, the public is becoming more litter conscious, but progress is slow. Also, the immense volume of valuable materials in our trash is stirring the interest of some waste-conscious and profit-seeking individuals who are making constructive efforts toward recycling certain materials.

AIR POLLUTION

While thousands of chimneys in the United States continually belch sulfur dioxide, 100 million motor vehicles add their version of insult through the emission of carbon monoxide (nearly 60% of smog) and other lethal gases.

Most of this occurs in or near cities, and the sheer bulk of big cities slows the cleansing winds. At the same time, rising city heat helps to create thermal inversions (a layer of warmer air above cooler air) that can trap pollutants for days.

Increasingly, air pollution is not confined to the vicinity of large cities in the East, Midwest, and West Coast. For example, Missoula, Montana, traditionally known as the Big Sky Country, is among the ten areas with the worst air pollution in the nation. Other cities in the Rocky Mountain region where air pollution has become a problem include Denver and Lewiston, Idaho. Also, in such places as the woodlands of Maine and Upstate New York, polluted air has settled poisons into the high mountain waters in such quantities as to kill fish and other marine life.

Another way air pollution detracts from our environment is by its effect on vegetation. In practically every urban area it has reduced vegetation from petunias to mighty oaks by 10% to 20%. It kills plants, blights new shoots, damages leaves enough to reduce nourishment, and produces premature old age.

Today unclean air threatens our health, corrodes our property, insults our peace of mind, and obliterates our scenery. Unclean air is no longer the exception in and near American cities—it is the rule.

Quality of environment, like freedom, must be protected and achieved anew by each generation.
—Lawrence S. Rockefeller, U.S. Department of the Interior, Environmental Report, Conservation Yearbook, 1971, p. 33.

Acid Precipitation

One of the most serious forms of air pollution is a chemical leprosy that is eating away at the face of our country. It is called "acid rain." The term *acid precipitation* is more descriptive because the acid fallout can come with rain, snow, sleet, hail, frost, fog, dew, and even dry particles. Further, it's not only a problem in this country but is common to all industrialized nations. In fact, it isn't even limited to industrialized nations because wind patterns carry the pollutants to faraway places.

A good piece of real estate is basic–from there on the quality of environment is a matter of human control.

Acid precipitation is caused by the emission of sulfur dioxide and nitrogen oxides from the combustion of fossil fuels. Natural sources, such as volcanoes, emit sulfur dioxide in the air, but about 90% of the sulfur in the atmosphere of industrial areas comes from man-made sources. Once aloft, the oxides of sulfur and nitrogen can be transformed into sulfuric and nitric acids by reacting with the moisture in the atmosphere, and the air currents can carry them hundreds, sometimes thousands, of miles. When these acids finally settle to earth, they have a devastating impact on plant and animal life. The effects vary in different locations, because the particular composition of the land, including land under water, influences the buffering effect.

In the United States acid precipitation falls almost continuously on land and water near industrialized areas. It has killed large amounts of fish and other aquatic life. In Maine it has been found that native brook trout have ceased reproducing in many of the lakes at high elevation because of the effects of acid fallout. In New York it has been documented that over 200 lakes and ponds in the Adirondacks have become acidified and incapable of supporting fish life. In Pennsylvania many of the mountain streams can no longer support rainbow trout and the more-tolerant brown trout are having difficulties. Further, in these same areas there is evidence of environmental damage to trees and shrubs. The damage is especially pronounced at the higher elevations, where there is more precipitation and the plant life is fragile. In Scandinavia, which is downwind from industrialized western Europe, acid precipitation has destroyed much of the fish life in hundreds of lakes and has damaged the salmon population in several rivers.

Further, this polluting menace is having a damaging effect on human health, as well as crops and forests, and it is disfiguring the surface of stone and brick buildings and monuments–including those in our nation's capital. According to many scientists, acid precipitation is now the single most serious environmental problem in North America, western Europe, and Scandinavia.

A jet belches a cloud of smoke at National Airport, Washington, D.C. (National Park Service)

The case pertaining to acid precipitation is clear and well documented. Yet, not nearly enough is being done to control it. The classic adage "pay now or pay later" is clearly applicable to this problem, and if it doesn't receive more attention, the problem could become an environmental disaster of the first order.

WATER POLLUTION

Most of the earth's total water supply is not drinkable by man, either because of its salty or polluted condition or its inaccessibility due to geographic location. The supply that is usable is held in precarious balance and is subject to drastic influences by people and industry. Of all our resources, we have mismanaged water the most, even though we know we cannot survive without it.

It seemed to our predecessors that we had enough good water to meet our needs for all time. Perhaps we were lulled in the early days by the reassuring platitude that "running water purifies itself." Perhaps we simply don't care. In any case, we have filled our streams with raw excrement and garbage. We have stained them with oil, coal dust, tar dyes, and chemical liquids discharged by industries. We have burned them with powerful acids that destroy aquatic life. We have turned them gray and murky with silt and sludge, smothering shellfish and other forms of bottom life. We have used them to dispose of residues containing long-lasting poisons, some so powerful that less than one part per million in a stream can kill fish. And, as though to show our contempt for nature, we have dumped billions of tons of trash in our once lovely waters—worn-out tires, old mattresses, rusty oil drums, refuse from hospitals, broken glass, dead animals, and junked automobiles. It is a dismal fact that we now have contaminated and despoiled most of the major rivers and bays in the entire United States.

Chesapeake Bay, like most of our major bays, long has been a receptacle for the pollution load from several dirty rivers and the sewage and oily wastes from heavy ship traffic. The Chesapeake's once clear waters have become turbid, and its bottom life is choked by silt and sickened by toxic pollutants. Particularly hard hit are the oysters, whose young depend on clean rocks on which to attach themselves. Fifty years ago the Chesapeake was the main harvest ground for the 10 million to 12 million bushels of oysters that Maryland then produced. Now, despite advances in oyster culture, the harvest is only one tenth of what it was. Each year large expanses of shellfish beds along U.S. shores are "uncertified" by health authorities; that is, they are found to be polluted and cannot be harvested.

Consider the mighty Hudson, first described in the logbook of Henry Hudson's *Half Moon*. As that explorer sailed up the river in 1609, searching for the fabled Northwest Passage, he was disappointed as the water lost its salty taste and became fresh. In our times anyone tasting water from the river would be risking his or her life. The Hudson is repeatedly contaminated by raw sewage before it flows past New York City, where it receives another colossal discharge.

Mark Twain in *Life on the Mississippi* called the Mississippi basin "the body of the nation" and wrote lovingly of "the great Mississippi, the magnificent Mississippi, rolling its mile-wide tide, shining in the sun." Today pollution experts call this once-proud river the garbage dump of mid-America. Along its winding 2350-mile (3790 km) length the river suffers all the indignities a society can heap on it. Hundreds of towns and cities use it as a sewer. Thousands of factories, packing houses, stockyards, refineries and mills drain into it their assortment of wastes: oil, toxic metals, slaughterhouse offal, pickling liquors, chicken feathers, garbage, chemical sludge, and other horrors. Water birds and fish on the Mississippi have been killed by oil slicks. Spawning beds have been smothered by silt and sludge. Occasionally, dead water, robbed of its oxygen by decomposing organic wastes, has slaughtered countless migrating fish.

In the great industrial complex of Detroit, municipal and industrial wastes are handled in Model T style. Among the daily items the Detroit River is supposed to absorb and carry away are thousands of gallons of oil, acid, and chemical salts. These are all in addition to the sketchily treated human wastes from a population of several million. The Detroit River is only one of the many polluted streams debauching Lake Erie.

It is a dismal fact that we now have polluted almost every large river, lake, and bay in the entire United States.

Then there is the once-pure Lake Tahoe, in the Sierra Nevada Mountains. Seen from an airplane, the bright blue lake, 20 miles long, looks as pure as it was years ago when Captain John C. Fremont discovered it. But along some of its coves telltale green splotches are starting to creep out from the shore—algae, a condition that is relatively new at Tahoe. Until recently the high, isolated lake had been a summer resort with a few homes scattered around its rocky shores. Then came the boom of people, and, with them, definite signs of pollution.

Fortunately, the future does not look as grim as the above information would make it seem. Today's advanced methods of waste treatment can purify water to about any level nec-

Sugar beet waste dumped into this stream in Ohio killed thousands of fish. (U.S. Department of Agriculture, photo by W. E. Seibel)

essary or desired. This means a city that usually disposes of 60% to 90% of its water after the first use, can significantly increase its water supply by cleansing its wastewater for recycling. Until recently, conventional treatment methods removed about 90% of the oxygen-consuming wastes. But, current methods can remove nearly 100% of these wastes. From this point of view, the future of water quality is promising. Even though the processes of water purification are very expensive, prevention and cure are both cheaper than the eventual alternative.

NOISE AND ODOR POLLUTION

Noise pollution is the presence of too much noise or unpleasant noise. The growling and honking of cars, the clatter of machines, and the constant roar of planes overhead are examples of pollution that detract from a peaceful life-style. For many people constant noise causes emotional stress, gradual loss of hearing, and job inefficiency. Further, it can detract from the serenity of a calm and peaceful environment.

Odor pollution is of a different type. It results from sulfur fumes and other industrial wastes, smoke, gasoline and diesel exhaust, and other combustion wastes, and sewage. Odor, like other kinds of pollution, can detract greatly from the qualify of life.

WHAT IS BEING DONE

There are four major aspects to the control of pollution and ugliness: personal, social, political, and economic. The *personal* aspect involves individual concepts of a desirable environment and its importance to society. One's perception of beauty and cleanliness and the desire for an attractive environment are personal qualities partly inherent and partly developed. These concepts are also a part of one's education.

The *social* aspect is expressed in the unity of thought and action by a group, or by society as a whole. Without unified thought and action, little can be accomplished toward controlling pollution. Probably of even greater importance is the *political* aspect. Many of the major problems of pollution require the passage and enforcement of laws at various levels and other governmental influence. Without effective political machinery–that is, without politicians who are committed to fostering a desirable environment–only a limited amount can be accomplished.

Many alarms have been sounded, but alarms by themselves do not put out the fire.

The fourth aspect, *economics*, is the thorn in our side, because many industrial managers and public officials claim that cleanup and prevention are often economically prohibitive. Yet what is or is not economically feasible depends largely on priority. When pollution reaches the critical stage, then control becomes feasible even at the expense of industrial or other kinds of development.

In 1963 Congress passed the Air Pollution Control Act (now amended and called the Clean Air Act), which represented the first major effort to clean up the air that Americans must breathe. This, along with some good efforts by states, local agencies, and some private industries, has produced worthy results. Yet the major causes of air pollution still await our solutions. The automobile industry now installs antipollution devices on new cars, but the increase in the number of cars will offset the effectiveness of these devices. Many industrial plants have reduced their contributions to pollution, but more factories are being built, and the total effect is more pollution instead of less. Some cities are working diligently to reduce pollution caused by the incineration of wastes, but the growth of cities offsets much of the results of the improved methods.

Significant steps have also been taken toward solving the problem of water pollution. In 1965 the Water Quality Act was passed by Congress, giving the states until July 1967 to develop standards of quality to be maintained on interstate streams within their boundaries. The act also established the Federal Water Pollution Control Administration to represent the government in this field. But, despite its value, the act is still a compromise, and its effects are quite limited. One of the most serious problems is that one fourth of our cities and towns still have no sewage-treatment plants of any kind, and half of the existing plants are outdated and not of the type that purifies water.

Land pollution is perhaps less critical than air and water pollution from the standpoint of health. But with regard to an attractive environment, land pollution is perhaps our greatest problem, and it is receiving only moderate attention. A few bold projects designed to beautify blight areas of cities have made a mark on the problem. Billboard controls, especially on interstate highways, have progressed. Much has been done to develop a litter-conscious public. And efforts are being made toward soil conservation, reforestation, and rehabilitation of land that has been strip-mined. Some of the sore spots still receiving little attention are neglected vacant lots, industrial sites, auto-salvage areas, and crowded residential districts within cities.

Despite the fact that some good efforts are being made, our waters, our air, and our land are becoming more polluted day by day. Our industrial expansion and population growth are progressing faster than our techniques for controlling pollution.

STIMULUS FOR LOCAL ACTION

It is significant that much of the pioneering of environment improvement comes from efforts by individuals and citizen groups that tackle a particular local problem with imagination and skill, and thus provide a model for others. Chances are, there are several immediate challenges for your community. It may be that more playgrounds are needed, that a stretch of roadside should be planted, or that a marsh ought to be saved. The project will be worth doing in its own right, and it may also serve as a wedge for other efforts.

The first step toward action should be to survey the local situation. Become informed about people's needs, interests, and opinions in regard to beautification and pollution control.

Pennsylvania countryside strip-mined for coal. It is practically impossible to recapture natural beauty once the area has been significantly modified for other uses. (U.S. Forest Service)

Find out which agencies and citizen groups will help to bring about desired results. Specifically, ask yourself the following questions:

1. How do elected officials stand on the matter of beautification and pollution control? Have they shown any significant interest in improving the environment? Has anyone approached them on the matter? Perhaps they need some public pressure to motivate them to act. You may be the one to convince them of strong public desire for a beautiful environment.
2. Is there a planning commission? Every community needs a planning commission to have a design by which to grow in an orderly fashion. Further, the commission members must be creative and foresighted.
3. Has a master plan been developed? Without a plan and an agency to implement the plan, a community will grow in a disorderly fashion.
4. Is there a park and recreation department? This is the one agency whose primary concern is the provision of adequate recreation opportunities. If the department has good leadership and adequate support it can make a great contribution toward building a livable community.
5. Is there an agency for waste disposal? Waste disposal and trash cleanup are important to the environment. The more populated a community becomes, the more attention must be given to this matter.
6. Is pollution of air and water receiving adequate attention? Does any agency have the power to control sources of air and water pollution and, if so, is it doing the job effectively?
7. Which civic groups and private organizations are available to join in the effort?

Action for Open Space

A certain amount of open space in and around populated areas can add to the quality of living. There are three important considerations with regard to open space: (1) amount, (2) convenience of its location, and (3) its quality or particular characteristics.

When considering action for open space, citizens or planners should consider the following questions:

1. Would a planning grant be justifiable in the case of your community? If so, such a grant might be obtained under the 701 section of the Federal Housing Act, which enables the federal Department of Housing and Urban Development to pay two thirds of the cost for a community planning study.
2. Are there areas in or around your community that would qualify for purchase and development under the Land and Water Conservation Fund Program, which is administered by the National Park Service? This fund is established for the specific purpose of enhancing the purchase and development of outdoor recreation areas.
3. Can the present open space, including parks and playgrounds, be upgraded to serve the public better?
4. Are there any private groups or individuals who may want to donate land for open space in the community?

5. Would it be desirable and is it possible to zone nearby agricultural land in such a way as to encourage its being retained for agricultural use rather than developed for residential or industrial uses?
6. Are there spots of such historic significance that they should be established as historic sites? Money and advice in support of such sites are available from the Department of Housing and Urban Development and the National Park Service.
7. Would changes in zoning help provide more open space in your community?

Action for a Better Landscape

What does a person perceive while driving home from work, or on the way to the supermarket? And what of the people on the wrong side of town? What do their eyes view? The critical, unifying parts of the community's landscape are the parts that the greatest number experience in common—the focal points.

Ask yourself these questions about the landscape of your community:

1. Is there need for an antilitter drive?
2. Should your community have a clean-up and paint-up day?
3. Do additional trees and flowers need to be planted? If so, which organizations are willing to help?
4. Should you press for underground utility lines?
5. Is the lack of billboard control detracting from the landscape?
6. Is there need for street benches and park picnic furniture?

A successful environmental reform will require much more than piecemeal dosages of technical antidotes for individual environmental problems. It will require a substantial renovation of the American life-style.

Action for Clean Air and Clean Water

Since the passage of the Water Quality Act of 1965, there has been authority for the establishment of water-quality standards for interstate and coastal waters. Fortunately all of the states have now submitted water-quality standards for their interstate waters. The enforcement of these standards will go a long way toward cleaning up our dirty waters.

Most states have agencies that provide some form of technical assistance to communities for water-pollution control. The field people of these agencies can help your community evaluate its needs and direct it toward the right assistance.

The 1967 passage of amendments to the Clean Air Act gives the government a new and powerful mandate to move forward with the enforcement of air-quality standards. Any incorporated community is eligible for project grants to help finance pollution control.

Most citizens who have fought to control pollution and ugliness have found the battle to be tough. But they have carried on under the inspiration of creating a better place for themselves and their children and for all those who follow. It is, without question, a battle worth fighting.

POSITIVE ASPECTS OF TECHNOLOGY

Composting leaves and twigs is an ancient agricultural process. Modern technology can make it work in cities, too. Using techniques developed by the Department of Agriculture, specially prepared soils can be mixed with sludge from sewage treatment plants to provide the necessary medium to support a healthy growth of sod and other vegetation. Giant concrete-mixer trucks have been used successfully for stirring the sludge together with natural soil and other components to produce the best mixture. This is only one example of how to use technology to benefit the environment.

It has been found that construction equipment and engineering techniques can be used to undo earlier damage, and in some cases improve on the natural setting. Heavy users of technology can improve a swamp for wildlife propagation rather than obliterate one. They can prepare forests and parks over the fertile soil of landfill dumps. They can level abandoned factories and warehouses and prepare these areas for attractive open-space developments. And they can make numerous other changes that contribute to a better environment.

The technological specialists are not all bad in the environmental sense. There are many engineers as well as biologists who are numbered among the environmentalists. The technologists have proved they can make crooked rivers straight. There are some instances where they could just as well make straight rivers crooked. They can destroy wetlands and estuaries, but they can also build dikes and rechannel water to create new water areas. Technologists have proved they can beautify highways, bridges, and buildings. The challenge is to get environmental issues high enough on the priority scale that they receive first-order attention by technology specialists.

ARE WE PROGRESSING?

With respect to nature, archeologists and historians have found that civilizations pass through four stages during the course of development. In the first stage we battle nature for our survival. We attempt to cope with nature and conquer it. In the second stage we cooperate with nature in an effort to become more civilized, and nature helps us to produce the goods that we need. The third stage involves exploiting nature by overharvesting the resources and overusing natural goods. After recognizing this error and the futility of this approach, we enter the fourth stage, that of rehabilitating nature, attempting to heal the wounds we have caused.

The divisions between these four stages are not clear-cut, and at a particular time a society may not be at the same stage in all respects. In America we have seemingly passed through the first and second stages, and for the most part have been in the third stage for quite some time. We are now, let us hope, entering the fourth stage. Though we have overharvested and overused our natural resources and are still doing so, finally many of us have recognized this error and are attempting to rectify it.

Like winds and sunsets, wild things were taken for granted until progress began to do away with them. Now we face the question of whether a still higher standard of living is worth the cost in things natural, wild, and free.

—Aldo Leopold, *A Sand County Almanac*, Ballantine Books, New York, 1978, p. xvii.

Discussion Questions

1.   It has been said that pollution is like the common cold in terms of its effect throughout the total population. Discuss the meaning of this. Do you agree? Why or why not?
2.   What is acid precipitation and how is it caused? Why is it a dangerous form of pollution?
3.   Discuss the purpose of the Clean Air Act and the Water Quality Act. How have these acts affected pollution? What promise do they seem to have for the future?
4.   Give specific examples of how pollution reduces or destroys outdoor recreation. Which kind of pollution problems are of particular concern to recreationists?
5.   What are some of the forms of pollution in the vicinity of your community? Is the problem growing or diminishing? What is being done about the problem? What more should be done?
6.   Pollution is said often to be a result of our unwise use of our environment. Can some forms of pollution occur regardless of human involvement? Explain.

Recommended Readings

Alexander, Tom."The Hazardous-Waste Nightmare." *Fortune*, 21 April 1980, pp. 52–58.

"The Clash Brewing Over Clean Air." *Time*, 6 July 1981, p. 64.

Cross, Robert F. "A Challenge for the Eighties: DEC's Goals for the Next Ten Years." *The Conservationist*, July–August 1981, p. 19.

"Hard Times Come to Environmentalists." *U.S. News and World Report*, 10 March 1980, p. 49.

Hendrey, George R. "Acid Rain and Gray Snow." *Natural History*, February 1981, pp. 58–65.

Jennrich, John H. "Environmental Control: Keeping the Good Earth Clean." *Nation's Business*, December 1979, pp. 73–76.

La Bastille, Anne. "Acid Rain: How Great a Menace?" *National Geographic*, November 1981, p. 78.

"1981 Environmental Quality Index." *National Wildlife*, February–March 1981, pp. 29–36.

"Outdoor Recreation and Environmental Concern: A Reexamination." *Leisure Sciences*, Vol. 2, No. 1, p. 1.

"Pro and Con: Relax Air Pollution Standards." *U.S. News and World Report*, 24 May 1982, p. 39.

"Resort Fever Is Changing the Face of Appalachia." *U.S. News and World Report*, 14 April 1980, p. 52.

"Retreat on Clean Air." *Consumer Reports*, April 1982, p. 177.

Rosencranz, Armin. "Economic Approaches to Air Pollution Control." *Environment*, October 1981, pp. 25–30.

Stokes, Bruce. "Housing: The Environmental Issues." *Sierra Club Bulletin*, September–October 1982, p. 45.

U.S. Environmental Protection Agency. *Recreation and Land Use: The Public Benefits of Clean Water.* Office of Environmental Review. Washington, D.C.: U.S. Department of the Interior, 1980.

Ward, Morris A. "Congress Confronts the Issues." *Environment*, July–August 1981, pp. 6–15.

CHAPTER 18

Planning Procedures

Planning is a vital part of overall management. It forces people to think beyond the present and consider the possible actions for both the near- and long-term future. Planning accomplishes at least two vital tasks: (1) it stimulates foresight, and (2) it encourages and enhances advanced decision making. Planning requires analysis of the past, consideration of the present, and preparation for the future. Here are some logical steps involved in planning:

1. Define the problem or need.
2. Determine what final results are desired.
3. Formulate alternative approaches for achieving the results.
4. Select the appropriate course of action.
5. Periodically evaluate your progress and your plan.

Through the planning process people learn about the social, physical, and economic conditions and the interrelationships that should be considered in the plan. Further, planning helps to clearly consider and correctly define goals, objectives, and aspirations. Planning is like a road map. It can help indicate both *where* to go and *how* to get there.

We shape our physical environment and, in turn, it shapes us.

PRINCIPLES OF PLANNING

There are several basic principles that should be considered in planning for parks and recreation. These are little more than common sense, and they apply to a variety of situations.

1. Park and recreation areas should provide opportunities for all persons regardless of race, creed, age, sex, or economic status.

2. To meet the needs in a particular geographic area, consideration should be made of all the resources available, including lakes and streams, woodlands, marshes, mountains, historical and archeological sites, and areas of scenic value and special interest.

3. Multiple use can often add to the total use of an area; therefore, multiple use should be considered, even though it is not always accepted.

4. Early acquisition of land based on a comprehensive recreation plan is essential. Unless sites are acquired well in advance of demand, land costs often become prohibitive.

5. Timely evaluation should be made of present recreational needs and future trends to accurately project for the future.

6. Insofar as possible, recreation areas and facilities should be properly distributed in accordance with the population, so that all of the people have approximately equal availability of recreational opportunities.

7. The design of individual park and recreation sites should be as flexible as possible to accommodate changing patterns of recreation in the given area.

8. Barriers should be avoided whenever possible to provide for easy access to recreation areas by the elderly, the handicapped, and others with mobility restrictions.

9. There should be citizen involvement in planning whenever possible, because this results in good ideas and added enthusiasm toward using the areas once they are developed.

10. Responsibilities should be defined and agreed upon by the various governmental and private agencies so that the duplication of areas, facilities, and services will be avoided and so the public will receive the best return possible on the dollars spent.

11. Park and recreation lands should be protected in perpetuity against encroachment and nonrecreation purposes. These areas should not be considered the path of least resistance for highways, public utilities, and buildings.

12. The plan for a particular recreation area or the plan for a system of areas and facilities should be carefully integrated with the total master plan for the particular agency or area. Park and recreation planning is not an isolated function. It should be integrated with the total plan.

LEGAL STRUCTURE

Planning must be done in accordance with the laws, regulations and policies that will govern or influence implementation of the plan. In a broad sense the legal structure includes federal, state, and local laws as well as the applicable regulations and policies. Of course, plans that are contradictory to any element of the legal structure are unsound and may be impossible to implement.

Among the most basic aspects of the legal structure are *organic documents*–documents that define the purposes, jurisdictions, and limitations of the particular agency or business entity.

It is especially important for planners to understand the organic definition of the agency they represent.

Federal laws are printed in the U.S. Code. They are categorized so as to show the current status of all legislation concerning a subject. Old versions are deleted as new laws and amendments supersede them. *Federal policies* are stated in the Code of Federal Regulations as well as in documents of the various federal agencies. The U.S. Code and the Code of Federal Regulations are available in most major libraries.

State laws are found in the state code for the particular state, and *local laws* appear in the local register of ordinances. These publications are also found in the major libraries of the particular locality.

One of the best methods of finding specific laws and obtaining legal interpretations and advice is from the particular government attorney, such as city attorney, county attorney, or state attorney general. Also, resource managers or recreation professionals can often be helpful to others on matters pertaining to the legal aspects of park and recreation planning.

PUBLIC INVOLVEMENT

In most situations the more successful activities are those planned with the people and not for them. Professionals in public agencies should not view themselves as decision makers in the autocratic sense. Instead, they should serve as coordinators of the decision-making process. This helps to make sure that public areas and facilities are used and managed according to the interests, needs, and will of the public. Methods of public involvement include the following:

1. Public meetings where people have a chance to hear proposals and voice their support or resistance.
2. Coverage in the news media. This exposes ideas and alternatives to the public and stimulates involvement.
3. The appointment of advisory committees to represent the public.
4. Public surveys or polls to provide information for the planning process.
5. Sensitivity to members of the public.
6. Presentations at the meetings of service clubs, political groups, and auxiliary organizations.

Managers of public agencies ought to demonstrate attitudes and procedures that encourage the interchange of facts and opinions in a cooperative atmosphere. The U.S. Forest Service[1] recommends the following attitudes for its personnel, and also the employees of other public agencies.

1. Recognize that public involvement is an essential part of decision making.
2. Discard notions that only professionals can judge actions affecting environmental quality; public concern may well outweigh scientific considerations and cause modification of proposals.

---

1. U.S. Forest Service. *Guide to Public Involvement in Decision Making,* Department of Agriculture, Washington, D.C., 1974, p. 14.

3. Be willing to accept criticism with a positive rather than a defensive attitude.
4. Keep records of public involvement and decision making; it allows full review before making final decisions and is a reference if the decisions are challenged.
5. Realize that involving the public does not relieve agency professionals of the final responsibility for the decision.
6. Give equal consideration to the opinions of past opponents of the agency and of past supporters; all interest groups are champions of some aspect of good resource management.
7. Allow ample time for public study of issues and the land under question.
8. Communicate objectives and procedures for specific issues in early stages of involvement.
9. Inform and involve all groups interested or affected by the issue.
10. After decisions are made, immediately inform all interested parties and the general public.
11. Keep the participation process visible and dignified to maintain public confidence.

It is important to recognize that almost every plan or aspect of the plan will have both support and resistance from different individuals and segments of the public. This is normal because each person sees a plan or proposal from his or her own point of view and evaluates it in light of that understanding. Also some individuals and groups have vested interests. Thus, it should not be expected that a plan or proposal will have universal support. The best that usually can be hoped for is a compromise that will produce the greatest good for the greatest number.

COOPERATION

Public and private-sector cooperation at all levels can result in accomplishments not otherwise possible. A cooperative approach usually results in filling the recreation needs in the most cost-efficient manner. Unwanted competition and overlap among agencies, groups, and individuals is minimized through mutual support from the public and private sectors.

Cooperation among government agencies is equally important. Local divisions of government such as the divisions of community planning, personnel, finance, purchasing, law enforcement, and city streets play important supportive roles. Also, cooperation from civic groups and local leaders is very beneficial.

Further, in planning it is essential for the local recreation and park agency to cooperate with state and federal agencies. It would be senseless and unjustified to have a lack of cooperation among government agencies, since all of them are supported by tax money and exist for the good of the people.

LEVELS OF PLANNING

The levels of planning can be viewed in different ways, but in the case of parks and recreation a logical hierarchy is one that relates to levels of government. In this hierarchy there are four levels: national, state, local, or site planning.

1. Nationwide planning involves the overall recreation needs and projected trends for the nation as a whole, including the roles of the different national agencies and the national policies that affect recreation opportunities.
2. State recreation planning contains essentially the same elements as planning at the national level except it is limited to the geographic area of the state.
3. Local planning is done by cities, counties, school districts, and other local agencies.
4. Site or project planning pertains to a single recreation site or facility.

Planning at each of these levels must feed into the next higher level, and each succeeding level should form a framework within which the levels below it can properly fit.

Some localities do not have adequate park and recreation areas because they don't *plan* to have them.

NATIONWIDE PLANNING

The outdoors has always been an important part of American life—first as a wilderness to be conquered and then as a source of inspiration and recreation. In this latter sense its importance is still increasing. Of course, recreation planning at the national level has occurred to some degree for a long time. Before a few decades ago, such planning was sketchy and inconsistent. The first comprehensive planning effort was done by the Outdoor Recreation Resources Review Commission, which began its work in the late 1950s.

Outdoor Recreation Resources Review Commission

Recognizing the need for a nationwide study of recreation opportunities and problems, Congress established the Outdoor Recreation Resources Review Commission in 1958. The commission consisted of eight members of Congress and seven private citizens appointed by the president, with Lawrence Rockefeller as the commission's chairman. Congress directed the commission to survey the outdoor-recreation needs of the people for the next 40 years and to recommend actions to meet those needs.

The commission took inventory of the nation's supply of outdoor recreation spaces, including such resources as parks, forests, and fishing and hunting areas. It questioned a large number of people to learn what people do for recreation and what they are likely to do in the future. It estimated recreation demands through the year 2000 and made more than 50 specific recommendations intended to ensure that the benefits of outdoor recreation would be available to all Americans, now and in the future. The final report to the Congress, made in 1961, included 27 volumes, with each volume written on a separate topic of special significance.

The commission found that adequate provisions were not being made for the rapidly expanding outdoor-recreation needs. It found that the gap between demand and supply would widen over the coming years if effective actions were not taken promptly. And it found

An accurately determined carrying capacity is one important aspect of planning.
(National Park Service, photo by Cecil W. Stoughton)

a qualitative as well as a quantitative lag. Many existing programs were not aimed at providing what most people actually wanted. Better-planned, bolder, and more imaginative efforts were required.

Soon after the commission had completed its work, several significant actions resulted from the recommendations: (1) numerous states authorized and helped finance recreation land-acquisition programs, (2) the national park system was expanded significantly, (3) the Bureau of Outdoor Recreation was established (the bureau has since been dissolved and its functions transferred to the National Park Service), (4) a national wilderness system was officially established, (5) the Land and Water Conservation Fund Program was inaugurated, (6) a wild and scenic rivers system was established, (7) a national trails system was started, and (8) an ongoing national outdoor-recreation planning procedure was developed.

In addition to these prominent developments, numerous lesser actions were prompted by the work of the commission. Obviously, the Outdoor Recreation Resources Review Commission caused a major and lasting impact.

Public Land Law Review Commission

In 1964, by act of Congress, the Public Land Law Review Commission was established to review the nation's land use and the laws and policies governing it. The final charge to the commission was to provide recommendations to Congress about the status of land use, the problems associated with it, and the changes that would be needed for the future. The commission published its report in 1970, and the report contained 452 recommendations. The recreation section of the report tied in closely with the Outdoor Recreation Resources Review

Commission report, and it supported many of the recommendations previously stated by the recreation commission. The Public Land Law Review Commission's report contained the following pertinent statement about the role of the federal government:

> The Federal Government should be responsible for the preservation of scenic areas, natural wonders, primitive areas, and historic sites of national significance; for cooperation with the states through technical and financial assistance; for the promotion of interstate arrangements . . . and for management of federal lands for the broadest recreation benefit consistent with other essential uses.

Among other recommendations, the commission confirmed the desirability of multiple use of Forest Service and Bureau of Land Management lands, with recreation being one of the basic uses. It also confirmed the importance of emphasizing the preservation concept in the management of national parks and monuments and the need for an expanded national wilderness system. Further, its report contained several recommendations pertaining to the importance of (1) improvements in land classification, (2) identification of prime recreation resources, (3) an aggressive acquisition program, and (4) new methods of financing acquisition and development of recreation areas and facilities. It recommended that the land purchases emphasize (1) right-of-way corridors (passages) through private lands in order to make public areas more accessible to recreationists, (2) additions to the National Park System, (3) expansion of the wilderness system, (4) acquisition of additional seashores, and (5) further development of the national wild and scenic rivers system and the national trails system.

The commission also made recommendations about the roles that ought to be played by state and local governments, and the private sector:

> The states should play a pivotal role in making outdoor-recreation opportunities available by the acquisition of land, the development of sites, and the provision and maintenance of facilities of state or regional significance; by assistance to local governments; and by the provision of leadership and planning.

> Local governments should expand their efforts to provide outdoor recreation opportunities, with particular emphasis upon securing open space and developing recreation areas in and around metropolitan and other urban areas.

> Individual initiative and private enterprise should continue to be the most important force in outdoor recreation, providing many and varied opportunities for a vast number of people, as well as the goods and services used by people in their recreation activities. Government should encourage the work of nonprofit groups wherever possible. It should also stimulate desirable commercial development, which can be particularly effective in providing facilities and services where demand is sufficient to return a profit.

Nationwide Outdoor Recreation Plans

In its early existence the Bureau of Outdoor Recreation (founded in 1965) was charged with the responsibility of developing and maintaining a national plan, and for coordinating the outdoor-recreation effort at the national level. After much work with federal, state, and local government agencies and with nongovernment groups and individuals, the first national plan was formulated in 1969, but it never was published. A national plan was first published in 1973, and it was titled *Outdoor Recreation: A Legacy for America*. The next published plan became available in 1979, and soon afterward work began on a plan to be published in the mid-1980s.

In 1978 the Heritage Conservation and Recreation Service was organized, and it encompassed the former Bureau of Outdoor Recreation. In 1981 the Heritage Conservation and Recreation Service was dissolved, and its responsibilities were given to the National Park Service. Consequently, the Park Service is now the main recreation-planning agency for the federal government. It also is the bank for the Land and Water Conservation Fund, which provides grants to states for the acquisition and development of recreation areas.

Public Law 88-29 directs the secretary of the interior to

> formulate and maintain a comprehensive nationwide outdoor recreation program, taking into consideration the plans of the various federal agencies, states, and their political subdivisions. The plan shall set forth the needs and demands of the public for outdoor recreation for the current and foreseeable future. Further, the plan shall identify critical outdoor recreation problems, recommend solutions, and recommend desirable actions to be taken at each level of government and by private interests.

The 1973 Nationwide Plan

The 1973 plan treated recreation as an important element in land-use planning. The plan committed the federal government to several actions. Specifically, it said that to *increase the availability of recreation resources*, the federal government will:

1. Complete a program of identification and selection and a plan for acquisition of those superlative areas needed to round out the federal recreation estate.
2. Continue to use the Land and Water Conservation Fund to acquire needed federal recreation lands and assist the states in doing the same.
3. Open to the public directly or through state and local entities those underused portions of federal properties or facilities having public recreation values, when such lands are not available for transfer.
4. Accelerate evaluations of proposed trails, wild and scenic rivers, wilderness areas, wetlands, and historical properties to ensure that those unique lands are preserved by federal, state, or local governments or private interests for the benefit of the public; and accelerate the evaluation of federal land holdings to determine if beaches, shorelines, islands, and natural areas can be made available for increased public recreation use.

Further, the plan stated that to *improve the management and administration of recreation resources* and programs, the federal government will:

1. Accelerate the identification and no-cost transfer of surplus and underused real property to state and local governments for parks and other recreation sites.
2. When the land is not available for transfer, and direct federal management is not necessary or desirable, take necessary steps to transfer management responsibility for existing recreational units to state and local governments.
3. Promote recreation developments on or near federal lands on the basis of regional land-use plans. Whenever possible, private investment should be used for the provision of these services.

4.   Undertake preparation of recreation land-use plans for all management units and coordinate such planning with all interested federal, state, and local government agencies and private entities.

The 1979 Nationwide Plan

The 1979 nationwide plan followed a format that was much different from the previous plan. It consisted of two major divisions: (1) an *assessment* of outdoor recreation; and (2) a recreation *action program.*

The *assessment* provides an overview of the benefits and impacts of recreation and discusses existing trends, needs, resources, and opportunities for future consideration. It also includes pertinent information about demographic characteristics, the agencies that provide outdoor recreation at the federal level, the national resource base, facilities, equipment, and program services, problems and issues, financing, and future directions. It is intended to be a reference document, and the issues that it discusses will be used as a basis for developing annual action programs until the next five-year assessment is completed.

An attractively designed walkway protects the natural features of this high-use natural area. (National Park Service, photo by Richard Frear)

The *action program* was finally narrowed to nine pertinent issues of national significance. These issues were condensed from a very large number of issues that were identified by numerous representatives from agencies of government of all levels and the private sector. Briefs of the nine issues composing the action program are stated here.

1. Federal land acquisition:

- A new and more effective planning and decision-making process will be instituted to identify and select lands eligible for the federal portion of the Land and Water Conservation Fund.
- A policy will be developed defining the federal role in protection and acquisition of land for conservation of natural, cultural, and recreational resources. This policy will encourage alternatives to outright acquisition.

2. Wild, scenic, and recreational rivers:

- New guidelines will be developed to shorten the time required to study potential wild, scenic, and recreational rivers.
- Federal agencies will develop guidelines to avoid adverse effects on potential wild and scenic rivers identified in the nationwide rivers inventory.
- Federal land-managing agencies will assess the potential of rivers identified in the nationwide inventory located on their lands and take steps to designate or manage these rivers as components of the national wild and scenic rivers system.
- Administration of the Clean Water Act and the Wild and Scenic Rivers Act will be better coordinated to ensure that investments made to clean up rivers and waterways provide maximum public recreation benefits.

3. National trails and trail systems:

- The Forest Service will establish 145 additional national recreation trails in the national forest system.
- Federal land-managing agencies will establish goals for creating additional national recreation trails on public lands other than national forests.
- The Department of the Interior will accelerate its efforts to encourage state, local, and private land managers to submit applications for new national recreation trails.
- A grass-roots effort will be undertaken across the country to assess national trail needs. This assessment will be made by representatives of state, local and private trail interests in cooperation with federal agencies.
- States, localities and private landholders will be more actively encouraged to develop trails on their lands and to participate with federal agencies and trails users in creating a national trails system to meet public needs.
- The accomplishments of the "rails-to-trails" program of the Railroad Revitalization and Regulatory Reform Act will be evaluated and further recommendations made to eliminate outstanding problems.
- State and local governments will be encouraged to develop appropriate types of bikeways using existing federal programs.

4. Water resources:

- Federal water-quality grants will be more closely examined to determine the degree to which they include recreation considerations.
- Nonstructural alternatives to flood control, including the preservation of open space for recreation, will be evaluated for their applicability in flood-prone communities.
- Actions will be taken to ensure that urban waterfront revitalization projects include considerations for recreation and public access.

5. Energy conservation. A program of energy conservation will be developed for all recreation lands, facilities, and programs, and guidelines will be issued for all federal recreation grant programs to state and local governments.

6. Environmental education. Guidelines will be prepared for all Department of the Interior agencies and coordinated with other federal agencies.

7. The handicapped:

- The Department of the Interior will provide improved access to recreation facilities.
- The Department of the Interior will establish procedures to involve disabled citizens in the development of recreation policy and programs.

8. The private sector. The feasibility of cooperative agreements between the private sector and public recreation agencies will be explored as an alternative method of improving public recreation opportunities, and appropriate demonstrations will be undertaken.

9. Research. A comprehensive national recreation-research agenda will be prepared.

Continuous Planning

To ensure that planning is continuous, a Division of Nationwide Planning has been established within the National Park Service. The mission of this unit includes the following: (1) to define and monitor the annual action programs, (2) to update the five-year assessment, (3) to conduct nationwide recreation surveys and coordinate more specialized federal surveys, (4) to compile and update a national research agenda for recreation, and (5) to promote long-range planning for the future of recreation in America. The Division of Nationwide Planning also gives guidance and technical assistance for statewide comprehensive outdoor-recreation planning, which occurs in all of the 50 states.

STATE OUTDOOR RECREATION PLANNING

For a state to receive financial assistance from the federal Land and Water Conservation Fund, the state must have a current plan that describes the ways in which it will help satisfy recreational needs at the various governmental levels within the state. A new plan must be prepared at least once every five years.

In preparing the plan, each state is encouraged to hold public meetings so that government officials and interested citizens can review the state's recreation policies. This enables citizens to suggest changes in policy and inform state officials of the local needs. Further, it is recommended that the state recreation plan include at least the following kinds of information:

1. A brief description of factors—such as climate, topography, wildlife, history, populations, and urbanization—that influence outdoor recreation in the state.
2. A list of the federal and state agencies that are responsible for creating, administering, and financially assisting publicly owned recreation areas.
3. An inventory of recreation areas that are publicly or privately owned, summarized by region or country, and a list of historic sites.
4. An estimate of the number of people who participate in each of several recreational activities, now and in the future, and an estimate of the frequency with which they participate.
5. A statement of recreation needs that will be met by the state, county, and local governments.
6. A statement of recreation needs of special populations, such as the elderly, the handicapped, and the poor.
7. A description of actions proposed for the next five years to provide more outdoor-recreation opportunities, such as proposals for acquisition and development, legislation, financial and technical assistance, and research.

The plan in each state is developed under the leadership of the state outdoor recreation liaison officer, and in most states it is this officer's responsibility to coordinate the implementation of the state plan with agencies of the federal government and with political subdivisions of the state. A copy of the plan for any particular state can be obtained from the state liaison office. A current list of these offices appears in Appendix D.

LOCAL PLANNING

The responsibility for local recreation planning is usually entrusted to one of two public agencies—the planning agency or the park and recreation agency. In a survey conducted by the National Association of County Park and Recreation Directors, it was found that most plans are prepared by the planning agency in cooperation with the park and recreation department. The planning agency usually has ready access to demographic data and other basic information used in planning. In addition, it is well situated to dovetail the park and recreation plan with other elements of the comprehensive plan for the community.

Although no one has a single best method of developing a plan, planners generally agree that the procedure can be divided into three major phases: (1) collection of data about past history and present status, (2) projection of future park and recreation needs, and (3) formulation of realistic proposals for both the near and long-term future.

Little is accomplished by comprehensive planning unless implementation occurs. Important aspects of the implementation include (1) a definite timetable, (2) adequate financial support, and (3) cooperation from other agencies and the citizenry.

In view of our increasing population and urbanization, it is essential that timely *zoning ordinances* be enforced to prevent overcrowding and disorderly conditions. Adequate zoning for parks and open space can greatly improve living conditions and result in long-term increases in property values.

In many cities and counties, local officials have adopted *land-dedication ordinances,* which require subdivision developers to dedicate a portion of the subdivision as permanent open space or to make a cash payment to the local government in lieu of land dedication. Such ordinances are predicated on the grounds that each subdivision increases the demand for recreation areas and that each subdivider should be required to furnish open space for the community in relation to the need created. This is justified on the same basis as the requirement to install streets, sidewalks, and other community improvements in connection with subdivisions. Theoretically the developer recovers the monetary cost by raising the price of the homes. Thus, the home owners who will benefit the most from the open space actually pay for it.

In some localities officials are taking steps to preserve open space in residential areas by enacting *cluster* or *density* zoning ordinances. A cluster zoning ordinance establishes an overall density for the area, usually in terms of acreage for each dwelling unit. However, it allows the developer to adjust the lot sizes and group the homes as long as the density limit is not exceeded. One section or tract may be developed at a high density and the remaining portions at a low density, or all development may be centered in one section with the remainder in open space for recreation purposes. These ordinances stipulate whether the open space is to be retained in private ownership or dedicated to the local government. Both the community and home owners may reap aesthetic, recreational, and economic benefits from cluster developments. Local government officials find this a practical way to preserve adequate open space.

Unless the high-potential recreation areas are acquired early, they become lost forever to other permanent uses.
–U.S. Department of the Interior, *River of Life,* Environmental Report, Conservation Yearbook Series No. 6, Washington, D.C., 1970, p. 72.

SITE PLANNING

The site plan (or project plan) might be for a campground in a scenic forest grove covering 3 acres (1.2 ha), or a major ski resort covering 1200 acres (490 ha) and ranging in elevation from 7000 to 10,000 feet (2100–3000 m), or a waterfront development including boating facilities, designated use areas, and shoreline and beach facilities. These are only three examples of a long list that could be given of the different kinds of recreational site developments.

One of the most important aspects of site planning is the preparation and submission of an environmental-impact statement. This is required in connection with all developments of much consequence. The exact procedures for doing this can be obtained from the state outdoor-recreation liaison officer (see Appendix D).

The initial aspect of site planning involves the gathering of as much useful information as possible. This might include the review of photos, on-site inspections, soil samples, information about surface and underground water, history of special problems, and questions about ownership, rights-of-way, or other legal matters.

Another important aspect is appropriate involvement by members of the public. The nature and size of the project will dictate the importance of this.

Each agency or planning organization has its own particular approach, but the approaches involve essentially the same elements. To serve as a model, the procedures used by the Forest Service are presented below. Notice that the procedures involve four major steps with numerous details under each step.

1. The drafting of a detailed site map, including:

    *   Land lines and boundaries as well as ownership
    *   A permanently established baseline and reference points
    *   The map scale (Usually no smaller than 1:600)
    *   Contour lines with an interval of 1 or 2 feet (0.3–0.6 m)
    *   Special natural features

2. A narrative report, consisting of three main parts:

    *   Analysis and discussion of the physical characteristics of the site as they may influence design and construction
    *   Analysis and discussion of the physical and aesthetic requirements of the use or uses and the desired level of experience of users
    *   Statement of design objectives–that which you intend to do with design to accommodate the desired uses within the capability of the site to withstand the use

3. A general development plan, usually made by tracing the detailed site map and adding proposed improvements. It would contain the following:

    *   An overall design scheme
    *   The type and placement of all facilities but not layout details
    *   Road plan
    *   Survey control baseline and description
    *   Map showing the site and surrounding area
    *   Orientation
    *   Legend
    *   Aerial photo coverage

4. A final construction plan, which conveys instructions to the contractor and includes:

    *   Road design
    *   Water and sewage system designs
    *   Grading plans, including all contour modifications
    *   Family unit layout and construction details
    *   Construction drawings of all facilities and structures
    *   Layout information for the location of all site improvements
    *   All necessary specifications

Discussion Questions

1. Consider the following statement: "Planning for parks and recreation should be done with people and not for them." Explain the meaning and significance of this. Do you agree? Why?
2. What are some of the methods used to obtain public involvement in planning and decision making? Which methods do you consider the most effective? Give examples of their use.
3. Why is cooperation between the private and public sectors and among government agencies so important in recreation planning?
4. What organization is currently the main recreation planning agency for the federal government? What are its principal planning responsibilities?
5. For a state to qualify for financial assistance from the Federal Land and Water Conservation Fund, the state must have a current state comprehensive outdoor recreation plan. Explain what is involved in this plan. How often must it be updated?
6. Describe what is meant by cluster or density zoning. What valid arguments can you present for and against this approach?

Recommended Readings

Brockman, Frank, et al. *Recreation Use of Wild Lands,* 3rd ed. New York: McGraw Hill, 1979. Chapter 14.
Christensen, Monty L. *Park Planning Handbook.* New York: John Wiley & Sons, 1977.
Crompton, John L., Charles W. Lamb, and Patric Schul. "The Attitudes of Recreation and Park Administrators Toward Public Involvement." *Leisure Sciences,* Vol. 4, No. 1, p. 67.
Knudson, Douglas M. *Outdoor Recreation.* New York: Macmillan Publishing Co., 1984. Chapters 22, 23.
U.S. Department of the Interior. *Handbook for Recreation Planning and Action.* Washington, D.C.: 1980.
Van Doren, Carlton S., George B. Priddle, and John E. Lewis. *Land and Leisure: Concepts and Methods in Outdoor Recreation.* Chicago: Maaroofa Press, Inc., 1979. Chapters 5, 22.

CHAPTER 19

Management Policies and Methods

Certain management policies, methods, and procedures have been discussed in earlier chapters, particularly in sections on the Park Service, Fish and Wildlife Service, Bureau of Reclamation, Forest Service, and various state agencies. For the most part those policies and methods pertain to the particular agencies or resources being discussed. Nonetheless, there are certain concepts or elements of management philosophy that ought to be understood because of their application to a broad range of natural resources. Some of the more significant concepts are discussed here.

The face and character of our country are determined by what we do with America and its resources.

—Thomas Jefferson

PRESERVATION CONCEPT

Preservation implies the status quo. In resource management it is an effort to protect resource areas from human influence. Preservation is associated closely with *nonrenewability*. Much of our attractive scenery and points of special interest are nonrenewable, at least within a reasonable length of time. Therefore, we attempt to *preserve* these features. In the practical sense, a stalactite that has developed over 1000 years is nonrenewable. The same is true of a 2000-year-old cedar or redwood. Also, the Old Faithful geyser is nonrenewable, as are the Pueblo Indian ruins at Mesa Verde National Park and some fragile features of the Everglades.

Certainly wildlife species that become extinct are totally nonrenewable. Should the last antelope vanish, all the biologists and politicians in the country couldn't do anything about it.

Surface soil is another characteristic that relates closely to nonrenewability. When soil is depleted, the foliage and, in turn, the wildlife of the area become reduced or extinct. Thus, preservation of surface soil and of the foliage which grows in it and replenishes it becomes fundamental to the perpetuation of any ecosystem. It is interesting that many of the so-called underdeveloped countries are actually overdeveloped in terms of long-term overuse and mismanagement of resources to a state of depletion.

Certainly, the application of the preservation concept in just the right balance with other procedures is fundamental to good resource management. Proper application of the preservation concept can greatly enhance long-term recreational opportunities.

CONSERVATION CONCEPT

While preservation relates to nonrenewable resources, conservation relates primarily to *renewable* resources. Conservation implies the *use* of resources in the most beneficial manner over the long term while avoiding waste. It means to reserve the resources for their best uses and to spread the uses over the proper time frame. It also means to *renew* or *replenish* as the resources become damaged or partially depleted. Conservation involves a cycle of intelligent use and timely replenishment.

A forest is an example of a renewable resource where the timber can be harvested and replenished on an acceptable time cycle. Also, deer and other game animals can be harvested in reasonable numbers and replenished. Further, the various forms of natural foliage are renewable, provided the soil and water conditions remain favorable.

The correct application of the conservation concept to renewable natural resources is important in terms of recreation management as well as for other reasons. The availability and quality of the renewable resources are dependent directly upon wise application of the conservation concept.

Conservation also applies in the case of *improved* recreation areas and facilities, such as golf courses and picnic sites, for example. A rotational approach is used in golf-course management to enable rehabilitation of worn areas. Also, strict use regulations and maintenance guidelines are applied to minimize damage and deterioration. Similar methods apply in the case of picnic sites or a number of other kinds of recreation areas.

WILDERNESS CONCEPT

Wilderness is of various kinds and degrees. For example, there is desert wilderness, forest wilderness, water wilderness, and coastal wilderness. There is wilderness at high elevations and at sea level. The definition of wilderness and the application of the concept have become very important in the management of natural resources.

Wilderness is often measured by *remoteness*. Generally, we perceive the mountain wilderness of interior Alaska as more wild than a wilderness coastline 100 miles from a city. Yet, in terms of native characteristics, one might be just as wild as the other.

Further, we generally associate wilderness with *rugged characteristics*. Thoreau referred to the wilderness of Walden Pond near Concord, Massachusetts. It was the closest thing to wild country that he knew at the time. Later he traveled to the forest regions of Maine where he was even more impressed with the wild characteristics of the rugged New England terrain.

Seal hunting is an important part of the Eskimo culture, but the application of appropriate conservation measures is necessary. (National Park Service, photo by Robert Belous)

Thoreau never experienced wilderness in the high Cascade Range, or the Rockies of western Canada, or the coastline of the Alaskan peninsula.

Another distinguishing characteristic of wilderness is official *status* or *designation*. We now have a national wilderness system that contains areas previously designated as wilderness by the Forest Service and the National Park Service. The fact that an area is designated as wilderness causes it to be so in terms of official status. In reality such areas are often no more wilderness than some undesignated areas; however, they might remain more wild as time passes, because wilderness designation will protect them from change.

Regardless of the different connotations of the term wilderness, the wilderness-preservation concept, wherever it is applied, influences the use and management procedures of that area. It causes the area to be managed with the objective of preserving the native characteristics for at least three reasons: (1) wilderness recreation for a relatively few visitors; (2) a preserved area to serve as a standard against which the changes of other areas can be measured; and (3) a haven where the native flora and fauna can survive in their natural state indefinitely.

The application of the wilderness concept will always be controversial because it results in restricted use, controlled use, and very low-density use of resources. There is more about wilderness in this chapter in the section entitled Carrying Capacity. Also, refer to the sections on wilderness in Chapters 7 and 8.

DISPERSED-USE CONCEPT

This management concept encourages the dispersion of users over the entire area, as opposed to concentrated use of portions of the area. The Forest Service encourages dispersed uses of certain kinds, and most of the recreational use of the forests is dispersed. Concentrated use is also encouraged in selected areas through the construction of campgrounds and picnic sites.

The Bureau of Land Management, too, encourages dispersed use, but with careful controls applied to fragile areas.

Other examples of the application of desirable dispersement of recreationists would be (1) boaters on a reservoir or lake, (2) fishers along a stream, (3) sunbathers on a beach, (4) bird watchers on a wildlife refuge, or (5) pheasant hunters afield.

The concept of dispersement also applies in wildlife management. Generally, it is desirable to manage habitat in a manner that will encourage animals to disperse over the entire region. This diminishes the possibility of depleting the foliage in certain areas and damaging the surface characteristics.

MULTIPLE-USE CONCEPT

In a general sense, the concept of multiple use means the resources will be managed in a manner that makes them available for a variety of uses. The concept applies to a broad base of resources and not to each specific resource or area. Within the multiple-use framework, certain areas may be administered under the single-use concept. For example, a developed campsite would be restricted to only recreational use, and a critical watershed might be restricted to watershed protection. These would be single-use sites that fit within the broad spectrum of multiple use of the larger resource areas.

The great majority of publicly owned land is managed under some form of multiple use. The managing agencies have definitive guidelines concerning appropriate uses and use priorities. The two largest land-management agencies, the Bureau of Land Management and the Forest Service, operate under legislative mandates concerning multiple use. It is true, however, that these agencies managed their lands under a multiple-use plan long before the mandates were passed. The laws simply gave legal status to multiple use and helped to clarify priorities.

Forest Service lands are administered under the Multiple-Use Sustained-Yield Act of 1960, which directs the "management of all the various renewable surface resources of the national forests so that they are utilized in the combination that will best meet the needs of the American people." The act describes the five major uses of national forest lands as *timber production*, *watershed protection*, *outdoor recreation*, *wildlife management*, and *range management*.

The lands under the jurisdiction of the Bureau of Land Management are managed under multiple use as described in the Federal Land Policy and Management Act of 1976. The act states:

> The public lands and their resource values shall be managed so their utilized combination meets the needs of the American people. . . . The combination of uses takes into account the

long-term needs of future generations for the renewable and nonrenewable resources, including but not limited to recreation, range, timber, minerals, watershed, wildlife and fish, natural, scenic, scientific, and historical values.

The multiple-use management concepts described here provide a basic framework for management. Within the broad structure there is sufficient room for the application of specific principles, guidelines, and decisions.

SINGLE USE

In contrast to the multiple-use policies governing most of the lands available to the public, there are some resources that are managed under the philosophy of single use, or restricted use. Perhaps the most prominent example is the national park system. The national park areas are to be *preserved* in essentially their present state for the "benefit and enjoyment of people now and in the future." Units of the national park system are not for the production and harvest of products or to produce profit. They are areas where people can benefit from the historical, archeological, cultural, and scenic characteristics of the particular areas in a fashion that is not destructive to these unique values.

Wilderness areas provide another example of restricted-use management. Pure wilderness is incompatible with any kind of use, even limited visits by recreationists. Any kind of intrusion by an outside element is at least mildly disruptive to the purely wild ecological

Public safety is an important aspect of management. (U.S. Fish and Wildlife Service)

system. This means that even our most remote wilderness areas are at least slightly diluted from their once-pure wilderness condition. The more use of any kind a wilderness area receives, the more it deviates from pure wilderness. Therefore, within the context of wilderness preservation, crucial decisions must be made as to how much and what kinds of uses will be permitted.

Wild and scenic rivers constitute another category of resources that are managed on a restricted basis. As explained in Chapter 7, the rivers included in this system are of three classes: *wild*, *scenic*, and *recreational*, with the classes descending from greater to lesser restrictions.

The managing agencies of single- or restricted-use areas are almost always under pressure from special-interest groups or lobbyists who want the restrictions modified or reduced. Naturally, these pressures will increase as our nation continues to develop, and there are greater demands for all kinds of resource use.

CARRYING CAPACITY

The first American to apply this management idea to people and the outdoors was probably Lowell Sumner. In 1942 he wrote an essay concerning the biological balances in wilderness areas and urged that visitation be kept "within the carrying capacity or recreation saturation point." Sumner defined this as the "maximum degree of the highest type of recreational use which a wilderness can receive, consistent with its long-term preservation."

Sumner's main concern was the *biological* carrying capacity–the amount of use that the biological characteristics can withstand without serious damage or deterioration. Another important aspect, and one that's harder to measure, is *psychological* carrying capacity–the impact of people on people. Of course, the cutoff point of psychological carrying capacity varies with the individual–a fact that vastly complicates the formulation of management policy.

In the case of most kinds of recreation areas, carrying capacity is elastic because it can be increased in several ways:

1. The durability of vegetation can be increased through watering, fertilizing, and selection of durable species.
2. Education programs that change visitors' behavior can reduce wear and tear on sites.
3. Increased development of physical facilities can reduce damage to natural areas.
4. Through physical developments or regulations or both, managers can shift visitors from overused sites to underused sites and thus better distribute the load within the recreation area.

One functional method of keeping use within the carrying capacity is through a *permit system*. This means that a specific number of permits are issued to users, after a study has determined how much visitation an area can withstand before the environment is damaged or the visitor's experience suffers. This method is still new and somewhat problematic, but it has

Park rangers on horseback are generally better accepted by the public than those afoot or in motor vehicles. (National Park Service, photo by Clare Ralston)

definitely become implanted in management procedures. There are several methods of issuing permits:

1. Advanced reservation, based on date of request.
2. Lottery, where the users are chosen randomly.
3. Queuing, where applicants wait on location and receive permits on a first-come basis.
4. Merit, where the most experienced or best prepared applicants receive priority consideration. (Though much discussed, this last method is not in use.)

Certification, or *licensing,* is another interesting concept that has application in the case of specialized recreation experiences, such as white-water rafting, wilderness travel, or big-game hunting. This method is based on the idea that the specialized recreation opportunities should go to those who have prepared themselves. The argument for this is along the line that those who are not prepared to protect others and themselves on the highways should not drive automobiles. Those who have not completed a course in hunter safety should not hunt; those who are unprepared to protect the environment and themselves in the wilderness should not go there; and so on.

It has been suggested that areas requiring certification or licensing be classified into different categories so that recreationists who are less prepared could qualify for the use of some areas but not for others. In the case of wilderness, Roderick Nash[1] recommends a well-defined five-category system, with class one being marginal wilderness and class five the most remote and wild areas.

Currently, policies pertaining to carrying capacity are in the hands of the separate resource-management agencies, and there is not a great deal of standardization and coordination among agencies on this matter. This is not to imply, however, that resource managers are negligent in this regard. The 1973 nationwide outdoor-recreation plan called for the determination of recreational capacity limits for all federal land-management units, and required that the areas be managed within those limits. Most of the agencies involved with recreationists have established fairly clear carrying-capacity guidelines, and they seem to be making honest efforts toward enforcement.

USE INCOMPATIBILITY

When two uses of a particular area are completely *incompatible*, the management alternatives are fairly simple, though the decision may be hard to reach: all of one, none of the other. For example, a forest area cannot be used for timber harvest and also for wilderness. One management objective must be chosen and the other excluded. The decision may rest upon estimates of economic value, biological considerations, social or philosophical convictions, or some other basis.

When two uses are completely *compatible* so that management for one purpose achieves management objectives for the other purpose, there is no problem at all; management for either is management for both.

In most cases, however, alternative uses are *reasonably* compatible but require some special management steps to make the combinations work. In a forest, timber harvest may have to be modified or specially structured to protect the watershed and the wildlife. Also, in wilderness, the pure wilderness concept has to be modified to permit restricted use by recreationists and scientists. Further, if a stretch of wild river is to serve as an area for direct enjoyment by people, it must be available to people under restricted use.

Here are some additional examples. Natural watershed is *fully* compatible with maintaining an attractive environment. Wildlife management is *generally* compatible with controlled timber harvest. Visits by recreationists, if properly controlled, are *moderately* compatible with wildlife.

To consider incompatibility in a more specific way, think of a trail which has several potential uses including hiking, horseback riding, bicycling, trail-bike riding, snowmobiling, cross-country skiing, and snowshoeing. Obviously, no trail can accommodate all of these uses without damaging the environment and frustrating the users. Therefore, trails are typically designed and designated for certain uses and not for others.

In the same area of a lake waterfront, powerboating, fishing, and swimming would be an incompatible combination. It would result in safety hazards and user dissatisfaction.

Like overuse, use incompatibility has two dimensions: *biological* and *psychological*. The biological considerations relate to the kind of use mixture that can be withstood by the

1. Nash, Roderick, "Protecting the Wilderness From Its Friends," *Backpacker*, April 1981, p. 15.

ecological characteristics of the area. The psychological considerations relate to the mixture of uses that can occur without detracting too much from user satisfaction.

USE ESTIMATES

Resource-management agencies have become more concerned about keeping records of visitor use. Some of the agencies have felt forced to do so because the data sometimes have budgetary implications.

In the 1973 nationwide outdoor-recreation plan it was declared that each federal land-managing agency will report annually on recreational use at each management unit. Even though this directive has been generally followed in concept, the particular procedures have been modified and they are still under study. Fortunately, some progress has been made toward standardizing the terminology and the methods, as exemplified by the following definitions.

A *visit* is defined as the entry of any person into a site. A recreation *visitor-hour* is the presence of one or more recreationists for continuous, intermittent, or simultaneous periods of time aggregating 60 minutes. A recreation *activity-hour* is the same as a visitor hour except identified with a particular recreation activity, such as swimming, picnicking, or hiking. A *visitor-day* is the accumulation of 12 visitor hours. The visitor-hour and the 12-hour visitor-day are now the most standardized measures, and they are the recommended methods of recording visitor use.

Sometimes it is necessary to make estimates when the actual counting of hours or days is not feasible. The following are methods of estimating, from least accurate to most accurate.

1. Estimates based on observation. This method involves no counting or sampling. It is simply a manager's best judgment of the number of visits to a particular area during a specified time. Obviously, with this method there is much room for error, and the errors tend to be on the high side.
2. The sampling method involves either direct counts of people or counts of a related element, such as number of cars. Generally, the larger the sample the more reliable the data. There is the problem of whether the sample is representative of the total situation.
3. The most accurate, but also the most cumbersome method, is a pure count of either individuals or a related phenomenon such as cars, entry fees, user fees, number of boats, campsite occupancy, or one of a number of other related elements.

In light of the several approaches used, there is obvious chance for error in the reporting of visitors. For this reason, it would be erroneous to place too much confidence in use statistics unless the methods used are clearly understood. To accept statistics at face value and make comparisons could prove both illogical and misleading.

Though some standardization of measuring visitation has occurred, it is unfortunate that visitor-use reporting procedures have failed to become *more* standardized at all levels of government and in the private sector. If the procedures were standardized, the data would be much more meaningful, and this would enable logical comparisons that would enhance both planning and management.

RETENTION OF PUBLIC LAND

Over the years the federal government has disposed of a tremendous amount of property, transferring it through different programs to private ownership. In a general sense, the policy has now changed from one of land disposal to land retention. Exceptions to this general rule involve individual tracts that still may be disposed of in the national interest.

The government's previous policy of land disposal dates back to the Revolutionary War. The Bureau of Land Management and its predecessors have been the agencies through which most of the disposed land has been handled. Other land-management agencies such as the Park Service, Fish and Wildlife Service, and Forest Service have acquired only the land transferred to them for specific uses. Agencies such as these generally do not administer land-disposal programs.

The federal government's new policy of land retention was clarified in the Federal Land Policy and Management Act of 1976. In the act it states that as a general policy, the United States will retain its public lands in federal ownership. "Public lands" refers to the 343 million acres (139 million ha) administered by the Bureau of Land Management.

Despite the retention policy, laws already on the books will cause a substantial reduction when these commitments are complete. The largest transfers already obligated involve lands to be transferred to the state of Alaska and the Alaskan natives.

There are several reasons why Congress adopted the retention policy, the most prominent being the realization that a concern for environmental values and open space had gradually replaced the drive for development and increased production. Further, in the 1976 act it was specified that "the public lands must be managed in a manner that will preserve and protect certain natural conditions; that will provide food and habitat for fish and wildlife and domestic animals; and that will provide for outdoor recreation."

SPECIAL MANAGEMENT PROBLEMS

It seems that every area of management has certain unique problems. Included here are brief descriptions of some special problems concerning the management of natural resources for recreation.

Crime

Crime, including vandalism, is a major management problem encountered by practically every resource-management agency. In addition to the direct effects of the criminal and abusive acts, there is a side effect known as the "perception of crime," which poses a constraint on recreation opportunities. Many people avoid public areas and facilities because they perceive crime as a problem even when it isn't.

The great majority of crimes in public recreation areas are of the nonviolent type. Larceny and breaking and entering account for nearly half of the crimes. It is a disturbing fact that nonviolent crimes of practically all kinds are spreading steadily in recreation areas throughout the country. The Park Service estimates that such crimes have increased 25% during the past five years in the national park system. Auto thefts have increased more than 50%. Similarly, many private and public campgrounds are plagued by break-ins of campers, tents, and recreation vehicles. Clearly, crime and the personal fear of crime have become major management concerns.

Vandalism is one of the most serious problems in delivering park and recreation services. Nationally, there has been a staggering escalation of graffiti, littering, breakage, and wanton destruction of park property.

The Forest Service reports that vandalism at its recreation areas is underreported. The problem in public campground facilities is about seven times greater than that experienced on private property. In addition, vandalism to the environment on public grounds is more than double that incurred on private recreational property. The Forest Service estimates its annual losses due to vandalism at more than $3 million for facilities and $1 million in damages to natural resources. According to research on vandalism at Corps of Engineers reservoirs, the most common type is destruction or breakage of material and equipment. Defacement and graffiti rank second, and ecological destruction ranks third.

Vandalism is also increasing throughout the national park system. In 1982 the Cape Cod National Seashore reported more acts of vandalism than any other Park Service site. A total of nearly 1200 incidents were recorded, costing taxpayers about $60,000. Park Service holdings in Washington, D.C., were second with about 500 reported cases costing nearly $40,000.

It should be clarified, however, that cases commonly called vandalism often do not stem from wrongful intent. This accidental behavior can range from a teenager or overweight child unintentionally breaking a toddler's swing to a careless smoker setting a building on fire.

Further, what is considered vandalism or improper behavior is not clearly defined. Many times an act of vandalism as defined by a manager may be viewed as acceptable by a user. In some cases, recreationists who have little contact with the environment may really not know what is defined as vandalism by managers. In other cases, they may know but disagree. Examples include throwing axes into trees, carving on tables and benches, chopping down trees in campgrounds for firewood or for more space. Even though rules prohibit such activities, the fact that users don't understand or agree with the rules may result in vandalism by discrepancy of definition. Research has documented this difference in interpretation between managers and some users.

There are numerous approaches or methods that can be applied toward solutions of the crime and vandalism problem. However, there is no magic solution, and no complete solution. Resource managers can only apply the best methods possible, and do so with consistency. Some of the more useful possibilities include the following:

1. Public education. Through the educational process people can be persuaded to be more respectful of other people and of personal and public property.
2. Direct supervision. Significantly less crime and vandalism occur in areas that are closely supervised.
3. Keeping areas and facilities in good repair. It is generally believed that people feel more respectful toward attractive, well-maintained areas and facilities than they do toward facilities that are in poor repair.
4. User fees. Some managers claim that vandalism and other behavior problems are reduced when fees are charged. If this is true, it might be because (1) those who are

unwilling to pay the fee are the ones who cause the problems, and (2) perhaps paying a fee has a positive psychological influence on the users in terms of respect for the area.

5. Reducing the opportunity for crime and vandalism, which can be accomplished to some degree by eliminating temptations for would-be criminals and vandals.
6. Detection of crime and enforcement of laws, policies, and regulations.
7. Involving recreationists in helping to solve crime and vandalism.

Many agree that after reasonable measures have been taken to control crime and vandalism, the final approach should be to treat it much like shoplifting–assume some will occur, and charge the customers (users) the resulting cost.

Off-Road Vehicles

The Council on Environmental Quality has estimated there are more than 10 million off-road vehicles, including snowmobiles, in the United States. Although certain forms of off-road vehicle use is acceptable, some aspects of this activity have become a plague to resource managers. Motorcycles, four-wheel-drive vehicles, and dune buggies have done extensive damage to vegetation, wildlife, and surface soil in our southwestern deserts and many other locations. Hill-climbing contests involving motorcycles and four-wheelers have marred the landscape on slopes throughout the nation. Off-road vehicles, including snowmobiles, have had a major disrupting effect on the peaceful existence of wildlife in their natural habitat. Further, the inappropriate use of these machines has diluted the backcountry experience of many recreationists.

Most off-road driving in the nation takes place on federal lands. In fact, over half occurs on lands managed by one federal agency–the Bureau of Land Management. Resource managers have grappled with this problem for the past two decades, and most of the agencies have now developed fairly acceptable guidelines and regulating procedures. However, the problem of education and enforcement continues.

As a Bureau of Land Management environmental-impact statement noted, "Silence is a resource." Direct encounters with off-road vehicles simply are not compatible with the quality of outdoor experiences being sought by most Americans.

The Forest Service estimates that under forest conditions the noise from an average motorcycle is detectable 7000 feet (2100 m) away. A quiet motorcycle is detectable at 4000 feet (1200 m) and a loud one at 11,500 feet (3505 m). With respect to quiet and solitude, off-road vehicles shrink the amount of land available for other recreationists.

Perhaps the prime example of resource abuse by off-road vehicles has been the case of the California desert. This problem became so extensive that members of the public became irate about the damage and abuse to the public lands. As a result, considerable public pressure was applied during the mid-1960s to the Bureau of Land Management. To gain the upper hand, the agency performed studies in the late 1960s to determine the extent of off-road vehicle use and the impact it was having on the desert's resources. The findings motivated the bureau to move quickly on a broad front to bring the situation under control. A two-pronged approach called the California Desert Program was designed. It included an Interim Critical Management Program to blunt the worst abuses, while a Long-Range Comprehensive Use Plan could be developed for the 12.5 million acres (5.1 million ha) of Bureau of Land Management desert holdings.

One objective of the interim plan was to immediately bring about some degree of management control. Enforcement officers (desert rangers) were hired and trained to accomplish this by use of a congenial approach. To minimize resource damage, the bureau began to require permits for off-road vehicle races, and rangers monitored these events. Another main objective of the interim plan was to remove off-road vehicles completely from areas that were highly susceptible to damage.

In the meantime, the bureau planning staff developed a long-range plan for regulating off-road vehicles. The plan was presented and discussed in a series of public meetings. This exposure provided significant public education. Under the plan, 1 million acres (400,000 ha) remained open to off-road vehicles under regulated conditions. On the remaining 11.5 million acres (4.6 million ha) of the desert, off-road vehicles were limited to designated roads. Ironically, the bureau was sued for being too lenient and also for being too harsh. But the courts upheld the plan and the restrictions were enforced.

Finally, in 1976 a more permanent solution to the problem was adopted. Congress passed the Federal Land Policy and Management Act. Title VI of the act established the California National Conservation Area. The act outlined the regulations and the enforcement procedures that were considered necessary to bring off-road vehicle use and other abuses of the desert under control.

**Much damage can be done to a natural area by just one thoughtless visitor.
(U.S. Department of the Interior)**

The California desert case was valuable nationwide because it brought to public attention the potential abuses of off-road vehicles and the critical need for resource agencies to enforce adequate controls. It helped to solidify the thinking of management personnel and members of the public. Further, it now serves as a model for other agencies with similar problems.

Executive Order 11989, signed in 1977 by the president, adds a new section to Executive Order 11644, signed by the president in 1972. It requires that whenever the director of a land-managing agency "determines that off-road vehicles will cause or are causing considerable adverse effects on the soil, vegetation, wildlife, wildlife habitat, or cultural or historic resources of particular areas or trails of the public lands, he must immediately close such areas or trails to the type of vehicle causing the effects." It seems that the resource-management agencies have become highly sensitive about off-road vehicles, and efforts are being made to adequately monitor and control their use.

Transportation and Access

Research indicates that in the United States 90% to 95% of all visitors to recreation sites outside of communities use private automobiles. Some of the problems relating to this are (1) traffic congestion in the more popular areas, (2) hazards for pedestrians and cyclists, (3) the need for extensive roads and large parking lots, (4) air pollution caused by automobile emissions, and (5) detraction from the native characteristics of the outdoor environment by all of the above.

Approximately one fifth of the people in the United States live in households that have no automobile, and alternative methods of transportation to outdoor recreation sites are very limited. Not much is being done to solve this problem, but the National Park Service is experimenting with a program that has some potential.

The Park Service has initiated numerous on-site transportation systems at national parks to relieve congestion and reduce interference with the native environment. There are currently more than 30 such programs in operation, most of which are shuttle-bus systems.

The National Park System Access Act of 1978 supports and encourages this and other approaches. The purpose of the act is to make the park areas more accessible in a manner consistent with good park management and energy conservation. To further comply with the act, the Park Service plans additional transportation projects, some of which will expand beyond the park shuttle-bus system. Undoubtedly, these efforts by the Park Service will serve as a useful model for other federal, state, and local agencies.

Another kind of problem is restricted access to public lands, which are landlocked by private holdings. Numerous Bureau of Land Management and Forest Service sites have this problem. Naturally, some private landowners do not want the public or government employees crossing over their property, and neither do they want the federal government infringing on their property rights.

As a general rule, federal land-management agencies can exercise the right of eminent domain to acquire access. This has recently been clarified in the Bureau of Land Management Organic Act (Federal Land Policy and Management Act of 1976) and in the National Forest Management Act of 1976. However, government agencies are reluctant to use this power because it is generally not accepted graciously. Even so, where the need for access justifies it, the right of eminent domain is used.

Planning for shorefront access was given emphasis by Congress in the Coastal-Zone Management Program of 1976. Participating federal and state agencies were strongly encouraged to develop policies to meet the growing demand for recreation. Recreation access, including urban waterfront redevelopment, is one of the four major areas currently being emphasized through this program.

Energy Conservation

The rising costs of energy will continue to increase the operating expenses of park and recreation agencies. To combat this, several options are possible: (1) reduce the level of service, (2) implement energy-saving procedures, and (3) replace energy-inefficient equipment with more efficient machinery.

Energy conservation education for employees has become quite popular. The National Recreation and Park Association has compiled energy-management materials that are used by some federal agencies and many state and local agencies. The Department of the Interior, in cooperation with the Department of Energy, has condensed its energy-conservation materials to make them more useful for its own personnel and state and local park and recreation agencies.

Fortunately, most agencies have shown serious concern and made dedicated efforts toward energy conservation. It has become a standard element of resource-management policy.

Dangerous and Feral Animals

Dangerous animals include a number of species, but the one that most often comes to mind as a problem among recreationists is the bear, especially the grizzly. Bears are scavengers, and so they are attracted to areas used by humans. For years, bears have been both an amusement and a nuisance as they have searched through garbage cans, frequented dump areas near campsites, and raided grub boxes. Unfortunately, these seemingly harmless activities occasionally result in encounters in which humans are hurt or killed. The main problem with bears has been in national parks, but the problem is by no means limited to these areas.

Management agencies have operated in precarious balance relative to the bear issue, because bears are part of the environment and they are one of the attractions. Further, there are contrasting points of view, with one being to reduce the number of bears in recreation areas and the other being to leave them alone and educate people about how to avoid encounters.

The National Park Service has taken some logical measures toward bear control, and according to the statistics of injuries and deaths caused by bears, the measures have had positive results. Among the measures have been the following: (1) habitually troublesome bears have been exterminated, (2) numerous bears have been trapped and transported to outlying areas, (3) certain recreation areas have been closed or restricted where encounters are likely, (4) several garbage areas and other features that attract bears have been fenced or eliminated, (5) educational and regulatory procedures pertaining to recreationists have been escalated.

There are numerous other examples of the problems caused by dangerous animals. But, most of them are of lesser concern and consequence. Recreationists are often warned to stay a safe distance from wild animals. Just how much emphasis this matter deserves in the management process depends largely on frequency of the problem.

The *feral* (or exotic) animal problem is not widespread, but it has become difficult in a few instances. In the Grand Canyon burros have become a nuisance because they have few natural predators there and harvesting them as game is not allowed or attractive. Further, they seem to thrive in the canyon environment. As a result, burros have become an infringement on the natural habitat and native wildlife. Further, their presence has a diluting influence on the enjoyment of recreationists who do not appreciate nonnative animals in the national parks.

The Park Service has considered complete extermination of the burros, but this has met resistance by the Humane Society and others who resist the slaughter of animals. Despite resistance, several hundred burros have been exterminated during the past decade to keep the numbers under control. Just what to do with this problem over the long term is a question that National Park officials have been unable to resolve.

While the Park Service has grappled with the problem of burros in the Grand Canyon, the Bureau of Land Management has tried to deal effectively with wild horses on the western desert regions. As the number of mustangs continues to increase, they compete with native wildlife and range animals for the sparse desert foliage. During the past few years, several hundred mustangs have been exterminated, but the bureau has found that a more acceptable control program is corraling the animals and selling them. This approach has also met with controversy, however, because it was found that many of the captured mustangs were hard to domesticate, and were being sold for meat processing.

The third prominent problem of this kind is the presence of more than 2000 boars in the Great Smoky Mountains National Park. This problem started several decades ago when a few boars gained freedom from a nearby game farm. Wild boars destroy vegetation and surface soil. Being energetic rooters, they have caused some locations in the national park to take on the appearance of a plowed field. More than 700 of these animals have been exterminated during the past few years, but this procedure has met great resistance by animal-rights advocates and by those who have developed a fondness for boar hunting.

A workable solution to the problem of unwanted animals has not been found. In general, the policy relative to these species is one of further study while maintaining an acceptable level of control in the meantime.

Discussion Questions

1. What is wilderness preservation and what is the rationale for preserving specific areas as wilderness?
2. What are the differences between preservation and conservation of natural resources?
3. What is meant by the dispersed-use concept? Explain its application by the U.S. Forest Service. Do you think dispersed use is overemphasized or underemphasized?
4. Define and give some examples of use incompatibility, overuse, and misuse of natural areas.
5. Define the following as applied by management agencies: visitor-hour, activity-hour, visitor-day, visitor.
6. What do you think are some possible solutions to the problems of feral and exotic animals in our national parks and other recreation areas?

Recommended Readings

"Attitudes Toward Outdoor Recreation Development." *Leisure Sciences,* Vol. 3, No. 2, p. 169.

Brady, Paul T. "A Practical Approach to Vandalism." *Parks and Recreation,* April 1981, p. 33.

Brockman, Frank, et al. *Recreation Use of Wild Lands,* 3rd ed. New York: McGraw Hill, 1979. Chapters 15 and 16.

Clark, Roger N. *Control of Vandalism in Recreation Areas: Fact, Fiction or Folklore?* U.S. Forest Service, General Technical Report PSW-17, 1976, pp. 62–70.

Cordell, H. Ken, and John C. Hendee. *Renewable Resources Recreation in the U.S.: Supply, Demand, and Critical Policy Issues.* Washington, D.C.: American Forestry Association, August 1982.

"Criminal Law Enforcement Authority of Park Rangers in Proprietary Jurisdiction National Parks–Where Is It?" *California Western Law Review* 13, pp. 126–152.

Ellerbrook, Mike. "Some Straight Talk on User Fees." *Park and Recreation,* January 1982, p. 59.

Gifford, Kenneth A. "Recreation: The Problematic Side of the Preservation Coin." *Parks and Recreation,* May 1981, p. 32.

Goldman, Don. "Land Use: The Multiple-Use Concept." *Environment,* October 1981, pp. 4–5.

Heinrichs, Jay. "Wilderness: Can We Have It and Use It Too?" *American Forest,* March 1980, p. 16.

Hope, Jack. "The Real Impact of Off-Road Vehicles on Public Lands." *Backpacker* 43 1981, p. 65.

Jubenville, Alan. *Outdoor Recreation Management.* Philadelphia: W. B. Saunders Co., 1978.

Knudson, Douglas M. *Outdoor Recreation.* New York: Macmillan Publishing Co., 1984. Chapter 31.

Leigh, Pamela. "The Managerial Woman in Parks and Recreation." *Parks and Recreation,* October 1982, p. 40.

Manning, Robert E., and Sidney C. Baker. "Discrimination Through User Fees: Fact or Fiction?" *Parks and Recreation,* September 1981, p. 70.

Miller, Pam. "Regulating the Last Slices of Wilderness." *Adventure Travel,* February–March 1981, p. 86.

"95,000-Mile Battle Line: America's Coasts." *U.S. News and World Report,* 4 August 1980, p. 62.

Rossman, J. Robert. "Evaluate Programs by Measuring Participant Satisfaction." *Parks and Recreation,* June 1982, p. 33.

Ruger, George. "The Ethics of Outdoor Recreation." *Field and Stream,* October 1980, pp. 40–43.

Schultz, Dr. John D. "Conservation, Preservation, and Environmentalism." *American Forest,* February 1980, p. 6.

Sharpe, Maitland. "The Sagebrush Rebellion: A Conservationist's Perspective." *Rangelands,* December 1980, p. 22.

Thayer, Ralph, and Fritz Wager. *Vandalism.* Arlington, Virginia: National Recreation and Park Association, 1981.

"20th-Century Battle of the Wilderness." *U.S. News and World Report,* 14 July 1980, p. 56.

Twight, Ben W., Kenneth L. Smith, and Gordon H. Wissinger. "Privacy and Camping: Closeness to the Self Vs. Closeness to Others." *Leisure Sciences,* Vol. 4, No. 4, p. 427.

U.S. Department of the Interior. *The Third Nationwide Outdoor Recreation Plan: The Assessment.* Washington, D.C.: 1979.

U.S. Department of the Interior. *The Third Nationwide Outdoor Recreation Plan: The Executive Report,* Washington, D.C.: 1979.

U.S. Forest Service. *Vandalism and Outdoor Recreation: Symposium Proceedings.* Washington, D.C.: 1976.

Van Doren, Carlton S., George B. Priddle, and John E. Lewis. *Land and Leisure: Concepts and Methods in Outdoor Recreation.* Chicago: Maaroofa Press, Inc., 1979. Chapter 7.

Watt, James. "World View: The Mandate for Multiple Use." *Backpacker* 45, 1981, pp. 19–20.

West, Patrick C. "Perceived Crowding and Attitudes Toward Limiting Use in Back Country Recreation Areas." *Leisure Sciences,* Vol. 4, No. 4, p. 419.

Woods, Lois E. "ORV's on the National Forest: A Classic Use of Listening." *American Forests,* November 1981, p. 41.

CHAPTER 20

Liability

This chapter[1] deals not with congressional or legislative acts or local ordinances, all of which are applicable to outdoor recreation but are discussed elsewhere. Instead, this chapter emphasizes the potential legal entanglements between managers of recreation resources and the users. The information is especially important both to employees of government agencies and owners and employees of commercial enterprises.

There is a concept known as Murphy's Law that states, "If anything can go wrong, it will." Some consider this to be a negative point of view and not the attitude that should normally prevail. However, constant awareness of Murphy's Law can help a manager remain alert to potential pitfalls.

There exists a serious problem with respect to injuries of recreationists and the liability burdens that are sometimes imposed on equipment manufacturers and providers of recreation areas and facilities. This legal liability problem is a growing threat to both private and public sponsors of recreation. Liability lawsuits have increased rapidly during the past two decades for recreation product-related injuries as well as for injuries received on recreation land and facilities.

The growing concern for individual rights has taken precedence over the traditional concept of *sovereign immunity*. Employees of government agencies at all levels are no longer necessarily immune from liability simply because they are employed by a branch of government. As a result, individuals involved in the management of areas and facilities for public use are obligated to give reasonable attention to safety and to make sure that the facilities are managed in a prudent manner and in accordance with the law.

---

1. Linda Carpenter, EdD, LLD, a professor of physical education and recreation at Brooklyn College, New York, furnished much of the technical information in this chapter.

Even though many outdoor activities involve accidental risk, managers should not be too apprehensive about providing adequate opportunities. Generally, the courts are aware of the inherent risks in these activities and acknowledge that the potential values exceed the risk expectancy, thus viewing normal participation as being within the parameters of *reasonable risk*. But still, liability suits against individuals in ownership, leadership, and management positions are definite possibilities. Thus, it is important to (1) be well informed about the laws that pertain to one's legal responsibilities, (2) exercise adequate caution and control in safety procedures, and (3) always act wisely and prudently in the case of accidental injury. The following are a few carefully selected legal terms or conditions that have application to outdoor recreation.

Act of God.   An unavoidable incident due to forces of nature that could not have been foreseen or prevented.

Assumption of risk.   Participation or involvement in an activity or situation where an element of risk is inherent. Voluntary participation can be interpreted as an acceptance of risk. In outdoor recreation there is an element of reasonable risk that the participant assumes through his or her decision to participate.

Attractive nuisance.   A facility, area, or situation that attracts participation and is hazardous. Examples are a footbridge in poor repair, a designated swimming area that is unsupervised or improperly regulated, children's play equipment in poor repair. Whether a situation would be legally declared an attractive nuisance would be influenced by the laws of the particular state, the age and competence of the injured person, and the various circumstances surrounding the incident.

Civil law.   Civil action implies a noncriminal infringement upon the rights of a person, agency, or corporation. Tort and contract disputes are examples of civil suits. Civil law is different from criminal law.

Common law.   That body of governing principles and rules of action derived from past practices, customs, and traditions.

Contributory negligence.   Where an individual's action was not the primary cause of negligence, but it was a contributing factor to the negligent act.

Equal protection of the law.   The right of equal treatment by the law and the law-enforcement agencies for all persons under similar circumstances.

Foreseeability.   The degree to which danger may have been expected or an accident foreseen.

Immunity.   Freedom or protection from legal action. Sovereign immunity refers to the protection of the government or the ruling body against possible suit or blame. It is based on the concept that "the king can do no wrong."

Injunction.   A prohibitive ruling issued by a court directing a person or agency to refrain from performing a specific act.

Liability.   Being responsible for a negligent act or other tort; having legal responsibility which was not fulfilled and resulted in injury.

Liability insurance.   Insurance policies that provide protection against financial loss from liability claims.

Mandatory legislation.   Enacted legislation that must be observed. Its opposite is *permissive* legislation.

Negligent. Not exercising the proper care or following the procedures that a person of ordinary prudence would do under similar circumstances. It can take the form of either commission or omission of an act.

Permissive legislation. Legislation that legalizes an action but does not require or mandate it. Its opposite is *mandatory* legislation.

Proximate cause. The situation or factor that was the main cause of an injury or incident.

Prudent person. One who acts in a careful, discreet, and judicious manner in view of the particular circumstances.

Statutory law. Law that is made through legislative acts.

Tort. A civil wrong or injustice, independent of a contract, which produces an injury or damage to another person or to property.

TORT LAWS

Tort is a word used to classify a group of civil wrongs as opposed to criminal acts. Negligence is one of the major torts. Other wrongs that fall into this category are trespass, nuisance, and defamation. Two important characteristics of tort are these: (1) torts are prosecuted by the injured persons rather than by law-enforcement officials, and (2) to prove a tort the injured party must demonstrate a preponderance (more than 50%) of the evidence supports his or her claim. This last characteristic differs from a criminal case, where proof beyond a reasonable doubt is required.

Under tort law a person who causes injury to another person for which a legal liability exists is frequently answerable to the injured person in monetary damages, although other forms of compensation are sometimes used. It must be emphasized that a person can be held liable for another person's injury or damage only when the first person intentionally, or negligently, causes or contributes to the injury. The injured person (plaintiff) must prove that the injuring person (defendant) was the proximate cause of the plaintiff's injury. Tort law has its most basic foundation in the concept of *fault*–with whom does the fault of injury lie?

Negligence

One of the most important aspects of tort is negligence. In the legal sense negligence is the failure to perform one's responsibilities at the level expected of a reasonable person under the particular circumstances. Good intentions alone are no safeguard, because negligence denotes an unintentional failure to do what is reasonably expected. When a person falls short of these expectations and this contributes to injury of another person, then negligence can be declared.

Any individual can file a suit against another for negligence, but whether the suit is successful is a decision to be made by the court. Negligence is often difficult to prove, and many individuals who are inclined to sue become discouraged when the grounds are weak or insufficient. For a person to be declared negligent, the following elements must exist:

1. The defendant must have a *duty toward the plaintiff*. Employees of recreation-sponsoring agencies clearly have certain duties toward participants. In most states a person does not have a legal duty toward a stranger even when the stranger is in dire

need of help. To encourage aid when needed, some states have passed *Good Samaritan laws*, which provide legal protection for a person who tries to assist another person.

2. The plaintiff must have been harmed by the tort or wrong committed by the defendant. This could be in the form of property damage, personal injury, or damage to one's character or reputation.

3. The individual having *duty* must have breached that duty by an act of omission (*nonfeasance*) or an act of commission (*misfeasance*). This means that a person who does nothing when something should have been done is often as liable as one who responds incorrectly.

4. The breach of duty mentioned in the previous item must have been directly related to the damage done the plaintiff. In other words the breach of duty was the proximate cause of the damage.

Situations of Potential Negligence

It is important to understand the potential hazards pertaining to negligence and deal effectively with them.

Faulty equipment for which an employee or leader is responsible can result in grounds for a suit if a participant becomes injured. Possible examples would be these: (1) injury to a skier due to malfunction or poor repair of the lift, (2) the loss of life due to the sinking of a boat that was rented from a concessionaire and was in ill repair, and (3) injury to a child due to defective or poorly designed playground equipment. In addition to the duty to prevent the use of defective equipment, there is a duty to periodically inspect the equipment with the intent to discover any defects.

Attractive nuisances can place the responsible party in a very weak position if someone is injured as a result of such a nuisance. These are examples: (1) hazardous equipment that is unsecured and unsupervised and which may attract persons (a loaded gun, bows and arrows, a climbing rope, scuba equipment, and unsecured watercraft, for example), (2) swimming pools and designated swimming areas that are unsecured or have no supervision.

Impudence involves the *duty of care* question, which is decided in court. The duty of care required to avoid tort liability is that which a reasonable person of ordinary prudence would exercise for the safety of others under the particular circumstances. The test to be applied is what the particular individual should have reasonably foreseen and done. This standard is often referred to as the *reasonable-man test*.

The conditions under which the visitor is present are an influencing factor. Visitors are entitled to various levels of protection, depending on their status. They fall into three categories:

1. A *trespasser* is one who enters another person's property without permission and not for the benefit of the property owner. The property owner has only minimal responsibility for the trespasser, but the owner is not totally free of responsibility. For example, the owner is not allowed to let the trespasser become exposed to known dangers or in any way purposely cause the trespasser to become injured.

2. A *licensee* is one who enters another person's property with consent (implied or stated) of the property owner, but not for the benefit of the owner. Examples of licensees

are snowmobilers who obtain permission to tour on private property, or one who has permission to hunt rabbits or quail on a landowner's property, or a fisher who receives permission to cross private land enroute to a destination. The property owner is required to prevent willful harm to the licensee, meaning that any known hazards must be pointed out so that it does not appear that the property owner entrapped the visitor.

3. An *invitee* is a visitor on either private or public property for the benefit of the property owner. Commercial recreation operations fall into this category. The owner or manager has an obligation to keep the property and equipment in good repair and to prevent injury to the visitor. This requires proper instruction, the elimination of unreasonably hazardous conditions, and the implementation of adequate precautionary and safety measures.

Defenses Against Negligence

Special attention should be given to the particular conditions that can keep a person free of negligence. Each of the following are defenses against negligence:

1. The absence of legal duty or of proximate cause would normally mean that liability does not exist. There must be a clear and direct link between the action of the defendant and the damage done to the plaintiff. Further, there must be evidence that the defendant had a responsibility and that the defendant's conduct actually contributed to the cause of damage.

2. The assumption of risk means that there is certain risk inherent in participation. Of course, the element of risk varies with different activities. For example, skiing, snowmobiling, scuba diving, rock climbing, and hang gliding are high-risk activities. When an individual voluntarily participates, he or she assumes the risk. Damages that result within the limits of a known risk do not constitute liability. However, conditions that create unreasonable risk can definitely constitute liability.

3. Contributory negligence by the injured person constitutes protection against liability on the part of the property owner. Suppose a participant takes more risk than is necessary or disobeys warnings or safety regulations, or acts unwisely under normally hazardous conditions. In such a case the injured person contributes to his own damage, and therefore is guilty of contributory negligence.

Handling Injuries

When someone is injured, the person supervising or handling the situation is placed in a precarious position, because the proper procedures must be followed, including first aid. A person could be found liable for not administering first aid measures when needed or for administering first aid incorrectly. This is especially true of individuals who have supervisory or protective responsibilities such as a lifeguard, or a ski patrol member. These individuals have responsibilities for both prevention and treatment. Further, the property owner or manager is expected to provide responsible supervisory personnel, such as qualified lifeguards and ski patrol members. In this regard there are four very important considerations: (1) strictly avoid placing or allowing participants in unreasonably hazardous circumstances, (2)

Preparation for rescue is an important aspect of good management. (National Park Service, photo by Richard Frear)

provide adequate supervision so there is a reasonable effort toward the prevention of injury, (3) when injury occurs, have the injured person cared for by a qualified individual who will act prudently, and (4) keep an accurate written record of every serious incident.

CONTRACTS

A contract is a legally binding agreement representing both sides and explaining the conditions of agreement. It is assumed that contracts are entered voluntarily in a spirit of agreement and with a legal purpose in mind. Outdoor-recreation leaders and managers become involved with contracts with employees, suppliers, constructors, concessionaires, and cooperating agencies. Contracts require the signatures of both parties, and once the signatures are fixed it is assumed that both parties understand the conditions of the contract and will abide. Any exception is considered a breach of contract and is subject to legal action. Contracts should not be viewed as legal devices or pitfalls. They should be forthright agreements designed to afford legal protection to the parties involved.

SOVEREIGN IMMUNITY

The concept of sovereign immunity pertaining to public agencies has existed for a long time. However, during the past couple of decades sovereign immunity has deteriorated significantly. In many cases the results have favored the individual against the public agency.

Because of the deterioration of sovereign immunity, employees of governmental agencies have had to become more alert and aggressive toward preventative measures and the enforcement of safety regulations. They have found it necessary to enforce safety standards whether recreation participants want it or not. Potentially dangerous trails, bridges, ski slopes, climbing sites, and swimming areas must be properly marked and carefully monitored, or else closed to participants.

The sovereign immunity concept has traditionally extended to nonprofit and charitable organizations, including youth-serving agencies and religious organizations. The deterioration of immunity of government agencies is likely to affect the liability of these quasi-public agencies. The trend is definitely toward socializing individual losses and shifting the financial burden of damages to society.

PRODUCT LIABILITY

Product liability is a legal obligation that may require compensation by a manufacturer of supply equipment used by a recreation consumer who is injured while using the equipment. There has been a proliferation of product-liability suits, and many of them have been profitable for the injured person. This has escalated the cost for the manufacturers because of court costs, increased insurance, and legal settlements. For the most part the increased costs get passed on to purchasers of recreation equipment. However, in some cases, the costs have been so great as to put some recreation companies out of business.

Each year many people are injured in recreational activities, among them, snow skiiing, waterskiing, and rock climbing. In some cases the injuries can be associated with poorly designed or faulty equipment. Thus, there is risk for both the participants and the equipment manufacturers. It is also a problem for recreation providers when they rent or lease equipment to consumers.

LAND AND FACILITY LIABILITY

Land and facility liability legally requires compensation by an owner or operator of recreation areas or facilities to a consumer who has been injured while using those facilities. Lawsuits have been directed against local park and recreation agencies, campground operators, and ski-area owners.

The National Ski Association estimates that during the last five years, a 300% insurance-premium increase has occurred for the ski industry.

Golf courses, campgrounds, and other private recreation land and facilities are also subject to liability suits. A large number of claims have been filed for broken automobile and house windows resulting from golf balls driven from fairways. Sometimes a golf ball hits a person and then the liability problem is much greater.

There have been many examples where suits have been attempted, and some have been successful against operators of private campgrounds. Further, wildlife-management agencies are concerned about the number of private landowners who have become reluctant about permitting access to their land for hunting and fishing because of the danger of a liability suit in case someone is injured on the property.

Recently in many states there has been legislation passed that provides additional protection for equipment manufacturers and recreation-property owners and puts more burden of responsibility on the participant. However, liability associated with design, construction, and supervision can only be legislated and adjudicated to certain limits. Beyond this the participant must be educated to recognize that the extent of his or her involvement is directly related to the assumption of personal responsibility and risk. Further, there will always be certain situations that will go to court because of their unique nature and differences of opinion as to where the fault lies for injury or damage incurred.

Discussion Questions

1. What is Murphy's Law and how can it be applied to accident prevention and in the prevention of legal liability?
2. Briefly define each of the following: act of God, civil law, assumption of risk, foreseeability, liability, negligence.
3. What is meant by tort and what are its characteristics? How does tort apply in the field of outdoor recreation?
4. For a person to be found legally negligent, what basic circumstances must exist?
5. Visitor status on private land is divided into three categories. What are they and what is the landowner's potential liability in connection with each category?
6. What are some of the conditions that can keep a person free from liability?
7. Do you feel that more or less legal responsibility should be placed on recreation participants as opposed to the owner or sponsor? Why? Be specific.

Recommended Readings

American Alliance for Health, Physical Education, Recreation and Dance. *Safety in Outdoor Recreational Activities.* Reston, Virginia: 1977.

Bury, Richard L. "Risk and Accidents in Outdoor Recreation Areas." College Station, Texas: Texas Agricultural Experiment Station, Texas A&M University, 1980.

"The Criminal Law Enforcement Authority of Park Rangers in Proprietary Jurisdiction National Parks— Where Is It?" *California Western Law Preview* 13, pp. 126–152.

Frakt, Arthur N. "Adventure Programming and Legal Liability." *Leisure Today,* April 1978, p. 42.

Howard, Dennis R., and John L. Compton. *Financing, Managing and Marketing Recreation and Park Resources.* Philadelphia: William C. Brown Publishers, 1980. Chapter 9.

Kozlowski, James C., JD. "Section 1983 Civil Rights Liability for Public Park and Recreation Agencies." *Parks and Recreation,* November 1982, p. 24.

Meier, Joel F., Talmage W. Morash, George E. Wilton. *High Adventure Outdoor Pursuits: Organization and Leadership.* Salt Lake City, Utah: Brighton Publishing Co., 1980. Part III.

Rankin, Janna S. "The Legal System as a Proponent of Adventure Programming." *Leisure Today,* April 1978, p. 12.

Van der Smissen, Betty, "Minimizing Legal Liability Risks." *Journal of Experimental Education,* spring 1979, p. 28.

Van der Smissen, Betty. "Where is Legal Liability?" *Parks and Recreation,* May 1980, p. 50.

CHAPTER 21

Education for Outdoor Recreation

To determine the role of education in meeting people's outdoor-recreation needs, two main groups must be considered: the *consumers* of outdoor recreation and the *producers* (leaders) of recreation opportunities. The former group is composed of the general public; the latter group includes those who plan, manage, and administer recreation resources and programs. In the case of both of these groups, adequate preparation is important.

The consumers must be educated about how to enjoy nature and benefit from outdoor experiences. Further, it is important for them to be informed about the fragile characteristics of the natural environment and the need for its wise use and protection.

The producers of recreation opportunities must be effective managers of both people and natural resources. They must help ensure that people's use of the resources will produce rewarding experiences, while at the same time the resources are properly managed and protected.

Next in importance to freedom and justice is education, without which neither freedom nor justice can be permanently maintained.

–James A. Garfield

EDUCATING THE CONSUMERS

Education is both basic and essential to human purpose and achievement; yet it is a complex process about which we have too little information.

Humans differ from the rest of the biological world in that the human character and personality are not determined primarily by heredity. At birth, we are largely unmade; hence, what we become is greatly influenced by our experiences–that is, by our education, both formal and informal. Ignorance or neglect of this fact about humans would be fatal to individual or group welfare. The human, uncultivated, is something more dangerous than other species. Each animal is guided by its special instincts including some crucial restraints. This is less true with humans, who have tremendous destructive potential and who are subject to powerful emotions. Humans are desperately dependent upon what they learn or fail to learn.

The process of "making a person" is education. In the case of outdoor education, the task at hand is essentially one of developing an informed and concerned public rather than merely managing natural resources.

The interdependence of outdoor recreation and education is clear. Each can make the other more meaningful. Education must precede and accompany outdoor experiences if those experiences are to be valuable. What we get from recreation depends largely on what we provide in education.

Terminology

Interest in nature and outdoor activities has stimulated a growing number of agencies to initiate programs of education about the outdoors. This has been done under a variety of labels, such as *interpretation education, conservation education, environmental education, outdoor education,* and *eco-education.* Whatever title is used, the focus is generally upon developing awareness of nature and natural processes through direct and indirect experiences. The primary methods involve firsthand experience–seeing, hearing, and touching objects in the environment. All of the terms have their proponents, and the proponents have their rationale. However, the author has chosen to use *environmental education* as the principal term in this

A quiet spot at the end of a canoe trip is especially conducive to expanding one's knowledge with a good book. (U.S. Forest Service)

case. It seems adequately descriptive, it aligns with the topic of this text, and it is as well accepted as any of the other terms.

One of the early meaningful definitions of the term appeared in the Environmental Education Act of 1970. The definition was modified slightly in the 1978 amendment of the act to read as follows:

> Environmental education means the education process dealing with man's relationship with the Earth and his effect on the Earth and his relationship with his natural and man-made surroundings, and includes the relations of energy, population, pollution, resource allocation and depletion, conservation, transportation, technology, economic impact, and urban and rural planning to the total human environment.

The Council on Environmental Quality defined environmental education as "the study of the relationships of man to the ecosystem, as well as man's dependence on, contributions to, and alterations of the ecosystem."

A park naturalist interprets the ecology of southern slough. (National Park Service, photo by M. Woodbridge Williams)

Jon K. Hooper[1] described it as a "multidisciplinary approach to teaching the interrelationships between people and their natural and man-made environments." He went on to explain that in total, environmental education refers to education *about* the environment (facts, concepts, and principles), education *for* the environment (attitudes and skills directed to conservation), and education *in* the environment.

Every woodland or forest in addition to yielding lumber, fuel, and posts, should provide those who frequent it a liberal education about nature. This crop of wisdom never fails but unfortunately it is not always harvested.

–Aldo Leopold, *A Sand County Almanac*,
Ballantine Books, New York, 1978, pp. 77–78.

Historical Development

As pointed out by George W. Donaldson and Malcolm D. Swan,[2] formal education programs about the environment have appeared only recently in the American educational scene. However, their roots can be traced to both people and movements of earlier times, especially in Europe. For example, the philosophy concerning firsthand experience with nature is clearly traceable to the 17th century, when European educator John Comenius (1592–1670) wrote:

As far as possible men are to be taught to become wise, not by books, but by the heavens, the earth, oaks and beeches, that is, they must learn to know and examine things themselves and not the testimony and observation of others about the things.

Swiss education reformer Johann Pestalozzi (1746–1827) stated:

Observation is the absolute basis of all knowledge. The first object then, in education, must be to lead a child to observe with accuracy; the second, to express with correctness the results of his observation.

German educator Friedrich Froebel (1782–1852) encouraged teachers to

allow the wee one to stroke the good cow's forehead, and to run among the fowl, and play at the edge of the wood. Make companions for your boys and girls of the trees and banks and the pasture land.

These and other elements of educational philosophy were carried from Europe to the United States by several prominent educators, including Louis Agassiz (1807–1873), an eminent European scientist who moved to Harvard to teach in 1848, and Edward Shelton, an

---

1. Hooper, Jon K., "Diffusion of Environmental Education: Adaption of Wildlife Ecology Education in California K–12 Schools." PhD dissertation, University of California–Davis, 1980, p. 44.
2. Donaldson, George W., and Malcolm D. Swan, "Administration of Eco-Education," AAHPERD, Reston, Virginia, 1979, p. 23.

American normal-school president, who studied in Europe in the late 1850s. They both stressed the importance of the study of nature.[3]

It was not until 1908 that education about nature had gained enough popularity to result in the formation of the American Nature Study Society. In 1910 the American Camping Association was established, and subsequently, several other organizations have been formed that emphasize nature study as part of their overall function.

Despite these early beginnings, early environmental education in the United States did not take hold until the 1940s. Donaldson and Swan[4] have characterized the decades of the 1940s, 1950s, and 1960s with the following description:

> The 1940s–a period of innovation, characterized by "school camping," the wholistic philosophical approach and the geographical spread to California, Missouri, Texas, and to numerous other locations.
>
> The 1950s–a time of expansion, consolidation, and the emergence of teacher-education programs.
>
> The 1960s–a period of (1) increased emphasis on the use of diverse resources other than the school camp, (2) a decrease in emphasis on the wholistic philosophy, and (3) a corresponding increase in subject matter emphasis. Also, while outdoor education programs had always stressed conservation, the 1960s marked a decided increase in what had come to be called Environmental Education. (Indeed, many programs changed their names as well as their emphasis.)

During the 1970s continued emphasis was given to the term *environmental education*. It seemed more inclusive and descriptive of the current educational needs. Also during this era, some leaders advocated the term *eco-education*. They believed such a term would clear up the terminology struggle. Whether this "inclusive" term will add or detract from the confusion remains to be seen.

Program Goals

Of all the aspects of life for which goals are important, education ranks near the top. Goals serve as guides for both effort and achievement. The Intergovernmental Conference of Environmental Education held in Tbilisi, Russia, in 1977 was probably the most broadly based and significant conference of its kind. From that conference came the following goals for environmental education:[5]

1. To foster clear awareness of, and concern about, economic, social, political, and ecological interdependence in urban and rural areas.
2. To provide every person with opportunities to acquire the knowledge, values, attitudes, commitments, and skills needed to protect and improve the environment.
3. To create new patterns of behavior by individuals, groups, and society as a whole toward the environment.

---

3. Ibid., p. 32.
4. Ibid., p. 36.
5. Hooper, *Diffusion of Environmental Education* p. 46.

Joel Goodman and Clifford E. Knapp[6] stated five general goals that are compatible with the goals stated previously but that provide a different approach.

1. Understanding yourself and others through exposure to new environments.
2. Respecting and enjoying the environment.
3. Living safely and healthfully outdoors.
4. Developing lifelong outdoor and environmental interests.

Categories of Environmental Education

The outdoor aspects of environmental education include three major categories: (1) education *in* the outdoors, (2) education *for* the outdoors, and (3) education *about* the outdoors. The three categories are closely related and they compliment each other. The first category occurs outdoors, but the other two categories may occur outdoors or indoors.

Vanishing attributes of this country are miles of open beaches where visitors can fish, stroll, and gather seashells. (U.S. Fish and Wildlife Service, photo by Rex Gary Schmidt)

6. Goodman, Joel, and Clifford E. Knapp, "Beyond a Philosophy of Outdoor Environmental Education," *Journal of Physical Education, Recreation and Dance*, April, 1981, p. 23.

Education *in* the outdoors involves direct outdoor experiences involving observation, study, and research outdoors in settings such as school sites, park and recreation areas, camps, forests, farms, gardens, zoos, refuges, preserves, lakes, rivers, and deserts.

Education *for* the outdoors involves learning skills and developing appreciation for outdoor participation. Included are camping and survival skills, fishing and hunting techniques, boating and watercraft skills, swimming, waterskiing, scuba diving, alpine and cross-country skiing, hiking and mountaineering, orienteering, and numerous other outdoor activities.

Education *about* the outdoors differs from the other two categories because it is primarily concerned with creating an understanding of how natural systems function. It emphasizes the learning and application of ecological concepts and principles. Various elements in this category can be taught indoors or outdoors.

The concept that nature is a community remains basic in the study of ecology. The idea that nature is to be loved and respected, however, is clearly a matter of ethics.

Role of the Schools

The outdoors has always been a great laboratory for learning. Children and youth are curious about their natural surroundings, and they enjoy learning by direct contact. From kindergarten up, students need the chance to learn about natural resources and processes. They need to analyze problems, plan projects, do useful work, and observe what happens as a result.

Environmental education should not be separated from other educational subjects but should be taught with the related subjects, such as the physical sciences and social sciences. Figure 21.1 provides general descriptions of curriculum content. Specific examples and recommendations can be found in textbooks and articles devoted to that topic.

Grades   K   1   2   3   4   5   6   7   8   9   10   11   12

Classroom-related field experiences, study, observation, and projects in outdoor settings.

Outdoor activities and skills—boating and swimming, winter sports, hiking and camping, and nature study.

Outdoor clubs, clinics, and special activities. Environmental field trips.

Figure 21.1. Environmental-education curriculum content at different levels.

The Environmental Education Act of 1970 (as amended in 1978) was designed to improve curricula and teaching methods. To promote better understanding about the environment, the act established an office of Environmental Education within the U.S. Office of Education. This agency distributes funds as grants and contracts to state and local educational agencies for the following purposes:

- To develop curricula
- To disseminate information relating to curricula
- To support environmental-education programs
- To train adult leaders
- To plan outdoor ecological study centers
- To conduct community-education programs for adults
- To prepare and distribute materials for mass-media use

Involvement of Government Agencies

Local park and recreation agencies have particular contributions to make to the environmental education effort in the following ways:

- Interpretation programs including field trips, publications and audiovisuals
- Visits to zoos, aquariums, botanical gardens, and similar places
- Special-interest clubs relating to the outdoors
- Instruction in outdoor skills, such as aquatic activities, winter sports, camping skills, survival techniques, and outdoor photography
- Field trips and excursions such as hiking, backpacking, bicycling and cross-country skiing

Moreover, state government is typically involved in environmental education in some fashion, including the departments of education, parks and recreation, fish and wildlife, forestry, recreation, and colleges and universities.

Several of the federal resource-management agencies conduct interpretative programs to enlighten visitors about environmental issues and conservation practices and to make their visits more enjoyable and meaningful. For example, the National Park Service provides lectures, films, scenic hikes, museums, and demonstrations. The Forest Service also conducts interpretative programs in certain localities in the form of nature hikes, demonstrations, interpretative signs and evening lectures and films. The following are brief explanations of how the different federal agencies are involved.

The *Extension Service* of the U.S. Department of Agriculture conducts workshops and publishes material on various topics relating to environmental protection. Further, it is the sponsoring agency of the 4-H program, which promotes environmental projects and conducts an extensive youth camping program.

The *Farmers Home Administration* prepares handbooks for teachers on environmental education. It also offers a curriculum guide on improving the quality of the environment.

The *U.S. Forest Service* has a nationwide environmental-education program involving teacher training, environmental study sites, and teacher guides. The main thrust is in the area of teacher preparation and workshops. This is in addition to the interpretation services that the Forest Service sponsors for visitors in some national forests.

The *Soil Conservation Service* furnishes technical assistance for environmental-education projects, including outdoor classrooms on school sites. The agency assists with teachers' workshops and supplies curriculum materials for a variety of courses, including recreation and land-use planning.

The *National Park Service* sponsors three environmental education programs: (1) NEED (National Environmental-Education Development) is designed to assist school systems through the development of interdisciplinary educational materials that supplement existing school curricula. Teacher guides and student materials are available. (2) NESA (National Environmental Study Areas) is a program of environmental study whereby schools use the resources of national parks in conjunction with an ongoing environmental-education curriculum at the schools. (3) NEEL (National Environmental-Education Landmarks) is designed to identify and preserve nationally significant environmental study areas. In addition to these education efforts, the Park Service carries on an extensive interpretation program for park visitors, including nature hikes, lectures, demonstration areas, museums and exhibits.

The U.S. Fish and Wildlife Service, Bureau of Land Management, Bureau of Indian Affairs, Bureau of Reclamation, Environmental Protection Agency, Office of Coastal Zone Management, and Tennessee Valley Authority all provide limited technical assistance and interpretation services. For example, the Bureau of Indian Affairs offers two environmental-education curriculum guides and assistance in setting up programs. The Bureau of Reclamation and the Bureau of Land Management each have a small group of environmental specialists who serve as consultants in connection with its own projects and to design educational experiences for the visitors.

Numerous other government agencies are involved in specific kinds of environmental education. In many cases their efforts are not geared toward youth or the general public. Instead, they become involved with workshops, clinics, and printed materials for the environmental education of engineers, scientists, teachers, and others whose jobs cause them to have impact on the environment. Such people need to be well educated in ecology and about conservation objectives and principles.

Nongovernment Agencies

Several private and voluntary organizations have become involved with environmental education. Among them are nature clubs and youth and citizen groups.

Nature centers first appeared in the United States in the late 1800s and began to gain popularity in the 1940s. The emphasis broadened to include elements of conservation and environmental education. Nature centers sponsor after-school, evening, and summer activities, frequently through the auspices of outdoor clubs. Such centers are often managed in cooperation with nearby schools as supplementary to the school curriculum. Numerous school districts have established nature centers of their own. Some such centers are compact and close to the schools and include both indoor and outdoor exhibit and experimental areas. Other centers are relatively large, often more remote, and oriented toward experiencing nature in a relatively unmodified state.

Youth organizations, such as the YMCA, YWCA, Boy Scouts, and Girl Scouts have long been involved with sponsoring a broad range of outdoor experiences. There are hundreds of

The public must recognize that man is only a cog in the ecological mechanism. If we work with it we can flourish; if we work against it, it will eventually grind us down. (National Park Service, photo by Richard Frear)

permanent youth camps across the country owned and operated by youth agencies. Many of them are church affiliated. In addition, there are thousands of organized camps and excursions sponsored each year by these same agencies in locations different from the permanent camps. Practically all of these events include elements of environmental education.

In addition, there are many other organizations that provide assistance to individuals and groups interested in outdoor projects. Listed below are selected organizations that are principally involved. (The addresses of several of these organizations appear in Chapter 15.)

Air Pollution Control Association
America the Beautiful Fund
American Conservation Association
American Forestry Association
American Nature Study Society
American Society for Ecological
    Education
Appalachian Trail Conference
Association of Interpretative
    Naturalists
Conservation Education Association
Conservation Services, Inc.
Defenders of Wildlife
Environmental Action, Inc.
Environmental Action Foundation

Friends of the Earth
Garden Clubs of America
Izaak Walton League of America
John Muir Institute for Environmental
    Studies
Keep America Beautiful, Inc.
League of Conservation Voters
National Audubon Society
National Environmental Education
    Development
National Parks and Conservation
    Association
National Recreation and Park
    Association
National Wildlife Federation

Speak to the earth and it will speak back with ages of wisdom. (Dinosaur National Monument) (National Park Service, photo by Richard Frear)

Natural Resources Council of America
North American Wildlife Foundation
Northern Environmental Council
Sierra Club

Soil Conservation Society of America
Western Interpreters Association
Wilderness Society
Wildlife Society

Interpreter-Naturalist Programs

The goal of the nature interpreter should be to help visitors have rich experiences with the natural environment and help them become better citizens in terms of environmental appreciation. The scope of interpreter programs includes nature hikes and tours conducted by naturalists, self-guided interpretative trails, talks, visitor centers, audio-visual productions, and demonstration areas. Environmental interpretation has unusual potential for enhancing visitor experiences and elevating people's sensitivity toward nature.

Numerous agencies, including the National Park Service, Forest Service, and many state park systems have year-round naturalists, as well as seasonal interpreters hired for the summer. Also, during recent years numerous local park and recreation departments have hired naturalists.

Freeman Tilden[7] enumerated these principles of interpretation:

1. Interpretation is revelation based upon information. Build a story into your presentation and incorporate the visitors into your stories. True interpretation deals not with parts but with the historical and spiritual whole.

7. Tilden, Freeman, *Interpreting Our Heritage*, Chapel Hill, North Carolina, University Press, 1962, p. 67.

An outdoor experience can result in a valuable lesson about both plants and people. (National Park Service, photo by Richard Frear)

2. Interpretation is art and can be taught. The story is art–not science. We are all poets and artists to some degree–images are adventures of the imagination. The interpreter must possess the skills of speaking and writing.

3. The chief aim is provocation, not instruction–to stimulate in the reader or hearer a hunger to widen his or her horizon of interests and knowledge. The national park or monument, the preserved battlefield, the historic restoration, the nature center in a public recreation spot are all places where interpretation blooms and flourishes. First stimulate the visitor's interest, and then stimulate him or her to see and understand.

4. Interpretation should aim to present the whole to the whole person. Toward a perfect whole, the interpreter works for a complete experience, using all five senses. The visitor should leave with one or more pictures in mind.

5. Interpretation programs for children should use a different approach. Children enjoy using superlatives, such as the largest this, the smallest that. They love to touch objects with their fingers and hands. Challenge their senses. The interpreter can help children relate to phenomena in terms they understand, without talking down to them.

The destruction of a natural wonder or historic artifact or the extinction of a plant or animal species is essentially painless if we know little enough about them. Education can help us to avoid such catastrophes.

As a practical example of an interpreter program, let us consider the Visitor Information Service, a program of the U.S. Forest Service started in 1960. The program has been implemented in some of the districts but not all of them, depending largely on the number and concentration of visitors. The Visitor Information Service objectives, which are stated below, will indicate the nature and the purpose of all nature interpretation.

1. To help visitors develop a better understanding and appreciation of natural resources, products, uses, and activities on national forestlands.
2. To acquaint visitors with recreation opportunities, natural and human history, and activities in the area.
3. To obtain greater public cooperation in protection against fire, vandalism, stream pollution, and littering.
4. To stimulate curiosity and satisfy the desire to understand natural resources and their relation to the environment.

Interpretative techniques include a broad spectrum of activities and experiences that expose visitors to different elements of the natural environment. Among the many approaches used are guided walks and tours, self-guided nature walks with interpretive signs or leaflets, campfire programs, visitor centers, trailside or roadside exhibits, posted bulletins, and plant labeling.

PREPARING LEADERS

Another responsibility of education related to outdoor recreation is to prepare individuals who will serve as leaders, planners, interpreters, managers, and administrators. A large number of these professional positions now require a bachelor's degree, some require a master's degree, and a few justify a doctorate.

A profession is regarded as covering a rather broad field, within which are areas of specialization. Medicine, for example, includes surgery, neurology, pediatrics, and other branches. Engineering includes civil, chemical, and electrical engineering. Recreation similarly has numerous branches, among which are school, municipal, industrial, therapeutic, and outdoor recreation.

Each profession must have an identified body of knowledge—a core content—to which is added material pertaining to the specialized branches. The professional preparation curriculum should provide the combination of *core content* and *specialization* required by each branch of the profession. The curricular content in the field of recreation, including outdoor recreation, is basic to the effective preparation of leaders.

Development of the Profession

As pointed out by Samuel T. Dana,[8] professional education in outdoor recreation (or outdoor-related education) has developed along two distinct but gradually converging lines. It was first associated with physical education, which dealt primarily with body development and sports. These activities obviously promoted health and provided the participants with recreation of a sort, often outdoors. Gradually, departments of physical education in the colleges evolved into departments of physical education and health, then into departments of physical education, health, and recreation, always with outdoor recreation receiving relatively little attention except for outdoor sports and camping skills. These were centered on people and on activity, and relatively little attention was given to natural resources.

No profession can be truly great unless its practitioners have the vision of greatness and the desire to relate its service to man's vital needs.

The second stage of the development of professional preparation was through natural-resources management. Those who prepared for management of natural resources found the resources being used more and more by recreationists. The problem of management, conservation, and preservation became ever more closely entwined with the recreational use of the land and water. The need for special preparation in outdoor recreation became so apparent that courses on outdoor recreation were added to the resource-management curricula.

A significant event in natural-resource management occurred in 1898 when Cornell University offered the first four-year professional forestry program. During this same year, the New England Association of Park Superintendents was formed, and their first annual meeting was held in 1899. This organization became the stepping stone for the origin of the American Association of Park Superintendents and later the American Institute of Park Executives.

Soon after the turn of the century, important professional publications began to appear. In 1902 the *Journal of Forestry* began, and in 1907 *Recreation Magazine* first appeared. *Landscape Architecture* magazine made its first appearance in 1910, and *Parks and Recreation*, the official publication of the American Institute of Park Executives, was first published in 1917.

The New York State College of Forestry at Syracuse University is given credit for offering the first program for training park superintendents, beginning in 1912. The emphasis was on municipal-park design and park administration.

The official recognition of the value of recreational use of natural resources took a major step forward in 1924 when President Calvin Coolidge called the first National Outdoor Recreation Conference.

The publishing in 1928 of L. H. Weir's book, *Parks: A Manual of Municipal and County Parks*, provided the first comprehensive book on park design, management, and administration. The book served to bring recreation specialists and park designers into a common fold, even though their professional associations remained independent.

8. Dana, Samuel T., *Education and Outdoor Recreation*, Department of the Interior, Bureau of Outdoor Recreation, U.S. Government Printing Office, Washington, D.C., 1968, p. 87.

The New Deal brought increased interest in national resource planning and development and a realization that academic training in the colleges and universities was needed. Recreation land-use courses were initiated at the University of Massachusetts, and a forest-management and recreation program was started at Utah State College in the early 1930s. By 1934 park-management courses were begun at Colorado State College, and a year later a recreation and municipal-forestry program was instituted at Michigan State College. In 1936 New York University added both undergraduate and graduate courses in recreation education. The University of North Carolina established an undergraduate curriculum in 1943, and Purdue University initiated a curriculum in industrial recreation in 1949.

In 1946, 78 institutions offered majors in recreation and parks; 33 offered graduate degrees. In 1948 a national conference on professional preparation of recreation personnel was held at New York University, and a similar conference was held in Washington, D.C., in 1954. A corps of educators and professionals resulted from these conferences to promote better curricular content and leadership methods.

Curriculum Development

One of the first productive efforts toward improving curricular content was the National Conference on Professional Preparation held in 1962 under the auspices of the American Alliance for Health, Physical Education, Recreation, and Dance. The conference emphasized the importance of a strong background of general education, which it felt should compose 50% of a four-year undergraduate program.

With respect to outdoor recreation, the conference recognized two specialized program areas—recreation and park administration, and camping and outdoor activities. The scope of the proposed coverage for each of these fields was indicated in some detail, but no attempt was made to prescribe specific courses.

Five years later, in 1967, AAHPERD held a conference on graduate education. This conference concluded that three principal areas of emphasis are observable in graduate-level recreation education: recreation programming, administration of recreation services, and natural-resource management for recreation. The knowledge regarded as essential for the last area included an understanding of the relationships between natural resources and of the principles involved in their management, but not the technical ability to direct their actual management for purposes other than recreation.

In 1965 the National Research Council established through one of its commissions a panel on natural-resource science. One of the tasks assigned to it was the preparation of recommendations for the development of undergraduate programs in the field of renewable natural resources. The panel came to the conclusion that the basic principles—and to a considerable extent the practices—involved in the management of natural resources have much in common, whether the major emphasis is on trees, wildlife, forage, water, or recreation. Therefore, it decided to recommend a unified but flexible approach to education for all aspects of natural-resources management.

The panel's specific proposal was that there be a single curriculum for the education of students preparing for service in the field of renewable natural resources. This curriculum would be followed by all students, but its structure would be such as to meet the needs of those intending to work in different areas, such as forestry, wildlife management, watershed management, and recreation management. It would be divided into four parts: (1) a basic core, (2) an area emphasis, (3) professional courses, and (4) electives. The first part would be uniform for all students, but the other three parts would permit specialization.

In 1968 the National Recreation and Park Association and AAHPERD held a national conference in Washington, D.C., on outdoor recreation and education. The conference program emphasized the need for more qualified leaders and more standardization of curricula in areas of education about the outdoors.

In 1978 the National Recreation and Park Association entered the business of accrediting college curricula. This procedure has gone a long way toward defining levels of expectation and specific areas of curricular content in the programs of colleges and universities.

In the United States more than 165 universities now offer curricula leading to a bachelor's degree in recreation. (A nearly equal number of two-year colleges offer recreation curricula.) Even though about half of these institutions claim a specialization in outdoor recreation, only a few are prepared to offer a truly thorough education in this field. Therefore, students who want to become true specialists should be selective about the institutions they attend. They should consider only programs that are well established and staffed by competent teachers. A complete list of the colleges and universities that offer degrees in recreation, along with a designation of specialized areas in each program, appears in *Opportunities in Recreation and Leisure* (see recommended readings).

Continuous Professional Preparation

Regardless of what else is done in support of any endeavor, the results will not exceed the level of its leadership. Leadership sets the tone and defines the limits within which any organization, program, or discipline can function. Some individuals take the limited view that leadership preparation is totally the responsibility of colleges and universities. This is not true. In any occupational field the primary role of the institutions of learning is to supply the profession with new people who have adequate basic education to enter the field and function effectively. The growth and development of professionals, however, must be continuous. This can come about with valuable on-the-job experience combined with in-service training, such as conferences, institutes, clinics, regular reading of professional literature, and tutoring from those who are professionally more mature and better prepared. The right combination of formal education and in-service preparation will create the caliber of leadership that the outdoor-recreation field will need in the future.

Discussion Questions

1. What characterized outdoor education in the 1940s, 1950s, 1960s, and 1970s?
2. List and briefly describe the three major categories of outdoor recreation.
3. What are some of the ways that different federal agencies are involved in outdoor recreation?
4. Why is it important for engineers, scientists, and teachers to be well educated about the natural environment?
5. What are some of the benefits that result from nature-interpretation programs?

6.	What we get from a recreation experience depends in large part on what we bring in terms of educational background. Do you agree with this statement? Why or why not?
7.	Do you feel that the principal responsibility for the outdoor education of young people rests with the public schools? Why?

Recommended Readings

Baker, Woodson C., III. "Year-round Camping Through Adventure Education Programs." *Camping*, January 1981, pp. 18–20, 25–28.

Darst, Paul W., and George P. Armstrong. *Outdoor Adventure Activities for School and Recreation Programs*. Minneapolis: Burgess Publishing Co., 1980.

Donaldson, George W., and Malcolm D. Swan. "Administration of Eco-Education." Reston, Virginia: AAHPERD, 1979.

Ford, Phyllis. *Principles and Practices of Outdoor-Environmental Education*. New York: John Wiley & Sons, 1981.

Grimm, Gary, and Larry Neal. "Outdoor Wilderness Program: A Campus Makes a Committment to the Individual." *Journal of Physical Education, Recreation and Dance*, April 1980, p. 45.

Hammerman, Elizabeth L., and Donald R. Hammerman. "Developing a Resident Outdoor Education Program." *Journal of Physical Education, Recreation and Dance*, March 1982, p. 49.

Henkel, Donald D. *Directory of College-University Programs in Recreation, Leisure Services, and Resources*. Alexandria, Virginia: National Recreation and Park Association, 1981.

Jensen, Clayne, and Jay Naylor. *Opportunities in Recreation and Leisure*, 3rd ed. Skokie, Illinois: National Textbook Co., 1983.

Jensen, Mary, and Briggs Anderson. "Alternatives for Outdoor Education Programming." *Journal of Physical Education, Recreation and Dance*, October 1981, p. 64.

Knapp, Clifford E., and Joel Goodman. *Humanizing Environmental Education: A Guide for Learning Nature and Human Nature Activities*. American Camping Association, 1981.

Knudson, Douglas M. *Outdoor Recreation*. New York: Macmillan Publishing Co., 1984. Chapter 26.

Link, Michael. *Outdoor Education*. Englewood Cliffs, New Jersey: Prentice Hall, Inc., 1981.

Lishman, Mark. "Outdoor Education." *Camping*, March 1981, pp. 10–14, 50.

Miner, Joshua L., and Joe Boldt. *Outward Bound USA*. New York: William Morrow and Co., Inc., 1981.

National Recreation and Park Association. *A Handbook for Interpreters*, 2nd ed. Alexandria, Virginia: 1976.

Radcliffe, Betty, and Gerlach, Luther P. "The Ecology Movement After Ten Years." *National History*, January 1981, pp. 12, 14–16, 18.

Sessoms, H. Douglas. "Education in the Eighties: The Forecast, the Change." *Parks and Recreation*, May 1981, p. 48.

Sharpe, Grant W. *Interpreting the Environment*, 2nd ed. New York: John Wiley & Sons, 1982.

Soil Conservation Service. *Outdoor Classrooms on School Sites*. Washington, D.C.: U.S. Government Printing Office, 1980, 22 pps.

Staley, Frederick A. "Outdoor Education in the Total Curriculum." *Journal of Physical Education, Recreation and Dance*, January 1983, p. 56.

Staley, Rebecca R., and Frederick A. Staley. "Outdoor Education: Catalyst for Change." *Journal of Physical Education, Recreation and Dance*, January 1983, p. 62.

Watz, Karyl. "Funding Outdoor Education Programs." *Journal of Physical Education, Recreation and Dance*, January 1983, p. 64.

Wilson, Renate. *Inside Outward Bound*. Charlotte, North Carolina: The East Woods Press, 1981.

CHAPTER 22

A Look at the Future

What we have done in the past and where we stand now are both less important than the direction we are heading. The past serves as our guide; the present represents our circumstances; and the future holds our hopes and aspirations. However, predicting the future with reasonable accuracy has become increasingly difficult because the future holds so many options. Yet we must make predictions and estimates about the future or we have little basis for planning and preparing. It seems that the most reliable prediction is that change in almost all aspects of our lives will be the overriding characteristic of the future.

SOCIOECONOMIC TRENDS

Fundamental to the future of outdoor recreation are the social and economic factors that set the stage for the kind of life-style we live. How will these forces affect our opportunities and preferences?

The *population* of our nation is presently increasing at about 1% annually. This means that the 237 million people in the United States in 1985 will increase to 250 million by 1990 and about 280 million by the year 2000–approximately double what it was in 1950. The average age of the population will continue to increase. In 1983 for the first time there were more people in the United States over 65 than there were teenagers. By the year 2020 those over 65 will outnumber teenagers two to one.

Currently, about three fourths of the people live in urban and suburban areas. By the year 2000, 78% of the 280 million people will live in these areas. By then, the Eastern Seaboard, the Great Lakes region, the West Coast, and the Southeastern-Gulf region will each contain a sprawling megalopolis. The Rocky Mountain and Sunbelt states will be much more populated than they are now. Obviously, with these changes some of our outdoor recreation patterns will also change.

As the population increases, certain aspects of our *transportation* system will require over-hauling. The large urban areas will need larger mass-transit systems, some of which will have to be underground or elevated above ground level. The surface of the land in the densely pop-ulated areas will certainly not accommodate all of the moving about that people will do. High-speed railway systems will take people rapidly from one point to another within the populated regions. Helicopter shuttles within cities will expand, with rooftops serving as landing platforms. Faster air travel, perhaps up to 2000 mph (3200 kph), will become avail-able across country and to foreign lands. The larger waterways will have to carry more boats and ships, some of them skimming across the open water at 50–75 knots. But, for the bulk of the people, the automobile will continue to be the main method of transportation. Cars will appear in ever-increasing numbers, and on the average they will become smaller, quieter, and less polluting.

With more people and better transportation, it seems inevitable that increased numbers will travel to the doorsteps of practically every outdoor recreation attraction, both in the United States and elsewhere. Granted, the energy problem will become more acute, but cer-tainly, suitable alternatives to gasoline engines will be developed.

Personal *income* has increased (with only a few setbacks) since the depression of the 1930s. Economists predict that the trend will continue upward, though there will be disrup-tions and irregularities. What our purchasing power will be by 1990 or 2000 is hard to predict, but indications are clear that Americans will have more purchasing power than they do now. There will be more money for goods and services of one's choice, and this will provide oppor-tunities for expanded participation in outdoor recreation.

The average level of *education* as measured by grade level achieved in school has gradu-ally increased over several decades. Present conditions indicate continuation of the upward trend, but at a slower rate. The increased education will cause improved earnings and also expanded interests in a variety of activities, including many forms of outdoor recreation. Fur-ther, there will be more need for environmental education, because Americans will become even more removed from nature's processes during daily living because of automated work conditions and urbanization.

Within the next two to three decades we will see the *average workweek* in industry and commerce lowered to about 32 hours. It is currently just under 40 hours, whereas 50 years ago it was 60 hours. Combined with the shorter workweek we will see an expansion of two other forms of leisure: vacations and retirement. At the same time, life expectancy will continue to move upward; thus, the period of retirement will expand in both directions. All of this *increased leisure* during one's life span will have a tremendous impact on outdoor recreation and our demands on the resources that support it.

During recent times we have had great advances in *technology*, and this has influenced practically every aspect of our lives, including what we do for recreation, where we do it, and how much time we spend. Future advances will have even greater impact on our recreation patterns. New devices used for participation will open new worlds of leisure activities. Tech-nology will be both a friend and an enemy to recreation. Though it will enhance recreation participation in both variety and amount, it also will be ever more destructive to the outdoor environment.

Regardless of how much time, money, and education we have, the factor that determines our recreation patterns more than anything else is our *philosophy*, including both our personal and our social sense of values. It has become clear that the *worthy use of leisure* really needs to be integrated more convincingly into our educational process and our recreational patterns. We ought to think more carefully about which leisure activities should be encouraged. Overall, we will have to do much better at selecting and promoting appropriate activities if leisure time is to serve society well.

In some respects this overview of future trends affecting recreation presents a bleak picture, perhaps giving the impression that our outdoor areas will be overrun by hordes of people, exploiting nature at every turn. Unfortunately, this could be the case. It does not need to be, however, and it will not be if we keep abreast of arising problems, and if we exercise proper planning and control. The future of outdoor recreation can be extremely bright if we give it proper attention. But we must face the fact that problems of the future will be more complex and the solutions will become increasingly difficult. Providing enriching opportunities for an expanded population will require the attention of our best planners and organizers. It will demand extensive foresight by political and professional leaders and much cooperation by the different levels of government and between government and nongovernment agencies. Finally, education of the public about the processes of nature, appropriate environmental controls, and principles of conservation and preservation will need increased emphasis.

Those who stay close to nature and understand its processes have a better basis for rational thought and behavior.

FUTURE NEED FOR OUTDOOR RECREATION

Even though great changes have occurred in our living patterns, our basic needs and desires have changed little. We are still a biological species living in an environment with which we have been compatible for thousands of years. We have the same basic drives, a need to belong, a need for security, a need for enjoyment and happiness, a need to understand our reasons for existence, and a need to control to some reasonable degree our circumstances and destiny.

For people everywhere it would seem that staying in close touch with nature and having an understanding of natural processes are fundamental to a meaningful life and the perpetuation of existence. But to Americans, the great outdoors has special meaning, because it is deeply imbedded in our heritage and woven into our history. The fact that we now live in a technicalized environment does not diminish the need for regular contact with nature. In fact, under these circumstances staying close to nature takes on even more significance. The crucial question is not whether this need will exist, but whether in the future there will be ample opportunities.

FUTURE SUPPLY AND DEMAND

The supply of basic natural resources for recreation will not increase. Certain modifications and improvements can enhance the usefulness of some of the resources, but such

There must always be natural beauty to awe the spirit and inspire the soul. (National Park Service, photo by Richard Frear)

revisions have limited potential. On the other hand, because of the increasing population combined with the other socioeconomic factors previously discussed, there seems to be no limit to the potential increase in demand. This simple relationship between supply and demand means that in the future we will need to (1) more clearly identify the areas with high recreation potential and prevent them from being committed to less essential uses, (2) continue at an increased rate to improve recreation areas so they will better serve the increased demands, and (3) modify our recreation patterns to fit the available resources. This whole matter will represent a complex problem that will require the involvement of government at all levels, private enterprise, and numerous professional and service organizations.

FUTURE PARTICIPATION TRENDS

While the population will approximately double during the 50-year period from 1950 to 2000, predictions are that participation in outdoor recreation will triple. Emphasis will continue to be on the simple and economical forms of recreation, such as hiking, cycling, fishing, hunting, swimming, and sightseeing. However, the increases will be above average in winter sports, especially cross-country and downhill skiing and snowmobiling; boating for pleasure, including sailing and waterskiing; health-related activities, with special emphasis upon physical fitness; adventure (risk) activities, especially adventure travel and wilderness experiences.

Beaches and waterways are particularly attractive for recreation, and the population tends to cluster along these areas for reasons of both commerce and recreation. Because of this, proper use and management of the beaches and water corridors will be of crucial importance. It is also true that places of unusual beauty or unique natural features will continue to grow in popularity at a disproportionate rate. Unfortunately, many of these areas have fragile features that must be protected from overuse; otherwise, the areas will lose the very characteristics that make them attractive. Preserving these features while attempting to accommodate the expanding use will be one of our great resource-management challenges.

All told, the most useful and the most-used outdoor-recreation areas will be those close to the population–the areas that are available on a daily and weekend basis. Such areas will be needed in abundant supply for walking, swimming, cycling, golfing, sailing, and other such close-to-home events. In addition to the heavy use of the nearby attractions, however, the remote areas with attractive characteristics also will be taxed to their limits. Outdoor recreationists will appear in ever-increasing numbers in every kind of activity and every location.

BETTER LEADERSHIP WILL BE NEEDED

Much of the future leadership in outdoor recreation will need to come from well-prepared resource-management specialists who are sincerely concerned about people's enjoyable use of areas and resources. Individuals with interdisciplinary backgrounds will be the best prepared for the high-level positions. Within the systems managed by those with multidisciplinary backgrounds, there always will be a need for specialists, such as landscape architects, interpreter-naturalists, horticulturalists, wildlife specialists, and programming specialists.

Some of the most important leaders will be well educated and sensitive connoisseurs, who have broad perspectives and keen insights into cultural change and individual tastes and preferences. These leaders, who will stand at the pinnacle of the park and recreation profession, will have to demonstrate an accurate feel for the needs of people and for the wise use of resources for both the short- and long-term. Such leaders will possess the ability to define and implement what is valuable in terms of outdoor recreation, and how these experiences can be provided now and still be available in the future.

We should wage a constant war–not a war against people, but a war for people, a war for all those things which are good for all of us.
–Sterling W. Sill, a speech at Brigham Young University, 16 February 1967.

MAINTAINING A LIVABLE ENVIRONMENT

Let it be repeated that the most useful recreation opportunities are those found in everyday life close to home. This stresses the importance of a *recreational environment*–an environment that contributes to the pleasantness of each day.

For most future Americans to live in this kind of environment we will have to reverse our direction in several respects. We will have to find ways to depollute the lakes, bays, and streams that we have vigorously polluted until now. We will need to escalate our efforts toward the control of air pollution–a problem that is still being largely ignored. We shall have to face the fact that we cannot destroy matter; we can only change its form. Once we make millions of cars, billions of cans and bottles, and millions of other objects that eventually become useless, then we must have acceptable methods of disposal or transformation of these objects. We must learn that we cannot continue to mar the landscape and clutter it with all sorts of unattractive litter and still have a pleasing environment. Our methods of antipollution have a long way to go before they catch up with our highly effective methods of pollution. Greater strides will have to be taken toward all aspects of pollution control if we are to survive–to say nothing of having an environment that can be enjoyed.

OTHER PROJECTIONS

The future for *wilderness preservation* and *nature conservation* looks generally promising. The value system of the population has improved, and both government and nongovernment agencies have stepped up their measures toward caring for the environment, with particular emphasis on our nonrenewable natural treasures. However, even with this generally positive tone, preserving and conserving natural resources at an acceptable level from the outdoor recreationist's point of view will become increasingly difficult in the face of heavier use by an expanding population.

Linear outdoor recreation areas are sometimes called recreation corridors. These include rivers, trails, shorelines, and parkways. Corridors offer special kinds of recreation because they afford unique forms of travel opportunities, and often they include a tremendous amount of high-quality recreation space. Moreover, corridors are among the most cost-efficient means of providing recreation opportunities, and they disperse the use and thereby diminish the chance for harmful impact. Many recreation corridors have greater future potential than their present level of use, and this potential will need to be realized.

Unfortunately, in terms of parks and open space, the *development of cities* has a grim history. The early planners of many of our large cities expressed fond hope and honest intent of having the cities develop in a manner that would provide adequate space for truly pleasant living. Chicago is a prime example, for at its beginning it adopted the motto *Urb sin horto*, meaning city in a garden. At the time Chicago was described as the city with the lakefront on one side and flowering landscape on the other three. But soon row-house developments and industrial complexes began to encroach on the surrounding landscape, and gradually Chicago became a very ordinary large city. Similar trends occurred in New York, Detroit, St. Louis, Los Angeles, and most of our other metropolitan areas.

Perhaps in the future we will have better success with the development of cities, but to do so, community and regional governments will have to (1) do more advanced planning with

Sometime in September a mountain stream comes to a lonely quiet time; summer has vanished like the wake of a canoe on a foggy day. (U.S. Forest Service)

respect to open space and recreation facilities, (2) be more intent about acquiring in advance those sites that have prime features and hold the line on preserving them for recreational use, and (3) show greater concern for the everyday living environment of people.

Indicators point toward the increasing *economic importance of outdoor recreation*. The combination of more participation and more purchasing power per individual will clearly result in more dollars spent in the pursuit of enjoyment of outdoor activities. Recreation expenditure is bound to be an item of first importance. This potential will be both challenging and exciting.

Private land and private enterprise will, of necessity, become more involved with outdoor recreation. Government agencies and resources will simply not be able to meet the ever-increasing demands. The majority of land in the United States is in private ownership (about 60%). Much of this land is close to the population, whereas most of the government acreage is far away from heavily populated areas. As a result, many landowners will seek opportunities and find ways to benefit from people's recreational needs. At the same time, the increased availability of private property will serve a worthy purpose for the public.

In certain areas the maximum *carrying capacities* will have to be determined and the use limited. This will be particularly difficult in wilderness areas and with the nation's more scenic places. To accomplish this, use permits will become much more prevalent. Also policies pertaining to hunting and fishing will become more stringent because of the inability of these resources to keep pace with the increasing demands.

The *back-to-nature surge* that started in the early 1960s is still very much intact and will probably continue. It's a contrast to the convenience-oriented life-style that otherwise dominates our lives. For this and other reasons this trend will continue to be a significant element in the leisure patterns of many Americans.

Even though the general trend is toward reduced involvement and *budgetary cutbacks* for state and federal agencies, it would be irrational for government to become too inactive in land-use planning. Future circumstances will require increased efforts toward identifying, developing, and managing the more desirable recreation attractions on government lands. This, plus other apparent needs in connection with recreation, will cause state and federal agencies to become involved even more than in the past.

Every citizen ought to be among those who look upon the future as a great opportunity.

SUMMARY

In the near future another author will be able to write about actual and projected changes that are even more dramatic than the changes discussed in this text. The author may talk about sightseeing tours in outer space or excursions deep under the sea. The author may lament the plight of the wilderness hiker before individualized flying devices became available to silently carry recreationists to mountain tops and to once-remote fishing, hunting, and scenic areas. The author will refer to new forms of computerized golf and baseball designed especially for less space. The author will talk of the more affluent individuals who have personal counselors to help select and arrange leisure pursuits. The author might even mention the reservation that he or she has on Moon Flight 732.

Certainly some of these ideas seem farfetched. But not many years ago it would have seemed just as farfetched to talk seriously about making 25 ski runs from the top of Beaver Mountain in a day and returning home refreshed, or taking a week-long hunting trip to Alaska, or waterskiing behind a powerboat at 25 knots.

Bolder projections are not really farfetched, and not even far away. The rapid rate of change in our living conditions will certainly continue. Where and when will it all stop, or will it stop, or will it even slow down? How will the various changes of the future affect our life-styles and how can we adjust to them? How successful will we be in preparing ourselves and others for the changing conditions that will prevail?

Even though the rapid increase in demand for outdoor recreation has taxed our resources and caused great need for concern, this does not necessarily mean that the future is dim. In fact, the future of outdoor recreation can be very bright. If we are careful and thorough in our delineation of the problems, meet them head on, and work out intelligent and timely solutions, then our opportunities can be even better than they are now or have been in the past. Outdoor experiences can continue to have positive impact on our lives, and this should remain one of the attractive features of life in America.

Discussion Questions

1. What can we anticipate in the future with respect to improved transportation, increased income, early retirement, population increases, and population shifts? How will these factors affect outdoor-recreation demands and opportunities?
2. How will technology in the future be both a friend and an enemy in terms of outdoor recreation?
3. What can be expected in the growth pattern of private enterprise in the field of outdoor recreation? Which aspects of recreation will depend the most on private enterprise? Which kinds of recreation have the best possibility of being financially profitable in the future?
4. How can recreation assist in combating the growing health problem related to sedentary living? How do you apply outdoor recreation to this problem in your own life-style?
5. In the future state governments will play a larger role in the growth of outdoor recreation. To achieve this, what are some of the areas that will need to be emphasized by the states?
6. What are some of your predictions concerning growing and changing trends in outdoor recreation in your own geographic area in the near future?
7. Do you think that we now will move more rapidly toward reclaiming many of the areas previously degraded or destroyed by pollution and carelessness, or will we continue to believe we can afford to exploit our natural resources?

Recommended Readings

Chubb, Michael, and Holly R Chubb. *One-Third of Our Time.* New York: John Wiley & Sons, 1981. Chapter 4.

Cross, Robert F. "A Challenge for the Eighties." *The Conservationists,* July–August 1980, pp. 2–7.

Dwyer, John. "Wilderness in Century III." *Parks and Recreation,* January 1981, p. 61.

Gold, Seymour M. "What the Leisure Field Can Do to Safeguard the Future." *Parks and Recreation,* May 1980, p. 45.

Gray, David E. "State of the Art–Future Challenge." *Parks and Recreation,* July 1980, pp. 22–28.

Gray, David E., and Seymour Green. "Future Perspectives II: The 1980's and Beyond," *Parks and Recreation,* May 1982, p. 52.

Knudson, Douglas M. *Outdoor Recreation.* New York: Macmillan Publishing Co., 1984. Chapter 34.

Shafer, Elwood L., George H. Moeller, and Russell E. Getty. *Future Recreation Environments.* U.S. Forest Service FS-316. Washington, D.C.: 1977.

Van Doren, Carlton S., George B. Priddle, and John E. Lewis. *Land and Leisure: Concepts and Methods in Outdoor Recreation.* Chicago: Maaroofa Press, Inc., 1979. Chapter 1.

APPENDICES

APPENDIX A

Legislative Acts Affecting Outdoor Recreation

Included in this appendix is a chronological list of the legislative acts that have had a significant effect on outdoor recreation. There are numerous other acts not included that have had minor or limited influence. The paragraph following the name of each act includes the federal agency primarily responsible for administering the conditions of the act, a condensed description, and a page reference to where the act is discussed in the text.

Creation Act of 1891. Forest Service. Created the original national forest reserve. Pages 134, 139.

Lacey Act of 1900. Fish and Wildlife Service. Established the Department of the Interior as the federal agency responsible for the government's role in the management of fish and wildlife. Also placed controls on interstate shipment of game. Page 172.

Reclamation Act of 1902. Bureau of Reclamation. Initiated the reclamation program that has since resulted in the construction of hundreds of water-management projects in the western states. Pages 31, 152–153.

Forest Service Act of 1905. Forest Service. Created the U.S. Forest Service as the managing agency of the national forest reserve. Page 135.

Antiquities Act of 1906. National Park Service. Gave the president the power to establish national monuments on public lands by proclamation. Pages 32, 121, 191.

Weeks Act of 1911. Several agencies. Enabled government purchase of lands to protect navigable streams. Most of the forest reserve in the eastern states has been acquired under this act. Page 139.

Term Lease Law of 1915. Forest Service. Authorized the Forest Service to issue long-term leases for summer homes, hotels, concessions, and other recreation and resort facilities. Pages 32, 139.

National Park Service Act of 1916. National Park Service. Created the National Park Service as the managing agency of the areas in the national park system. Page 122.

Migratory Bird Treaty Act of 1918.   Fish and Wildlife Service. Provides various controls for the protection of migratory birds. Page 172.

Recreation and Public Purposes Act of 1926.   Department of the Interior. Authorizes exchange, sale, or lease of federal lands to states and political subdivisions for recreational purposes. Pages 144–145.

Migratory Bird Conservation Act of 1929.   Fish and Wildlife Service. Enhanced the development and management of migratory-bird refuges. Page 172.

Shipstead-Newton-Nolan Act of 1930.   Forest Service. The act was landmark legislation for forest recreation. It applied only to northern Minnesota, but it set a precedent for the protection of aesthetic qualities for forest lakes by prohibiting leasing or timber harvest within 400 feet of the shorelines. The policy now applies extensively to both national and state forests.

Tennessee Valley Authority Act of 1933.   Tennessee Valley Commission. Established the TVA for the purpose of developing and managing Tennessee Valley water projects. Page 162.

Fish and Wildlife Coordination Act of 1934.   Amended in 1958. Fish and Wildlife Service. Requires that wildlife conservation receive equal consideration and be coordinated with other features of water-resource development. Page 172.

Historic Sites Act of 1935.   National Park Service. Broadened the president's power to add historic sites to the national park system by proclamation. Page 191.

Migratory Bird Hunting Stamp Act (Duck-Stamp Act) of 1934.   Fish and Wildlife Service. Requires a fee for all persons over age 16 who hunt waterfowl. The funds have helped substantially toward the expansion of refuges. Pages 33, 172.

Park, Parkway, and Recreational Studies Act of 1936.   National Park Service. Directed the National Park Service to do a comprehensive study of public park and recreation areas and programs of the nation, the individual states, and their political subdivisions. The results were used in planning and coordination efforts.

Flood-Control Act of 1936.   Corps of Engineers. Established a national flood-control policy with specific guidelines for implementation. Page 159.

Pittman-Robertson Act of 1937.   Fish and Wildlife Service. Established an excise tax on sporting arms and ammunition. The proceeds go to state wildlife agencies for wildlife management. Page 172.

Flood-Control Act of 1944.   Corps of Engineers. Greatly expanded the Corps' responsibilities for providing recreational facilities at civil-works projects. Pages 159–160, 162.

Surplus Property Act of 1944.   Several agencies. Allows the sale of federal property at 50% of appraised value to states and political subdivisions for park and recreation purposes. Pages 189, 202.

Dingell-Johnson Act of 1950.   Fish and Wildlife Service. Established a manufacturer's excise tax on fishing equipment. The revenue is used by states for fishery management. Pages 33, 172.

Refuge Recreation Act of 1952.   Fish and Wildlife Service. Allows development of lands adjacent to refuges and hatcheries for recreational use. Page 172.

Recreation and Public Purposes Act of 1954.   Department of the Interior. Expanded the provisions of the Recreation and Public Purposes Act of 1926. Increased the sale and lease program of public lands to public and quasi-public organizations for recreation purposes. Page 33.

Watershed-Protection and Flood-Prevention Act (Small-Watershed Act) of 1954. Soil Conservation Service. The act authorized the participation of the federal government in small-watershed management projects and enabled financial assistance for the development and management of recreation and fish and wildlife in connection with the projects. Pages 33, 166.

Housing Act of 1954.   Sections 701, 702, and 704, as amended. Department of Housing and Urban Development. Contains provisions for federal government financial and technical assistance to enhance urban planning and development, and to acquire and build park and recreation facilities and urban open spaces.

Fish and Wildlife Act of 1956.   Fish and Wildlife Service. Established the Fish and Wildlife Service in approximately its present form and enlarged the participation of the federal government in wildlife management. Page 172.

Colorado River Storage Act of 1956.   Bureau of Reclamation. Directed the secretary of the interior to give more attention to the recreation and wildlife potential of reservoir projects. This has set a precedent with reclamation projects that has greatly benefited water-based recreation in the West. Page 155.

National Wildlife Refuge System Administration Act of 1956.   Fish and Wildlife Service. Describes and refines federal policy with respect to the national wildlife refuge system. Page 172.

Outdoor Recreation Resources Review Act of 1958.   Congress. The act established the Outdoor Recreation Resources Review Commission and clarified the commission's assignments. Pages 34, 313–314.

Multiple-Use Sustained-Yield Act of 1960.   Forest Service. Clarified and further defined the concept that national forests are to be administered on a multiple-use basis with five primary uses—outdoor recreation, watershed, range, timber, and fish and wildlife. Pages 34, 139, 141, 327.

Senate Document Number 97 of 1962.   Water Resources Agencies. Specifies that full consideration be given to outdoor recreation and fish and wildlife enhancement in the planning and development of water-resources projects. Pages 151, 160.

Air Pollution Control Act of 1963 (now amended and called the Clean Air Act). Environmental Protection Agency. Defines the clean air expectations and requirements, and explains procedures toward the attainment of these goals. Page 303.

Wilderness Act of 1964.   Forest Service, Park Service, and certain other agencies. Established the national wilderness system and placed numerous areas already designated as wilderness into the system. Pages 34, 97–98, 126, 140–141, 144.

Small Reclamation Projects Act of 1964.   Bureau of Reclamation. Provides for federal financial and technical assistance for nonfederal public agencies to construct small water projects, and provides for recreation planning and development in connection with the projects.

Economic Opportunity Act of 1964.   Department of Labor. Provides for federal assistance for various kinds of training and work programs, some of which have significant impact on the development of recreation areas and facilities. Such programs as the Neighborhood Youth Corps and the Job Corps exist under the provisions of this act.

Highway Beautification Act of 1964. Department of Transportation. Furnishes specific guidelines and the framework for significant funding for the beautification of the nation's highways. Pages 34, 194.

Public Land Law Review Act of 1964. Congress. Established the Public Land Law Review Commission and specified its assignments. The commission's work has had significant influence on the land-use policies of the federal government. Pages 314–315.

Land and Water Conservation Fund Act of 1965. National Park Service. Provides additional sources of revenue and appropriated funds for outdoor recreation and enhanced planning procedures for recreation. The fund applies to several agencies of government at the various government levels. It is one of the most significant pieces of outdoor-recreation legislation ever enacted. Pages 34, 140, 144, 159, 187, 214, 231, 316, 319.

Federal Water Projects Recreation Act of 1965. Federal water-resources agencies. Specifies that full consideration shall be given to recreation and fish and wildlife enhancement in connection with all federal water-resources projects. Pages 144–145, 151–152, 155.

Water Quality Act of 1965. Environmental Protection Agency. Specifies the responsibility of assuring an adequate supply of water suitable in quality for recreation and the propagation of fish and wildlife. Pages 103, 303, 306.

National Historic Preservation Act of 1966. National Park Service. Authorizes matching grants to states and to the National Trust of Historic Preservation. To participate, a state must have a current comprehensive plan for historic preservation. Pages 113, 191.

Air Quality Act of 1967 (Clean Air Act) as amended. Environmental Protection Agency. Describes air-quality standards and the procedures for implementation of the act. Page 306.

National Trail System Act of 1968. National Park Service. Established the framework for the development of a National Trail System and designated two trails for initial inclusion. Pages 34, 109, 140, 188.

Estuary Protection Act of 1968. Department of the Interior. Designed to help control or prevent the continuing destruction of estuaries in the United States. Page 177.

Wild and Scenic Rivers Act of 1968. Park Service, Forest Service, and other agencies. Established the national wild and scenic rivers system and designated certain rivers as initial entries in the system. Pages 34, 99, 101–104, 140, 144, 188.

National Environmental Policy Act of 1969. Environmental Protection Agency. Among other elements, the act furnishes guidelines and requirements concerning environmental protection of land and water resources administered by federal government agencies. Page 144.

Environmental Education Act of 1970. Office of Education. Encourages new and improved curricula and methods to enhance environmental quality and maintain ecological balance. Has application for a large number of agencies concerned with environmental education. Pages 351, 356.

Federal Boat Safety Act of 1972. Department of the Interior. Provides regulations and guidelines to enhance boat-safety education and enforcement.

Water Pollution Control Act of 1972. Environmental Protection Agency. Among other provisions, the act specifies that water-quality planning must include consideration of water recreation. Pages 34, 196.

Endangered Species Act of 1973.   Fish and Wildlife Service. Designed to protect and propagate endangered and threatened species of animals and plants. Pages 173, 182, 183.

Forest and Rangeland Renewable Resources Planning Act of 1974.   Forest Service. To improve planning and management by the Forest Service, including planning and management for recreation. Page 140.

National Forest Management Act of 1976.   Forest Service. Provides improved management guidelines and priorities for the national forests. Page 140.

Federal Land Policy and Management Act of 1976.   Bureau of Land Management. Clarifies the land-management policies to be implemented by the Bureau of Land Management. It is the bureau's organic act. Pages 34–35, 143–144, 147, 327, 333, 336–337.

Urban Park and Recreation Recovery Act of 1978.   National Park Service. Provides matching grants to local governments in designated urban areas to rehabilitate existing recreation facilities and to demonstrate innovative approaches in park and recreation management. Page 187.

National Parks and Recreation Act of 1978.   National Park Service. Clarifies that it is the policy of Congress to preserve wilderness, enhance wildlife conservation, and improve park and recreation values of real property owned by the United States. Pages 35, 197.

Alaska National Interest Lands Conservation Act of 1980.   National Park Service. Altered boundaries of previously established units and redesignated several units as national parks and national preserves. The act greatly enlarged the size of the national park system. Pages 123, 144.

Addresses of Federal Resource Agencies

LAND-MANAGEMENT AGENCIES

National Park Service
Headquarters Office
Interior Building
18th and C streets NW
Washington, DC 20240

North Atlantic Region (Maine, New Hampshire, Vermont, Massachusetts, Rhode Island, Connecticut, New York, New Jersey): 15 State Street, Boston, MA 02109

Mid-Atlantic Region (Pennsylvania, Maryland, West Virginia, Delaware, Virginia): 143 South Third Street, Philadelphia, PA 19106

National Capital Region (Washington, D.C., including nearby Maryland, Virgina, West Virginia): 1100 Ohio Drive SW, Washington, D.C. 20242

Rocky Mountain Region (Montana, North Dakota, South Dakota, Wyoming, Utah, Colorado): 655 Parfet Street, Box 25287, Denver, Colorado 80225

Western Region (Arizona, California, Nevada, Hawaii): 450 Golden Gate Avenue, Box 36063, San Francisco, CA 94102

Southwest Region (Arkansas, Louisiana, New Mexico, Oklahoma, Texas): Box 728, Santa Fe, NM 87501

Southeast Region (Alabama, Florida, Georgia, Kentucky, Mississippi, North Carolina, South Carolina, Tennessee, Puerto Rico, Virgin Islands): 1895 Phoenix Boulevard, Atlanta, GA 30349

Midwest Region (Indiana, Michigan, Wisconsin, Illinois, Minnesota, Iowa, Missouri, Nebraska, Kansas): 1709 Jackson Street, Omaha, NE 68102

Pacific Northwest Region (Alaska, Idaho, Oregon, Washington): 601 Fourth and Pike Building, Seattle, WA 98101

U.S. Forest Service
Chief Forester's Office
Department of Agriculture
Independence Avenue
Washington, DC 20240

Region 1 (Northern): Federal Building, Missoula, MT 59807

Region 2 (Rocky Mountain): 11177 West Eighth Avenue, Box 25127, Lakewood, CO 80225

Region 3 (Southwestern): Federal Building, 517 Gold Avenue, SW, Albuquerque, NM 87102

Region 4 (Intermountain): Federal Office Building, 324 25th Street, Ogden, UT 84401

Region 5 (California): 630 Sansome Street, San Francisco, CA 94111

Region 6 (Pacific Northwest): 319 SW Pine Street, Box 3623, Portland, OR 97208

Region 7 (Southern): Suite 800, 1720 Peachtree Road, NW, Atlanta, GA 30309

Region 8 (Eastern): Clark Building, 633 West Wisconsin Avenue, Milwaukee, WI 53203

Region 9 (Alaska): Federal Office Building, Box 1628, Juneau, AK 99801

Bureau of Land Management
Office of the Director
U.S. Department of the Interior
Washington, DC 20240

Denver Service Center
Denver Federal Center
Building 50
Denver, CO 80225

State offices:

Alaska: 555 Cordova Street, Anchorage, AK 99501

Arizona: 2400 Valley Bank Center, Phoenix, AZ 85073

California: Federal Office Building, 2800 Cottage Way, Sacramento, CA 95825

Colorado: Room 700, Colorado State Bank Building, 1600 Broadway, Denver, CO 80202

Idaho: 398 Federal Building, 550 West Fort Street, Boise, ID 83724

Montana: Federal Building, 222 North 32nd Street, Billings, MT 59107

Nevada: 3008 Federal Building, 300 Booth Street, Reno, NV 89502

New Mexico: Federal Building, South Federal Place, Santa Fe, NM 87501

Oregon and Washington: 729 NE Oregon Street, Portland, OR 97208

Utah: Federal Building, 125 South State, Salt Lake City, UT 84147

Wyoming: Federal Center, Cheyenne, WY 82001

Eastern states office: 7981 Eastern Avenue, Silver Spring, MD 20910

Bureau of Indian Affairs
Office of the Director
1951 Constitution Avenue NW
Washington, DC 20245

Federal Highway Administration
Office of the Director
400 Seventh Street SW
Washington, DC 20590

RESERVOIR PROVIDERS

Bureau of Reclamation
Office of the Director
U.S. Department of the Interior
Washington, DC 20240

Pacific Northwest Region: Box 043, U.S. Court House, 550 West Fort Street, Boise, ID 83724

Mid-Pacific Region: 2800 Cottage Way, Sacramento, CA 95825

Lower Colorado Region: Box 427, Boulder City, NV 89005

Upper Colorado Region: Box 11568, Salt Lake City, UT 84111

Southwest Region: Herring Plaza, Box H-4377, Amarillo, TX 79101

Upper Missouri Region: Box 2553, Billings, MT 59103

Lower Missouri Region: Building 20, Denver Federal Center, Denver, CO 80225

U.S. Army Corps of Engineers
Office of the Chief of Engineers
Pulaski Building
20 Massachusetts Avenue
Washington, DC 20314

Lower Mississippi Valley Division: Box 80, Vicksburg, MS 39187

Missouri River Division: Box 103, Downtown Station, Omaha, NE 68101

North Atlantic Division: 536 South Clark Street, Chicago, IL 60605

North Pacific Division: 220 NW Eighth Avenue, Portland, OR 97209

Ohio River Division: Box 1159, Cincinnati, OH 45201

Pacific Ocean Division: Building 230, Fort Shafter, HI, APO San Francisco, CA 96558

South Atlantic Division: 510 Title Building, Atlanta, GA 30303

South Pacific Division: 630 Sansome Street, San Francisco, CA 94111

Southwestern Division: Main Tower Building, 1200 Main Street, Dallas, TX 75202

Tennessee Valley Authority
Headquarters Office
400 Commerce Avenue
Knoxville, TN 37902

Soil Conservation Service
Headquarters Office
Department of Agriculture
Box 2890
Washington, DC 20013

WILDLIFE RESOURCES

United States Fish and Wildlife Service
Office of the Director
U.S. Department of the Interior
Washington, DC 20240

Pacific Region (Hawaii, California, Idaho, Nevada, Oregon, Washington): 1500 Plaza Building, 1500 NE Irving Street, Portland, OR 97208

Southwest Region (Arizona, New Mexico, Oklahoma, Texas): Federal Building, U.S. Post Office and Court House, 500 Gold Avenue SW, Albuquerque, NM 87103

North-Central Region (Illinois, Indiana, Michigan, Minnesota, Ohio, Wisconsin): Federal Building, Fort Snelling, Twin Cities, MN 55111

Southeast Region (Alabama, Arkansas, Florida, Georgia, Kentucky, Louisiana, Mississippi, North Carolina, South Carolina, Tennessee): 17 Executive Park Drive, Atlanta, GA 30329

Northeast Region (Connecticut, Delaware, Maine, Maryland, Massachusetts, New Hampshire, New Jersey, New York, Pennsylvania, Rhode Island, Vermont, Virginia, West Virginia): McCormack Post Office and Courthouse, Boston, MA 02109

Alaska Area: 813 D Street, Anchorage, AK 99501

Denver Region (Colorado, Iowa, Kansas, Missouri, Montana, Nebraska, North Dakota, South Dakota, Utah, Wyoming): 10597 Sixth Street, Denver, Colorado 80225

FINANCIAL AND TECHNICAL ASSISTANCE PROGRAMS

In Chapter 11 are descriptions of the financial and technical information available from the agencies already listed, plus those listed below.

Department of Agriculture
Independence Avenue Between 12th and 14th Streets SW
Washington, DC 20250

Department of Transportation
400 Seventh Street SW
Washington, DC 20591

Department of Housing and Urban Development
451 Seventh Street SW
Washington, DC 20410

Department of Labor
200 Constitution Avenue NW
Washington, DC 20210

Department of Commerce
14th Street and Constitution Avenue NW
Washington, DC 20230

Small Business Administration
1441 L Street NW
Washington, DC 20416

Environmental Protection Agency
401 M Street SW
Washington, DC 20410

General Services Administration
Central Office
F Street NW
Washington, DC 20405

Council on Environmental Quality
722 Jackson Place NW
Washington, DC 20006

Community Services Administration
1200 19th Street NW
Washington, DC 20506

Federal Energy Regulatory Commission
825 North Capitol Street NE
Washington, DC 20585

State Agencies Involved in Outdoor Recreation

State	Agencies With Principal Responsibilities in Outdoor Recreation	Agencies With Limited Responsibilities in Outdoor Recreation
Alabama	Department of Conservation Division of Water Division of State Parks, Monuments, and Historical Sites Division of Game and Fish Division of Seafoods Division of Outdoor Recreation	Mound State Monument
Alaska	Department of Natural Resources	
Arizona	Game and Fish Commission State Parks Board Outdoor Recreation Coordinating Commission	Highway Commission Office of Economic Planning and Development
Arkansas	Game and Fish Commission Department of Local Services Department of Parks and Tourism	Ozarks Regional Commission (joint federal-state agency) Geological Commission Forestry Commission Industrial Development Commission State Highway Department

State	Agencies With Principal Responsibilities in Outdoor Recreation	Agencies With Limited Responsibilities in Outdoor Recreation
California	Resources Agency Department of Parks and Recreation Department of Navigation and Ocean Development Department of Conservation Department of Forestry Department of Fish and Game Department of Water Resources	Department of Public Works Bureau of Health Education, Physical Education, and Recreation State Lands Commission Water Pollution Control Department of Health California Transportation Agency Wildlife Conservation Board California Coastal Zone Conservation Commission
Colorado	Department of Natural Resources Division of Parks and Outdoor Recreation Division of Wildlife	State Historical Society Department of Highways State Board of Land Commissioners
Connecticut	State Department of Environmental Protection	State Department of Health State Department of Transportation
Delaware	Department of Natural Resources and Environmental Control Division of Parks and Recreation Division of Soil and Water Conservation Division of Environmental Control Department of Community Affairs and Economic Development Division of Economic Development Department of State Division of Historical and Cultural Affairs Department of Public Safety Department of Health and Social Services	State Archives Commission State Highway Department State Development Department State Board of Health Water and Air Resources Commission Soil and Water Conservation Commission
Florida	Department of Natural Resources Division of Recreation and Parks	Department of Agriculture and Consumer Services

State	Agencies With Principal Responsibilities in Outdoor Recreation	Agencies With Limited Responsibilities in Outdoor Recreation
Florida continued	Game and Fresh Water Fish Commission	Division of Forestry Department of Education Department of Transportation Department of State Division of Archives, History, and Records Management Department of Health and Rehabilitative Services Department of Environmental Regulation Water-Management Districts Department of Veteran and Community Affairs
Georgia	Georgia Department of Natural Resources Parks and Historic Division	Jekyll Island State Park Authority Stone Mountain Memorial Authority Lake Lanier Development Authority Georgia Department of Transportation

Hawaii	Department of Land and Natural Resources
	   Division of State Parks, Outdoor Recreation, and Historic Sites
	   Division of Aquatic Resources
	   Division of Forestry and Wildlife
		Department of Transportation
		   Harbors Division

Idaho	State Park and Recreation Board Fish and Game Commission	Department of Transportation State Department of Tourism and Industrial Development State Historical Society State Land Department

Illinois	Department of Conservation
	   Division of Parks
	   Division of Historic Sites
	   Division of Land Management
	   Division of Wildlife Resources
	   Division of Fisheries
		Department of Public Works and Buildings
		Department of Registration and Education
		Department of Public Health
		Illinois State Youth Commission

State	Agencies With Principal Responsibilities in Outdoor Recreation	Agencies With Limited Responsibilities in Outdoor Recreation
Illinois continued	Division of Forestry	Department of Business and Economic Development
Indiana	Department of Natural Resources Division of Fish and Wildlife Division of Forestry Division of State Parks Division of Reservoir Management Division of Nature Preserves Division of Museums and Memorials Division of Outdoor Recreation	State Highway Department State Board of Health State Commission on Aging and the Aged and the Governor's Youth Council Division of Tourism
Iowa	State Conservation Commission Division of Administration Division of Fish and Game Division of Land and Waters	State Soil Conservation Department Iowa Development Commission State Department of Transportation Office of Planning and Programming
Kansas	State Park and Resources Authority Kansas Fish and Game Commission Joint Council on Recreation	State Department of Transportation State Recreation Consultant State Historical Society Department of Economic Development Kansas Water Office
Kentucky	Department of Local Government Department of Fish and Wildlife Department of Parks Heritage Commission Division of Forestry Division of Special Programs	Division of Water Division of Conservation Division of Highways Historical Society
Louisiana	Office of State Parks Department of Culture, Recreation and Tourism	Department of Highways Department of Public Works Department of Commerce and Industry Louisiana Tourist Development Commission

State	Agencies With Principal Responsibilities in Outdoor Recreation	Agencies With Limited Responsibilities in Outdoor Recreation
Maine	Department of Inland Fisheries and Wildlife Baxter State Park Authority Department of Conservation State Development Office	Atlantic Sea-Run Salmon Commission Department of Maine Resources Department of Transportation Department of Human Services
Maryland	Department of Natural Resources Capital Programs Administration Maryland Forest and Park Service Maryland Wildlife Administration Maryland Tidewater Administration Natural Resource Police Force Water Resources Administration Department of State Planning State Highway Administration Department of Economic and Community Development	
Massachusetts	Department of Environmental Management Division of Fisheries and Game Division of Water Resources Division of Forests and Parks Division of Marine Fisheries Metropolitan District Commission Parks Engineering Division Department of Public Works Fisheries Forestry Wildlife Bureau of Water Management Water Development Service Commission on Pollution Air Pollution Control Solid Waste Management	Department of Public Health Department of Commerce Department of Correction Department of Youth Services Department of Fisheries, Wildlife, and Recreational Vehicles
Michigan	Department of Natural Resources Division of Recreation	Water Resources Commission Mackinac Island Park Commission

State	Agencies With Principal Responsibilities in Outdoor Recreation	Agencies With Limited Responsibilities in Outdoor Recreation
Michigan continued	Division of Forestry Division of Fish and Game	Waterways Commission State Tourist Council Division of State Lands
Minnesota	Department of Natural Resources Division of Forestry Division of Game and Fish Division of Parks and Recreation Division of Enforcement Trails and Waterways Unit	Department of Transportation Historical Society Iron Range Resources and Rehabilitation Commission Pollution Control Agency Energy Planning and Development Agency Legislative Commission on Minnesota Resources Minnesota-Wisconsin Boundary Area Commission
Mississippi	Mississippi Game and Fish Commission Mississippi Park Commission Mississippi Bureau of Outdoor Recreation	Pat Harrison Waterway District Pearl River Basin Development District Tombigbee River Valley Water Management District Mississippi Department of Archives and History Mississippi State Highway Department Grand Gulf Military Monument Commission Pearl River Valley Water Supply District Mississippi State Board of Health Mississippi Board of Water Commission Mississippi Agricultural and Industrial Board Yellow Creek Watershed District Bienville Recreation District Mississippi Boat and Water Safety Commission
Missouri	State Conservation Commission State Department of Natural Resources State Tourism Commission	State Highway Commission Division of Commerce and Industrial Development

State	Agencies With Principal Responsibilities in Outdoor Recreation	Agencies With Limited Responsibilities in Outdoor Recreation
Montana	State Fish, Wildlife, and Parks Department	State Highway Department Board of Health State Historical Society State Department of Lands State Department of Natural Resources and Conservation
Nebraska	Game and Parks Commission	Department of Health Department of Roads State Historical Society Department of Economic Development Natural Resources Commission Extension Division (University of Nebraska)
Nevada	Department of Conservation and Natural Resources Fish and Game Commission Division of Parks	Department of Economic Development Department of Highways State Museum Division of Forestry
New Hampshire	Department of Resources and Economic Development Division of Parks Fish and Game Department	Natural Resources Council Water Resources Board Water Pollution Commission State Historical Commission Department of Public Works and Highways
New Jersey	Department of Environmental Protection Division of Parks and Forestry Division of Fish, Game, and Shellfisheries Division of Water Resources Division of Marine Services	Department of Community Affairs Division of State and Regional Planning Division of Local Government Services Department of Transportation Department of Health
New Mexico	Natural Resources Department Administrative Services Division Game and Fish Department	Commerce and Industry Department Tourism and Travel Division State Highway Department Department of Education

State	Agencies With Principal Responsibilities in Outdoor Recreation	Agencies With Limited Responsibilities in Outdoor Recreation
New York	Office of Parks, Recreation, and Historic Preservation Bureau of Recreation Services Operations and Maintenance Marine and Recreation Vehicles Historic Preservation Bureau of Historic Sites Department of Environmental Conservation Division of Lands and Forests Forest Recreation Environmental Education Winter Recreation Division of Fish and Wildlife Bureau of Recreation and Field Operations	Department of Education Department of Health Division for Youth Office for the Aging Department of Commerce Division of Tourism Promotion Office of General Services Department of Transportation
North Carolina	Department of Natural and Economic Resources Grants Administration Division of Resource Planning and Evaluation Division of Parks and Recreation Division of Community Assistance Regional Offices Division of Economic Development Wildlife Resources Commission	Department of Cultural Resources Department of Transportation
North Dakota	State Parks and Recreation Department State Game and Fish Department State Forest Service State Water Commission	State Health Department State Historical Society State Soil Conservation Committee State Highway Department State Tourism Promotion Division Economic Development Commission
Ohio	Department of Natural Resources Division of Parks and Recreation Division of Wildlife Division of Forestry	Department of Natural Resources Division of Civilian Conservation Department of Transportation

State	Agencies With Principal Responsibilities in Outdoor Recreation	Agencies With Limited Responsibilities in Outdoor Recreation
Ohio continued	Division of Watercraft Division of Natural Areas and Preserves Office of Outdoor Recreation Services	Department of Economic and Community Development Department of Health Department of Education Department of Agriculture Ohio Historical Society Environmental Protection Agency Rehabilitation Services Commission Commission on Aging
Oklahoma	Department of Tourism and Recreation Division of State Lodges Division of State Parks Office of Outdoor Recreation and Planning Wildlife Conservation Department Fisheries Division Game Division	Department of Agriculture Division of Forestry Department of Highways
Oregon	Department of Transportation, Parks and Recreation Division Department of Fish and Wildlife Marine Board Fair Board Assistant to the governor, natural resources	Division of State Lands Department of Forestry Columbia River Gorge Commission Department of Environmental Quality Department of Land Conservation and Development
Pennsylvania	Department of Community Affairs State Fish Commission State Game Commission Department of Environmental Resources	Department of Commerce Department of Welfare Department of Health Department of Transportation Historical and Museum Commission Office of State Planning and Development
Rhode Island	Department of Natural Resources Division of Parks and Recreation Division of Forest Environment	Department of Health Department of Economic Development

State	Agencies With Principal Responsibilities in Outdoor Recreation	Agencies With Limited Responsibilities in Outdoor Recreation
Rhode Island continued	Division of Fish and Wildlife Division of Coastal Resources Division of Planning and Development Division of Boating Safety	Division of Tourist Promotion Department of Administration Statewide Planning Division
South Carolina	Forestry Commission Department of Parks, Recreation, and Tourism Wildlife and Marine Resource Department	Department of Highways and Public Transportation Department of Health and Environmental Control State Development Board State Budget and Control Board Public Service Authority Patriots Point Authority Water Resources Commission
South Dakota	Department of Game, Fish, and Parks Wildlife Division Parks and Recreation Division Custer State Park Division	Commissioner of Schools and Public Lands Department of Transportation Department of Education and Cultural Affairs Department of Water and Natural Resources Department of Tourism and Economic Development
Tennessee	Department of Conservation Division of State Parks Division of Forestry Division of Planning Division of Facilities Management Wildlife Resources Agency	Department of Tourism
Texas	Parks and Wildlife Department	Department of Highways and Public Transportation Tourist Development Agency Department of Community Affairs State River Authorities General Land Office Department of Water Resources Air Control Board Historical Commission

State	Agencies With Principal Responsibilities in Outdoor Recreation	Agencies With Limited Responsibilities in Outdoor Recreation
Utah	Department of Natural Resources and Energy Outdoor Recreation Agency Division of Wildlife Resources	Department of Transportation Travel Council Utah National Guard Division of State Lands Division of State History Division of Water Resources
Vermont	Agency of Environmental Conservation Planning Division Department of Forests, Parks, and Recreation Department of Water Resources and Environmental Engineering Water Resources Board Environmental Board	Agency of Transportation Department of Highways Agency of Development and Community Affairs Department of Development Agency of Human Services Department of Health Office on Aging Vermont Council on the Arts Department of Education
Virginia	Department of Conservation and Economic Development Division of Forestry Division of Parks Commission of Game and Inland Fisheries Commission of Outdoor Recreation	Department of Highways Breaks Interstate Park Commission Water Control Board Department of Health Agencies Administering Historic Sites Historic Landmark Commission Marine Resources Commission
Washington	Department of Natural Resources State Parks and Recreation Commission Department of Game Interagency Committee for Outdoor Recreation Department of Fisheries	Highway Department Department of Health Department of Ecology Department of Commerce and Economic Development Office of Community Development Department of Water Resources
West Virginia	Department of Natural Resources Division of Game and Fish Division of Forestry Division of Parks and Recreation Division of Water Resources Division of Reclamation Public Lands Corporation	State Road Commission Department of Health Department of Agriculture Department of Education

State	Agencies With Principal Responsibilities in Outdoor Recreation	Agencies With Limited Responsibilities in Outdoor Recreation
West Virginia continued	Department of Commerce Office of Federal-State Relations	

Wisconsin	Department of Natural Resources
	   Division of Forestry, Wildlife,
	     and Recreation
	   Division of Tourism and
	     Commercial Recreation
		Department of Natural Resources
		   Division of Environmental
		     Standards
		   Division of Enforcement
		Department of Business
		   Development
		State Historical Society
		Department of Transportation

Wyoming	Recreation Commission Game and Fish Commission Board of Charities and Reform Travel Commission	Highway Department Forestry Division

APPENDIX D

State Outdoor-Recreation Liaison Offices

Each state has a particular office that is identified as the focal point for the state's involvement in outdoor recreation. In addition to other responsibilities, this office coordinates the outdoor-recreation planning of the state with the federal government. In particular, it is the office responsible for the administration of Land and Water Conservation Funds that are allocated to the state. Further, the liaison office is the central location for outdoor-recreation information for the state.

Alabama
Department of Conservation and
Natural Resources
Administrative Building
Montgomery, AL 36130
(205)832-6361

Alaska
Alaska Division of Parks
619 Warehouse Drive
Suite 210
Anchorage, AK 99501
(907)274-4676

American Samoa
Department of Parks and Recreation
Government of American Samoa
Pago Pago
American Samoa 96799
633-1191 (call thru overseas operator)

Arizona
Arizona Outdoor Recreation
Coordinating Commission
1333 West Camelback Road
Suite 206
Phoenix, AZ 85013
(602)255-5013

Arkansas
Arkansas Department of Parks and
Tourism
1 Capitol Mall
Little Rock, AK 72201
(501)371-2535

California
Department of Parks and Recreation
Box 2390
Sacramento, CA 95811
(961)445-2358

Colorado
Division of Parks and Outdoor
Recreation
Department of Natural Resources
1313 Sherman Street
Room 618
Denver, CO 80203
(303)886-3437

Connecticut
Department of Environmental
Protection
117 State Office Building
Hartford, CT 06115
(203)566-2904

Delaware
Department of Natural Resources and
Environmental Control
Edward Tatnall Building
Box 1401
Dover, DE 19901
(302)736-4403

District of Columbia
District of Columbia Recreation
Department
3149 16th Street NW
Washington, D.C. 20010
(202)673-7665

Florida
Division of Recreation and Parks
Department of Natural Resources
3900 Commonwealth Boulevard
Tallahassee, FL 32303
(904)488-6131

Georgia
State Department of Natural
Resources
270 Washington Street SW
Atlanta, GA 30334
(404)656-3500

Guam
Department of Parks and Recreation
Box 2950
Agana, Guam 96910
477-9620 (call through overseas
operator)

Hawaii
Board of Land and Natural Resources
Box 621
Honolulu, HI 96809
(808)548-6550

Idaho
Department of Parks and Recreation
Statehouse
Boise, ID 83720
(208)334-2154

Illinois
Department of Conservation
605 William G. Stratton Building
400 South Spring Street
Springfield, IL 62706
(217)782-6302

Indiana
Department of Natural Resources
608 State Office Building
Indianapolis, IN 46204
(317)232-4020

Iowa
State Conservation Commission
Wallace State Office Building
Des Moines, IA 50319
(515)281-5384

Kansas
Kansas Park and Resources Authority
503 Kansas Avenue
Box 977
Topeka, KS 66601
(913)296-2281

Kentucky
Department for Community and
Regional Development
Capitol Plaza Tower, Second Floor
Frankfort, KY 40601
(502)564-2382

Louisiana
Department of Culture, Recreation,
and Tourism
Office of Program Development
Box 44247
Baton Rouge, LA 70804
(504)925-3384

Maine
Bureau of Parks and Recreation
Department of Conservation
Station 19
Augusta, ME 04333
(207)289-3821

Maryland
Department of Natural Resources
Tawes State Office Building
Annapolis, MD 21401
(301)269-3043

Massachusetts
Department of Environmental Affairs
Leverett Saltonstall Building
100 Cambridge Street
Boston, MA 02202
(617)727-9800

Michigan
Michigan Department of Natural
Resources
Stevens T. Mason Building
Box 30028
Lansing, MI 48909
(517)373-2682

Minnesota
Department of Natural Resources
Centennial Building
Box 51

St. Paul, MN 55155
(612)296-6235

Mississippi
Bureau of Recreation and Parks
Department of Natural Resources
Box 10600
Jackson, MS 39209
(601)961-5244

Missouri
Department of Natural Resources
Box 176
Jefferson City, MO 65102
(314)751-4422

Montana
Montana Department of Fish,
Wildlife, and Parks
1420 East Sixth Avenue
Helena, MT 59601
(406)449-3750

Nebraska
Nebraska Game and Parks
Commission
2200 North 33rd Street
Box 30370
Lincoln, NE 68503
(402)464-0641

Nevada
Nevada Division of State Parks
Capitol Complex
Carson City, NV 89710
(702)885-4384

New Hampshire
Department of Resources and
Economic Development
Box 856
Concord, NH 03301
(603)271-2411

New Jersey
Department of Environmental
Protection
Box 1390
Trenton, NJ 08625
(609)292-0432

New Mexico
Natural Resources Department
119 Villagra Building
Santa Fe, New Mexico 87503
(505)827-2143

New York
Office of Parks and Recreation
Agency Building 1
Empire State Plaza
Albany, NY 12238
(518)474-0443

North Carolina
Department of Natural Resources and
Community Development
Box 27687
Raleigh, NC 27611
(919)733-4984

North Dakota
North Dakota Parks and Recreation
Department
Pinehurst Office Park
1424 West Century Avenue
Box 700
Bismarck, ND 58502
(701)224-4454

Ohio
Department of Natural Resources
Fountain Square
Columbus, OH 43224
(614)466-3770

Oklahoma
Oklahoma Tourism and Recreation
Department
500 Will Rogers Memorial Building
Oklahoma City, OK 73105
(405)521-2413

Oregon
State Parks Administrator
525 Trade Street SE
Salem, OR 97310
(503)378-6305

Pennsylvania
Department of Environmental
Resources
Box 1467
Harrisburg, PA 17120
(717)787-7160

Puerto Rico
Puerto Rico Development Company
Box 2827
San Juan, Puerto Rico 00903
(809)725-0140

Rhode Island
Department of Environmental
Management
Veterans Memorial Building
83 Park Street
Providence, RI 02903
(401)277-2771

South Carolina
Department of Parks, Recreation, and
Tourism
Suite 113, Edgar A. Brown Building
1205 Pendleton Street
Columbia, SC 29201
(803)758-7705

South Dakota
Division of Parks and Recreation
Department of Game, Fish, and Parks
Sigurd Anderson Building
Pierre, SD 57501
(605)773-3387

Tennessee
Department of Conservation
2611 West End Avenue
Nashville, TN 37203
(615)741-1061

Texas
Department of Natural Resources
Box 1007
San Marcos, TX 78666
(512)477-3236

Utah
Department of Natural Resources
and Energy
1636 West North Temple
Salt Lake City, UT 84116
(801)533-5356

Vermont
Agency of Environmental
Conservation
State Office Building
Montpelier, VT 05602
(802)828-3130

Virgin Islands
Department of Conservation and
Cultural Affairs
Box 4340
Charlotte Amalie
St. Thomas, Virgin Islands 00801
(809)774-3320

Virginia
Virginia Commission of Outdoor
Recreation

James Monroe Building
101 North 14th Street
Richmond, VA 23219
(804)786-2036

Washington
Interagency Committee for Outdoor
Recreation
4800 Capitol Boulevard KP-11
Tumwater, WA 98504
(206)753-3610

West Virginia
Office of Economic and Community
Development
Building 6, Room B-553
Charleston, WV 25305
(304)348-4010

Wisconsin
Office of Intergovernmental Programs
Department of Natural Resources
Box 7921
Madison, WI 53707
(608)266-0836

Wyoming
Wyoming Recreation Commission
604 East 25th Street
Cheyenne, WY 82002
(307)777-6308

Index

Student Survey
Clayne Jensen
OUTDOOR RECREATION IN AMERICA
Fourth Edition

Students, send us your ideas!

The author and the publisher want to know how well this book served you and what can be done to improve it for those who will use it in the future. By completing and returning this questionnaire, you can help us develop better textbooks. We value your opinion and want to hear your comments. Thank you.

Your name (optional) _____ School _____

Your mailing address _____

City _____ State _____ ZIP _____

Instructor's name (optional) _____ Course title _____

1. How does this book compare with other texts you have used? (Check one)

    ☐ Superior   ☐ Better than most   ☐ Comparable   ☐ Not as good as most

2. Circle those chapters you especially liked:

    Chapters: 1 2 3 4 5 6 7 8 9 10 11 12 13 14 15 16 17 18 19 20 21 22

    Comments:

3. Circle those chapters you think could be improved:

    Chapters: 1 2 3 4 5 6 7 8 9 10 11 12 13 14 15 16 17 18 19 20 21 22

    Comments:

4. Please rate the following (check one for each):

	Excellent	Good	Average	Poor
Logical organization	( )	( )	( )	( )
Readability of text material	( )	( )	( )	( )
General layout and design	( )	( )	( )	( )
Match with instructor's course organization	( )	( )	( )	( )
Illustrations that clarify the text	( )	( )	( )	( )
Up-to-date treatment of subject	( )	( )	( )	( )
Explanation of difficult concepts	( )	( )	( )	( )
Selection of topics	( )	( )	( )	( )

5. List any chapters that your instructor did not assign. _____

_____

6. What additional topics did your instructor discuss that were not covered in the text?

_____

7. Did you buy this book new or used?   ☐ New   ☐ Used

    Do you plan to keep the book or sell it?   ☐ Keep it ☐ Sell it

    Do you think your instructor should continue to assign this book? ☐ Yes   ☐ No

8. After taking the course, are you interested in taking more courses in this field?
    ☐ Yes   ☐ No

    What is your major? _____

9. GENERAL COMMENTS:

May we quote you in our advertising?   ☐ Yes   ☐ No

Please remove these pages and mail to: Mary L. Paulson
                                           Burgess Publishing Company
                                           7108 Ohms Lane
                                           Minneapolis, MN 55435

THANK YOU!